# THE SHAKESPEARE'S MINE

# THE SHAKESPEARE'S MINE

## ADAPTING SHAKESPEARE IN ANGLOPHONE CANADA

EDITED BY RIC KNOWLES

PLAYWRIGHTS CANADA PRESS
TORONTO • CANADA

**Playwrights Canada Press**
The Canadian Drama Publisher
202-269 Richmond Street West, Toronto, ON M5V 1X1
416-703-0013 • info@playwrightscanada.com • www.playwrightscanada.com



We acknowledge the financial support of the Canada Council for the Arts, the Ontario Arts Council (OAC), the Ontario Media Development Corporation, and the Government of Canada through the Canada Book Fund for our publishing activities.

Canada Council for the Arts Conseil des arts du Canada
ONTARIO ARTS COUNCIL
CONSEIL DES ARTS DE L'ONTARIO
an Ontario government agency
un organisme du gouvernement de l'Ontario
Canada
Ontario
Ontario Media Development Corporation

Front cover photo of Monique Mojica, Michelle St. John, Clifford Cardinal, Jani Lauzon, Craig Lauzon, Falen Johnson, and Sara Sinclair. Photo by Nina Lee Aquino.
Cover design: Blake Sproule
Production editor: JLArt

Library and Archives Canada Cataloguing in Publication

The Shakespeare's mine : adapting Shakespeare in anglophone Canada /
Ric Knowles, ed.

Includes bibliographical references.
ISBN 978-1-77091-854-2

1. Shakespeare, William, 1564-1616--Adaptations. I. Knowles, Richard, 1950-

PR3109.C3S534 2009 822.3'3 C2009-901464-5

First edition: May 2009.
Printed in Canada by Imprimerie Gauvin, Gatineau.

*To Christine*

# CONTENTS

Introduction: *Adapting to Shakespeare*
by Ric Knowles iii

***Cruel Tears***
by Ken Mitchell and Humphrey & the Dumptrucks 1

***Claudius***
by Ken Gass 73

***Mad Boy Chronicle***
by Michael O'Brien 143

***Harlem Duet***
by Djanet Sears 237

***Shakespeare's Will***
by Vern Thiessen 311

***Death of a Chief***
by Yvette Nolan and Kennedy C. MacKinnon 379

# ADAPTING TO SHAKESPEARE

Ric Knowles

*"The Shakespeare's mine, but you can have it."*

Spoken by Othello's black first wife, Billie, in Djanet Sears's *Harlem Duet* (1998) when she and Othello are divvying up their books at the end of their marriage, these words characterize the conflicting attitudes towards Shakespeare in most adaptations—Canadian or otherwise—of his life and work. Adapters, for the most part, want at once to lay claim to the cultural authority represented by the Bard—"the Shakespeare's mine"—and to shuck the oppressive weight of his influence—"but you can have it."

Adapting Shakespeare has its rewards, as playwrights from a broad spectrum of backgrounds piggyback on his cultural capital, using his name to gain access and recognition. It's no accident, for example, that Tom Stoppard's *Rosencrantz and Guildenstern are Dead*—*Hamlet* seen from the point of view of its most clueless characters—is one of the most-produced twentieth-century plays, often at Shakespeare festivals, often accompanied by productions of *Hamlet*, often with cross-casting between the shows to enhance the intertextual frisson. And it's not alone. In English Canada, plays evoking Shakespeare seem to have a special place in the canon. *Harlem Duet* was the first play by a person of African descent to be produced at either the Canadian Stage Company (in 1997) or the Stratford Festival (in 2006). *Harlem Duet* is also one of a disproportionate number of Shakespeare adaptations to have won Canada's highest literary prize, the Governor General's Literary Award for Drama—the others being Ann-Marie MacDonald's *Goodnight Desdemona (Good Morning Juliet)* (1990) and Timothy Findley's *Elizabeth Rex* (2000), the latter almost unique among Canadian plays in actually premiering at Stratford. Vern Thiessen's *Shakespeare's Will* (2005) was not simply produced, but commissioned by a Shakespeare festival, before premiering at a large regional theatre, Edmonton's Citadel, and going on to productions at Stratford and beyond.

But adapting Shakespeare also has its perils. After all, his is a hard act to follow, and audiences may be forgiven for wondering on occasion why they're not getting the Real Thing (to conjure Stoppard once again) instead of the hack work of some contemporary upstart crow dressing themselves in Shakespeare's feathers, even as he—the ultimate adapter—was accused of dressing himself in those of his urban, university-educated betters. And the enormous cultural weight that Shakespeare now represents can also make it difficult for any adapter to crawl out from under that baggage and be heard. For anyone using Shakespeare to mount a cultural critique—usually from the post-colonial position of "talking back to Empire" or the feminist position of talking back to patriarchy—the very rewards that can accrue to adaptation can also have an overwhelmingly stifling effect, operating as the lethal embrace of a "high" culture that has taught "us" to love, unconditionally, everything associated with the Swan of Avon. Anti-racist, anti-colonialist, and feminist critiques are easily embraced under such rubrics as "poking fun at the Bard," leaving "his" cultural authority entirely intact and their critique muffled.

So why do it—apart from the material rewards for those willing to risk seeking the bubble reputation even in the canon's mouth? Sometimes the purposes are merely ludic displays of wit or virtuosity, a category into which work such as Leon Rooke's carnivalesque novel, *Shakespeare's Dog* (1983), Rick Miller's wildly comic *MacHomer* (*Macbeth* delivered via *The Simpsons*, first produced in 1996), or many of the endless virtuosic one-person versions of *Hamlet* or twenty-minute versions of the complete works. Sometimes Shakespeare has been adapted into other forms, genres, and languages in order for "him" to travel, or to popularize an increasingly remote Bard in the genres of the day, whether that means the thousands of paintings and sculptures of characters or scenes from the plays (think of the influence of Millais's *Ophelia*), Italian operas (Verdi's *Macbeth*), poetry (Auden's *The Sea and the Mirror*), fiction (Carole Corbeil's *In the Wings*), film (from *Romeo + Juliet* through *O* and *Scotland, PA* to *My Own Private Idaho* and *Last Action Hero*), or an ever-expanding number of pop-culture and televisual citations, musical remixes, comics, and graphic novels.

Perhaps the most frequent form of adaptation consists of probing more deeply into the lives of Shakespeare's minor characters. Falstaff is a popular one, having in one sense been adapted by Shakespeare himself when he plopped the fat knight from the history plays into the middle of his very Elizabethan comedy, *The Merry Wives of Windsor*. The character has reappeared, often in the leading role, in plays, poems, operas, and novels by the likes of Giuseppe Verdi, Bernard Shaw, and Orson Welles ever since, most recently, as I write, at Canada's National Arts Centre in 2007 in a double adaptation by John Wood and Roger Forbes of Robert Nye's novel, *Falstaff*. *Hamlet* alone has spawned dozens of plays based on the expanded stories of most of its minor characters: Rosencrantz and Guildenstern, Gertrude, Ophelia, Claudius. Even a figure from *Hamlet* who is frequently cut from productions of the play itself has been grist for the revisionist mill in Lee Blessing's 1991 play, *Fortinbras*. But perhaps *The Tempest*'s Caliban wins the Oscar for most adapted versions of a character in a supporting role, in work such as Aimé Césaire's foundational 1968 adaptation, *Une Tempête* and dozens of subsequent post-colonial versions and reinterpretations that talk back to Prospero as colonizer.

But adaptation has often been undertaken over the centuries as a corrective to Shakespearean errors, misrepresentations, or perceived blemishes. This type of revisioning began, possibly in Shakespeare's lifetime (the dating is disputed), when his colleague and collaborator John Fletcher penned *The Woman's Prize; or the Tamer Tamed*, a proto-feminist response to *The Taming of the Shrew* with the gender tables turned. And examples occur in every century since. In the eighteenth century his plays were adapted to make them conform to neo-classical conceptions of dramatic decorum—*Lear*'s happy ending restored to what it was before Shakespeare messed with *his* sources, *Macbeth* deprived of its indecorous Porter, and so on. In the nineteenth century Shakespeare was staged in conformity with that age's ideas about historical verisimilitude, the text radically cut and rearranged to accommodate lavish, "historically accurate" settings, in spite of Shakespeare's own historical and geographical imprecision (most famously, Bohemia with a coastline in *The Winter's Tale*). In print in the same period, the Shakespeare canon was adapted to the temper of the times and published in versions that excised the dirty bits and placed the author in the familiar position of being the source, even in his afterlife, of a newly minted word: "bowdlerization." And of course the twentieth and twenty-first centuries have seen him endlessly updated and relocated in order to demonstrate his supposed universality, "to diminish the gap between Shakespeare's world and our own" (Carley), or to "talk back" to empire and patriarchy from feminist, anti-colonialist, and anti-racist stances. Shylock, Caliban, Desdemona, and Kate have all been given independent voice and agency in play after play after novel, film, and poem.

But Shakespearean adaptation is undertaken with equal frequency for its instructional or educative value in anything ranging from the arts of rhetoric and proper English speech, through the modelling of uplifting moral values, to the production of good (docile colonial and appropriately gendered) citizens. Many such works have been written from the position of the colonizer, intending to teach or model appropriate civilized (English) behaviour to peoples construed as either savages or settlers, both Willy-nilly (as it were) subjects of "the Crown." In Winnipeg in 1915, Sister Mary Agnes assembled *A Shakespeare Pageant* for commencement day at Saint Mary's Academy in order to provide graduates of the Catholic girls' school "a lovely garland of maxims for the young [...], most valuable lessons for young girls entering the broader fields of life" (S.M.A. 79). The pageant is representative of many such uses of Shakespeare in the schools, as it is of the myriad of adaptations of Shakespeare for children, beginning, perhaps, with Charles and Mary Lamb's *Tales from Shakespeare* in 1807. Post-colonialist scholars from India, South Africa, Australia, and Canada have demonstrated the use-value for empire in locating Shakespeare at the centre of school curricula that shore up conceptions of universal human identity and value by placing the source and measure of that value in Shakespeare as the heart of the Western canon. Materialist scholars, meanwhile, have done parallel work on the use of the Bard in the British education system and elsewhere to shore up social hierarchies and class divisions. Not all of this work focuses on adaptation as such, but arguably the filtering of "Shakespeare" through schools and other institutions (such as large Shakespeare festivals), functioning as ideological state apparatuses, is inevitably a form of adaptation, more powerful, perhaps, for being invisible as such.

Which brings us to the thorny question of what constitutes (an) adaptation, together with what constitutes Shakespeare, and what constitutes the Canadianness of Shakespeare adaptation. Definitions and taxonomies, useful in organizing bodies of knowledge and ways of thinking into fields and disciplines, are also ways of policing the generic borders around bodies of work that might otherwise get out of hand, dangerous, or "unsettling." And adaptation, like the parallel activities of translation, theatrical production, and critical interpretation, is almost *by* definition a crossing of these and other borders: it is fundamentally a question of accommodation to new circumstances or purposes. I tend, then, to agree with Mark Fortier, who in a recent article makes the case, in the face of restrictive definitions, for "wild adaptation": "adaptation," he argues, "is, quite literally, anything you can get away with." I also agree with Fortier that "Shakespeare" is whatever we make of him; that is, "he" is the history of the uses to which he has been put by, among others, his adapters, and this includes what has been made of his life, works, and reputation (Fortier, "Wild")—Fortier elsewhere calls Shakespeare Canada's "cultural undead"—"the past that refuses to vanish" ("Undead" 342). But the words that we use to refer to adaptation are nevertheless worth looking at, on the way to laying out some principles by which the selections were made for this volume.

Linda Hutcheon, in her 2006 book *A Theory of Adaptation*, points out that the noun "adaptation" is used to refer to both a *process* and the work that the process produces, both something you *do* and the *result* of that doing (22). One engages in adaptation in order to produce an adaptation. I would add to this the observation that as a verb "adapt" can be transitive or intransitive: you can adapt something, or you can adapt *to* something—or you can engage in adaptation (the process) as a way of both adapting *and* adapting to, which seems to me what most dramatic adaptations of Shakespeare in Canada have done. Canadians have adapted Shakespeare as a way of adapting to the fact of his overwhelming cultural presence *as* undead—as a ghost that haunts the collectivity like the ghost of Hamlet's father (a role, apocryphal tradition has it, first played by Shakespeare himself). What makes *an* adaptation of Shakespeare "Canadian" is unclear—Canadian adaptations have been almost infinitely various, and to try to address their linked "Canadianness" would be both tedious and futile. What may be the case, however, is that adaptation *to* Shakespeare has been and remains, in Canada, and especially in an English-Canadian theatre community that's living in the shadow of the Stratford Festival, necessary. Ever since the Europeans first "discovered" Canada (much to the chagrin of the people inhabiting the land at the time), residents of the particular slice of Turtle Island constituted by the settler/invaders as Canada have of necessity been adapting to Shakespeare and everything that he has come to represent. Adaptation, therefore, is an ongoing and self-perpetuating process in Canada rather than a canon of works. It is a process of subject formation, of working out—negotiating—who, as a collective, "we" *is*. And there is no better site for such a negotiation than the live, public forum that is theatre.

The adaptations included in this volume and its companion collection, *A Certain William: Adapting Shakespeare in Francophone Canada*, edited by Leanore Lieblein, represent the very small tip of a very large iceberg. Indeed, the Canadian Adaptations of Shakespeare Project at the University of Guelph includes over 450 dramatic adaptations in its database and counting. The selection here from that massive body of work is, in Fortier's sense, "wild": it includes work that for various reasons would not be considered to be adaptations by the definitions of Linda Hutcheon, who requires that an adaptation call attention to its relationship to an original, and function as "an extended intertextual engagement with the adapted work" (8). *Cruel*

*Tears*, by Ken Mitchell with Humphrey and the Dumptrucks, does not announce itself as an adaptation, unless one recognizes the two-word title or, late in the play, an adapted "Willow Song," as deriving from *Othello*. Mitchell relocates the adapted plot of the play to Saskatoon, changes the characters' names, and cites "Shakespear" (along with Geraldi Cinthio and Brian Sklar) only cryptically in the acknowledgements to the published text. *Harlem Duet* also draws upon *Othello*, and *does* announce its relationship to Shakespeare, but it does not adapt the play's action, preferring to provide backstory in the form of a prequel. *Shakespeare's Will* would be excluded by Hutcheon's definition on the grounds that it adapts the life rather than the work of Shakespeare (though one sonnet, left intact, is crucial to its effect). But even as an adaptation of the life, the play and its title character are decentred, since Shakespeare is dead when the play opens, and his voice is heard only through his (indomitable) "will." Once again, he ghosts the play as its and our undead. *Death of a Chief*, too, fits the rubric of adaptation oddly, since the words spoken in the play are almost exclusively unaltered lines from Shakespeare's *Julius Caesar*; only the stage directions, cuts, and rearrangements (for those who recognize them) betray the play's status as adaptation. Even Michael O'Brien's *Mad Boy Chronicle* sets out with scissors and glue "to deface the greatest play of all time," not through updates or relocations, but by returning to and adapting Shakespeare's *own* sources for *Hamlet*. Among the plays published here, only Ken Gass's *Claudius* would squeak in under traditional (or Hutcheon's) definitions of adaptation—in this case, again, of *Hamlet*—and even here, the character Emilia puts in a guest appearance, smuggled in to the play from *Othello* after the death of her husband, and Hamlet is provided with a mistress named Genevieve, smuggled into the play from under the sheets.

And in what sense are these plays *Canadian* adaptations? *Harlem Duet*, though it has a secondary character named Canada, is set in Harlem. *Mad Boy Chronicle* is set in a Viking Denmark. *Shakespeare's Will* takes place in seventeenth-century Stratford-on-Avon. And the setting for *Claudius*, well, could be any number of places—the transposition of Emilia from *Othello's* Venice to *Hamlet*'s Denmark suggests that we're really in the "Shakespearosphere" rather than any actual geographical location. But in any case, we're not in Canada. Only *Cruel Tears* and *Death of a Chief* announce their Canadian (re)location and explicitly address Canadian issues, even if the latter retains a very un-Canadian blank verse.

So why have I chosen these particular plays, all of which in their wildly various ways, I would argue, are adapting to Shakespeare in Canada? First, because I like them. Each builds a powerful dramatic world inhabited by compelling characters doing and saying interesting things. Second, because they are teachable: together they represent a range of responses to Shakespeare, constitute the text for a course I'd like to teach, and speak to one another in interesting ways across their differences. It's also for the sake of the classroom that I have limited the selection to adaptations of only three plays, so that it would be possible in the course of a single semester to read all of the adaptations against one another and against their Shakespearean sources. And for a similar reason—to make them roughly comparable—I have limited the representation of Shakespearean adaptations to the contemporary period, beginning with *Cruel Tears* (first produced in 1975) and ending with *Death of a Chief* (2008). Finally, taken together the plays published here raise a range of questions that I believe are worth asking. What does it mean to efface the Shakespearean source of an adaptation—to use the story without acknowledging it—rather than engage openly in dialogue with that source? What does it mean in any adaptation, but particularly those that mount class, gender, or race based critiques of social hierarchies, to differentially reward audiences based on their knowledge of Shakespeare, perhaps provoking a self-congratulatory discourse: aren't I clever, I understood that allusion; aren't I well-educated, I recognize the source of that phrase? Does dividing an audience between those who are and are not "in" on Shakespearean citations create a special class of readers, thereby undercutting anti-hierarchical critiques? What does it mean to piggyback on Shakespeare's cultural capital while speaking back to his authority? What does it mean for a marginalized group to claim the right to *speak* Shakespeare's words rather than rewrite them, to claim access to the power that is his language? What does it mean to adapt a life rather than a work? What does it mean to view African diasporic history and ideas through the frame of a role that was performed for centuries in racist blackface? And of course readers and audiences will come to the plays with their own questions.

Adaptations are not read or viewed in the same way as other plays. *Should* these plays be read alongside their Shakespearean sources? Should a reader know the Shakespeare well before tackling the adaptation, or should the adaptation be read independently, relying on the general knowledge of Shakespeare that's in the ether, in Canada as elsewhere? Or should these plays be read ignoring Shakespeare altogether, assuming that as stand-alone plays they need to "work" independently or not at all? And should they be read for their commentary on Shakespeare or on the contemporary world, on life? Should they be read for their representation of Canada? Of gender? Of race, class, ethnicity? Different readers will bring different questions, and emerge with different answers. But *as* Canadian adaptations of Shakespeare, the plays published here all serve as examples of different ways in which Canadian playwrights have addressed the strange doubleness of claiming and rejecting, citing and rewriting, represented in my epigraph. "The" Shakespeare *is* unavoidably ours, and we have to decide what to do with it.

**Works Cited and Suggested Further Reading**

Brydon, Diana and Irena R. Makaryk, eds. *Shakespeare in Canada: A World Elsewhere?* Toronto: U of Toronto P, 2002.

Canadian Adaptations of Shakespeare Project. 14 October 2008. http://www.canadianshakespeares.ca.

Carley, Rod. "Bardomania: Adapting Shakespeare within a Canadian Political Context." Fischlin, *Canadian.*

Fischlin, Daniel, ed. *Canadian Shakespeares.* Special issue of *Borrowers and Lenders: The Journal of Shakespeare and Appropriation* 3.1 (Fall/Winter 2007). 6 April 2009. http://www.borrowers.uga.edu/cocoon/borrowers/previous_issue.

———. "Giving Shakespeare Meaning, Canadian Style: Canadian (?) Shakespeares." Fischlin, *Canadian.*

———. "Nation and/as Adaptation: Shakespeare, Canada, and Authenticity." Brydon and Makaryk 313–38.

Fischlin, Daniel and Mark Fortier, eds. *Adaptations of Shakespeare: A Critical Anthology of Plays from the Seventeenth Century to the Present.* London: Routledge, 2000.

Fischlin, Daniel and Ric Knowles, eds. *Adapting Shakespeare in Canada. Canadian Theatre Review* 111 (2002).

Fortier, Mark. "Undead and Unsafe: Adapting Shakespeare (in Canada)." Brydon and Makaryk 339–52.

———. "Wild Adaptation." Fischlin, *Canadian.*

Hutcheon, Linda. *A Theory of Adaptation.* New York: Routledge, 2006.

Knowles, Ric. *Shakespeare and Canada: Essays on Production, Translation, and Adaptation.* Brussels: Lang, 2004.

Salter, Denis, ed. *Shakespeare and Postcolonial Conditions. Essays in Theatre/Études théâtrales* 5.1 (1996).

S.M.A [Sister Mary Agnes]. *A Shakespeare Pageant: Dialogue for Commencement Day. Canadian Theatre Review* 111 (2002): 78–86.

Wilson, Ann, ed. *Shakespeare in Canada. Canadian Theatre Review* 54 (1998).

# CRUEL TEARS

KEN MITCHELL AND
HUMPHREY AND THE DUMPTRUCKS

## *OTHELLO* AT THE BLACKTOP

Ken Mitchell is something of a legend. A novelist, short-story writer, screenwriter, literary critic, prairie regionalist, Sinophile, anthologist, teacher, performer, cowboy poet, and above all, playwright, Mitchell was born in 1940 and raised on the outskirts of Moose Jaw. Although he worked briefly as a journalist and studied sociology at the University of Regina, he began writing stories and radio plays while still a student, and in 1967, after receiving his M.A., found himself teaching creative writing at Regina, where he has remained on faculty ever since. In 1969 he helped establish the Saskatchewan Writer's Guild, from 1970–75 he was director of creative writing at Saskatchewan School of the Arts, and in 1982 he helped found the Saskatchewan Playwrights Centre. He has held visiting professorships across Canada and internationally, and his contributions have been recognized by his induction into the Order of Canada in 1999 and his receipt of the Saskatchewan Order of Merit in 2001.

Throughout his career Mitchell has been an ardent advocate for prairie—or more specifically, Saskatchewan—culture, while also maintaining a fascination (and lived relationship) with China. The latter manifests itself in books such as *Through the Nan Da Gate: A China Journey* (1986) and *Stories of the Dalai Lama* (1993), and in two of his major plays—*The Great Cultural Revolution* (premiered 1979) and *Gone the Burning Sun* (1984). The former is apparent in most of his over thirty books, from *Wandering Rafferty* (1972), a novel set in Regina beer parlours, to both *Rhyming Wranglers: Cowboy Poets of the Canadian West*, an anthology he edited in 2007, and *No Ordinary Cowboy*, the cowboy poetry show in which he now performs. In addition to those already mentioned, his plays include *This Train* (1973), *Heroes* (1975), *The Medicine Line* (1976), *Davin, the Politician* (1978), *The Shipbuilder* (1978), *Chatauqua Girl: A Musical Show for Young People* (1982), *The Plainsman* (1985), *Tommy* (1986), and of course, *Cruel Tears.*

*Cruel Tears* premiered at Persephone Theatre in Saskatoon in 1975, directed by Brian Richmond and designed by Joan Paih and Gie Roberts, with music composed and performed by Humphrey and the Dumptrucks—hence their credit as co-authors of what Mitchell considers to be a country opera. Humphrey—(Gary "Humphrey Dumptruck" Walsh) and the Dumptrucks (Michael "Bear" Millar and Michael "Ernie" Taylor) was a popular Saskatoon country-folk group and jug band active between 1967 and 1981. The show toured nationally, was first published in 1977 by Talonbooks, was nominated for a Chalmers award for outstanding Canadian play in 1978, and has been frequently remounted ever since.

*Cruel Tears* is a populist hybrid that wears its Shakespeare, Grand Opera, and (in the first production, masked) Greek chorus lightly. But the play is firmly rooted in its time and place: the trucker's culture of mid-1970s Saskatchewan, which is conjured with evocatively selective detail and what now feels like "period" dialogue. There the "Yewkeranian" Johnny falls in love with Kathy, the boss's daughter, inciting the jealousy of his trucker buddy Jack Deal and activating the "prejudices" of everyone. There are traces of *Romeo and Juliet*—or more properly, Leonard Bernstein's musical adaptation, *West Side Story*—throughout, as in echoes of the musical's "There's a Place for Us," and the angry lyric, "stick to your own kind," but the main Shakespearean source is of course *Othello*. Mitchell's adaptation is coy about this, perhaps not wanting to alienate the populist crowd. Only those who recognize the title as derived from *Othello* will come to the play watching for parallels, until near the end Kathy sings a surprisingly faithful country version of Desdemona's "Willow" song, and Johnny, otherwise inexplicably in 1970s Saskatoon, talks of snuffing out the candles at the climax of the action. But the plot closely parallels that of the Shakespearean source, Johnny and Kathy standing in for Othello and Desdemona, Jack Deal and his wife Flora playing a mean Iago and unhappy Emilia, Ricky a "hippy" trucker version of Cassio, and Kathy's father Earl standing in for an omnibus Brabantio, the Duke, and the Venetian Senate.

Mitchell replaces race with ethnicity (the only black things in the play are the asphalt highway and the Blacktop Bar), and in spite of a soft "Liberated Lady" song by a miniskirted Debbie-Lou (Bianca) looking for a man, it more or less replicates the masculinist gender politics of the original. But the real strength of *Cruel Tears* is its perceptive attention to class, in both form and content. Mitchell is acute in his depiction of Frank Deal's manipulation of class pride and class betrayal to feed various jealousies and prides, and the poignant scene of class misunderstanding between Kathy and Flora brilliantly reconceptualizes the Renaissance mistress-servant relationship of Desdemona and Emilia through more subtle but very real Canadian prairie hierarchies. And Mitchell's attention to class also extends to form. He has said in interviews that in writing *Cruel Tears* he had wanted to reclaim both Shakespeare and opera as popular forms:

> I wanted to write a political play. It's political in the sense that I wanted to break down some of the barriers between art and politics; I wanted to reach a different kind of audience. We haven't broken through yet to this audience, a different audience than the university-educated, regular, theatre-going audience—the elite, if you want to call it that. (Mitchell 40)

The broad popular success of the play in production suggests that he may well have succeeded.

**Work Cited**

Mitchell, Ken. "Prairies." Interview with Alan Twigg. *For Openers: Conversations with 24 Canadian Writers*. By Alan Twigg. Madeira Park, BC: Harbour Publishing, 1981. 163–73.

*Cruel Tears* was commissioned by and first performed at Persephone Theatre in Saskatoon, Saskatchewan on March 15, 1975, with the following company:

| | |
|---|---|
| JOHNNY Roychuk | Winston Rekert |
| KATHY Jensen | Dorothy-Ann Haug |
| JACK Deal | David Stein |
| Florazarea (FLORA) Deal | Janet Wright |
| EARL Jensen | Larry Ewashen |
| RICKY Yates | Robert J. Wright |
| ROY Carter | David Miller |
| BARTENDER | Larry Ewashen |
| DEBBIE LOU Belinsky | Janet Wright |
| POLICEMAN | Larry Ewashen |
| HITCHHIKER | Andrew Czaplejewski |
| CHORUS | Marcella Cenaiko, Tamara Hrechuck, Andrew Nahachewsky, Thomas Nahachewsky |
| VOCAL CHORUS | Humphrey and the Dumptrucks |

Directed by Brian Richmond
Designed by Joan Paih and Gie Roberts
Choreographed by Bohdan E. Wowk
Music by Humphrey and the Dumptrucks

## CHARACTERS

JOHNNY Roychuk, 28, a truck driver
KATHY Jensen, 19, his sweetheart and wife
EARL Jensen, 45, owner of Motormack Express
JACK Deal, 30, Johnny's friend
Florazarea (FLORA) Deal, 30, Jack's wife
RICKY Yates, 22, a driver
ROY Carter, 40, a driver
FILTHY PHIL, a driver
DEBBIE LOU Belinsky, 25–45, a waitress
POLICEMAN
CHORUS, dancers and mimes
VOCAL CHORUS, three singers

## PLACE

Saskatoon, Saskatchewan

## TIME

May–June, 1974

## SET

The stage is divided into four levels. Upstage right is the highest level, Level 1, a small platform that serves as the bedroom. Opposite, upstage left, is a platform at a slightly lower level, Level 2, where the VOCAL CHORUS stands. Between these two platforms, upstage, is the third level, Level 3. The lowest level, Level 4, the floor, roughly half the stage, is where most of the action and the larger scenes take place.

# CRUEL TEARS

## ACT ONE

*The house lights are off; the stage is black. The VOCAL CHORUS begins to make the sound of the prairie wind moaning. The first chords of the verture are heard. As the overture is played, the lights come up slowly, suggesting the rise of a bright prairie sun in early May. The sound of a meadowlark trilling is heard. As the overture reaches full tempo, the light becomes hot. A mime suggests a prairie environment. The overture ends.*

*The VOCAL CHORUS sings "Cruel Tears Talking Blues."*

**VOCAL CHORUS** *Well we got a song about the West,*
*But we don't want you to get all depressed.*
*Now it's all about people and it's kinda sad,*
*'Cuz you know some are good and some are bad.*
  *Call it "Cruel Tears."*
  *(refrain) "Cruel Tears."*

*Like this land that we live in here,*
*Our story don't go too far to cheer,*
*But hear it even if yuh choke*
*You might even know some of these folks.*
  *They're all country people.*
  *"Westerners"*
  *Like they say in Ottawa. Wa.*

*We been through a lot, you and us,*
*We licked the winters and fought the dust.*
*We struck the thirties up Bennett's ass*
*Now we're waitin' for the time to pass,*
  *Good times we mean to say,*
  *Lookin' for 'em every day,*
  *But she's tough.*

*Why did they struggle, all of them years,*
*Breakin' their backs and cryin' cruel tears?*
*Looking for rain and chewing on dirt,*
*Schoolin' the kids so they don't get hurt.*

*That's what it's all about—*
*For the children.*
*The future*
*(refrain) If it ever comes.*

*You know who's gonna change this world?*
*Those sunburned boys and blushing girls.*
*Doesn't feel right when they go away,*
*But farming these days don't seem to pay*
*So it's off to the city.*
*High-rise apartments.*
*Okay economy.*

*You can't make a bundle, if you don't get caught*
*Tearin' down homes for parking lots.*
*You meet a lot of people in the push and shove,*
*Tryin' to buy success, what they need is love.*
*[Too expensive!]*
*City lights.*
*Every night a party.*
Good *times!*

*We're gonna show 'em at work and show 'em at play.*
*We'll show you the place where they spend their pay.*
*The men drive trucks and the girls keep house.*
*They do what they can, or they do without.*
*Cruel Tears.*
*Taste a little like whiskey.*
*Hurtin' like sin.*

*Cruel Tears!*

*The lights go up on Level 3, where JOHNNY Roychuck appears driving his truck. He sings "The Lonesome Trucker Blues."*

**JOHNNY** *Well, I been pushing this White Freightliner twenty hours,*
*Take another twenty 'fore I stop.*
*Logbook says, "Take your time,"*
*But on a day like this I'm flyin'*
*And the only one I'm cheatin' is the clock.*

*Drifting along under endless skies*
*Racing my shadow down the road*
*Born for courtin' danger,*
*Often lonesome as a stranger,*
*This diesel is my best friend and my home.*

*The boys will all be waiting at the Blacktop.*
*The harder we been workin', the rowdier we are.*
*There'll be money in the jukebox,*
*And boozin' till the door's locked,*
*My friends'll all be waitin' at the bar.*

*The lights go up on the Blacktop Bar. Instrumental music continues in the background. JACK, RICKY, and ROY have entered the bar. JACK is neat, handsome. ROY is old-fashioned, "straight." RICKY has long hair and fancy denims.*

**ROY** You buyin' the first round, Jack?

**JACK** This one's on me, boys!

**RICKY** Yer lookin' pretty fat, arnchuh?

*(to ROY)* Didjuh check the new chrome stacks on his Kenworth?

**ROY** Hey, yuh gonna get a set of moon discs, eh, Jack?

**JACK** Just cuz you were dumb enough to buy 'em for that old Jimmy a yours! And then lose one the next day at a railroad crossin'!

*They laugh.*

**RICKY** Yeah—but how about all that crummy red plastic you stuck inside yer cab? I keep seein' pieces of it blowin' down the ditches on Number Eleven!

**JACK** Don't worry, hippie! It'll last longer'n that dumb shag carpeting in that gutless Mac of yours.

**ROY** Yeah, he don't call it a shaggin' wagon fer nuthin'! Haw haw!

**RICKY** Shaggin' wagon! You should talk!

*(to JACK)* You know that redhead waitress at the Husky House?

**JACK** *(already laughing)* Yeah.

**RICKY** Guess whose truck I saw at six o'clock this morning, parked behind the gradge? Roy's!

**ROY** *(embarrassed, but pleased that they noticed)* Awwwwww!

**JACK** Yeah, but diddenshuh see? It wasn't the redhead he had in his bunk—it was the *husky*!

*They all laugh uproariously. Freeze. The lights dim on the bar.*

**JOHNNY** *For a trucker there's no limit to the ladies.*
*Some are easygoin' and some you can't get near.*
*Married women are callin' in,*
*Mona wonders, "Where you bin?"*
*And Debbie Lou keeps layin' on the beer!*

*The lights go up again on the bar. The instrumental music continues. There is a vacant chair for JOHNNY at the table in the bar.*

**JACK** *(calling to the back)* Hey, Debbie-Loooooo! Quit waterin' the rye! Come on out here—we're all gettin' dry!

**ROY** Yeah, gettin' thirsty!

**RICKY** Hey nurse! Time for my shot!

*DEBBIE LOU enters with a tray. She is heavily made up, still looking for her man. She could wear a very short skirt emblazoned with trucking crests.*

**DEBBIE LOU** Why don't I just bring the whole bar over here? You guys got hollow legs fer pourin' it down?

*The men laugh. FILTHY PHIL enters. His name refers to his style, not his hygiene. FILTHY PHIL has a wide repertoire of obscene words, gestures, and leers.*

**FILTHY PHIL** Hey Debs, *I* got a hollow leg. Wanna see it?

**DEBBIE LOU** *(right back)* Well, I hope it's bigger'n last time!

**JACK** Wanna check mine out for size?

**DEBBIE LOU** Well, I'd take a chance on anything—but *Mrs.* Deal might have somepin to say 'bout that.

**ROY** Haw haw. She got yuh there, Jack! She's lookin' for a *single* guy! Right, Debbie Lou?

**DEBBIE LOU** Maybe I'm not lookin' at all! I'm perty choosey, yuh know.

**RICKY** *(shaking his locks)* Yeah—she's goin' for the dry look! Arnchuh, Debs?

**DEBBIE LOU** You said it—dry behind the ears!

*Laughter.*

**JACK** Hey, yer in there like a dirty shirt, hippie!

**ROY** *(an old joke)* We'll hafta trim your hair first, though! Right, you guys?

*He laughs by himself.*

**FILTHY PHIL** No, no—she dozen' want *Ricky*! She's savin' herself fer—ole Roy!

*Freeze.*

**JOHNNY** *But life is pretty hollow if yuh haven't got a plan,*
*And you never try to find that special one.*
*Now there's a woman I can trust*
*And all my travellin's just become*
*A better way of gettin' close to home.*

**RICKY** Hey Filthy! How come yer in so late?

**FILTHY PHIL** Aaa, got held up by a couple a mothertruckin' Smokies—just outside a Chamberpail.

**ROY** Juh see Johnny?

**FILTHY PHIL** Naw, the big Yewkeranian was ahead a me! Must a bin in some kind a hurry—Mona said he only stopped there for a minute.

**ROY** I don't believe it! One minute fer the Manitoba Muffin?

**JACK** You better convoy down there and look after her, dummy!

**DEBBIE LOU** You guys quit buggin' Roy. You go puttin' notions in that so-called brain a his and there's gonna be trouble.

**FILTHY PHIL** *(elbowing ROY)* Go on, Roy, now's yer chance!

*The boys laugh, jabbing each other in the ribs.*

**DEBBIE LOU** Same again here, fellas?

**JACK** Yeah, hit us again! Roy's round!

**DEBBIE LOU** *(pointing around the table)* Right. Eight and a juice, rye and a Seven…

*Pointing to JACK.*

One M.G.…

*Pointing to RICKY.*

Rum and coke…

*Pointing to FILTHY PHIL.*

Couple a Heidelberg, one Pil, and a Blue, and a Blue!

*Pointing to ROY.*

**ROY** *(interrupting)* And uh—yuh got a ride home after work—yet?

**DEBBIE LOU** *(not even listening)* Hey, where's Johnny tonight?

*Freeze.*

*JOHNNY sings the last stanza of the song.*

**JOHNNY** *The chair they're holding will have to wait.*
*There's a prairie lady lookin' for me soon,*
*With promise in her smile,*
*That stays with me all the while*
*I head this big old rig on back to Saskatoon.*

*JOHNNY crosses to Level 1, where KATHY is waiting. As the instrumental music ends, he reaches her and the lights go black on Level 1. Everyone is drunker in the bar.*

**ROY** Hey, it's ten o'clock! Thought yuh said Johnny was comin'!

**JACK** *(snarling)* He's comin'!

**RICKY** Yeah? How do you know?

**JACK** 'Cause I make it my bizness to know!

**RICKY** That must be why you're the boss, eh?

**JACK** I ain't the boss!

**RICKY** Yer the union boss, arnchuh? Same thing.

*JACK grabs RICKY, threatening. The others react.*

**JACK** We got no union at Motormack! And there isn't gonna be one as long as *I'm* around.

**RICKY** *(placating him)* Okay, hear the spokesman!

**ROY** Yeah, we *elected* him spokesman, Rick.

**RICKY** Okay, spokesman, when are yuh gonna talk to old man Jensen about gettin' us that pay raise?

**JACK** I'm lookin' after it.

**FILTHY PHIL** Yeah. Keep the faith, Ricky!

**RICKY** Faith's cheap. It's the foldin' green I need. I wanta put a CB in my cab and I got no bucks.

**JACK** Don't worry, hippie, you'll get what's comin' to yuh.

**ROY** Whatssat, Jack? Gonna give 'im a haircut?

*He laughs by himself.*

**JACK** *(to RICKY)* I'm way ahead of yuh, loverboy! I got an appointment to see Jensen tomorrow.

**RICKY** Well, be sure 'n' kiss his ass for *me*, eh?

**JACK** *(rising)* You wanna step outside and show us how it's done?

**DEBBIE LOU** *(intervening)* Hey, Ricky—where'd all the music go?

*Seductively.*

Wanna plug my Wurlitzer?

**RICKY** *(hesitating, grinning)* Sure, Debs—whucha like to hear? "Our Song"?

*DEBBIE LOU dances RICKY over to the jukebox, clowning. ROY and FILTHY PHIL hoot and laugh.*

**DEBBIE LOU** G-7.

*RICKY plugs the jukebox. JACK remains sitting at the table while the others dance with DEBBIE LOU. Eventually, JACK joins in. They sing "One More for the Women."*

**VOCAL CHORUS & RICKY**

*Well it's one more for the women,*
*And one more for the road.*
*Gas my truck, wish me luck, it's time to go.*
*Tell old Debbie at the Blacktop Bar,*
*I ain't goin' all that far—*
*But I got a heavy load.*
*So give me one more for those women,*
*One more for the road.*

**RICKY**

*Now I'm the kind a guy who likes to travel.*
*My home is wherever I go.*
*Women are found in damn near every town,*
*That's something you oughta know.*
*It always makes them cry*
*When you gotta say goodbye,*
*But when you gotta go, you gotta go.*

**ALL**

*Give me one more for the women,*
*One more for the road.*

**RICKY**

*Let me get my rig out on the highway,*
*I want to see those headlights glow.*
*I'll be there with time to spare,*

*You're gonna hear my air horn blow.*
*The cops on Number One*
*You know I keep them on the run.*
*I ain't known for bein' slow.*

**ALL** *So give me one more for those women,*
*One more for the road.*

**RICKY** *There's a chick waiting for me in Regina.*
*And one 'bout halfway down the road.*
*Lots of gals, good old pals,*
*Best I've ever known.*
*They'll back you up, when you're outta luck,*
*True Knights of the Road.*

**ALL** *Give me one more for those women,*
*One more for the road.*
*So give me one more for those women,*
*And give me one more for the road.*

*Everyone takes their drinks and sits down. DEBBIE LOU goes out for more drinks.*

**ROY** Wish ole Johnny was here.

**FILTHY PHIL** Aa, he's out chasin' skirts! You know Roychuck!

**JACK** Don't talk crap! I seen him dodge two weigh scales one Friday tuh get here for the boozin'! He's comin'!

**RICKY** *(realizing something)* Hey, I know where he is!

**ROY** *(now thoroughly drunk)* He's gotta get here fer th' party.

**JACK** Aaa, go slobber on Debbie, will yuh?

**ROY** *(blubbering)* She dozen wamme, neither!

**RICKY** He's got a girlfriend!

**JACK** *(to RICKY)* Aw, yer full of it! The last guy who's gonna get trapped up in this town is Johnny Roychuck!

**RICKY** That's how much you know! This time he's *hooked*!

**JACK** You wanna bet?

**FILTHY PHIL** How 'bout it, hippie? Who is she?

*DEBBIE LOU re-enters.*

**DEBBIE LOU** Last call, boys.

**RICKY** *(delighted with himself)* Little—Kathy—Jensen!

**FILTHY PHIL** *Earl's kid?*

**ROY** *(stunned)* Kathy Jensen?

**RICKY** Yeah, he's took her out a couple of times. And last week she picked him up at the loading dock!

**JACK** *What?*

**RICKY** In the old man's station wagon!

**ROY** Well whudya know? Good ole Johnny!

*A big uproar. JACK slams his fist down angrily, knocking over some glasses. DEBBIE LOU squeals.*

**RICKY** Hey, watch out!

**JACK** That's a load of bull!

*JACK slams out the door. There is an awkward silence.*

**FILTHY PHIL** What's with him?

**RICKY** Aaa—just pissed off Johnny's havin' a good time. Jealous!

*The bar lights flash off and on.*

**ROY** Hey, lash call!

**FILTHY PHIL** More beer, Debbie Lou!

**RICKY** Let's have another song.

**DEBBIE LOU** Too late. Jukebox's awready shut off.

*The men give catcalls and groans.*

**FILTHY PHIL** Come on, sweet-thighs, yuh owe us a couple.

**RICKY** How 'bout it, Debs? I'll give yuh a ride home if you let me plug it in.

**ROY** Yeah—me too!

**DEBBIE LOU** *(relenting)* Oh, awright. But yuh gotta promise to keep him…

*To ROY.*

…in his cage.

*She goes to the jukebox below the VOCAL CHORUS.*

Which one?

**ROY** A real *romaaaanic* song!

**DEBBIE LOU** *(decisively)* B-3.

*The instrumental music for "The Love Duet" begins. The lights come up on the bedroom, Level 1, where JOHNNY and KATHY are together on the bed.*

**JOHNNY** *Kathy, you know I'm not much with words.*
*It's been hard to say things how I mean 'em.*
*When I look at you, those words don't ring true,*
*And I'm the damn fool that just said 'em.*

**KATHY** *Oh Johnny, words are only a screen.*
*Fine talk is for lawyers and statesmen.*
*What I see in your eyes makes speeches all lies.*
*Just hold me all night till the morn'.*

**JOHNNY** *But you know that I love you!*
*Though I'm not worthy of you,*
*'Cause I grew up somewhere on the wrong side of town.*
*And your family won't want to*
*Admit I'm the one to*
*Put their baby in a wedding gown.*

**KATHY** *Why waste our time on marriage and morals?*
*Let's only try to be happy tonight.*
*Don't try to possess me,*
*Just lie and caress me,*
*Why promise a future too bright?*
*Just lie here and love me all night.*

**TOGETHER** *Together we'll find a way.*

**KATHY** *Let's take it day by day.*

**JOHNNY** *Just tell me I am the one.*

**TOGETHER** *And we've got the world on the run.*

*An instrumental break as they rise from the bed.*

**JOHNNY** *We got to make plans for a family wedding*
*And think out our life together.*

**KATHY** *I don't need a ring to prove I love you,*
*Or stay with you through stormy weather.*

**JOHNNY** *No, it's got to be done right,*
*With a priest and a ring.*
*Common law ain't the way I was taught.*
*I'll go to your father and ask for his blessing.*
*And then we can go tie the knot.*

**KATHY** *It isn't that simple! When I get married,*
*It's going to be forever.*
*There's no turning back*
*Or changing your mind.*
*You must be sure from the start.*

**JOHNNY** *That's just what I feel in my heart!*
*I'll go right away to your father and say:*
*I want your daughter's hand in marriage,*
*And if he listens to me,*
*He'll just have to see...*

**KATHY** *He'll never consent to our wedding.*

*The lights come up as the sun rises. It is dawn.*

**JOHNNY** *Let's go together and talk to him now.*
*We don't have to wait anymore.*

**KATHY** *Oh Johnny, I love you.*

**JOHNNY** *And I—love you too.*

**TOGETHER** *We don't have to wait anymore.*

**JOHNNY** *It's our life that we're fighting for.*

**TOGETHER** *Together we'll find a way.*
*To face the world wide awake.*
*People can say what they will.*
*I will be here with you still.*

*An instrumental bridge.*

**VOCAL CHORUS** *There the lovers stand,*
*Making future plans.*
*They will love each other,*
*Come what may.*
*(refrain) Come what may.*

*They sing their love song,*
*And nothing can go wrong.*
*They will love each other.*
*Come what may.*
*(refrain) Come what may.*

*The bedroom goes black. The instrumental music for "Jack's Soliloquy" begins. The lights come up on Level 3—JACK Deal's mobile home. FLORA Deal enters from the back looking tired and harassed, yawning. She is in a housedress, and while she is sloppy and haggard, she was once an attractive woman.*

**FLORA** *(calling to the back)* Jack! Come on, Jack! Get outta bed. It's nine-thirty.

**JACK** *(off)* Hey—where's my shirt?

**FLORA** Right where you dropped it last night!

**JACK** *(entering, half-dressed)* Fix me a Bromo, will yuh? I'm dyin'!

*He puts on his shirt.*

Maybe yuh better throw some rye into it. I got a sore throat.

**FLORA** *(sweetly)* How about some Drano?

**JACK** Very funny.

**FLORA** How come yuh hafta go in on a Saturday, anyway?

**JACK** Hafta see Earl about somethin'.

**FLORA** Gonna ask him about the raise?

**JACK** *(downing a Bromo)* 'At's confidential, Flora—you know that.

**FLORA** Yuh got in perty late last night.

**JACK** Yeah, well—you know.

*He grins.*

Friday night with the boys, eh?

**FLORA** Johnny there?

**JACK** Who wants to know?

**FLORA** *(shrugs)* Just askin'.

**JACK** *(looking around)* Wherejuh put my good jacket?

**FLORA** *(pointing)* Here.

**JACK** *(heading for the door)* You got anythin' on today?

**FLORA** Yeah, sure. The mayor's comin' for *tea*.

**JACK** Uh-huh. Well—just have supper ready by five, eh? Wanna watch the Flyers tonight.

*Heading out the door.*

And tell those kids to keep their goddamn tricycles off the driveway!

*He goes out the front door.*

*Why is it always me has to look like the heavy?*
*Tryna do right for everybody—*
*What kind a thanks do I get?*
*What kind a thanks do I get?*

*A pause.*

*I work my butt off for two whole years.*
*To get these boys organized.*
*And what sort a thanks do I get?*
*A union couldn't a got 'em what I got 'em:*
*Decent contracts, weekends off.*
*And what kind a thanks do I get?*

*All y'hear about is Johnny.*
*Johnny. Johnny does this.*
*Johnny does that.*
*Come have a beer with us, Johnny!*

*An instrumental break.*

*Kathy Jensen, that stuck-up bitch!*
*Big Johnny—the truck drivers' hero!*
*The big bohunk and the boss's daughter!*

*An instrumental break.*

*Well, Johnny, friends can help you out,*
*And Jack's yer buddy, realize it or not.*
*Realize it or not.*
*Okay, kid, so you're naive.*
*Dumb as a gopher.*
*You got no idea what women can do.*
*You just don't understand 'em.*
*Just don't understand.*

*An instrumental break.*

*You did okay for a while, though,*
*Didn't yuh? Eh?*
*It's always you quiet guys get the most.*
*You and Ricky. The pretty boys.*
*I wonder about Flora, the way she talks...*
*Prob'ly got it on with both of 'em.*
*Well, good for them!*
*Good for her!*

*An instrumental break.*

*I got more bedrooms on the road*
*Than she ever even dreamed about.*
*Give 'em the old killer smile—boom!*
*Jack Deal scores another chicken.*
*Chalk up another kill*
*On the side of his cab.*

*The music ends. The lights go up on EARL Jensen, working inside at his desk. JACK knocks at his door.*

**EARL** Yeah—who is it?

**JACK** *(stepping inside)* Yuh free for a minnit, Mr. Jensen?

**EARL** What's on your mind, Deal?

**JACK** It's about the contract, Mr. Jensen.

**EARL** Contract talks are in September. You better see me then.

**JACK** Well, the boys are havin' it pretty tough with all this inflation. Cost a livin's goin' up alla time!

**EARL** Cost? Don't tell *me* about cost!

*He shows JACK the clipboard he has been working on.*

There's the fuel bill for this outfit last month.

*JACK looks. He whistles sympathetically.*

That's right—you guys never see it from my viewpoint.

**JACK** How about *our* viewpoint? We gotta *live*. It isn't just a matter of balancin' books, you know. We got kids to feed—

**EARL** Every driver in the company signed that contract—!

**JACK** Yeah, we signed, Mr. Jensen, but if it means we hafta work to rule just to get our fair share—well—

**EARL** That sounds like *union* talk to me, Deal.

**JACK** No unions here, Mr. Jensen.

**EARL** That's right. Your job was to keep the teamsters *out*.

**JACK** Yeah—okay.

*He shrugs and grins.*

Can't blame a guy for tryin'. We gotta keep the boys happy, don't we?

**EARL** *(getting out a bottle of whiskey)* That's right, Deal. Humour the boys. Have a slug?

**JACK** Say no more!

*EARL pours a drink for JACK. A pause. JACK toasts him.*

Well—management wins again!

*JACK laughs and drinks. EARL turns back to his work, waiting for JACK to leave. JACK sets his glass down.*

**EARL** What now?

**JACK** Well. I uh—don't know how to start—I'm not very good at talking about this kind a thing—I guess it's best to just come right to the point, not beat around the bush—

**EARL** What's the problem now?

**JACK** Oh, there's no problem—with the company. It's uh sorta—personal—matter.

**EARL** *(indignant)* Personal?

**JACK** Yuh see, there's this—talk goin' around the depot, and it's—well, kinda gross.

**EARL** *(standing)* Get to the point!

**JACK** Well—this story—I won't mention any names—has it there's a sweet little girl from the suburbs involved in some pretty funny business on the other side of town—

**EARL** *(impatient)* So?

**JACK** It's a real sideshow. You know—animal act—like the kind a stuff you were tellin' us *you* saw down in Vegas.

*He grins.*

Remember?

**EARL** Yeah?

**JACK** Yeah! Over on the other side a the river! I know you don't get into that part of town much, Mr. Jensen—lotta DP's, yuh know. Indians. But there's this big dumb bohunk over there who's got a *perfect* set-up—yuh know, bachelor pad, lotsa booze, the whole bit—

**EARL** *And?*

**JACK** And this sweet little chick from the suburbs gets the blocks put to her by the bohunk—every night, when her old man thinks she's at her pottery class!

**EARL** *(stunned)* What?

**JACK** So this story goes.

*A pause.*

**EARL** *Katharine?*

**JACK** *(hastily)* No, Earl—*no.* It's just *gossip*, like I said. I only mentioned it because I thought maybe you should—put a stop to it—

**EARL** It's a lie!

**JACK** Sure—*I* know it's a lie. I wouldn't even a repeated it—but you gotta face facts. It's the kind a thing could ruin Kathy's reputation fer good.

**EARL** *(getting hold of himself)* Who—told you this?

**JACK** Let's see, I guess it musta been Ricky. What was it the hippie said—? "Now she's used goods, man."

*EARL reacts to this.*

Course, nobody ever believes a thing he says, anyway. Just a loudmouth—you know the kind. Always lookin' fer the worst in people.

**EARL** I'll put a stop to this nonsense right away.

*A pause.*

I appreciate it, Jack.

**JACK** Appreciate?

**EARL** Your—honesty. And, uh—one more thing. Who's the—culprit?

*A long pause.*

**JACK** Now, that's askin' a bit much, Earl. Don't forget I gotta *work* with these guys.

**EARL** *One of my drivers?*

**JACK** Well—I don't wanta get anybody in trouble. Maybe there's nuthin' to this. You see, in my position—

**EARL** What's it worth to you?

**JACK** I didden come here fer money, Earl.

**EARL** *(angrily)* Well, what *did* you come for?

*A pause. JACK shrugs.*

**JACK** *(smiling)* The cost-a-livin' hike? Remember?

**EARL** *(pausing)* Okay. Ten percent, across the board!

*A pause.*

And your usual commission.

**JACK** I can't rat on a driver, Earl!

**EARL** Who is it?

*A pause. JACK looks pained.*

**JACK** No, I just can't do it. Not to a buddy.

**EARL** *Roychuck?* I'll—!

**JACK** Hey, take it *easy*, Earl!

**EARL** I—I'll look after this now.

*In control.*

I can destroy this—rotten lie.

*A pause. EARL pours two drinks.*

Of course, none of this discussion will leave the office.

**JACK** Right you are, Earl.

*JACK salutes and drinks his whiskey.*

I'll, uh move along then.

**EARL** *(distantly)* Okay.

**JACK** *(going out)* And I'll bring that contract down next week! For your John Henry.

**EARL** Yeah—sure. Sure.

*The instrumental music for "Earl's Aria" begins.*

*Oh my God—not Kathy.*
*She's just a little girl!*
*She's still my baby daughter!*

**JACK** *(off) Now she's used goods, Earl.*

**EARL** *All these drivers are like animals.*
*They sneer about my wife.*
*They've been lusting after Kathy*
*And trying to wreck her life.*

*My whole life's been a struggle*
*To keep her sweet and pure.*

*I did everything a father could*
*And now it's spoiled for sure.*

*I dreamed some day she'd marry*
*An up-and-coming man.*
*But now that's all been shattered.*

**JACK** *(off) You gotta face facts, man.*

**EARL** *(angrily) Well, it's my turn now for action.*
*I'll find his crummy den.*
*I'll have him beaten like a dog,*
*And then—!*

*EARL smashes the table with his glass. The music ends.*

*JOHNNY and KATHY appear, laughing and holding hands. KATHY's high spirits play off JOHNNY's nervousness as they approach the door of EARL's office.*

Katharine!

**KATHY** Daddy, I have some *fantastic* news for you!

**JOHNNY** Kathy! Would you just let me—?

**KATHY** Oh, all right—he wants to tell you.

**JOHNNY** I—we came—to ask you something, Earl. You see, Kathy and I have been—getting to know each other for a while and we—well, we thought it was time to come and talk about doing the right thing—

**KATHY** *(giggling at his embarrassment)* Listen to him. Isn't he quaint?

**EARL** Be quiet!

**KATHY** Pardon?

**EARL** Katharine—go inside while I deal with this—animal.

**JOHNNY** Now, hang on, Earl. You're making a mistake.

**EARL** When it's time to hear from you, I'll give your cage a shake!

**KATHY** *(confused)* Daddy—what's *wrong*?

**EARL** Will you go? This isn't for you to hear!

**JOHNNY** Stay where you are, Kathy. You're old enough now.

**EARL** *I'll* decide on her maturity, Roychuck! I make the decisions for *my* daughter! Not you!

**JOHNNY** We already decided! *We* did! Kathy and me are getting married!

**EARL** Married!

*The instrumental music for "The Struggle Trio" begins.*

*What's wrong, Kathy, are you crazy?*
*Is this respect for your family?*
*I know this kind. They're all the same.*
*To get your money he'll steal your name.*

**KATHY** *Oh, Daddy, how can you say those things?*
*We haven't rushed into this without a thought.*
*There'll be all kinds of trials we have to face—*

**JOHNNY** *(angrily) Tell her what you mean, Jensen.*
*Tell her how the bohunks beat their women.*
*Go on! Tell her those worn-out lies again.*

**EARL** *There! He said it himself. Did you hear him?*
*They drink and fool and tear around,*
*But the women sit home till they're old*
*And worn right down.*
*God, live with him.*
*But don't get married!*
*You think you're pretty smart, Roychuck.*
*But you'll never drive a rig of mine again.*

**JOHNNY** *(right back) That's fine with me—Boss!*
*You can take your truck and stick it!*
*(to KATHY) Come on! We're gettin' outta here!*

*JOHNNY moves toward the exit.*

**KATHY** *Now just hold on—the* two *of you.*
*Yelling and fighting won't get us through!*
*Neither of you is being honest—*
*Johnny, where's all that cool you promised?*
*And Daddy, you're being so unkind.*
*Give him a chance to speak his mind.*
*It must be the shock of finding out*
*That your little girl is growing up.*
*You've got to consider it while there's still time:*
*I'm ready to be his, and he'll be mine.*

**EARL** *No daughter of mine would marry his sort.*
*They've all got a girlfriend in every port.*

**JOHNNY** *We made a big mistake coming here to you,*
*We should'a just took off without even telling you.*
*But I gotta do things straight and right—*
*Not sneakin' round like a thief,*
*In the middle of the night.*

**EARL** *You listen to me, you worthless bum,*
*It cost me a fortune to bring her up.*
*She's used to having* everything*—*
*Brand spanking new!*

**KATHY** *Don't tell stories you know aren't true!*

**JOHNNY** *I know what you're saying, tryna put me down.*
*Okay, I come from the wrong side of town.*
*But I learned early how to earn my own,*
*And if you're talking about wild oats,*
*They're already sown.*
*I'm gonna marry her—I can treat her right.*
*I didn't come here to start a fight.*

**KATHY** *I know the kind of boy that you'd pick out,*
*But Johnny's the only man I'll ever love.*

**EARL** *(trying another tack) Listen to me—you're both still kids.*
*Let's forget about the things you did.*

**JOHNNY & KATHY** *We're* not *ashamed of what we're doing.*

**EARL** *You'll forget all about him pretty soon.*

**KATHY** *Now I'm old enough to live my own life.*

**JOHNNY & KATHY** *And with or without you,*
*She'll (I'll) be my (his) wife.*

**KATHY** *So please smile and wish us all the best.*
*I know my Johnny'll take care of the rest.*

**JOHNNY** *I can start my own business just like you.*
*I've been driving long enough to know what I'm doin'.*
*We'll build a home, and we'll get by.*

**JOHNNY & KATHY** *I will always be right by your side.*

**EARL** *Do you know what it is that hurts me most?*
*The father is always the last to know.*

*But I guess if you both really mean what you say—*
*I won't be the one to stand in your way.*

**KATHY** *Oh, Daddy, you're an angel! I love you so.*

**JOHNNY** *Mr. Jensen, there's something you ought to know.*
*We wouldn't have done it without your okay,*
*'Cause I always did respect what you got to say.*

**EARL** *Well, we'll have to start thinking in terms of you.*
*Maybe there's a better job you can do.*
*I'm not getting any younger, as you can see.*
*Someday you'll have to take over from me.*
*It's a good chance for you to see what you got.*
*Johnny, why don't you give it some thought?*

**KATHY** *Everything's happening! It's just like a dream!*

**JOHNNY** *The only thing that matters is you with me.*

**EARL** *Kids these days are growing up too fast!*

**JOHNNY & KATHY** *Ours is a love that's going to last.*

**EARL** *Well I'm sorry, but I've got work to do.*
*From here on in, it's up to you.*

**KATHY** *I'll ask Mother to start the plans.*

**JOHNNY** *Sir, I'd like to shake your hand.*

**EARL** *From now on, John, it's Dad—or Earl.*

**KATHY** *Daddy, you've made me a happy girl!*

*At the end of the song, all three are standing together. The instrumental music for "The Wedding Song" begins. JOHNNY takes his place at the altar as the characters assemble in church for the wedding. EARL and KATHY march down the aisle.*

**VOCAL CHORUS** *She's all in white. He's by her side.*
*Today they're becoming man and wife.*
*Choir begins to sing. He gives her the ring.*
*She feels like a queen, and he's her king.*

*The ceremony ends. KATHY and JOHNNY leave the church as the crowd, including JACK, FLORA, RICKY, EARL, and the DANCERS, throws rice. They reassemble for the wedding reception and dance. A bar is set up downstage.*

*The instrumental music for "The Sugar Waltz" begins. EARL approaches KATHY and JOHNNY, downstage centre.*

**EARL** Well. Am I entitled to the first dance?

**JOHNNY** Sure—you go ahead—Dad.

*They dance away to the right.*

But have her back before midnight.

*FLORA and JACK approach from the left.*

**JACK** Hey, good buddy! Can I buy a drink for the ole married man?

*He laughs.*

Sucker!

*JACK puts his arm around JOHNNY and takes him off to the bar at right, leaving FLORA alone, downstage centre. DEBBIE LOU and RICKY dance past.*

**RICKY** Hiya, Flora!

**DEBBIE LOU** How's tricks, Mrs. Deal?

**FLORA** Oh—Debbie. Don't tell me *you* got an invite!

**DEBBIE LOU** Johnny *said* I could come!

*ROY enters dressed up in new, but outrageous, clothes.*

**ROY** Hey, Flora! Wanna cut a rug?

**FLORA** Whudja, finish yer Arthur Murray course?

*ROY and FLORA dance off in real style. EARL and KATHY dance past.*

**KATHY** Daddy, I'm so happy, I could—explode!

**EARL** Now Punkin, you shouldn't expect too much at first.

**KATHY** Oh Father—*stop* it!

*JOHNNY intercepts them from the right, a drink in his hand.*

**JOHNNY** You don't mind if I cut in now, do you?

**EARL** You're certainly impatient, I'll say that.

**JOHNNY** Aa—it's just the ole "Ukrainian" in me—Dad.

*He puts the drink in EARL's hand and dances off with KATHY. EARL goes to the bar, passing JACK, who meets RICKY and DEBBIE LOU dancing past. JACK cuts in.*

**JACK** *(to RICKY)* Well, they really got this shindig organized in a hurry, didn't they? Didjuh see Earl's shotgun at the door?

*He laughs.*

**FLORA** *(dancing past him)* Oh shut up, Jack. Why don't yuh enjoy yourself for once?

*RICKY cuts in on ROY as JACK and DEBBIE LOU dance off. FILTHY PHIL appears.*

**FILTHY PHIL** *(to ROY)* Well, whuddayuh think? Bride looks a little plump around the middle of her wedding dress—eh?

**ROY** *(staring)* Gowan!

*FILTHY PHIL laughs and shoves ROY over toward the bar. KATHY and JOHNNY dance past.*

**KATHY** What are you looking so scared for?

**JOHNNY** The boys! I wonder if any of 'em found out where we're staying tonight?

**KATHY** *(feigning innocent curiosity)* Why—was it supposed to be a secret?

*JOHNNY looks around in horror. She smiles and hugs him. Suddenly, the Roychuck family enters dressed in traditional Ukrainian costume—the dancers.*

**JOHNNY** Dobray Vetcheer!

*Response.*

**JACK** *(to anyone)* Roychuck's family's here! Kin smell the garlic from here!

**JOHNNY** Hey—Kolomeyka!

*The waltz ends.*

*The dance floor clears as the "Kolomeyka" dance music begins. JOHNNY and KATHY are invited to participate, and do. Gradually, all the dancers join in, led by RICKY, who is enticed into the dance by a YOUNG WOMAN.*

**JACK** Go on, hippie! Don't let 'em show yuh up!

**KATHY** Try it out, Ricky!

**DEBBIE LOU** If you dance with *her*, I'm goin' home with Scrotum!

*The dancing builds to a display of wild rhythm accompanied by shouting and stomping. There is a great final shout and the stage suddenly goes black.*

## ACT TWO

*In the darkness, the instrumental music for "Cruel Tears" begins. The lights come up on the VOCAL CHORUS and on KATHY and JOHNNY in their home, Level 1. JOHNNY prepares to leave for work in the morning.*

**VOCAL CHORUS** *A month goes by, that's not much time,*
*But our couple's settled in just fine.*
*Got a little suite just built for two*
*In a modern block called the "Normanview."*
*Two years lease,*
*No pets, no kids. (refrain) No fun.*
*Right behind the shopping mall.*
*(refrain) On the bus line.*

*Johnny's a foreman, climbin' real fast.*
*He wears a tie and his pants get pressed.*
*Kathy's in the kitchen cookin' up a storm*
*Sewin' all the curtains for their cozy little home.*
*Blind stitchin'!*

*JOHNNY leaves for work as KATHY bustles about in her kitchen. The instrumental music for "The Catalogue Blues" begins. FLORA comes to the door and knocks.*

**KATHY** Hello?

**FLORA** Hiyuh.

**KATHY** Oh! Uh—Flora?

**FLORA** 'At's right. We met at the wedding, remember?

**KATHY** Sure. You're uh—Jack's wife?

**FLORA** Yeah—Jack's wife.

*She laughs nervously.*

'At's me, awright.

**KATHY** Come in, come in!

*A pause.*

How is—Jack?

**FLORA** Oh, real good. He always is.

**KATHY** I was, uh, just putting the kettle on. Would you like some tea?

**FLORA** *(appalled) Tea?*

**KATHY** Oh, I have coffee too! It's only instant though. We haven't got our coffee maker yet.

**FLORA** No, no—tea's real good.

*KATHY goes out to fill the kettle.*

**KATHY** *(from the kitchen)* Would you like to try a cookie?

**FLORA** A what?

**KATHY** Oatmeal cookies! I'm learning a new recipe!

**FLORA** *(to herself, looking around)* Oatmeal cookies. Frilly curtains in the kitchen. I'd forgot what it was like. Hmph. And all this new stuff.

*KATHY returns.*

Got a lotta nice things at the reception, eh?

**KATHY** Yes—everybody was so generous! It was fantastic. And look!

*She gets out an elaborately designed, expensive-looking neck scarf.*

Johnny's mother gave me this beautiful scarf! Look at the *embroidery*!

**FLORA** Yeah—real nice. Makes a difference when you get—personal things.

*She hands it back.*

Used the waffle iron yet?

**KATHY** *(confused)* Waffle iron? Oh—yes!

*She smiles.*

Thank you very much. That was very—original.

**FLORA** Yuh didden get no others, eh?

**KATHY** *(laughing)* No! But we now have three toasters!

**FLORA** Yeah, Jack 'n me got four electric can openers at ours!

*She laughs.*

Well—as long as yuh got everythin' yuh need! Can't complain if it's free!

**KATHY** Oh, we had to buy a *few* things—most of the big, expensive ones.

**FLORA** Well, I hope they last till yuh pay 'em all off.

**KATHY** I beg your pardon?

**FLORA** Our stuff fell apart before the first anniversary! Wherejuh get yours? Korman's Cut-Rate House of Bargains?

*The VOCAL CHORUS sings "The Catalogue Blues."*

**VOCAL CHORUS** *This year's hottest buy*
*Is the deluxe range you'll need.*
*Auto-cleaning oven, four oven racks,*
*Self-basting rotisserie.*
*With a camouflaged storage drawer*
*To hide away all your pots and pans;*
*Console light, oven light,*
*Illuminated broiler, and*
*A prismachrome, bastomatic roast meter*
*To end those burnt-supper blues.*

*This five-cycle automatic washer*
*Is the queen of versatility.*
*Ten wash-spin speeds,*
*Hot-cold water—selectivity!*
*Heavy-duty agitator, lint trap,*
*With stop-action safety lid,*
*Genuine imitation steel construction*
*With plastic-coat front and sides,*
*Porcelain-enamelled basket and top.*

*Our finest quality dryer,*
*Along with the washer too,*
*Has automatic dry cycles, normal*
*And permanent press for you.*
*No-heat cycle fluffs your towels.*
*Safety stop switch, drum light.*
*Comes in avocado, harvest gold,*
*Ordinary beige, and white,*
*Mellow-tone green, little boy blue*
*And deeeeep olive.*

*(refrain) Our couple can own some wonderful things*
*In just a year or two.*
*Once they've made the small down payment,*
*They're almost through.*

*How about a twenty-speed blender?*
*With eight push-button controls?*
*High-low selector switch,*
*Pulse-action works, with a durable plastic bowl.*

*Five-cup graduated glass container*
*And a one-ounce removable top,*
*With electronic time for split-second blending,*
*Also an automatic stop.*
*Removable blade assembly, and*
*At no cost to you, a full-colour cookbook!*

*Here's a honey of a buy, top of the line,*
*One a frost-free two-door fridge—*
*Good family size, lots of shelves*
*With trim along the ridge.*
*With a butter compartment and one for cheese,*
*And a big meat-keeper too,*
*Egg buckets, crisper,*
*And a freezer dispenser for your juice,*
*Charcoal filter, dual controls.*
*Limit of two per customer, please.*

*You absolutely need a brand new carvomatic*
*Slicelectric knife,*
*With stainless steel double-hollow-ground blades*
*That'll stay sharp all its life.*
*You'll get a push-button blade release*
*Complete with automatic stop.*
*Comes with exclusive wall rack table stand,*
*Set in a plastic chest*
*And a handy fingertip on-off button,*
*Our ultimate in value, super-exclusive, this week only!*

*(refrain) You can own some wonderful things*
*In just a year or two.*
*Once you've made that small down payment—*
*You're almost through!*

**FLORA** Yuh know, I just didden think you'd be the type to take up cookin' and cleaning and all that.

**KATHY** Well—neither did I. Just *no way* Kathy Jensen was going to be trapped into a traditional housewife role—

**FLORA** Now wait a minute!

**KATHY** *(laughing)* Anyway, I *do* like cooking. Isn't that weird? I feel *great*, trying out new recipes. Making this place look like a home.

**FLORA** *(gazing at her)* Uh huh.

*A pause. The VOCAL CHORUS sings the refrain of "The Catalogue Blues."*

**KATHY** *(making conversation)* Did you uh—walk over?

**FLORA** No. No, I drove. Thought I'd be neighbourly and see how you're settlin' in tuh married life. Jack gimme the car today to get the groceries, so I dumped the kids off at Suzy's and—

**KATHY** Oh, that's fan*tas*tic! You have kids!

**FLORA** Yeah—four of 'em.

**KATHY** Gee, you're lucky. Someday—!

**FLORA** Every one of 'em an animal!

**KATHY** Oh.

*A pause.*

The water's boiling!

*KATHY goes to the kitchen.*

**FLORA** *(calling)* So you really got yourself a prize, eh?

**KATHY** Pardon?

**FLORA** Johnny! I was sayin' he's some catch!

**KATHY** *(still in the kitchen, making tea)* Well, I think he is!

**FLORA** *(to herself)* Half the wimmen in this town tried to snap him up! Single *and* married. But he held out. "Lookin' fer somethin' special," he sez. Just *like* a Uke.

*KATHY re-enters with the tea and some cups and saucers.*

**KATHY** Sorry— What were you saying?

**FLORA** Just pumpin' air, sweetie.

**KATHY** What do you take?

**FLORA** *(automatically)* Cream'n'sugar.

*A pause.*

Hey, tell me somethin'! Did you have some kind a plan, or what? Or was it *real love*? You know—stars fell on the Saskatchewan when I held you in my arms, eksetra, eksetra?

**KATHY** *(laughing)* No, I think it just happened.

*A pause.*

Maybe it *was* the stars. He's a Leo, you know.

**FLORA** He's a *what*?

**KATHY** Leo—the lion? That's his sign.

*The instrumental music for "The Homemaker's Duet" begins.*

**FLORA** *(ignoring KATHY's last line)* Honey, you got any *idea* how many girls tried to trap up Johnny Roychuck?

**KATHY** That's in the past, Flora! Sure—I know Johnny used to run around a lot, but we're married *now*. The past isn't important.

**FLORA** I don't wanna disillusion yuh, kiddo, but it has a way of comin' back tuh haunt yuh, eh?

**KATHY** Maybe that happens with other people, Flora.

**FLORA** *(laughing sharply)* Yeah, maybe. But it's funny how long those old flames take to flicker out sometimes. Six months after Jack and me got married, he was comin' home from his road trips smellin' like cheap perfume.

**KATHY** *(uncomfortable)* Well, I'm not saying married people don't have—problems. But I wouldn't have got married if Johnny wasn't really special.

**FLORA** Everybody thinks *that*, sweetie-poo. One minute you're standing up to your knees in rose petals, just dazzled by the godalmighty glory of it all!

**KATHY** Yes!

**FLORA** And the next, yer up to yer ass in dirty dishes and the old man's whining he doesn't have a clean shirt! To go out boozing with the boys!

**KATHY** *(turning away)* Yeah—I suppose.

*A pause.*

**FLORA** Aw, I didden come over to ruin yer day. Maybe you *have* got it together. Who knows what we really want, eh?

*KATHY begins to sing "The Homemaker's Duet."*

**KATHY**
*Oh, Flora, I'm so happy I got a good man.*
*I couldn't ask for more.*
*He's strong and yet he's gentle*
*And he treats me like*
*I've never been treated before.*

*It might sound silly to talk this way,*
*Like an empty-headed trucker's wife,*
*But listen to me, Flora—*
*I'm a woman,*
*And there's a reason why I chose this life.*

*(refrain) Living together with the one you love,*
*Sharing all the work and play,*
*Two people facing whatever comes along,*
*Anticipating each new day.*

**FLORA** *Listen honey, just you wait,*
*Let me tell you 'bout the life I've led.*
*Waitin' fer that truckin' man of mine,*
*Sleepin' in an empty bed,*
*I bin talking to the radio lonely nights,*
*Phoning up the Fifth Wheel Show,*
*Knowin' he's livin' it up real high,*
*Somewhere down the road.*
*I'm wipin' runny noses, there's dirty diapers*
*Soakin' in the biffy sink.*
*It's an easy life for a trucker's wife,*
*That's what I used to think.*
*Our castle turned out to be a garbage dump,*
*My hair is turnin' grey.*
*It's a far cry from what he promised me*
*On our weddin' day!*

*(refrain) Livin' together with the one you love,*
*Sharin' all the work and play.*
*Two people facin' whatever comes along,*
*Anticipatin' each new day!*

**KATHY** *I know it won't be an easy road,*
*It's full of twists and bends.*
*But Johnny and I are going down it,*
*Until we reach the end.*
*Maybe he's the driver, but when I got married,*
*I learned how to read the maps.*
*I can be a housewife, but not some loser*
*Living in a laundromat.*

*A musical bridge.*

**FLORA** *Let me tell yuh, sweetie—*
*You don't know nothin' till yuh got four kids!*
*Sherry's got the measles, Mark'll be next.*
*And Angie's got a real boyfriend.*

*I'm run ragged from dawn to dusk*
*Picking up their odds and ends.*
*Jack drops in for a change of clothes,*
*He forgot about the times we had,*
*Baby Brent spends the whole day cryin'*
*And he looks just like his dad.*

**FLORA & KATHY** *(refrain) Living together with the one you love,*
*Sharing all the work and play.*
*Two people facing whatever comes along,*
*Anticipating each new day.*

**FLORA** *Pay no mind to what I say,*
*I just been kicked around.*
*Maybe it's true you'll have a good life,*
*If your man keeps his feet on the ground.*
*If he treats you right, the way he should,*
*He'll always have your respect—*
*And you'll always have colourful things.*

*A pause.*

*Like that scarf around your neck.*

*The music continues instrumentally behind the dialogue. KATHY removes her scarf.*

**KATHY** Here. Take it, Flora—maybe it'll bring *you* some joy.

**FLORA** I can't! It's from Johnny's—

**KATHY** I want you to have it.

**FLORA** Won't he be—mad?

**KATHY** *(smiling)* He'd better not be! It's my scarf.

**FLORA** *(touched)* Thanks.

*A pause.*

Well, I better go get the rations.

*They go to the door.*

**KATHY** I want you to come over any time you feel like it. And bring your kids!

**FLORA** Yeah—you too. Now it's your turn to visit me.

**KATHY** Okay.

**FLORA** Just—gimme a call before yuh come over, eh?

*She goes.*

See yuh!

**KATHY** Bye bye.

*The instrumental music for "The Loading Dock Aria" begins. It is a simple percussion rhythm. ROY, JACK, and RICKY are loading a truck—ROY's. At the other side, FILTHY PHIL and the MALE NON-VOCAL CHORUS are loading a truck with boxes. JACK stops work first.*

**JACK** *What're we doin' on the loadin' dock,*
*Liftin' heavy boxes till the boss says stop?*
*Johnny was our friend, but now he's on top*
*Watchin' us sweat on the loading dock!*

**RICKY** *We're workin' for the money.*

**FILTHY PHIL** *It ain't fer fun.*

**ROY** *We gotta do the work 'cause it's gotta be done.*

**RICKY** *We're part of the company, according to John.*

**ROY** *Sweatin' for the money, not the fun.*

**RICKY** *We got plenty a muscle to make our way,*
*If it's work by week or work by day.*

**FILTHY PHIL** *It don't matter too much when or where,*
*If the pay is good and it's always there.*

**JACK** *This plan a his is a rip-off scheme!*
*It ain't as good as he makes it seem.*
*On an hourly rate we could featherbed;*
*Work by the mile and we're screwed instead!*

*Now if you listen to me, I got a plan.*
*Don't listen to Johnny, he's a company man.*

*Silence for one line.*

*Don't listen to Johnny, he's a company man.*

*RICKY and ROY stop work. The others continue.*

**RICKY** *Come on—we're all brothers. Johnny is too.*

**ROY** *He'll get us more bucks for what we're doin'.*

**JACK** *If you wanta slave, go and dig ditches.*
*Better 'n makin' these bastards rich. If*
*A man drives truck, he don't swing puck.*

*An archy-tect won't lift no bricks.*
*You guys run rigs, not garbage vans.*
*A Knight of the Road is a driving man!*

*As the second group continues to work, JOHNNY enters with a clipboard. He is surprised to see RICKY, ROY, and JACK idling.*

**JOHNNY** What's up? Truck loaded awready?

**JACK** Naw, we took a little break.

**JOHNNY** *(checking his watch)* Little break? This ain't no government office, boys—it's a truck depot! Now get movin', eh?

**JACK** *(to the others)* See what I say? Give a guy a bit of power and first thing you know yuh got a little Hitler on your hands.

*Laughter.*

**JOHNNY** Okay, you guys—cut the crap and get on with it. This truck's due in Winnipeg by midnight. Roy, aren't you supposeta be haulin' this?

**ROY** I'm just havin' a breather. All this liftin's gettin' us down, Johnny. We ain't used to it.

**JOHNNY** Well, you better get used to it.

**JACK** Hey, catch that, boys! Whatsa matter, big stud? Not gettin' enough from the ole lady?

**JOHNNY** *(bristling)* What was that?

**RICKY** *(quickly)* Hey, Johnny! Payday today! How about comin' over to the Blacktop and drawin' a few with us! Like old times!

**JOHNNY** I uh, don't think I can manage it today.

*He concentrates on the clipboard.*

**JACK** Old man Jensen keeps him on a short leash!

*ROY laughs.*

**JOHNNY** Well, if it's any a yer business, Kathy and me got something planned.

**JACK** Well then—we'll just hafta carry on by ourselves, eh, boys? *Somebody's* gotta keep up the tradition.

**RICKY** Couldenchuh drop by—fer a couple a quick ones? On your way home like?

**ROY** Yeah—a couple a quick ones!

**JOHNNY** I know what you guys mean. A couple of quick kegs!

**JACK** Okay, buddy, you go home and crawl between the sheets. We wouldn't wanchuh to hit the boudoir polluted with…

*Camping.*

…"alcohol"!

**JOHNNY** *(laughing)* You should talk! 'Member that night you were supposed to be home early for your anniversary dinner? I drank *you* right under the table!

*They all laugh, including JACK.*

**JACK** Yeah, that was a bash and a half!

*He shakes his head.*

Good times.

**ROY** How 'bout it, Johnny? Gonna come and bite the head off a few weasels?

**JOHNNY** Well—we'll see. Meantime, you guys get that pig *loaded*!

*To ROY.*

And I don't know why *you're* so eager! You're gonna be in Winnipeg tonight!

**ROY** Aw, I'll get somebody to take my run—if yer gonna come 'ave a few wit' us. This is the real *celebration*!

**JOHNNY** I'm not promisin' nuthin'! Now git those trucks looked after or we'll be here till this time tomorrow tryna do yesterday's work.

*The work rhythm begins again. JOHNNY goes out. JACK salutes him.*

**JACK** See you later—boss.

*The men laugh and chant the last stanza of the song.*

**TRUCKERS** *We got plenty a muscle to make our way,*
*If it's work by week, or work by day.*
*It don't matter too much when or where,*
*If the pay is good and it's always there.*

*As they work, they move the boxes and props out and set up the scene for JACK's trailer. A raucous buzzer goes off. They drop everything and head out to the beer parlour as the lights go down.*

**FILTHY PHIL** Hey—order me a rum! I gotta go drive my mum home!

**ROY** *(to JACK)* C'mon! Let's get Johnny!

*They exit.*

*In the darkness, the instrumental music for "Florazarea's Song" begins. The lights go up on FLORA, who is made up and looking prettier, in her trailer. She goes to the phone and dials.*

**FLORA** Yeah, is Jack Deal there? Well, could you call him to the phone? I see. No, it's not important. He must be on the way now.

*She hangs up.*

*Oh why do you treat me the way that you do?*
*Why do you treat me this way?*
*You're leaving me waiting while time goes along,*
*Do you still love me today?*

*I found you in the summertime,*
*When the grass was green and the sun it shined,*
*Now you're gone from these arms of mine.*
*Oh why do you treat me this way?*

*What went and happened to our yesterdays,*
*Those days of laughter and mine?*
*We treasured pressed roses and photographs*
*Now crumpled and faded with time.*

*We used to hold hands at the pitcher show,*
*Kissing and watching our dreams unfold,*
*But the screens went dark many years ago.*
*Oh why do you treat me this way?*

*You told me that first night you loved me*
*And whispered you'd always be true,*
*That maybe we'd have a few cloudy days*
*But I could depend, darlin', on you.*

*(spoken) Then you started calling home "late from work."*
*Around you I could hear all that beer parlour sound.*
*I had to struggle to hold back my tears:*
*"Okay, sweetie, now don't let me down!"*

*Why did it have to turn out this way?*
*I'm so scared of bein' alone.*
*I've wasted my life away livin' this lie*
*And crying when you're never home.*

*I found you in the summertime,*
*When the grass was green and the sun it shined,*
*Now you're gone from these arms of mine.*
*Oh why do you treat me this way?*

*A baby is heard crying, off. FLORA turns and exits. The music continues, but at a lower volume, as JACK appears downstage left, staggering drunkenly toward the door of his home. He is carrying a paper bag with a bottle in it. He stumbles into the trailer, cursing, and goes to the radio, turning on the switch.*

**JACK** *(calling)* Flora! Where are yuh?

*The instrumental music shifts to a fast version of "Florazarea's Song," very loud. FLORA re-enters hastily and turns down the volume. It will gradually rise again through this scene.*

**FLORA** Will you shut up? I just got the kids tuh bed.

**JACK** Lissen, getcher self fixed up. There's people on their way over here!

**FLORA** What?

**JACK** I invited the boys over for a little party!

**FLORA** Over *here*?

**JACK** Yeah! We haven't had a Friday night wingding fer a *long* time!

**FLORA** Oh shit!

**JACK** Come on, *hustle,* will yuh? They're gonna be here any minute! Just went home to collect the wimmen.

**FLORA** Well, call 'em up and tell 'em the whole thing's off. I'm not up to no party tonight.

**JACK** Hey, don't be an ole granny now! You're always bitchin' that we never do nothing or see nobody!

**FLORA** Well, there's such a thing as lettin' me know when—

**JACK** Okay, I'll call it off! Just don't come whining tuh me the next time yer feelin' "lonely"!

**FLORA** Well, if that doesn't take the goddamn cake! I had to carry all the groceries in here by *myself*! *After* I took the car into the garage!

**JACK** What?

**FLORA** The clutch fell outtuv it again!

**JACK** *Wimmen drivers!* I don't know why I even let you drive it!

**FLORA** Cuz if you didn't, you'd hafta do all the errands yourself.

**JACK** *Oh yeah?*

**FLORA** Then you woulden' have time to tear around, gettin' hammered up and chasin' wimmen in the beer parlours! Why do you bother even comin' home?

**JACK** Good question! Maybe cuz I was dumb enough tuh *marry* yuh!

**FLORA** Well, you didn't have to ask.

**JACK** I never asked! I was told!

**FLORA** Well, what was *I* supposeta do? Have the kid in a granary?

**JACK** Maybe yuh should've. Then yuh wouldn't be *bitchin'* about it alla time!

**FLORA** *Me* bitching? You're never here to listen! If I ever got started on all the things that—!

**JACK** Well, *don't* start! Get this damn trailer cleaned up so my friends don't think we live in a pigsty!

*The music has reached a peak in volume and FLORA turns down the radio. The music goes quiet again.*

**FLORA** You clean it up! It's you wants the party.

**JACK** *(dangerously)* You're gonna make me do something both of us are gonna be sorry for.

**FLORA** You can't scare me with that kind a hard talk. Not with all yer friends comin' over. Don't want 'em to get all upset at the sight of blood—*do* we?

*The music ends. One of the VOCAL CHORUS breaks in like a radio announcer.*

**VOCAL CHORUS** Temperatures in downtown Saskatoon a balmy seventy-eight degrees. *And* here's a new cut off the latest album from The Dumptrucks!

*The instrumental music to "Florazarea's Song," slow version, begins.*

*JACK pours himself a drink.*

**JACK** Roychuck's comin' over.

**FLORA** Johnny?

**JACK** Yeah—thought that'd cheer yuh up.

**FLORA** Is—Kathy comin' too?

**JACK** He says she is. Went home to get her, anyways.

*He laughs.*

**FLORA** What's so funny?

**JACK** I'd like to see the look on her face, when he gets home!

**FLORA** Why?

**JACK** Aw—him and Ricky got involved in a little chug-a-lug contest!

*He laughs again.*

They're both half-pissed!

**FLORA** Tryna start trouble awready?

**JACK** Hell, no! Just tryna show him what he got himself in for!

**FLORA** I hope they come.

**JACK** Aaa—forget it. She isn't gonna lower herself to take in a truck driver party! He'll hafta knock some sense into her first.

**FLORA** You don't know anything about her!

**JACK** Izzat so? Well, what would I *want* to know?

**FLORA** *(pausing)* It wouldn't make any difference. You gonna gimme a hand to clean this up?

**JACK** *(giving her a kiss)* Lissen, I gotta take a shower! Armpits smell like a farmer's socks!

**FLORA** *(protesting)* Well, look at this place. It'll take at least an hour!

**JACK** Aa, do whutchuh can.

*He notices the scarf around her neck that KATHY gave her.*

Hey, wherejuh get that?

**FLORA** *(pausing)* I bought it.

**JACK** To hell you did! You can't afford *that* kind a silk!

*He seizes the scarf.*

Where'd you get it?

**FLORA** A friend gave it to me.

*He twists the scarf.*

**JACK** Friend? What friend? The milkman? Or you started takin' *hippies* in off the street?

**FLORA** *(choking)* Kathy.

**JACK** You're lyin'. She don't know *you*!

**FLORA** I went over to visit her.

**JACK** And she *donated* you a fifty-dollar scarf? Just like that?

**FLORA** Yes.

**JACK** Who's she think she is—the Salvation Army?

**FLORA** She didn't need it.

**JACK** Neither do you. So you can hand it right back.

**FLORA** I could wear it tonight.

**JACK** Like hell you can. Think I want my wife wearing cast-offs—like some welfare bum? Take it off!

**FLORA** No.

**JACK** *(shouting at her in a fury) You take it off!*

*He tears the scarf from her throat, throwing her to the floor. The lights go up on the downstage area as ROY and DEBBIE LOU enter. ROY is carrying a case of beer. JACK exits through the rear.*

**ROY** Hey, juh hear that?

**DEBBIE LOU** What?

*They listen.*

**ROY** Jack and Flora—havin' another lovers' quarrel.

**DEBBIE LOU** Gee, maybe the party's off.

**ROY** Naaa—give 'em a minute tuh cool down.

*A pause.*

Like a beer? Sorta nice out here, izzen it?

**DEBBIE LOU** Yeah—giss so.

*ROY opens the case of beer. He uncaps two bottles with his teeth and hands one to DEBBIE LOU.*

**ROY** Wanna go and sit over by them lilacs?

**DEBBIE LOU** Lissen, dummy—you said "a ride to the party." I don't wanchuh droolin' all over my dress again.

**ROY** Awww!

**DEBBIE LOU** *You* go over by the lilacs!

*ROY goes over to pee. The instrumental music for "Roy's Aria" begins.*

**ROY**

*I can see you standing*
*In your satin evening gown.*
*You'll dance with all the fellas here*
*But you just put me down.*
*I'm good, I'm bad, I have my faults,*
*I'm just like all the rest—*
*But still you make me feel that*
*I am less than second best.*

*When I come a-callin',*
*You're never there at home.*
*There's a light up in your window,*
*And I'm standin' here alone.*
*But when you never answer*
*It hurts me, I confess.*
*Still you make me feel that*
*I am less than second best.*

*When they play the last waltz*
*And all the lovers dance,*
*I'll come up and ask you,*
*But I won't stand a chance.*
*I know you'll laugh and turn away*
*And think I'm just a pest.*
*Still you make me feel that*
*I am less than second best.*

*Still you make me feel that*
*I am less than second best.*

*DEBBIE LOU replies, singing "Liberated Lady."*

**DEBBIE LOU**

*I know you see me every night*
*Slingin' trays of foam,*

*The boys all grabbin' at my butt*
*And tryna get me home.*

*But when the lights flick off and on*
*And it's time to think of bed,*
*I want a dude*
*That isn't rude*
*To spread butter on my bread.*

*(refrain) I'm a liberated lady*
*And I'll just wait and see.*
*I got a lotta Friday nights*
*To get what's in store for me.*

*To love some mother's darlin'*
*You'll spend your life alone*
*Waitin' for that Romeo*
*To ring your telephone.*

*An instrumental break.*

*They tell me that I'm burnin' out*
*My candle from both ends.*
*I'm old enough to know better*
*But young enough to do it again.*

*No one claims this heart of mine,*
*Nobody owns my soul.*
*Life is short,*
*So come on, sport,*
*And let those hot dice roll!*

*(refrain) I'm a liberated lady*
*And I'll just wait and see.*
*I got a lotta Friday nights*
*To get what's in store for me.*

*RICKY, FILTHY PHIL, and the FEMALE NON-VOCAL CHORUS enter carrying more beer.*

**RICKY** *(drunk)* Hey, zis where the party is?

**DEBBIE LOU** Yeah, you're here! Roy's over waterin' the lawn.

**FILTHY PHIL** Hey Jack! We're comin' in, ready or not!

**DEBBIE LOU** Party! We're gonna have a party!

**RICKY** *(pounding at the door) Heeyy!* Any stompers at this soiray?

**ROY** Jack! We're here!

*FLORA opens the door.*

**FLORA** Will you guys shut up? You'll wake up the whole trailer court!

**DEBBIE LOU** Hi Flora.

*Going in.*

Not puttin' yuh to any trouble, are we?

**FLORA** Well, don't let it get you down, Chastity.

**ROY** *(going in)* Where'za bar, Flora?

**FILTHY PHIL** *(crowding in behind with the girls)* Hi Flora! Hey, let's have some music!

**DEBBIE LOU** *(to ROY)* Whudjuh bring, dummy?

**ROY** Whud I *bring*? Kar-Tel's Fifty Greatest *Hits*!

*He takes out his record and puts it on the record player. They all freeze, listening.*

**VOCAL CHORUS** *This is the shortest song in the world.*

*JACK enters, dressed up.*

**FILTHY PHIL** Hey, where's your handbag?

**JACK** I was gittin' worried you guys weren't gonna show. Crack me a beer, will yuh, hippie?

*RICKY opens JACK a beer.*

What sorta music yuh gonna give us tonight, dumbbell?

**ROY** All the golden oldens!

*Freeze.*

**VOCAL CHORUS** *Moose Jaw, Plunkett, Pile of Bones*
*Amazon, Climax, Yellowgrass.*
*Zelma, Zenon Park, Goin' Home,*
*Saskatoon, Elbow, Gopherzazz!*

**JACK** Where's alla potato chips and stuff, Flora?

**FLORA** You'll hafta go down to the store and get it!

**JACK** Who's gonna entertain our guests? Jeez, somebody's gotta look after things.

*FLORA shrugs and leaves.*

And while yer out, pick up a couple a six-packs!

*Freeze.*

**VOCAL CHORUS** *Bacon for people who like their eggs fried greasy,*
*Glass of milk and a coffee to go.*
*Who's got time for a meal, when you're cooking up a deal?*
*You got the runs on the road.*

**JACK** Who'd you come with tonight, Debbie Lou?

**DEBBIE LOU** Oh, nobody special—Roy gimme a ride over.

**JACK** *(putting his arm around her)* Don't go away, I got somethin' to show you later on.

**DEBBIE LOU** Well, I hope it's bigger'n last time!

*Freeze.*

**VOCAL CHORUS** *Keep your hands to yourself,*
*'Cause what I got is mine, all mine.*
*Keep your hands in your pockets,*
*'Cause what you want is mine, all mine.*

**FILTHY PHIL** Hey Roy! Yer old flame's comin' over tonight!

**ROY** Who?

**FILTHY PHIL** Kathy Jensen! I mean, Roychuck.

**ROY** Yeah—remember when she was a little kid, she used to ride her bike out to the depot?

*To the others.*

Filthy Phil always stayed late, so's he could watch her climb off in her skirt!

*The all laugh. Freeze.*

**VOCAL CHORUS** *I'm just a moan-in' moan-in' over you.*
*Just a moan-in' moan-in over you.*
*Why can't you be true? Be true? Be true? Be true?*

**ROY** Hey—my record!

**JACK** Dammit, Ricky, if you can't stand up, get away from the stereo!

**DEBBIE LOU** Anybody know if Johnny's comin' over?

**FILTHY PHIL** S'pose to. Why?

**DEBBIE LOU** I dunno, just like to see him again.

**FILTHY PHIL** Look at her—gonna pine away!

**RICKY** Forget him, Debbie Lou! *I'll always* love yuh!

*Freeze.*

**VOCAL CHORUS** *Don't push that button 'less you mean it,*
*Or you're in for the shock of your life!*
*Well, the sign said "Danger," but I couldn't read it,*
*'Cause I left my bifocals at home.*

*During the previous exchange, FILTHY PHIL has been preparing his coat hanger trick, which is to fasten a coat hanger to ROY's belt, cover it with a towel, then urge him to stand up.*

**DEBBIE LOU** *(pleased with the trick)* Oh, you dirty thing!

**JACK** *(laughing)* Know what, Roy? Kathy told me at the wedding she was really disappointed in you.

**ROY** Huh? Why?

**JACK** Said if you'd come on to her like a big stud—she wouldn't a married the Yewkeranian!

**ROY** G'wan!

**JACK** It's true! She had a crush on you for *years*. And yuh never gave her *nuthin'*.

**ROY** G'wan!

*JACK whips the towel off the coat hanger, laughing uproariously.*

**JACK** Didn't know you never *had* nuthin'!

*Freeze.*

**VOCAL CHORUS** *Ne pas actionez le chaise*
*Quand le train est en gare.*
*Don't tell me that*
*You just don't care.*

**RICKY** Hey, don' start buggin' *Roy*, or he'll end up doin' somethin' crazy again.

**JACK** Who cares?

**RICKY** I care! He shouldn't be scarin' hell outta Kathy! She isn't the kinda chick you're useta boogyin' around with.

**JACK** *(pausing)* Oh? Somethin' special, is she? You sayin' she's better'n our bohunk friend deserves?

**RICKY** I d'int say that!

*JACK takes out a mickey of rye.*

**JACK** Yer slurring your words. Better have a drink.

*Freeze.*

**VOCAL CHORUS** *Because I'm drinking more and enjoying it less,*
*Since you walked out on me—baby.*

*JACK takes RICKY to one side.*

**JACK** I been thinkin', Rick. How did a great guy like Johnny get mixed up with—Kathy Jensen?

**RICKY** Yeah, lucky bugger! I coulden' get to firs' base with her.

**JACK** Aa, but she's a stuck-up bitch. Be just like every other broad in a year.

**RICKY** Not her—too much class.

**JACK** Well, she'll be sorry she married a Knight of the Road. You know what a chick like her needs? Somebody really, you know, *far out*.

**RICKY** *(laughing)* Like you?

**JACK** *(pausing)* So you used to be kinda sweet on her, eh, Rick? Have another shot of rye.

*He pours him a drink. Freeze.*

**VOCAL CHORUS** *Just give me one more drink*
*Of good old number one—*
*Then you can carry me home.*

**ROY** Hey Debbie, you wanna go and check out Jack's bedroom?

**DEBBIE LOU** What for, fer cryin' out loud?

**ROY** He might have some gin stashed in there! Wanna go look?

**DEBBIE LOU** You dummy! Think I'd fall for that one?

**FILTHY PHIL** How about *this* one?

*He gooses her. Freeze.*

**VOCAL CHORUS** *She had long red hair*
*Streamin' down her back.*
*None of her head,*
*Just on her back!*

**RICKY** So—what're yuh tellin' me all this for?

**JACK** Well, I was talkin' to sweet little Kathy at the wedding, Rick. She's still stuck on yuh, buddy. Didjuh know that?

**RICKY** What?

**JACK** You know—on your wavelength? In fact, she passed on this scarf of hers.

*JACK takes out KATHY's scarf, which he has had in his pocket.*

**RICKY** Whaaah?

**JACK** Beautiful, isn't it?

*RICKY takes the scarf and fondles it.*

**RICKY** Jus—like—her.

**JACK** Just like her.

*Freeze.*

**VOCAL CHORUS** *I don't stand a chance*
*If I don't know the dance.*
*I didn't come all the way to Calgary,*
*Just to see you with another man.*

*The lights come up on JOHNNY and KATHY who are near the trailer, apparently arguing. FLORA enters with the groceries and the beer. The instrumental music for "The Party Boogie" quietly begins.*

**FLORA** Hi, you guys!

*She goes to JOHNNY and KATHY.*

What're you doin' out *here*?

**KATHY** *(at the same time as JOHNNY)* Looking for something.

**JOHNNY** *(at the same time as KATHY)* Just got here.

**FLORA** Hey! You two fightin' awready?

**KATHY & JOHNNY** Nooo!

**FLORA** I kin always tell. Come on, what happened?

**KATHY** Flora, it's so damn—silly—

**JOHNNY** It's *nuthin'*. Guess I was a little late gettin' home from the Blacktop—

**KATHY** I didn't mind you being late—if you'd just *called*—

**FLORA** Aaa—that's nothin' to fight about! Ferget about it! Come on in and have a good time!

*FLORA enters the trailer with KATHY and JOHNNY. "The Party Boogie" instrumental music comes up loud. Everybody dances enthusiastically.*

Look who I found outside waitin' fer an invitation!

**ROY** Hey, Johnny's here!

**JACK** And *Mrs.* Roychuck!

*The crowd greets them lustily. RICKY, at a gesture from JACK, jams the scarf into his pocket.*

**JOHNNY** Hi ever'body!

**KATHY** Hello.

**JACK** Okay—now we're all set to *boogie*!

*Freeze on gestures of drinking, dancing, feeling, with JACK overseeing it all.*

**VOCAL CHORUS** *Everybody's gonna have a real good time*
*Knocking back the beer, chugging five-star rye,*
*Dancing up a storm to the stereo!*
*You gotta watch out, boy, or you'll let it go.*

*This is no ordinary paycheque spree,*
*Drinkin' all night, coppin' feels for free.*
*Things are goin' on that you just don't see;*
*There's gonna be trouble! Jack's the key!*

*The instrumental music continues. JACK leads JOHNNY to the exit step of the trailer, ostensibly to give him a drink. KATHY is left alone. FLORA goes toward her, but RICKY arrives there first. He is drunk.*

**RICKY** H'ya, Kathy!

**KATHY** Hi, Ricky. Long time no see.

**RICKY** Howya bin doin'?

**KATHY** Oh—okay.

**RICKY** Hey, you wanna dance?

*KATHY looks around for JOHNNY.*

**KATHY** Well uh—sure. I'd love to.

*There is no room to dance in the trailer, so RICKY takes her outside past JACK and JOHNNY. RICKY and KATHY begin dancing in a way that indicates they have danced before. RICKY becomes quite lewd. KATHY thinks he is clowning and laughs at the joke.*

**JACK** Kathy sure does a mean two-step, don't she?

**JOHNNY** *(sourly)* Yeah, so it seems.

**JACK** She's a real nice chick, Johnny.

*RICKY makes a suggestive gesture.*

**JOHNNY** Yeah.

**JACK** Aaa—don't worry about that. Ricky isn't gonna do nuthin' outta line. Had a few too many!

**JOHNNY** He never could hold his liquor.

**JACK** *(calling to KATHY and RICKY)* Hey, you two! Don't get all hot and bothered. This ain't a cathouse!

*He laughs.*

Guess he don't realize you're the boss now, eh, Johnny?

**JOHNNY** What's that got to do with anything?

**JACK** Well—yer his *supervisor*.

**JOHNNY** You don't have to be a supervisor to straighten Ricky out.

**JACK** That's for damned sure! But Ricky doesn't need straightenin' out. He's a good driver!

**JOHNNY** *(snarling)* Is that a fact?

**JACK** Hey, take it easy. I didden say *nuthin'*!

**JOHNNY** He's a back-door creeper! You gotta watch his kind.

**JACK** Ricky? Naaa.

*A pause.*

Oh, you mean, when they useta go to high school together, they, uh—you know?

*JOHNNY shrugs.*

Hey, *careful*, John…

*JOHNNY rises violently.*

Now, take it easy, ole buddy. We're all friends here tonight. Knights of the Road—remember?

**JOHNNY** *(ominously)* Kathy!

*KATHY and RICKY don't hear.*

Katharine!

**KATHY** *(laughing)* Sorrrrry! Card full. You'll have to wait till the next dance!

**JOHNNY** That's enough.

**KATHY** Can't hear yoooooou!

**JOHNNY** *(shouting at her)* Stop dancing!

*The music stops abruptly. The crowd moves outside. KATHY moves anxiously toward JOHNNY.*

**KATHY** Johnny?

**RICKY** Hey, where yuh goin'? Arnchuh gonna finishuh dance?

**JOHNNY** Finish it yourself, lover boy!

**RICKY** Whatsat supposetuh mean?

**JOHNNY** It means you got trouble if you don't start walkin'!

**RICKY** "J.R." speaks!

**JACK** Okay boys—we don't want any trouble!

**JOHNNY** There isn't gonna be no trouble.

**JACK** There's other ways of settlin' fights, yuh know.

**KATHY** *(upset)* They're not fighting! Listen, Johnny—we were *dancing*—there's nothing to be ashamed—

**JOHNNY** *(cutting her off, speaking to RICKY)* I hear yer turnin' into a hotshot driver.

**RICKY** I'm makin' my way!

**JOHNNY** And now yer goin' around braggin' about bein' the top driver in the company!

**RICKY** *(grinning)* Can't disappoint the ladies, "J.R."

**JOHNNY** Think yer good enough to beat my time on a run to Edmonton?

**RICKY** Chrise, pick a tuffy! I beat that one months ago!

**JACK** Now don't get all *serious* about this, you guys. You need somethin' you kin settle right *now*!

**KATHY** Johnny, don't you do anything silly!

**JOHNNY** Canchuh see? He's just *beggin'* fer a lickin'!

**KATHY** Johnny!

**JACK** Whuchuh say, hippie, gonna take that?

**KATHY** *(terrified)* Johnny—let's go home *now*!

**RICKY** *(backpedalling)* I don't wanta fight you, Johnny.

**JOHNNY** I'll tell you what, hotshot! You got your car outside? Any distance you want! Start from the front door for our cars, and the first guy back wins.

**JACK** Right! And the loser quits the company?

*The crowd reacts.*

**RICKY** Soun's fair! Less go!

**KATHY** Please don't, Johnny!

**JACK** Okay, here's yer route! Out the freeway to Number Eleven, around the cloverleaf and back here to the front door!

**FLORA** Jack, you better stay outta this.

**JOHNNY** First one back to the party, right?

**RICKY** Have a beer ready for me!

**KATHY** Johnny, I won't let you!

**JOHNNY** Let *go* of me, will yuh?

**KATHY** If you get into that car, I'm walking home!

*JOHNNY hesitates.*

**RICKY** *(nearly unconscious)* C'mon, quit stallin', *Boss*!

*He staggers and nearly falls.*

**FLORA** Jack, you gotta stop this! Ricky's stoned outtuv his mind.

**ROY** Naw, he's okay.

**RICKY** Surrr! I'm okay!

**JACK** Atsa spirit, hippie! Now, yuh both know where yer goin'?

**KATHY** Johnny, I warned you!

**JOHNNY** *(snarling at her)* Yeah, yuh warned me. Now get inside and *shut up*!

*He pushes her roughly aside. She retreats offstage in slow motion. The instrumental music for "The Race Ballad" begins. JOHNNY and RICKY step to their cars in duel-like slow motion. The lights fade to black.*

**JACK** On your marks! Get set! GOOOOO!

**ROY** Come on, hippie—lay rubber!

**FILTHY PHIL** Get that Barracuda movin', yuh big hunky!

*The lights come up on the VOCAL CHORUS. They sing "The Race Ballad." There are special lighting effects on JOHNNY and RICKY and on the singer in the VOCAL CHORUS who is singing "The Race Ballad."*

**VOCAL CHORUS** *Now all you blacktop truckers,*
*Who think you know the road:*
*Be wary of the bottle*
*'Cause it can take control.*
*With whiskey, hate, and stupid pride.*

*A mixture to avoid,*
*The tale we'll tell is all of this,*
*So listen closely, boys.*

*The folly of a reckless man*
*Is very plain to see;*
*A test of manhood from the glass*
*Will end in misery.*
*Will surely end in misery.*

*It started at a party,*
*A crazy, drunken spree.*
*Ricky had his foolish pride,*
*And Johnny, jealously*
*Ricky said to Johnny,*
*"I'm just as good as you!"*
*Johnny said, "You son of a bitch,*
*I'll prove that isn't true."*

*They run outside blind with rage*
*And start up their machines.*
*The night is dark, but stars blaze down*
*Upon this frantic scene.*
*Tires just a-screamin',*
*They take off on their ride,*

*And hit the freeway flyin',*
*Wild fever in their eyes.*

*The 'cuda hits the Ruth Street ramp,*
*Huggin' to the line.*
*Ricky with his Charger floored*
*Isn't far behind,*
*By Preston they are neck and neck,*
*Blood rushing through their veins,*
*But the cloverleaf is comin' fast,*
*Just a single lane.*

*Ricky puts it to the mats,*
*He's doin' ninety-five.*
*The exit sign says twenty per;*
*Can he take the turn alive?*
*He hits the inside shoulder,*
*Goes fishin' round the curve,*
*Johnny hard upon his tail,*
*Straining every nerve.*

*They take off from the Eighth Street curve,*
*Burning up the night,*
*The city-centre ramp appears,*
*Glaring in their lights.*
*Squealing through the cloverleaf,*
*Heading back to town,*
*Johnny edging closer,*
*Tryin' to shut him down!*

*Back along the freeway,*
*They're locked in overdrive.*
*Fighting for position,*
*Holding side by side,*
*Rick looks out his window,*
*Sees Johnny's face all white,*
*All Johnny sees is Kathy's face,*
*Ghost-like in the night.*

*Nearly at the finish ramp,*
*Ricky shoots ahead,*
*But this time his number's up,*
*The curve beats him instead.*
*Johnny sees the Charger*
*Go spinning through the air,*

*Slowing down.*

*Burning, twisting, crazy,*
*Like a pinwheel at the fair.*

*There is a shattering explosion of metal and glass, or a stylized musical effect such as a broken string. The lights fade slowly on the VOCAL CHORUS as they sing the song's refrain.*

*The folly of a reckless man*
*Is very plain to see;*
*A test of manhood from the glass*
*Will end in misery.*
*Will surely end in misery.*

*The stage goes black.*

## ACT THREE

*Darkness. The sound of wind blowing is heard. The instrumental music for "Lady Two" begins as the lights come up very dimly to reveal RICKY lying face down, lower left, and JOHNNY wandering around in the darkness.*

**JOHNNY** Ricky! Where are you? *Ricky!*

**RICKY** *(moaning)* Ohhhh!

*JOHNNY goes to RICKY.*

**JOHNNY** Hey, come on, buddy! You're okay. You can't fool me!

**RICKY** Ohhhhh…

**JOHNNY** See—you're okay!

*He forces a laugh.*

Come on, get some life into yuh! Crowd's gonna be here any minute!

*RICKY coughs painfully.*

Okay, yuh just got the wind knocked outta yuh. Sit up now.

*He helps RICKY sit up.*

Is that better?

**RICKY** Uhhhh.

**JOHNNY** Okay, now stand. Attaboy. Startin' tuh come back to you now?

**RICKY** Yeah…

**JOHNNY** Man, the way you came off that ramp!

*He laughs.*

Looked like Awful Knawful jumpin' Blackstrap Canyon!

*RICKY laughs painfully.*

**RICKY** Boy, we sure do some crazy things!

**JOHNNY** Okay, don't worry. It's all over and done with.

**RICKY** *(still dazed, shaking his head)* Like idiots!

**JOHNNY** Here comes the party. Got it together?

**RICKY** I remember! You thought I was—messing around—with Kathy.

*A pause.*

**JOHNNY** Awright—forget it!

*ROY runs in with JACK and DEBBIE LOU.*

**ROY** *(surveying the wreckage)* Holy Hannah!

**RICKY** *(grinning)* I pulled out to pass th' ramp!

**JACK** That car is *lunched!*

**JOHNNY** Don't worry. We got it all looked after.

**JACK** Cops are on their way. Looks like Ricky's got some explainin' to do.

**JOHNNY** I said it's under control.

*Sirens begin, off.*

**RICKY** You don't hafta get mixed up in this, Johnny. It's my car. I can take the rap.

**JOHNNY** You keep quiet and do exactly what I tell you.

**RICKY** Whuddayuh mean?

**JACK** He said—keep your mouth shut!

**JOHNNY** I'm the supervisor! I can handle the cops.

**RICKY** *(angrily)* Lissen, this isn't your hassle!

**JOHNNY** Like hell it isn't! I'm responsible for the company—and if the paper hears about this, it means bad PR.

**RICKY** Bad *PR*! For the *company*!

**JOHNNY** Now relax and let me take care of it.

**ROY** I hope you got a good story, Johnny. That car looks like it drove through a rolling mill.

**JOHNNY** *(to RICKY)* You got blood on your face. Better get it wiped off.

*RICKY takes out KATHY's scarf and begins to wipe his face.*

**RICKY** Zat got it?

**JOHNNY** What's that?

**RICKY** *(startled)* What?

**JOHNNY** *(advancing)* Where'd you get that scarf?

**RICKY** *(staring at the scarf)* Well—it's just an old piece of—

*He realizes whose scarf it is and tries to hide it.*

**JOHNNY** Let—me—see it!

**ROY** Hey, what's goin' on?

**DEBBIE LOU** What's happenin'?

**RICKY** Johnny, lissen—it doesn't mean anything—

**JOHNNY** I want that—

**RICKY** She didn't—

**JOHNNY** —scarf—

**RICKY** —do nuthin'—

**JOHNNY** —*now!*

**RICKY** Hey!

*They fight. JOHNNY punches RICKY to the ground, then begins kicking him in a frenzy.*

**JOHNNY** You sneaking—lying—bastard!

**ROY** Johnny, cool it!

**JACK** Grab him! He's flippin' out!

**DEBBIE LOU** Stop it, you guys!

**ROY** Cops are comin'!

*JOHNNY is subdued. A COP appears.*

**COP** Okay—what's going on here?

**JACK** Nothing.

**ROY** Little—accident.

**COP** Yeah? What happened?

**JACK** Ricky got thrown outta the car. Kinda bad shape.

*The COP looks at RICKY on the ground.*

**COP** What's that?

**JOHNNY** *(dazed)* She gave him—the scarf—

**COP** *(turning to him)* Whudjuh say, son?

*Silence.*

**JACK** He's takin' it pretty hard, officer. They're close buddies!

**COP** Anybody phone the ambulance?

**DEBBIE LOU** Flora went back to call from the house.

*JOHNNY kneels to take the scarf from RICKY.*

**COP** Hey, what do you think *yer* doin'?

**JOHNNY** Taking this.

**COP** Don't touch nuthin'. That hanky might be evidence.

*JOHNNY reacts to this and takes the scarf, putting it inside his shirt and moving away.*

You heard—put that back!

**JACK** It's awright, officer. He should have it—sentimental value. Ricky and him were really tight.

**DEBBIE LOU** Here's the ambulance.

**JACK** You guys give the policeman a hand lookin' after Ricky. I'm gonna take this boy home—he's really shook up. Roy'll give yuh the story. Okay, Roy?

**ROY** Sure, I'll give yuh all the dope.

*ROY and the COP and DEBBIE LOU carry RICKY off. The instrumental music for "The Cheatin' Aria" begins. JACK takes JOHNNY over to the side of the road where they sit. JACK takes out his mickey of whiskey and they drink.*

**JOHNNY** It's true…

**JACK** Whudjuh say?

**JOHNNY** You were right.

**JACK** Right about what, old buddy?

**JOHNNY** Once they get their hooks into you—

**JACK** You said it!

**JOHNNY** They tear you apart!

**JACK** No, listen, John, you got it all wrong.

**JOHNNY** Eh?

**JACK** You're just dreamin' alla this up.

**JOHNNY** It's no dream.

**JACK** Well, I can't believe it! Other women, yeah—they might be rotten to the core—but not *Kathy*. She's too good.

**JOHNNY** That's what I thought.

**JACK** Yeah—too good.

**JOHNNY** *(taking out the scarf)* Jack—my mother *gave* it to her.

**JACK** Zatta fact?

**JOHNNY** And my grandmother gave it to her! It belonged to the women in my family for—generations!

**JACK** Yeah—the wimmen.

*A pause.*

Always the wimmen.

*JACK begins to sing "The Cheatin' Aria."*

*You made your bed, you gotta lie in it.*
*You got a pillow just to cry in.*
*You come into this world just to die in it.*
*Women are the cause of it all.*

*I seen it happen to all my friends.*
*One by one they found it out,*
*That women love to cheat and lie.*
*It's a cryin' shame, without a doubt.*

*Now Kathy's different, she's good as gold.*
*It's the other ones you gotta watch.*
*They'll play around without thinkin' 'bout you,*
*And act like saints when they get caught.*

**JOHNNY** *I won't let it get me down, Jack.*
*I figgered out it's all a line.*
*I know women love to torture us,*
*Now I know it happens all the time.*

**JACK** *Yeah, Kathy's fine, you're a lucky man.*
*Don't ever worry about her bein' true.*
*Oh she may slip up, once or twice,*
*But she'll come crawling back to you.*

**JOHNNY** *She wasn't like all them other girls,*
*Drivin' me crazy with her runnin' around.*
*Now I see she was laughing at me.*
*All that time I really was the clown.*

**JACK & JOHNNY** *You made your bed, you gotta lie in it.*
*You got a pillow just to cry in.*
*You came into this world just to die in.*
*Women are the cause of it all.*

**JACK** *(getting up)* Come on, I got another mickey under the seat. One more for the road—eh?

*They go out as the lights fade. The lights come up on the bedroom. KATHY is in her nightgown waiting anxiously for JOHNNY. She sings "The Willow Song" a cappella.*

**KATHY** *The poor soul sat sighing by a sycamore tree,*
*Sing all a green willow,*
*Her hand on her bloom, her head on her knee,*
*Sing willow, willow, willow.*
*The fresh streams ran by her moans,*
*Sing willow, willow, willow,*
*Her salt tears fell from her softened the stones,*
*Sing willow, willow, willow.*

*Sing all a green willow must be my garland,*
*Let nobody blame him. His scorn I approve.*

*I called my false love, but what said he then?*
*Sing willow, willow, willow,*
*If I court more women you'll couch with more men,*
*Sing all a green willow.*
*We found our vows drifting like leaves in the wind,*
*Sing willow, willow, willow,*
*And now who is able to gather them in?*
*Sing willow, willow, willow.*

*Sing all a green willow must be our prayer,*
*Restoring the tenderness we once did share.*

*My love turns away when I whisper his name,*
*Sing willow, willow, willow,*
*Now I weep without solace in shadows of pain,*
*Sing all a green willow.*

*Sing all a green willow must be my plea.*
*Such love is not simple. Please come home to me.*

*She lies down on the bed. JOHNNY enters, distracted. KATHY descends from the bedroom. The instrumental music for "The Die Aria" begins.*

Johnny?

**JOHNNY** Yeah.

**KATHY** Where have you been?

*A pause.*

I was so worried!

**JOHNNY** Were you?

**KATHY** Of course I was. I've never seen you like that before.

**JOHNNY** Like what?

**KATHY** So—violent.

*Silence.*

It looked like you were going to *hit* Ricky—

**JOHNNY** You worried about him?

**KATHY** Then taking off on that stupid race—both of you *drunk*. Leaving me behind in that—madhouse!

**JOHNNY** Madhouse.

**KATHY** That wasn't a party—it was a circus!

**JOHNNY** Yeah.

**KATHY** *(pausing)* Sweetheart, has something happened I don't know about?

**JOHNNY** Yeah, something happened. To Ricky.

**KATHY** He isn't—hurt, is he?

*A pause.*

Johnny?

**JOHNNY** In the hospital.

**KATHY** But—?

**JOHNNY** —*Why?* You wanta know why?

*A pause.*

**KATHY** Oh! No!

**JOHNNY** That's right!

**KATHY** Johnny—I was *dancing* with Ricky—only dancing!

**JOHNNY** Dancing with Ricky.

**KATHY** He's only a—friend!

*A pause.*

Don't you realize—there's nothing *wrong* with that?

*A pause.*

Johnny, we *agreed* before we got married that we'd never try to possess each other! We have to be *free*—to have our own friends and—interests!

**JOHNNY** "Interests"!

**KATHY** *I* wouldn't be jealous if *you* danced with somebody else. It's the only way it'll work. Don't you see?

*He gestures her toward the bedroom. She sighs.*

Okay. It's been a long day. We've done too much talking already.

*She takes his hand. He removes it and pushes her ahead of him toward the bedroom.*

You know, I'm so scared, when you're not here. I need you—to put me to bed.

**JOHNNY** I will.

**KATHY** Promise me you'll always be here to put me to bed, Johnny.

**JOHNNY** I promise.

*They ascend to the bedroom where they sing "The Die Aria." The lighting effects follow the song.*

*Now snuff out the candles*
*And let the smoke be drawn up*
*To the heavens waiting patiently above.*
*My vision is fading,*
*Darkened by the dying of the light*
*That once shone in your smile.*

**KATHY**
*Why must we retreat into darkness*
*To make love as if in shame*
*When no one can crush this flame?*
*Look—the light from the stars*
*Will illuminate two lovers*
*Seeking out the way.*

*JOHNNY closes the curtains.*

**JOHNNY** *And yet a cloud passing by*
*Can extinguish that light*
*Leaving both of us drifting in the dark.*

*KATHY removes JOHNNY's jacket.*

**KATHY** *But you are my world*
*Revolving in the orbit of these arms*
*Till we meet in the golden dawn.*

**JOHNNY** *The summer always fades.*
*The frozen sea of winter*
*Kills the prairie lily blowing in the sun.*

*KATHY draws him to the bed.*

**KATHY** *But life comes full circle,*
*And ice melts into water that*
*The sleeping lilies drink into life.*

*Lovers turn to earth,*
*And earth becomes the flowers,*
*Countless flowers turning to the sun.*

*You are my sun and earth,*
*And I will journey with you*
*Through a universe without time or end.*

*JOHNNY takes out the scarf and strangles her with it.*

**JOHNNY** *But if the heavens open*
*And the planets all collide,*
*None of us will see the dawn again.*

*JOHNNY sits up, still embracing her as he sings the last stanza again a cappella.*

*But if the heavens open*
*And the planets all collide,*
*None of us will see the dawn again.*

*There is knocking at the door. The knocking is repeated louder. It is FLORA. She enters and looks around in the semi-darkness.*

**FLORA** Kathy? It's Flora, Kathy!

*JOHNNY does not hear her. FLORA ascends to the bedroom.*

Kathy?

*She enters the bedroom.*

Oh uh, 'scuse me. Everythin' okay?

*A pause.*

Jack just called from the Blacktop. He uh said you were pretty shook up.

*She looks at KATHY.*

Is she uh sleeping?

*She sees the scarf.*

How did she—?

*A pause.*

Kathy?

*A pause.*

Oh no. Oh—noooooo! *Jack*, what'd you do? Kathy gave the scarf to me!

**JOHNNY** *(faintly)* Jack?

**FLORA** *(accusing)* He—killed—her!

*A pause.*

You *all* killed her!

*She backs out in horror and runs off as the lights fade on the bedroom. The lights come up downstage as DEBBIE LOU and ROY enter, walking down the street. "The Party Boogie" begins instrumentally and rises in volume as they approach the Blacktop Bar.*

**DEBBIE LOU** Well, I giss Ricky'll be okay. What are you gonna do now?

**ROY** I dunno. Wanna stop in to the Blacktop and tell them about the hospital?

**DEBBIE LOU** The Blacktop? On my night off? You gotta be *kiddin'*!

**ROY** Alla boys'll be there, Deb.

**DEBBIE LOU** *(disgusted)* Yeah, all the boys!

**ROY** *(wistfully)* Might even be some girls.

**DEBBIE LOU** Yeah?

**ROY** *(realizing this is his last chance)* Maybe I could—escort yuh—to thuh beverage room?

*DEBBIE LOU looks at him critically.*

**DEBBIE LOU** Oh! Ohhhh—kay, Roy. Then you kin drive me home—if you're good.

*ROY gallantly reaches to open the door to the Blacktop Bar. "The Party Boogie" instrumental opens up to full blast. There is not much action, however, as the lights go up on the scene. JACK and FILTHY PHIL are getting drunk.*

**FILTHY PHIL** Hey—there's Debbie Lou!

*He calls to her.*

Over here, Debs! How's Ricky?

*He grabs JACK.*

Jack—Roy's here!

*JACK's head goes up, but he is blind drunk. He offers only an unintelligible garble. They talk and joke as JOHNNY descends into the bar.*

Hey—Johnny!

**DEBBIE LOU** *(knowing something is wrong)* Johnny?

*JOHNNY crosses slowly to JACK. JACK sees him, grins and rises. The lights begin a slow fade.*

**JACK** Johnny, y'ole bohunk! Bin waitin' fer yuh. C'mon, say hello to yer good—buddy.

*JACK crosses to meet JOHNNY and hugs him in an embrace. In slow motion JOHNNY takes out a knife and stabs him in the guts. The others begin to retreat from the bar. The instrumental music for "Lady of the Prairie" begins. JOHNNY drops JACK's body to the floor and returns slowly to Level 1 as the VOCAL CHORUS sings "Lady of the Prairie."*

**VOCAL CHORUS** *She was a lady of the prairie,*
*And though she thought she'd never marry,*
*I stole that gal and we left that one-horse town.*
*She said she'd always call me papa*
*If I would treat her proper,*
*And I swore I'd never let that good gal down.*

*The lights go up on the VOCAL CHORUS.*

*My life was a barrel of fun,*
*My world was in my arms.*

*She had me up there sittin'*
*On a cloud that was gold-spun.*

*JOHNNY sits on the bed and takes KATHY in his arms.*

*I took her far off to the city,*
*And she was lookin' pretty,*
*Until I turned one day and saw*
*That she was gone.*

*Yodelling through one stanza with dobro accompaniment.*

*Well I went downtown to find her,*
*There was another man behind her,*
*And they looked like they was out to have some fun.*

*I said come on home now, sweet momma,*
*Back to the arms of your own papa.*
*We'll forget the past and let what's done be done.*

*The lights go out on JOHNNY and KATHY. The light on the VOCAL CHORUS goes to red and fades slowly through the last stanza of the song.*

*Then she melted like a vision,*
*Though I still can taste her kisses.*
*She left me standing in the glaring*
*Evening sun.*

*The stage goes to black. The VOCAL CHORUS yodels the last stanza of the song, which fades into the sound of the wind moaning. This sound in turn fades into silence.*

*The end.*

# CLAUDIUS

**KEN GASS**

## THE THRUST BEHIND THE THRONE

Ken Gass was a pioneer of the so-called alternative theatre movement in Toronto in the 1970s. Born in Abbotsford, BC, two months before the end of World War II, he studied theatre and creative writing at the University of British Columbia before moving to Toronto in 1968, where he got his first directing jobs moonlighting at Theatre Passe Muraille and the Garrett Theatre while teaching high-school English. In 1970 he founded Factory Theatre (then Factory Theatre Lab) above an auto-body shop on Dupont St., the first theatre in Toronto to focus exclusively on Canadian work, and the one that has done so most consistently since. He remained artistic director at Factory until 1979, producing fifty new Canadian plays and launching the careers of dozens of playwrights, including David Freeman, Michael Hollingsworth, himself, and most notably George F. Walker. In 1985 he founded the Canadian Repertory Theatre with the goal of reviving important works from the repertory at a time when they were in danger of disappearing, and in November 1996 he resumed the artistic directorship at Factory Theatre, which, having moved to its now familiar location at Adelaide and Bathurst in 1983, was teetering on the brink of bankruptcy. Drawing mightily on the work of Walker, Gass brought the theatre back to solvency, to the degree that in 1999 the company bought the 1868 heritage building that houses it now. He remains artistic director of Factory (while also teaching at the University of Toronto), and in recent years he has, not without controversy, used the theatre to try to address the cultural mix now visible on Toronto's streets and streetcars, producing work by Anishnaabe playwright Ian Ross, African-Canadian Andrew Moodie, co-producing with theatres representing various cultural communities, and hosting CrossCurrents, an annual intercultural play-development festival.

Gass's first stage play, *Light*, was produced in 1970 as part of the famous Festival of Underground Theatre at Toronto's St. Lawrence Centre for the Arts, which served to galvanize the nationalist theatre scene of the day. But the bulk of his work in the '70s and '80s premiered at Factory. *The Red Revolutionary* was part of the theatre's first season. *Hurray for Johnny Canuck*, first produced in 1974, has remained popular for its cartoon characterizations ever since, particularly in classrooms and university theatres. In 1976 Gass directed an ambitious production of his play *The Boy Bishop* with an unheard of (for Canadian plays) cast of twenty-three—a feat rarely replicated since. In the subsequent season at Factory many found his provocative play *Winter Offensive*, in which Albert Eichmann's wife hosts an orgy for Nazi officers, offensive, but the play shared with all of Gass's work a desire to shake audiences up, and few shows have ever suffered from public outcry. *Private Chambers* was also produced at Factory in a staged reading in 1981 as part of the Brave New Works series, not under the direction of Gass himself, but of playwright and director Hrant Alianak. In the 1990s Gass's stage plays—he has also written for radio and television—were produced at Canadian Repertory Theatre, again under his own direction. These include *Amazon Dream* (1994) and of course *Claudius*, which was nominated for a Chalmers (outstanding new play) award when it was first produced in 1993. His work has returned to Factory in 2002 with a production of *Slip Knot* and in 2005 with a reading of his latest play, *Gulag America*.

*Claudius* is, of course, an adaptation of *Hamlet*, and most of the main characters are there: Hamlet, Claudius, Gertrude, Polonius, Ophelia, Laertes, even Osric. There's no Rosencrantz or Guildenstern (it's been done) and, alas, there's only the briefest mention of Fortinbras, Gass's play being more concerned with domestic and sexual rather than global politics. As Claudius says, "Fuck the king of Norway, cut to the chase." Hamlet's father, however, is inexplicably renamed Theodore, Emilia puts in a guest appearance from *Othello*, there's an expanded, delightfully distorted, role for the snivelling Priest, and Hamlet has a newly minted mistress, Genevieve, with whom he spends much of the play in bed. But the action follows a recognizable, if significantly altered, *Hamlet* plot, and among the joys of watching or reading it is recognizing the precision with which specific scenes are messed with. The play is about, as Hamlet and Genevieve indicate when sharing a bed with the recording Priest, "sex," "politics," "marriage," "murder"—and, to answer the Priest's question, yes, they're connected. *Claudius* is notable for the sheer energy of its language, the vitality of its characters, and the randyness of the passions it portrays. And for me, in spite of the male title characters of both source and adaptation, it's most interesting for its representations of Ophelia's complex relationship to the materiality of l-l-language (on which she stumbles, but which she literally devours) and Gertrude's crowning genius for the politics of power.

*Claudius* was first produced by the Canadian Rep Theatre at Factory Theatre, Toronto in September, 1993, with the following company:

| | |
|---|---|
| CLAUDIUS | Michael Ayoub |
| PRIEST | David Bolt |
| LAERTES | Tom Barnett |
| EMILIA | Julia Donovan |
| OSRIC | Alex Fallis |
| POLONIUS | Dean Hawes |
| GERTRUDE | Susan Hogan |
| HAMLET | Peter Outerbridge |
| GENEVIEVE | Jane Spidell |
| OPHELIA | Victoria Tengelis |

Directed by Ken Gass
Set design by Marian Wihak
Costume design by Lea Carlson
Lighting design by Peter Freund
Fight direction by John Stead
Original music by Wayne Kelso
Stage management by Paul Mark

## CHARACTERS

CLAUDIUS
GERTRUDE
HAMLET
OPHELIA
POLONIUS
LAERTES
PRIEST
OSRIC
GENEVIEVE
EMILIA

# CLAUDIUS

## Scene One

*A royal wedding. Fanfare. The whole works. GERTRUDE makes a stunning entrance up the aisle, wearing an elegant gown with a long train. She arrives at the altar and smiles at CLAUDIUS, who stands waiting. In positions of prominence we find POLONIUS, LAERTES, OPHELIA, EMILIA, and OSRIC, among others. The music ends.*

*Then an awkward pause as the PRIEST, rather dishevelled, enters from the side, trips on his way to the altar, and fumbles for the correct passage in his book.*

**PRIEST** Sorry, I'm late. Sorry…. Your Majesties… *(smiling at the congregation)* Hi…

*The PRIEST clears his throat, adjusts his collar, then begins in a loud voice.*

Dearly beloved…. There are only three words to describe a marriage. Good. Good. Good. Yes, my friends, marriage is God's good work. God loves a good marriage. God says, and I quote, be good, be married. And He expounds on this. God says marry young, marry old; marry rich or poor, but marry. Marry your friend, your enemy. Marry your neighbour, your neighbour's wife, I mean, widow. Marry your cousin, your niece—some of you

dispute this, I know, but it's been done, and worse. Much worse. Marry your aunt, your uncle, yes, even he, the drunken lout, and if the old fool dies, take his money and marry again, marry three times, ten times, but for God's sake, marry. Because marriage, my friends, is the way to bliss. *(beat)*

And you can read all about it in my little pamphlet, which I just happen to have right here. *(holding it up)* "How to Marry and Reap the Material Rewards of the Hereafter." Clear, simple instructions on how to obtain a favoured seat in heaven for all eternity, with a good view of the southern constellation. Yes, folks, you can buy this pamphlet for ten pfennings, that's right, only ten pfennings, at the back of the hall after the ceremony.

This pamphlet comes, by the way, with a money-back guarantee. I will be held accountable!

**GERTRUDE** Please hurry along, for goodness' sake.

**PRIEST** Of course…

*The PRIEST grabs his ceremonial book, then drops it, knocks over a chalice, and stumbles on the floor trying to retrieve it.*

Sorry… sorry… sorry…

**LAERTES** Who is this fool?

**POLONIUS** The bishop refused to perform the ceremony so soon after Theodore's death. Claudius sacked him and hired a country priest instead.

**PRIEST** *(regaining control)* Where was I? Oh yes, the royal wedding. Weddings are… *(smiling)* there's no other word, is there?… wonderful! I explain the whys and wherefores here in another pamphlet, also ten pfennings, *Nuptial Bliss*, or, *Sexual Safety in the Age of Treachery*. Treachery is only a subtheme, actually, it's mainly about nuptial bliss. I know what you're thinking! You're thinking, as a priest, I probably know bugger all about it. But, even forgetting the Middle Ages where priests knew more about sex than the queen of Gomorrah, you're also ignoring the power of divine intervention! Divine knowledge. Which is passed on from up there, down here, around the Church, through me, and directly over to you. An incredible journey when you think of it. And you'd better think about it! The consequences for not thinking about it are spelled out right here, in this pamphlet, which you can take home to bed for a mere ten pfennings. That's right, folks, ten measly pfennings, back of the hall, next to the holy water. See… *(flipping the pages) Nuptial Bliss. Sexual Redundancy*. Illustrated and explained by yours truly, Father Ben. All legal, doubly guaranteed—

**CLAUDIUS** For Christ's sake, will you get on with it!

**PRIEST** Anyways, not to digress… *(to CLAUDIUS)* Sure. Sorry, Your Majesty, Majesties… sorry… sorry…

*The PRIEST reopens the marriage book, clears his throat rather loudly, then turns to the congregation once more.*

Sorry…. We are here to join in holy matrimony his recent Royal Majesty, Claudius, to our royal queen, Gertrude, recently bereaved widow to our late, beloved King Theodore, whom we remember as—

**GERTRUDE** Skip that.

**PRIEST** Excuse me?

**CLAUDIUS** Move on.

**PRIEST** Shouldn't I—

**GERTRUDE** Get to the vows, please.

**PRIEST** Oh, fine then. Have it your way. *(slamming the book shut)* You first, Your Majesty.

**CLAUDIUS** *(seething)* I, Claudius, Royal King of Denmark, do hereby take thee, Gertrude—

*CLAUDIUS indicates he wants a prompt. The PRIEST pretends to read the Scriptures.*

Do take thee, Gertrude—

**GERTRUDE** *(quickly, firmly)* Thou, Claudius, dost hereby take me, Gertrude, to be thy royal queen, as I, Gertrude, do hereby take thee, Claudius, to be my king and lord, et cetera, et cetera, while trading rings… *(She snaps her finger and OSRIC brings the rings.)* …we each other wed, become husband and wife, the priest says "Amen," and we kiss and are done.

**PRIEST** But I haven't finished the homily…. And I have other pamphlets that may well be of—

**POLONIUS** *(whispering loudly in his ear)* It's only fair to warn you, Priest. Your life is in mortal peril.

**PRIEST** I see… *(loudly)* Okay, moving right along then to the—

**GERTRUDE** Amen.

**PRIEST** What?

**EVERYONE** Amen!

**PRIEST** Okay, okay. Amen.

*The PRIEST makes the sign of the cross. CLAUDIUS and GERTRUDE kiss. Everyone applauds.*

**POLONIUS** Bravo. Bravo.

*The lights dim. Firecracker displays go off in colourful bursts to the accompaniment of music. With each of the flashes a series of photolike tableaux of CLAUDIUS, GERTRUDE, and the wedding guests. In some, members of the crowd toast the bride and groom; in others we see CLAUDIUS kissing GERTRUDE in a ceremonious manner.*

*Then in the final sequence, which includes sudden thunder and lightning and the sound of rain, we discover HAMLET, off to one side, up to his knees in mud, in a grave, holding a shovel, exhuming his father's corpse.*

*Blackout.*

## Scene Two

*The royal bedroom. CLAUDIUS staggers in, carrying GERTRUDE across the threshold.*

**GERTRUDE** A little more… a little more…

*CLAUDIUS finally throws GERTRUDE on the bed. They laugh. Kiss.*

Over at last.

**CLAUDIUS** Thank God!

**GERTRUDE** Thank God!

*They kiss again. Then CLAUDIUS gets up and locks the door.*

What a party. But, oh, Claudi, that priest… where did you find him?

**CLAUDIUS** I asked for a simple country parson. How was I to know he'd be a complete idiot as well? Sonofabitch, I'll have his head for breakfast.

**GERTRUDE** No you won't—

**CLAUDIUS** He can't get away with—

**GERTRUDE** Hush! It's over now, and there will be no reprisals. It would spoil everything. Claudi? For me? Promise?

**CLAUDIUS** All right… all right…

*CLAUDIUS smiles. They kiss again.*

**GERTRUDE** I'm your wife now, your queen, your lover, your mistress, all legally wrapped in one.

**CLAUDIUS** Yes.

*They kiss passionately for a moment or so, then break apart and begin to undress. There are many layers of clothing to unravel.*

**GERTRUDE** *(indicating the back of her dress)* Help me?

**CLAUDIUS** Of course.

*CLAUDIUS forces open one of the buttons and unfastens the hooks on the back of her dress.*

**GERTRUDE** Thank you. I wish—and it's only a wish—that we were both still virgins now.

**CLAUDIUS** Why?

**GERTRUDE** Wouldn't you enjoy making love to me all the more if I were completely innocent?

**CLAUDIUS** No.

**GERTRUDE** Really?

**CLAUDIUS** Virgins are boring, generally speaking. What excited me most was making love to you when you were Theodore's wife.

**GERTRUDE** All right, forget virginity. But suppose, just suppose, this were the very first time we'd ever been alone together. Think how we'd be trembling now, acting silly, our bodies moistening, tingling with anticipation.… No, definitely, we should've waited.

**CLAUDIUS** *(pouring two glasses of brandy)* I liked our secret liaison. It was—

**GERTRUDE** Dangerous?

**CLAUDIUS** Yes. And—

**GERTRUDE** Sexually gratifying?

**CLAUDIUS** Very.

**GERTRUDE** Yes…

**CLAUDIUS** You were my universe.

**GERTRUDE** You were my joy, my despair. My reason for living.

**CLAUDIUS** And mine. How I loved you, Gertrude.

**GERTRUDE** I loved you as well. I do love you, Claudius. I always will.

*They finish the brandy, then kiss each other ravenously. GERTRUDE pulls CLAUDIUS on the bed. A sense of mounting excitement, frustrated by a web of corsets, straps, belts, footwear, etc.*

**CLAUDIUS** My God, all this harness…

**GERTRUDE** *(laughing)* I know. I'm a prisoner.

*With CLAUDIUS's help GERTRUDE unfastens the rest of her skirts and accessories and stands in her petticoat. CLAUDIUS sits on a stool and takes off his boots.*

It's funny. I remember my first honeymoon. No, I do. For a lot of women I think it's a total blur. But I remember every detail…. Would you like to hear about it?

**CLAUDIUS** No thanks.

**GERTRUDE** Jealous?

**CLAUDIUS** Not really.

**GERTRUDE** Good…

*GERTRUDE kisses CLAUDIUS and playfully runs her hands through his hair and beard.*

I wonder… if Theodore hadn't died such a horrible death…. Would you and I still be secret lovers? Or would we have eloped by now, run away together?

**CLAUDIUS** I never run away. Never.

**GERTRUDE** Poor Theodore, he was so soft and gentle. In fact, I was the one who usually took the sexual initiative. But he was a wonderful lover all the same. Very… considerate. Not like you. That first time on the stairwell? My God—

**CLAUDIUS** Don't pretend you didn't want me to.

**GERTRUDE** Oh, I wanted you to, all right. Absolutely. Although I would've preferred a little tenderness, and some poetry afterwards. Still, if you hadn't taken me I think I would've ravished you at the first opportunity. You were my passion. My salvation.

*GERTRUDE kisses him hard on the lips. CLAUDIUS pulls her petticoat down off her shoulders and caresses her delicately.*

**CLAUDIUS** No more secret stairwells. We can have each other openly now. Openly, tenderly, poetically, night after night after night after night…

**GERTRUDE** My darling…

**CLAUDIUS** Angel…

*They fall back on the bed and begin to make love in earnest now. Then the door opens slowly. HAMLET enters silently, holding a skeleton key. He is covered in mud and carries a small shovel and a dirty shroud. After a beat he closes the door.*

**HAMLET** I think my father was murdered.

*GERTRUDE screams. CLAUDIUS jumps up, instinctively reaching for his sword beside the bed.*

**CLAUDIUS** What the goddamn hell—

**GERTRUDE** Hamlet. How dare you—

*GERTRUDE pulls a sheet over her breast.*

**HAMLET** Stabbed in the back…

**CLAUDIUS** Get out or I'll—

**HAMLET** …between the shoulder blades…

**GERTRUDE** Who?

**HAMLET** Your husband.

*GERTRUDE and CLAUDIUS look at each other.*

Sorry. Your first husband. My father. His brother. Your "gentle, considerate lover."

**CLAUDIUS** Get out—

**HAMLET** I know. I'm being rude. Sorry. It's just I've had this skeleton key for years, and—

**GERTRUDE** *(firmly)* Hamlet, leave. Now.

**HAMLET** Of course. *(beat)* Night, Mother.

*HAMLET impulsively kisses GERTRUDE on the cheek.*

**GERTRUDE** For God's sake, you're covered in mud.

**HAMLET** I know. Sorry, it was pouring in the graveyard, and I— *(sees CLAUDIUS glaring)* Night, Uncle Claudius.

*HAMLET attempts to kiss CLAUDIUS on the cheek. CLAUDIUS makes a threatening gesture with the sword. HAMLET smiles and backs off towards the door. Then stops, turns.*

I dug up his coffin. Yeah, gruesome, I know. The corpse, it's decomposing, naturally, but I saw everything clearly. The spine was hacked. From *behind*. Isn't that awful? I thought, being king and all, you'd want to know as soon as possible.

**CLAUDIUS** Your father committed suicide. The inquiry established that beyond any doubt.

**HAMLET** Yeah, I read the report. But it doesn't make sense. I mean, *why*? With such a beautiful queen in his bed, night after night after night after night—

**GERTRUDE** Hamlet, you're being extremely childish. Get out. Now!

**HAMLET** *(opening the door)* Okay, okay, I'm leaving. Maybe I was never here. Maybe you dreamt this. Both of you. Simultaneously. *(exiting, his voice trailing from offstage)* Maybe my father's alive. And his murderer's dead. Who can tell anymore?

*HAMLET has gone. CLAUDIUS closes and bolts the door.*

**CLAUDIUS** Your son's a goddamn lunatic.

**GERTRUDE** It's a trying time for him.

**CLAUDIUS** He'll pay the price if he thinks he can fuck with me. I won't put up with it. *(beat)* He did commit suicide, you know.

**GERTRUDE** Who?

**CLAUDIUS** Theodore, of course.

**GERTRUDE** Oh. *(beat)* I guess he did. He was always brooding. He had morbid, philosophical thoughts about everything. It destroyed his passion for living. Hamlet takes after him. I can see it now. He'll go off to university, read pessimistic books, and that'll be the end of him.

**CLAUDIUS** Change the subject.

**GERTRUDE** Sorry. *(beat)* This is our wedding night. Isn't it?

*GERTRUDE gets into bed and lies under the covers. CLAUDIUS kneels over her and slowly draws the covers back from her breasts. He leans over to kiss her.*

Please, not now…

*GERTRUDE turns away, her passion clearly spent. CLAUDIUS turns his head sharply towards the door, in HAMLET's direction.*

*Blackout.*

## Scene Three

*CLAUDIUS and POLONIUS in a government chamber.*

**CLAUDIUS** There's no reason to wage a goddamn war.

**POLONIUS** There's always a reason for war. Stick a feather in someone's nose, what do they do? Hmm? Ignore it, you say? For a while, perhaps, but eventually they brush it aside. My, my. The instant they do that you slap them across the face. They get hot and reach for their sword. Very nice. You pull out a gun and shoot them in the head. Bingo! The first volley fired. Then, retreat. Wait. Their well-armed relatives come running. They want revenge. Oh, good. You just happen to have a small army waiting in the bushes. Bang, bang. Boom, boom. Casualties—aha!—avenged by more casualties. Escalation. Aha! Aha! In no time, what have we got? Full-scale hostilities. We win, of course. So at the end of the day we take their money, their horses, and the best of their beautiful, tear-stained women. (Thanks very much.) A year later we sign
a peace treaty and sell the whole lot back for twice its worth and all is forgiven. And that, my friend, is the art of war.

**CLAUDIUS** It's not as simple as that. I'm not as popular as Theodore. In the countryside they still call me the Pretender.

**POLONIUS** So pretend you're a leader and wage a fucking war!

**CLAUDIUS** *(beat, coldly)* Don't fuck…

**POLONIUS** What?

**CLAUDIUS** …with me—

**POLONIUS** I'm merely trying to illustrate—

**CLAUDIUS** We are not fucking amused! And you, my friend, are about to lose your head.

**POLONIUS** Me? My head? Ha! If it wasn't for me you wouldn't have the crown. You'd still be old cousin Claudi.

**CLAUDIUS** You want to take credit for it now, is that it?

**POLONIUS** No, but—

**CLAUDIUS** Fine. You plotted the whole thing. Take the consequences as well.

**POLONIUS** *What* consequences? It was a textbook assassination. We didn't even have a local rebellion to put down. Consequences? What *are* you talking about?

**CLAUDIUS** Prince Hamlet. He's dug up Theodore's body. Even more thrilling, he's brought it back to the castle so he can play witch doctor with the stab wounds.

**POLONIUS** Hamlet's deranged. He's a royal fuck-up. Very *emotional.* Takes after the queen, though probably not as good in bed. *(He breaks into a coarse laugh, then notices CLAUDIUS glaring.)* Sorry, that just slipped out. Really, I find it very hard to take all this serious—

**CLAUDIUS** *(exploding)* I don't need Theodore's corpse lying outside my bedroom door the morning after my wedding night! *(beat)* Hamlet may be crazy, but he's not stupid. We need a cover-up.

**POLONIUS** As in cover up the body?

**CLAUDIUS** The politics. Cover up the smell.

**POLONIUS** More intrigue. Mmm. Delicious. Where's old Theodore now?

**CLAUDIUS** Lying in state. For the second time this month. I've a contingent of guards watching over him.

**POLONIUS** *(snapping his fingers)* Cremation.

**CLAUDIUS** What?

**POLONIUS** Cremation. Obviously. Let's burn the son of a bitch, bones and all this time. After that, any talk of stab wounds will be pure conjecture, which we can punish as treasonous speculation.

**CLAUDIUS** Fine. But keep your ear to the ground. Remember, if I go down, you go down with me.

**POLONIUS** Relax, it's nothing but table talk. Gossip. After the cremation why don't you declare a public holiday in honour of Theodore's birth.

**CLAUDIUS** What for?

**POLONIUS** To show you *care*, dummy. *(quick beat)* Sorry. To show your royal concern. *(smiling)* If Hamlet's a pain in the ass after that we'll send him off to war. *(as CLAUDIUS stares at him)* Take it from me. War *is* a wonderful concept.

*Blackout.*

## Scene Four

*Darkness. Sounds of lovemaking. Lights up to find HAMLET and GENEVIEVE lying in bed, buried completely under a white sheet, perhaps just their feet exposed.*

**HAMLET** Genevieve, you're amazing. Amazing. Nothing makes me happier than seeing you naked.

**GENEVIEVE** Perhaps. *(emerging from under the sheets)* But, as we both know, eventually you'll have to marry Ophelia, and that, sweet prince, will be that.

*GENEVIEVE buries herself back under the covers for a moment, then begins to dress herself.*

**HAMLET** *(also emerging)* Not necessarily.

**GENEVIEVE** Oh yes. Don't expect me to hang around and be your mistress.

**HAMLET** Mistress, whore. What's the difference?

**GENEVIEVE** Political. As a whore I know where I stand.

**HAMLET** You're not a whore.

**GENEVIEVE** I am—

**HAMLET** You're not—

**GENEVIEVE** You just said I was.

**HAMLET** I didn't mean it.

**GENEVIEVE** I did. I was before you. And I will be again. So what, it's a living.

**HAMLET** You're too complicated to be a whore.

*HAMLET reaches for a flask of wine and pours some into a goblet.*

Kiss me.

**GENEVIEVE** You kiss me first.

*HAMLET does. GENEVIEVE kisses him back, full on the mouth. They lie together in silence, sharing the wine.*

**HAMLET** Did you know my father was murdered?

**GENEVIEVE** I didn't know your father. Professionally, I mean. King Theodore was a very rare man. Married *and* satisfied. *(She laughs, beat, then sudden realization.)* What do you mean, murdered?

**HAMLET** Axed. Bumped off. Assassinated.

**GENEVIEVE** What are you? Crazy?

**HAMLET** I exhumed the body, Genevieve. His spine was hacked. Seven blows to the neck and shoulders. Three in the lower back. One right through the heart. He was murdered, all right.

**GENEVIEVE** Oh my God. But who—

**HAMLET** Isn't it obvious?

**GENEVIEVE** Oh my God. *(beat)* Are you sure?

**HAMLET** Not entirely.

**GENEVIEVE** Why are you telling me this?

**HAMLET** I need your help.

**GENEVIEVE** No! I'm having nothing to do with this.

*GENEVIEVE jumps out of bed, puts on her blouse.*

**HAMLET** Genevieve—

**GENEVIEVE** No! Shut up. Your mouth, just shut it. If I know anything they'll kill me too.

**HAMLET** *(holding her)* No one will hurt you. Genevieve, you have my word.

**GENEVIEVE** Right, thanks. I'll put it in the bank.

**HAMLET** Listen, I have evidence. I have suspicions. I have hunches. I need you to help me find proof.

**GENEVIEVE** How?

**HAMLET** Work on Claudius. Seduce him. If his conscience is pricking, he'll talk about it in bed.

**GENEVIEVE** You want me to fuck a murderer? What would that prove?

**HAMLET** You don't have to go that far. Just get him on his knees. Promise him things. Be his confessor. I'll be there, listening. Once he incriminates himself I'll take care of the rest.

**GENEVIEVE** It sounds messy. I hate the sight of blood. I don't even know if I trust you. Should I?

**HAMLET** I'll be there, I promise. *(beat)* My father, the king, was murdered. I have to bring his killers to justice. Will you help me or not?

*GENEVIEVE turns away. Pause.*

**GENEVIEVE** Are you done now? Shall I finish dressing?

**HAMLET** No. Stay. Please. Stay?

*Blackout.*

## Scene Five

*LAERTES sits moping, talking to himself.*

**LAERTES** What a wasted life. I *hate* this. I hate this place! *(groaning loudly)*

*OPHELIA enters.*

**OPHELIA** Laertes. You're still here. That's wonderful. I thought you were on your way to Wittenberg.

**LAERTES** I can't go to Wittenberg. I'm broke. Unless you want to lend me some money.

**OPHELIA** My dear sweet brother, you know I have none of my own. Except my dowry.

**LAERTES** So? Cash it in.

**OPHELIA** What? My d-dowry?

**LAERTES** Yeah. Sell it. That and your hope chest.

**OPHELIA** My d-d-dow—

**LAERTES** It's no use to you. Cash it in and let's split the proceeds.

**OPHELIA** N-no. It's for m-me a-a-and—

**LAERTES** Hamlet? The lunatic prince?

**OPHELIA** He's n-not…

**LAERTES** Course he is. What kind of marriage would that be? Two crazy cuckoos baked in a pie? Get real. Cash the stupid dowry and lend me some money. Please?

**OPHELIA** You're n-not very sensitive to my f-f-feelings, Laertes.

**LAERTES** Economic times, kid.

**OPHELIA** Why w-wouldn't Hamlet m-marry me?

**LAERTES** Because you're stupid and you s-s-stutter.

**OPHELIA** I d-do not. Only when I'm n-nervous. And I'm n-not stupid, you a-asshole.

*OPHELIA begins slapping him furiously.*

**LAERTES** Hey, hey… cut it out. I'm sorry.

**OPHELIA** *(still slapping him)* N-no you're n-not…

**LAERTES** Yeah, yeah…. Ow—I am…

*OPHELIA stops. Sits on the floor.*

**OPHELIA** Hamlet and I, we get along just fine.

**LAERTES** Oh yeah? I haven't seen him carrying any long-stemmed roses lately.

**OPHELIA** I know. *(beat)* What's wrong with everyone all of a sudden? It used to be if a man proposed marriage and was refused twice but had the nerve to come back a third and a fourth and a fifth time he'd be accepted, then the church bells would ring, there'd be a week of drunken rejoicing, and a wedding would consummate society's love affair with form and etiquette. Ceremony is all dead. Instead p-p-people have s-sex, they fight, break up, then get m-m-married on impulse. I may as well give up my d-d-dowry. The concept is archaic anyway.

**LAERTES** You mean you'll do it, you'll sell—

**OPHELIA** Y-y-yes. Just w-w-wait until I s-sort it out, o-k-kay?

**LAERTES** You don't think you could spring an advance? I don't even have beer-drinking money right now.

**OPHELIA** There's liquor in the dining hall.

**LAERTES** Please! I need to get out of here, into the real fucking world, or I'll become a basket case like the rest of you. Ophelia?

**OPHELIA** *(screaming)* I'll s-s-see what I c-c-can d-do, all right?

*HAMLET enters, his hair and clothes looking wild and dishevelled.*

**HAMLET** Stop torturing my sister.

**LAERTES** *(simultaneous)* She's not your—

**OPHELIA** *(simultaneous)* I'm n-not your—

**HAMLET** Twins, the two-two of you-you.

*OPHELIA giggles. HAMLET kisses her hand playfully.*

Sweet mistress Ophelia.

**OPHELIA** Hello, Hamlet.

**HAMLET** The love of Laertes's life.

**OPHELIA** Hamlet!

**LAERTES** I'm leaving. *(exiting)*

**HAMLET** Wander not into the prickly thorns, dear lad. Your father awaits for you.

**LAERTES** Oh, piss off…

*LAERTES completes his exit. Beat.*

**POLONIUS** *(offstage)* Laertes!

**LAERTES** *(offstage)* Ah, shit.

**POLONIUS** *(offstage)* Where the goddamn hell do you think you're off to? Get over here. Now!

**HAMLET** I knew he wouldn't believe me if I spoke the truth.

**OPHELIA** You're c-c-cruel sometimes.

**HAMLET** Cruel, cruel world, my love.

**OPHELIA** Stop talking like that. Your m-mad games are b-b-boring.

**HAMLET** Sorry. You're the only one who sees through me.

**OPHELIA** Not hard. You're like a pale glass of water.

**HAMLET** True. I'm a hollow, shallow, sham of a man.

**OPHELIA** Stop, stop, stop, stop, stop. You're avoiding again. With p-p-poetic ph-phrasings. Your images p-pound my brain. I feel them before the words even reach the air. You h-hate me. You think I'm an id-idiot. You b-believe there's no f-f-future. For anyone. For u-us, esp-p-pecially. I'm very sweet, s-say you, even though I'm gawkish. And n-n-nervous. You s-sometimes l-like me. But I'm P-P-Polonius's daughter. And y-y-you'd rather be back with G-G-G-G-Gen….

*OPHELIA starts to cry in large, wailing, choking sobs. HAMLET puts his arms around her.*

**HAMLET** Hush, hush… sweet angel of mercy…

**OPHELIA** *(breaking away)* Enough. I'm s-stronger than you th-think. M-more m-mad than you are. Even if you ask a hundred times. I'll k-k-kill myself before I m-marry you. So there.

*OPHELIA runs out.*

**HAMLET** So will I, love. So will I.

*CLAUDIUS has entered quietly.*

**CLAUDIUS** Hamlet—

**HAMLET** This man stole my father.

**CLAUDIUS** No, I did not—

**HAMLET** And my mother.

**CLAUDIUS** Your mother and I married for love. I'm sorry if you find that hard to believe.

**HAMLET** Ah, the mysteries of woman.

*POLONIUS enters, dragging LAERTES back in by the ear.*

**POLONIUS** Sons will be the death us all, Your Majesty. Look, I just caught mine trying to sneak out towards town.

**LAERTES** No, I wasn't—

**HAMLET** Take it from me, he was.

**LAERTES** Oh, dry up, you asshole. *(seeing the look from CLAUDIUS and POLONIUS)* Uhhh…

**CLAUDIUS** Hamlet vexes us all, Laertes, but he is our heir apparent.

**LAERTES** Right. I know. Sorry, Your Majesty—

**POLONIUS** *(cuffing him)* Miscreant. I ought to put you in military school. It's your only hope.

**LAERTES** Why can't I go to Wittenberg—

**POLONIUS** Oh shut up. Wittenberg, indeed.

**HAMLET** Indeed. *(smiling)*

**POLONIUS** Come along, can't you see His Majesty and the prince want to be alone.

*POLONIUS drags LAERTES offstage.*

**CLAUDIUS** Hamlet, let's try to have a reasonable discussion, just you and I, man to—

**HAMLET** Man to mouse. I'm the mouse. Squeak, squeak.

**CLAUDIUS** You're not fooling me with this pretense. I understand you better than you think.

**HAMLET** Then you'll give me back my father?

**CLAUDIUS** Your father died a tragic, self-inflicted death. The truth isn't always easy to accept.

**HAMLET** No, it's not.

**CLAUDIUS** All right, we're alone here. There are no witnesses. Put your fucking cards on the table. What? You think I killed him? My own brother? And orchestrated a conspiracy to keep it quiet? Try keeping anything secret around these halls. Hamlet, you're deluded. You've never liked me much, I don't know why. I used to be your favourite uncle. I took you hunting when you were ten. Helped you bag your first pheasant. Why are you against me now? Because of Gertrude. You were very close to your mother and the idea of her sleeping with anyone but your father is upsetting. I understand that, but, goddammit, Hamlet, you're not a child. Life has to go on. The state has to continue. What, you would've preferred she marry a foreigner? Or become a nun? Yes, I love your mother, I've admired her from the beginning. Yes, perhaps we rushed things, but someone had to clean up the mess Theodore left behind. He was a weak ruler, if truth be known. Too artistic in temperament. Once your mother and I decided to marry it became politically expedient to do so as quickly as possible so that the government could function without all this uncertainty. There. I've told you everything. From the heart.

**HAMLET** My father was stabbed in the heart.

**CLAUDIUS** Whatever wounds there were, were self-inflicted.

**HAMLET** He told you that, did he?

**CLAUDIUS** Who?

**HAMLET** Theodore.

**CLAUDIUS** Of course not—

**HAMLET** He told me. Oh yes. Walking on the parapets one night, his spirit flew by and told me the truth. I know. I intend to tell the world.

**CLAUDIUS** All right. I promised your mother I'd make a serious attempt to reason with you. If you're determined to be theatrical, I can see it's a waste of breath.

**HAMLET** *(imitating a ghost)* Oooohhh. My bwother… Claudiuth… he thabbed me, thabbed me, thabbed me…. Ooohhh…

**CLAUDIUS** Let me warn you for the last time. Hamlet. I'm the reigning monarch here. And if you say that again, even in jest, I will take off your fucking head.

**HAMLET** Do. Perhaps I'll return the favour.

**CLAUDIUS** You're a dangerous lunatic, Hamlet. Dangerous to yourself. Two can play this game. Suppose I decide to go mad for a couple of months. I could cut your throat in a midnight frenzy, and even be forgiven. People like success stories. Think about it. Prince Hamlet.

*CLAUDIUS exits. HAMLET's arm begins to shake violently.*

*Blackout.*

## Scene Six

*GERTRUDE sits, brushing her hair. OSRIC enters, carrying a small glass urn.*

**OSRIC** Excuse me—

**GERTRUDE** Go away. I don't want to be disturbed.

**OSRIC** I'm sorry, my lady. His Royal Majesty asked me to bring this right over.

**GERTRUDE** What?

**OSRIC** Theodore's ashes. Oh. Sorry. You didn't know? He was cremated this morning. *(as GERTRUDE looks aghast)* Oh. *(beat)* Do you want them then, or shall I—

**GERTRUDE** No, no, leave them… here… yes…. Put them down.

*OSRIC places them on a table. GERTRUDE stares at the urn, then notices OSRIC watching.*

Thank you, Osric.

**OSRIC** Any time. Sorry, I mean… *(bowing)* My lady…

*OSRIC leaves. GERTRUDE lifts up the glass urn and slowly opens the lid. Pause.*

**GERTRUDE** Why did he burn my husband's body? Odd words. Husband. Body. Body. Burn… *(peering into the urn)* Darling Theodore. Is this really you? All that's left? I remember…. What? Almost nothing, as if…. *(beat)* You were my first lover, my only lover until— No, don't go back, mustn't… *(beat)* Oh, Theo, poor baby Theo…. You died, didn't you? Ended your life, gave me freedom to— Why? Because you knew I was unfaithful? With your brother? Should I be suffering guilt now? Claudius doesn't, I don't think…. But why did he burn my husband's body? *(pause)*

I want to remember you, Theodore, I want to, but— It's as if you never existed. Except vaguely in another lifetime. Strange, how I feel absolutely no guilt about that, either. Perhaps if there was a god I'd feel guilt. Guilt would have purpose then, meaning. But there's only ashes. That's all, obviously, that we are…

But I do take responsibility. And remember… marrying you, and the purity I felt the first time you touched me, and yes, how your breath smelled of lilac that night…. No, Claudius wears lilac, you wore…. I can't remember, remember only the sweetness of it… and your body, thin, frail almost, but firmly muscled, and, yes, I remember your beard, softer than Claudi's, and very blue eyes, no, grey, grey like the stones I gave you, and, yes, you made me pregnant, and I remember the pain giving birth to Hamlet, and the waters breaking, and you laughing, but why is everything else like a foggy sea, like a pale, empty parchment…

Why did he burn my husband's body? What am I supposed to do with these ashes? A mantelpiece ornament? Poor Theodore, locked in a jar like a Persian genie. How do I let you out?

*GERTRUDE sits on the floor, then reaches in the jar, touches the ash, and puts it to her lips.*

Yes. I can taste you. Even your smell is coming back to me. The smell of your soft skin, against mine, and our bodies' fluids, that strange odour, the first time we—

*GERTRUDE presses the urn against her breast. CLAUDIUS enters.*

**CLAUDIUS** What are you doing? Get off the floor. You're disgusting.

**GERTRUDE** Why did you burn my husband's body?

**CLAUDIUS** What was I supposed to do? Let him rot on the palace floor?

**GERTRUDE** You could have told me in advance. Given me the choice—

**CLAUDIUS** It was a political decision. Hamlet's running amok. Pretending to be mad to hide the fact that he's dangerous. Inventing subversive lies about stab wounds in the goddamn corpse—

**GERTRUDE** Watch your mouth. He was my husband.

**CLAUDIUS** My brother.

**GERTRUDE** All the more reason to show him respect.

**CLAUDIUS** Get it through your pretty-faced head—

**GERTRUDE** Don't say— Don't you dare call me that—

**CLAUDIUS** *(overlapping)* This is tantamount to a state of war.

**GERTRUDE** *(overlapping)* I can think for myself. I'm not your pretty-faced puppet—

**CLAUDIUS** No, you're my queen, the Queen of Denmark—

**GERTRUDE** *(overlapping)* Find yourself a whore if that's what you think…

**CLAUDIUS** *(overlapping)* —which means you have responsibilities.

**GERTRUDE** *(beat)* Why did you burn my husband's body?

**CLAUDIUS** I've already told you—

**GERTRUDE** No reason. Unless you're afraid of the truth.

**CLAUDIUS** Oh, for God's—

**GERTRUDE** Are you afraid of the truth?

**CLAUDIUS** What truth? Truths that happened, or lies made credible by madmen who puncture corpses in order to—

**GERTRUDE** So his body was punctured? Like Hamlet said?

**CLAUDIUS** Apparently. But not by me.

**GERTRUDE** I wasn't implying—

**CLAUDIUS** Of course you were. You're infected with the idea like every other rumour-and-gossip monger.

**GERTRUDE** All right. What are you trying to hide, Claudius? Stab wounds bleed, but ashes are dry. And silent. Is that it?

**CLAUDIUS** Are you accusing—

**GERTRUDE** Don't tamper with his memory, my memory, the one thing I have left of him. Why am I suddenly burdened with his martyrdom?

**CLAUDIUS** He's not a martyr. He was a weak old king who killed himself. If it was anything else, you wouldn't have married me.

**GERTRUDE** I'm not so sure. Evil is very attractive, it's sexy, it seduces. I wedded myself to it. I was your partner in lust. What am I supposed to do now? Repent? Make these ashes into a shrine?

**CLAUDIUS** Shut up. You're becoming hysterical—

**GERTRUDE** I am very calm. *(beat)* Claudius… I want you to swear, over Theodore's remains—

**CLAUDIUS** Put the goddamn urn down. It was a mistake to let you have it.

**GERTRUDE** Swear—

**CLAUDIUS** Fuck off! Give them—

*CLAUDIUS tries to grab the urn. GERTRUDE screams.*

**GERTRUDE** No! I won't— *(pulling away)* I won't let you defile his—

**CLAUDIUS** Gertrude, stop—

*They struggle for possession of the urn. During the scuffle the urn smashes against the wall, scattering ashes over both of them. Dead silence.*

**GERTRUDE** Look at me! This is obscene! You couldn't leave his body— you couldn't even leave his ashes alone, could you? You had to eradicate every last trace of him.... Why? *(crying)* Because he was a greater king than you'll ever be—

*CLAUDIUS puts his hand over GERTRUDE's mouth, forcefully silencing her as he presses her against the wall. She stares at him coldly.*

**CLAUDIUS** I will not tolerate rebellion in my own kingdom. Not even from you. The crown is mine. Mine. Even if I sullied my hands to get it. I will not give it up. Not for you. Not for Hamlet. Not for anyone. *(letting her go)* Clean up this mess. And don't ever talk about Theodore in my presence again.

*CLAUDIUS leaves. GERTRUDE slowly wipes the ashes off her face. Lights fade.*

*Blackout.*

**Scene Seven**

*Dark shadows. The clock strikes. Then the PRIEST enters, a little tipsy, drinking from the bottle.*

**PRIEST** No one likes me here. No one talks to me. No one abuses me. There's no cerebral debate. They all just leave me alone. To hell with them. I may as well go back to the country. Sheep farmers make lousy conversationalists but at least they show respect. At least they buy my pamphlets now and again. I haven't sold one since I got here. I have to threaten people with eternal damnation just to get a free bottle of wine. What kind of life is that for a student of religious pornography?

*OSRIC enters.*

**OSRIC** Priest.

**PRIEST** Ah, yes. Osric, right? Could I interest you in my latest pamphlet, it's an index to pleasure spots in the heavenly spheres. It'll give you a definite advantage in the afterlife.

**OSRIC** I'm afraid not. But perhaps I could interest you in my little parchment.

**PRIEST** I've no money.

**OSRIC** It's free. Here, read it out loud.

**PRIEST** *(reading)* By command of His Royal Highness, Claudius the First, this shall serve as full sufficient death warrant for one country priest and pamphleteer, Father Ben, whose immediate execution… *(beat)* Excuse me, is this fact or fiction?

**OSRIC** I'm afraid it's the bitter truth.

**PRIEST** You're saying I'm more or less doomed?

**OSRIC** I'm saying you're royally fucked.

**PRIEST** Oh. *(beat)* I don't suppose you're susceptible to bribes or other forms of corruption?

**OSRIC** Not from you.

**PRIEST** I don't blame you. I guess my charms are few. *(beat)* And you wouldn't advise just trying to run for it?

**OSRIC** Not a chance. *(drawing his sword)*

**PRIEST** Wait—

**OSRIC** You're wasting what little breath you have left.

**PRIEST** I don't get it. I'm just trying to make a living. Don't you people have any sense of humour? Wait. One last taste…

*The PRIEST takes a large swig from his bottle, then clasps his hands and closes his eyes. OSRIC brings the sword to his throat.*

I'm so young. Barely middle-aged. Isn't there some way out?

**OSRIC** Unfortunately, there is one.

**PRIEST** *(opening one eye)* Excuse me?

*OSRIC pulls back his sword.*

**OSRIC** The queen has taken pity on you and, angel of mercy that she is, has insisted you be given a place in court as official biographer. You have five seconds to accept.

**PRIEST** Well, I… I…. What are the terms? I'm interested, of course, but I'll have to speak to my—

*OSRIC puts the sword back to his throat.*

*(quickly)* Accepted with thanks.

*Blackout.*

## Scene Eight

*EMILIA is dressed in black. She lights a candle and peers into the flames.*

**EMILIA** *(hoarse whisper)* Husband.... Lover.... Villain.... Bastard.... Are you there?

*GERTRUDE enters.*

**GERTRUDE** Emilia, what are you doing?

**EMILIA** *(startled)* My lady. I'm sorry. I-I thought you'd gone to bed. *(snuffs out the candle)*

**GERTRUDE** I couldn't sleep. I've a headache. My period's starting. And Claudi's out roaming the corridors.

**EMILIA** Do you want me to find him for you?

**GERTRUDE** No. Leave him. I prefer to be alone. There's politics going on. It's all Claudius seems to care about now.

**EMILIA** He's the king—

**GERTRUDE** So what? The state could run by itself if it had to. I could run it if I had to. But Claudius is addicted. *(beat)* Emilia, tell the truth. Were you angry at me when I married him?

**EMILIA** Of course not.

**GERTRUDE** People were gossiping—

**EMILIA** People always gossip. It's jealousy. In your place we'd all do the same.

**GERTRUDE** Do you think my husband's corrupt?

**EMILIA** I think all men are corrupt. Mine was a murderer. Now no one will touch me.

**GERTRUDE** *(beat)* Is Claudius capable of murder? Would he be if he had to?

**EMILIA** It's not murder if it's an act of the state.

**GERTRUDE** That's what they try to tell us. Like war. Justifiable homicide. We don't really believe that, do we?

**EMILIA** I think the less we know the better.

**GERTRUDE** Fear of drowning?

**EMILIA** Excuse me?

**GERTRUDE** In puddles of blood?

**EMILIA** I don't want to be an accomplice—

**GERTRUDE** Ah, but we are. We are. Your husband betrayed his general with a handkerchief you provided.

**EMILIA** I didn't know—

**GERTRUDE** You didn't ask.

**EMILIA** No…

**GERTRUDE** If Claudius made a similar demand of me, how would I respond? Would I lie? Could I commit murder if I had to? If he asked me?

**EMILIA** I'm sure His Majesty wouldn't—

**GERTRUDE** No? *(pause)* I wonder, Emilia. I wonder.

*Blackout.*

## Scene Nine

*CLAUDIUS and POLONIUS enter, followed by OSRIC.*

**CLAUDIUS** What else?

**OSRIC** The king of Norway—

**CLAUDIUS** Fuck the king of Norway. Cut to the chase.

**OSRIC** Excuse me?

**CLAUDIUS** Hamlet!

**OSRIC** Oh, right. The prince has petitioned you and begs an audience, uh, tomorrow morning.

**CLAUDIUS** What do you mean, petitioned? Since when has he had the courtesy to even ask for an appointment?

**OSRIC** I believe he wishes to bring his father's former lawyers with him, in order to discuss legal proceedings—

**CLAUDIUS** Petition denied.

**OSRIC** Yes, Your Majesty.

**POLONIUS** Tell him to bugger himself in hell.

*OSRIC smiles, then bows and leaves.*

**CLAUDIUS** He's written letters to every courtier and every goddamn government official, demanding a new inquiry into Theodore's death. I won't be able to keep a lid on this much longer.

**POLONIUS** Hmm. Listen. The English are fishing in our waters again. What do you say we raise an army and make them pay for it? Hamlet can be the field commander.

**CLAUDIUS** He won't do it. And if he did, we'd lose the war.

**POLONIUS** It doesn't matter if we lose the war, as long as people are distracted and Hamlet gets skewered on the battlefield. *(CLAUDIUS looks doubtful.)* We have to try. I've read his latest memos. Taking potshots at me as well now, some very thinly veiled accusations.

**CLAUDIUS** So maybe now you'll take the problem seriously.

**POLONIUS** All right, I was slow off the mark, but I'll make up for it. I'll cut him to ribbons in broad daylight if I have to.

**CLAUDIUS** Just be careful. He's stirred up a lot of sympathy. People are questioning why he gave up the throne. If he dies in suspicious circumstances, fingers will be pointing in our direction.

**POLONIUS** There are ways around that. Besides, Hamlet's mad. People know he's cuckoo. All right, all right, I see your point, but if we fight ourselves a little war—

**CLAUDIUS** If we fight a useless war and lose, I'll be the one taking the blame. I intend hanging onto this crown. In fact, I intend going down in history as the most beloved king this nation ever had.

**POLONIUS** Exactly. And the way to do that is to start a war, fight a juicy, bloody, stinking, self-sacrificing, little war… and win!

*CLAUDIUS suddenly exits. POLONIUS turns and follows.*

It's so simple. I fail to see the problem…

*Blackout.*

## Scene Ten

*Spotlight on OPHELIA. She sits on the floor, writing in her diary. Her clothes are somewhat askew. During the scene she takes pieces of her clothing off, putting them back on different parts of her body.*

**OPHELIA** With him I am chaste only in deed. My body is still, not even twitching, but my mind is racing, galloping over lips, cheeks, lips again, again. I love Hamlet. I love the idea of Hamlet, the notion of Hamlet stirring my body into liquefied madness. I love the concept of Hamlet's fingers, wringing milk from my skin. Nothing is dry anymore. I'm an ocean of desires. Mad, watery desires. Wet, delirious, excruciating, blazoning, disgusting, delicious wet, wet, wet, wet, wet, wet Hamlet desires…

*Blackout.*

*A spotlight on HAMLET. He sits on a throne, his legs sprawled over the sides. Smoking a cigarette.*

**HAMLET** The wheel's in motion. The royal maggots are buzzing around the corpse of the old king, my father, while Claudius, the living corpse, is twitching. Visibly. So why am I so depressed?

What have I done except speed up my death? They'll have to kill me now, there's no other way out. *(beat)* How will they kill me? Knife in the back like my father? A public hanging on trumped-up charges? Or some weird, complicated scheme too stupidly nightmarish to even imagine.

I *could* fight back. Probably even win. What for? To wear a crown and become a killer like Claudius just to stay in power? There'd be no other way. We haven't evolved to the point where anything else is possible.

Two choices now. One, disappear into the night. Two, continue seeking Claudius's destruction. And my own. It's a game. We both play it well, and we're learning to trade in deadlier poisons. Right now I'm sending Claudius anonymous death threats. To amuse myself. And to keep him off guard.

*Blackout.*

*Spotlight on CLAUDIUS. He opens a letter, glances at it, then tears it into pieces.*

**CLAUDIUS** He's trying to break me. Trying to make me crack. Hah! Does he think I'll roll over just like that? Abandon the throne, run into exile? Because of conscience? Guilt? Is that what he's playing on? Hah! He's living in the wrong century for that.

What can he do, anyway? I'm the one in power. I'm the one wearing the fucking crown. I can use it or abuse it any way I like. Naturally, I'd prefer to have a benign image, but if I have to become "efficient…" so be it. I'm unassailable. Unless I become careless. Like Theodore. And Hamlet becomes cunning like… *(beat)* I will *not* become careless. Guards!

*Blackout.*

## Scene Eleven

*GERTRUDE, wearing an elegant evening gown, sits at her dressing table. She puts on makeup, while EMILIA combs out her hair. The door is open. CLAUDIUS's voice can be heard echoing down the hallway.*

**CLAUDIUS** *(offstage)* Guards. I want more guards at the door. I want these letters stopped. I know who they're from. I want him caught. Red-handed…

**GERTRUDE** Emilia, please—

**EMILIA** Yes, my lady.

*EMILIA quickly closes the door, then returns to GERTRUDE.*

**GERTRUDE** Endless scheming. Relentless intrigues. Will the corridors never be quiet?

**EMILIA** Not likely. My husband used to say that silence was a waste of subtext. *(beat)* I think we need a change.

**GERTRUDE** Of course. But how to bring it about?

**EMILIA** I meant… your hair. *(GERTRUDE stares at her.)* Perhaps if I just pin it up? Like this?

**GERTRUDE** *(irritated)* Fine. Do what you wish.

*CLAUDIUS enters.*

**CLAUDIUS** Am I intruding? Do you want to be alone?

**GERTRUDE** A little late for that.

**CLAUDIUS** I meant—

**GERTRUDE** I know what you meant. *(beat)* Thank you, Emilia. I'll finish it myself now.

**EMILIA** As you wish, my lady.

*EMILIA curtsies quickly and exits, but giving CLAUDIUS a lingering look before she departs. CLAUDIUS watches her leave, then walks over and stands behind GERTRUDE.*

**CLAUDIUS** Why are you dressing up?

**GERTRUDE** You've forgotten?

**CLAUDIUS** I'm sorry. What?

**GERTRUDE** Never mind. I'll skip it.

**CLAUDIUS** What did I forget?

**GERTRUDE** It doesn't matter!

**CLAUDIUS** Another goddamn charity ball, I suppose. *(harshly)* Forgive me. I'm preoccupied. Your son is insane.

**GERTRUDE** Well. First he was goddamn crazy. Then he was a goddamn lunatic. Now he's simply insane. I call that progress.

**CLAUDIUS** I don't.

**GERTRUDE** I prefer the word "troubled."

**CLAUDIUS** Talk to him, Gertrude. Tell him there are boundaries. I can't keep covering up for him—

**GERTRUDE** Covering up for him? Is that what you think you're doing?

**CLAUDIUS** If he keeps on slandering the throne, I'll have to take action, eventually. Whether you like it or not.

**GERTRUDE** And if he's telling the truth?

**CLAUDIUS** What are you saying? You believe—

**GERTRUDE** If he *thinks* he's telling the truth, that his father was…. Isn't he obliged to ask a few questions?

**CLAUDIUS** If I thought Theodore was murdered, I'd ask questions too. We all would. But Hamlet doesn't believe that any more than I do. He's inventing this murder mystery to get at me for marrying you.

*Knock on the door.*

**GERTRUDE** Yes?

*HAMLET enters.*

**HAMLET** May I come in?

**GERTRUDE** Of course. As long as you remain polite.

**HAMLET** Don't worry. My insanity's in remission.

**CLAUDIUS** Glad to hear it. *(beat, then to GERTRUDE)* I'll leave the two of you alone.

**HAMLET** You don't have to go, Uncle.

**CLAUDIUS** I do. I'm running a little country called Denmark.

**HAMLET** As long as you're not leaving on my account. I'm quite at ease in the company of criminals.

**GERTRUDE** Hamlet—

**HAMLET** Pickpockets, thieves, rapists. Even traitors and fratricidal murderers.

**CLAUDIUS** What did I tell you? Insane.

**HAMLET** But not criminally insane.

**GERTRUDE** *(suddenly exploding)* Hamlet, shut up! I won't put up with this. If you're going to behave like a child, you can get the hell out and never come back for all I care. I mean it.

*Beat. HAMLET is stunned by the ferocity of her attack.*

**CLAUDIUS** In any case, I am leaving. *(to GERTRUDE)* I'll get dressed. The music gala, wasn't it?

*GERTRUDE nods wearily. CLAUDIUS smiles and exits.*

**HAMLET** So. Is this war? Or a state of emotional siege?

**GERTRUDE** You're too extreme, Hamlet. You have to learn moderation. Don't laugh. What's wrong with moderation, as a concept? It doesn't make headlines, but it gets results. With moderation and compromise life can go on!

**HAMLET** My father, your husband, was murdered—

**GERTRUDE** You don't *know* that.

**HAMLET** It's what I believe. It's my religion.

**GERTRUDE** Because you don't believe in goodness.

**HAMLET** Of course I don't.

**GERTRUDE** I do. I believe in "evolutionary justice." Wrongs can be overcome, mistakes can be forgiven. Love can heal.

**HAMLET** Excuse me while I go slash my wrists.

**GERTRUDE** Hamlet! You always were a difficult child. Difficult, moody, and melodramatic.

**HAMLET** You were always a perfect mother. A saint.

**GERTRUDE** No I wasn't—

**HAMLET** Yes, Mother. You were.

**GERTRUDE** Oh. And what am I now? *(beat)* Go on, say it!

**HAMLET** You say it.

**GERTRUDE** Whore. Bitch. Slut. Strumpet. Trollop. Tramp. Tart. Harlot. Wanton. Woman. Is that what you mean?

**HAMLET** Give or take a syllable. *(as GERTRUDE slaps HAMLET across the face)* Well. Now we both know where we stand.

*HAMLET turns to leave.*

**GERTRUDE** Hamlet, please. I'm sorry. *(as HAMLET turns back)* No, I'm not sorry. You deserved that. I'm fed up with your whining, your conspiracy theories, your accusations. Theodore is dead. I loved him, I mourned him, now I have to move on. We all do. If you can't live with my choices, too bad. You'll get your turn soon enough.

**HAMLET** So you intend to defend Claudius, even if he's wrong?

**GERTRUDE** Yes.

**HAMLET** Even if he's a murderer.

**GERTRUDE** You're using that word again. As if it answered everything. How simplistic. Paint the king villainous and have yourself a pretty scapegoat. Politics is more artful than that; if you haven't learned that by now it's time you did. There are numerous other theories about Theodore.

**HAMLET** Such as?

**GERTRUDE** He may have killed himself, just as the inquiry suggested. Or it may have been an accident, which they misinterpreted as suicide. Or it may have been suicide designed to look like an accident so as not to cause despair among his survivors. Or he may have killed himself and made it look like murder to wreak havoc among us. Or, more likely, he staged his death in an ambiguous manner, like the rest of his ambiguous, poetic life, in order to sow confusion and to force us to wade into these philosophical quagmires. Or, all right, he may indeed have been… killed. Murdered, if you insist. By accident, by design, by persons known or unknown, by those among us, by total strangers, or by one of a hundred political opportunists of whatever persuasion. However a king dies, some will suffer, and some will reap the rewards. All I hope is that somehow, somewhere, we can strike a morally justifiable balance.

*Beat. GERTRUDE looks exhausted. She pours herself a drink.*

Would you like one?

**HAMLET** I'm in despair. Maybe I'll follow my father. And sleep. Or maybe I'll wake up finally and do my duty.

**GERTRUDE** What do you mean?

**HAMLET** Become a good son to my mother. Become the crown prince of Denmark. Would you like that?

**GERTRUDE** Yes, Hamlet. Yes I would.

**HAMLET** No you wouldn't. Not one bit. *(jumping up suddenly and moving to the door, then turning)* Goodnight, Gertrude.

*HAMLET exits. GERTRUDE sits down, tosses back the drink.*

**GERTRUDE** I don't understand him. Maybe he *is* mad…

*CLAUDIUS comes in, dressed in formal attire.*

**CLAUDIUS** Gertrude… I owe you many apologies.

**GERTRUDE** It's not necessary—

**CLAUDIUS** I'm not just being formal. I'm appalled at what I've put you through. I-I love you. Very much.

**GERTRUDE** Yes… I love you, too. In fact, I'm terrified of what I'd do without you. That's a very weak position for a woman to be in.

**CLAUDIUS** We have to give each other strength.

**GERTRUDE** Even at the expense of honesty?

**CLAUDIUS** Honesty. The word has a wonderful ring to it, but when you analyze it, it's a vague, meaningless term.

**GERTRUDE** Perhaps…

*CLAUDIUS approaches GERTRUDE, takes her hand. Kisses it tenderly.*

**CLAUDIUS** Shall we go to the gala then? Together?

**GERTRUDE** No. *(beat)* Let's just stay in. Do you mind?

**CLAUDIUS** Not at all. In fact… *(kissing the back of her neck)* I'd like that very much…

*CLAUDIUS kisses GERTRUDE again. She reaches up and touches his cheek.*

*Blackout.*

## Scene Twelve

*HAMLET and GENEVIEVE are sitting up in bed, naked probably, but under a white sheet. They are sharing a goblet of wine.*

**GENEVIEVE** So that's it then?

**HAMLET** More or less.

**GENEVIEVE** You're going to marry Ophelia.

**HAMLET** Probably.

**GENEVIEVE** And become king of Denmark.

**HAMLET** In all likelihood.

**GENEVIEVE** Fucking great. I knew you were a waste of time.

*A knock on the door.*

**PRIEST** *(offstage)* Prince Hamlet?

**HAMLET** What is it?

**PRIEST** *(entering)* Hi. Sorry, they told me you'd be here and I— *(beat, seeing them)* Oh, excuse me. *(turning his back)*

**GENEVIEVE** Get out, you asshole.

**HAMLET** It's all right, come in.

**PRIEST** If you're in the middle of a carnal act, I could come back later.

**HAMLET** Don't worry. It's fine.

**PRIEST** You're sure now?

**HAMLET** I'm sure.

*The PRIEST turns around, smiles sheepishly, and pulls out a large notepad.*

**PRIEST** Hi. I'm writing a book. I was hoping to interview you and—

**HAMLET** Of course.

**GENEVIEVE** *(angry)* Jesus, Hamlet.

*GENEVIEVE rolls over and wraps herself under the sheet.*

**PRIEST** As you may know, I've been commissioned to write the royal biography—

**HAMLET** Of Claudius?

**PRIEST** Yes. I was hoping to get a few quotes.

**HAMLET** Bastard. Scumbucket. Crook. Scoundrel. Murderer. Will that do?

**PRIEST** Uh, do you think you could elaborate?

**HAMLET** *(patting the pillow)* Sure, sit up here. I'll tell you the whole story.

**PRIEST** Do I have to take my clothes off?

**HAMLET** Not unless you want to.

**PRIEST** Um. Maybe just my boots.

*The PRIEST begins removing his boots.*

**GENEVIEVE** Oh for Christ's sake. I'm leaving.

**HAMLET** No, please. Genevieve… *(touching her gently)* Stay?

*GENEVIEVE glares at HAMLET but stays. The PRIEST climbs into bed between them.*

**PRIEST** *(to GENEVIEVE, extending his hand)* Father Ben.

**GENEVIEVE** Go fuck yourself.

**PRIEST** I would, but I've taken a vow of chastity. Generally I manage to sublimate my desires with literature and alcohol. *(indicating the wine)* May I?

**HAMLET** *(handing him the goblet)* Of course.

**PRIEST** Thanks.

*The PRIEST quickly drains the glass. HAMLET refills it.*

**HAMLET** Genevieve?

**GENEVIEVE** *(softening)* All right.

*HAMLET teases GENEVIEVE with the wine, forcing her to reach way across the PRIEST to get it. She laughs.*

**PRIEST** I see God has endowed you rather well. I hope you thank Him in your daily prayers.

**GENEVIEVE** Yeah, God, thanks a bunch for making me a terrific whore. *(She drinks the wine.)*

**HAMLET** *(to PRIEST)* More?

**PRIEST** Absolutely. *(HAMLET pours.)* This is such a treat. Like the day after Christmas. You know, after all the boring obligatory sermons? *(holding out his glass)* A little more, if I'm not being greedy.

**GENEVIEVE** You are. And your feet stink.

**HAMLET** *(pouring)* But so what? Genevieve?

**GENEVIEVE** *(extending her arm)* Why not? *In vino veritas.*

**PRIEST** I agree.

*They all raise their glasses and drink.*

What shall we talk about? Aside from my book and the subject at hand.

**GENEVIEVE** Sex.

**HAMLET** Politics.

**GENEVIEVE** Marriage.

**HAMLET** Murder.

**PRIEST** Yes. Interesting topics, all of the above. Is there a connection?

**GENEVIEVE** Ask Hamlet. He's the one getting married.

**PRIEST** Really? Can I officiate?

**HAMLET** I'll have to ask Ophelia. *(to GENEVIEVE)* She doesn't know.

**GENEVIEVE** You haven't asked her yet?

**PRIEST** You're marrying Ophelia?

**HAMLET** *(to GENEVIEVE)* No.

**GENEVIEVE** Why the hell not?

**HAMLET** *(to PRIEST)* For political reasons. To fulfill my destiny and avenge my father's murder.

**PRIEST** Monumental tasks. If you need guidance…

**HAMLET** *(to GENEVIEVE)* I'm afraid she might refuse me.

**PRIEST** …I've just written a philosophical pamphlet that may be of relevance—

**GENEVIEVE** *(to HAMLET)* Bloody liar. You're messing with her head just like you messed with mine.

**HAMLET** *(to PRIEST)* On what theme?

**PRIEST** Actually I was lying. Trying to impress. But I'd be happy to write one for the occasion. On spec, of course, though I wouldn't say no to a few bottles of wine—

*HAMLET refills his glass.*

**HAMLET** Perhaps we could co-author one. On the subject of Claudius's usurpation of the throne.

**PRIEST** Oh. *(beat)* Oh. *(beat)* I smell conflict of interest. You see, the queen—

**HAMLET** The queen's putting makeup on a bad piece of skin. It won't work. The people see through it.

**GENEVIEVE** *(to HAMLET)* Did it ever occur to you Ophelia might have thoughts of her own, even if she is a fucked-up, fucked-over moron?

**PRIEST** *(to GENEVIEVE)* Don't you think you're being more than a little harsh—

**GENEVIEVE** *(to PRIEST)* Butt out, beet face!

**PRIEST** Immediately.

**HAMLET** *(to GENEVIEVE)* Ophelia has too many thoughts. Just like me. It's why she needs me. And why I need and love you.

**GENEVIEVE** You expect me to—

**PRIEST** What you're saying is…

**GENEVIEVE** Really?

**PRIEST** …the king and queen are corrupt at best, murderers at worst, and if I lie in bed with them, figuratively speaking—

**HAMLET** You'll be fucked, fried, and freeze-dried.

**PRIEST** Right. On the other hand…

**GENEVIEVE** I don't believe you.

**PRIEST** …I can tell what you're up to. It's unsavoury at best, a mortal sin at worst.

**HAMLET** I swear it.

**PRIEST** So if I ally myself with you, Claudius & Co. will do me in, or vice versa if I— *(to GENEVIEVE)* Does that make sense to you?

**GENEVIEVE** You got it, pal. You'll be killed by them if you do and by us if you don't.

**HAMLET** So choose.

**GENEVIEVE** *(to HAMLET)* You really need me?

**HAMLET** Desperately.

**GENEVIEVE** Love me?

**PRIEST** Personally, I prefer to die in bed.

**HAMLET** *(to GENEVIEVE)* Isn't that obvious?

**PRIEST** However, this may be a moment of truth. You know, the kind the monks used to write epic poems about? Ah well. Destiny is nothing if not bizarre. On the other hand, we could just ignore reality and all get drunk together?

**GENEVIEVE** You get drunk if you want to. I'm going to make love to Hamlet.

*GENEVIEVE crawls over the PRIEST and wraps herself in HAMLET's arms.*

Is that okay with you, my prince?

**HAMLET** Yes. *(kissing her)* Yes. Yes…

**PRIEST** *(extricating himself)* Um, I'll just slide over here. *(sliding onto the floor, propping his head against the end of the bed)* I won't be able to resist listening, but I'll try not to peek. Is that all right?

*HAMLET and GENEVIEVE are beginning to make love.*

**GENEVIEVE** You'd better talk to Ophelia about the wedding. And quick.

**HAMLET** I will, love, I will.

**PRIEST** Yes, life is full of surprises. Perhaps I'll write a novel about this. Or a gossip column. Perhaps I'll just shut up and get royally pissed on my own. *(looking over his shoulder)* Interesting.

*The PRIEST crawls around the side of the bed, not to watch, but to retrieve the bottle of wine.*

That's better.... Here's to both of you. Cheers.

*Blackout. Intermission.*

## Scene Thirteen

*OPHELIA sits with a pile of open books on her lap. HAMLET is kneeling beside her.*

**OPHELIA** No. *(beat)* Ask me again.

**HAMLET** Will you marry me?

**OPHELIA** No. *(beat)* Keep asking.

**HAMLET** Ophelia, will you marry me?

**OPHELIA** No. *(giggling)*

**HAMLET** I love you. *(She giggles again.)* Do you love me?

**OPHELIA** I love books. There's something about the printed word that conjures up a spiralling imagination. Books are my passion. I eat words, I devour syllables, I suck, chop, chew into vowels with a violence that language itself is powerless to describe. I love archaic words, words that defy meaning, words whose meanings are obscure, hidden in time, suggestive only in the traces of their lettering. I feed on etymology and symbiotics. I fantasize on the power of alliteration, assonance, onomatopoeia, rhythm, symbolism, allusion. I fuck myself with foreign alphabets, syllogisms, structural grammar. I breathe linguistic paradox. There's no need for marriage. My life *is* language.

**HAMLET** Ophelia, sweet—

**OPHELIA** Don't say any more. Especially pale words like sweet and love and queen. If you must talk, use brave talk with compound nouns and a lack of adverbs.

**HAMLET** Will—

**OPHELIA** Of course, I'll marry you. *(beat)* Now that we understand each other.

*Blackout.*

## Scene Fourteen

*GERTRUDE and EMILIA. In the garden with cake and coffee.*

**GERTRUDE** But why is he getting *married*?

**EMILIA** Why not? Ophelia needs a man, and Hamlet needs balance and stability. On top of it, they may actually love each other.

**GERTRUDE** Nonsense. People in love sleep together, but marriage is always political.

**EMILIA** I wish I had a man again. Someone younger. A lusty, very lusty, younger someone. I could survive the next ten years with that.

**GERTRUDE** Oh, hush.

**EMILIA** Well it's easy for you to talk. You've got Claudius. The most sexually rampant devil around. I'd give anything to have a beard like his running loose all over my body.

**GERTRUDE** Hush. His need for sex I understand. But why is he—

*HAMLET enters, suddenly.*

Why are you getting married?

**HAMLET** Why did you get married?

**GERTRUDE** Hamlet! Answer me.

**HAMLET** To prepare myself for the throne. As the legitimate heir apparent a queen would be useful, don't you think?

**GERTRUDE** *(to EMILIA)* See? It *is* political. *(to HAMLET)* Ophelia isn't fit to be queen. She's vague, stupid, neurotic, not useful at all. And you don't want to be king anyway. You publicly repudiated the throne.

**HAMLET** I was suffering from depression.

**GERTRUDE** And madness.

**HAMLET** A lot of monarchs are mad, aren't they?

**GERTRUDE** Why Ophelia?

**HAMLET** Why Claudius?

**GERTRUDE** Don't avoid my question.

**HAMLET** *My* question. Why Theodore's brother? And who killed Theodore, anyway?

**GERTRUDE** How would I know?

**HAMLET** Did you?

**GERTRUDE** What?

**HAMLET** Do it?

**GERTRUDE** *(beat)* You are mad. Why do you insist on believing your father was murdered? Once and for all, he killed himself. There's no proof of anything else.

**HAMLET** What about the stab wounds? Gone, of course, in the big fire. Mind you, I have pictures.

**GERTRUDE** What do you mean, pictures—

**HAMLET** Pictures of the eleven stab wounds. Drawings. Done by independent artists on the night of your wedding. I've decided to have them published.

**EMILIA** I think I'd better leave. I don't want to hear any of this.

*EMILIA exits.*

**GERTRUDE** I don't believe you.

**HAMLET** Read tomorrow's papers.

*HAMLET pulls out a drawing from his vest pocket and hands it to GERTRUDE. She glances at it nervously, draws in a breath, then quickly hands it back to him.*

**GERTRUDE** It wasn't Claudius.

**HAMLET** Who had access to the king? Access to his private corridor? Who knew the pattern of his nightly walks? Claudius. Claudius. Claudius.

**GERTRUDE** Among others, many others.

**HAMLET** Who organized the speedy inquiry? Who ordered the sudden cremation? Who sits on Theodore's throne and sleeps with

Theodore's queen? *(pause)* Motive, opportunity, tampering of evidence. I'm building a fairly good case, wouldn't you say?

**GERTRUDE** A case for what?

**HAMLET** The new judicial inquiry. *(smiling)* I intend to become King of Denmark and put Claudius on trial for murder.

*GERTRUDE gets up, backs away in horror.*

**GERTRUDE** You don't know what you're saying! You're risking your life, Hamlet. And mine. You have to stop this. Now!

**HAMLET** Too late, Mother. The pamphlets are printed and on their way to the newspapers, the marketplace, and the judges. There's no turning back now. For any of us.

*GERTRUDE glares at HAMLET then runs out of the room. HAMLET sits, begins eating the cake.*

*Blackout.*

## Scene Fifteen

*CLAUDIUS, POLONIUS, and LAERTES.*

**POLONIUS** The only answer is to go to war and make sure Hamlet gets killed in the war. Then you can give him a hero's funeral and everyone will be happy.

**CLAUDIUS** You may be right. The only way out now is war, total war.

**LAERTES** I don't get it. A whole war, and all that that entails, just to kill one goofy guy. Why don't we stab the fucker in the back?

**CLAUDIUS** It won't work. There are political complexities—

**POLONIUS** Which you know nothing about.

**LAERTES** You're right. I don't. Why can't I just go to Wittenberg and get laid like everyone else my age?

**POLONIUS** Because we need you here. It's time you grew up a little.

**CLAUDIUS** Yes. You're adult enough. Take some responsibility.

**LAERTES** Why me? I didn't make this mess.

**POLONIUS** You'll inherit none of it either. I'll leave you penniless.

**LAERTES** I am penniless. I have to beg for booze and whore money as it is.

**POLONIUS** That's because you lack gumption. If you want an allowance, earn it.

**LAERTES** How?

**POLONIUS** Stick a hatpin in Hamlet's bladder.

**LAERTES** Me? Do your own dirty work.

**CLAUDIUS** Enough. We need an organized plan. Hamlet must be killed. And it needs to look like an accident.

**POLONIUS** An accidental war, I tell you—

**CLAUDIUS** No. No, the risks are too high. We'll organize a fencing tournament. Hamlet's rapier can be weakened and made to break, then bingo! An accidental thrust to the heart. Or failing that, he receives a light wound on the shoulder, which becomes infected from a slow poison we place on the tip of the foil.

**LAERTES** It sounds complicated. I don't know if I can—

**CLAUDIUS** Never mind, Osric'll do it. He knows about things like that. We'll hold the tournament the day after tomorrow. One way or another, we'll engineer Hamlet's death. Then two weeks of mourning and the whole mess will be over.

**POLONIUS** All right. But if this fails we declare war on England or Spain or Poland immediately. Agreed?

**LAERTES** Agreed.

**POLONIUS** *(cuffing him)* Who asked you?

**CLAUDIUS** *(beat)* All right.

**POLONIUS** Good. A decision at last. *(smiling)* Personally, I hope Osric fucks up. I haven't worn my good suit of armour in years. I'm looking forward to it. Charge of the fat brigade. *(laughing)* Now who's going to tell Hamlet?

*Blackout.*

### Scene Sixteen

*GERTRUDE sits, writing a letter.*

**GERTRUDE** Dearest Hamlet. Don't be angry with me. I should have told you sooner, but I've only recently discovered this myself.

You're right, of course. Theodore was killed. Murdered. There, I've said the word. I don't know by whom, but if you must avenge his death, don't be blinded by jealousy and rage. I love you, darling boy. If I've sinned in your eyes, please try to be forgiving. In reality truth is elliptical, often bordering on the mysterious.

*A spotlight comes up on HAMLET in another area. He is reading the letter.*

Claudius is not what you think, though perhaps he has too often turned a blind eye to the machinations of those around him. To find what you seek, Hamlet, go to the source of knowledge. Not to my husband. You know who I mean. For Ophelia's sake I thought it best not to mention this before.

*GERTRUDE hesitates, writes a little more, then seals the letter.*

**HAMLET** "What you do now I leave to your conscience. With deepest affection. Your loving Mother."

*Light fades on GERTRUDE.*

My conscience?

*Blackout.*

### Scene Seventeen

*POLONIUS is putting on an old suit of armour. Now, half-dressed, he stops and stares into the mirror.*

**POLONIUS** Tell me if I'm a liar, you look nothing short of amazing.

[Do I now?] Absolutely. [Well thanks. But… *(whispering)* are you sure?] Oh yes. In fact, you look like a king. [Really? You're not just flattering?] *(feigns a shocked reaction, then smiles)*

I think so too. *(goes back to flirting with his mirror image, bowing several times)* Yes, Sire. Of course, Highness. Indeed, Majesty— *(releases a loud fart toward the mirror, then chuckles and continues dressing)*

Yes, I could've had the throne if I'd wanted it. Why bother? Living in fear and watching your rear. Like poor cousin Claudi. Hah! Give me the back rooms of power any day.

*POLONIUS begins strapping on a breast plate of armour.*

This I wore in the Turkish campaign. I cut a very stunning figure. Even Gertrude took notice. Hamlet was there too. With old daddy Theodore. Should've cut out both their livers when I had the chance. Accidentally, of course. *(reaching for a helmet with a gaudy plume)* And now for the pièce de résistance…

*HAMLET has entered quietly from the shadows. POLONIUS puts on the helmet and suddenly finds a dagger over his throat.*

*Blackout.*

*Lights up on the king's bedroom. HAMLET drags a screaming POLONIUS into the room, locks the door, then corners him on the bed. Some of POLONIUS's armour has now fallen off.*

**HAMLET** Who killed—

**POLONIUS** No, please…. No, Hamlet…

**HAMLET** —my father? You know.

**POLONIUS** No, I swear, I don't…. By God— *(HAMLET jabs him)* Ow—

**HAMLET** Who killed—

**POLONIUS** I don't—

**HAMLET** —my father?

**POLONIUS** I don't know! I swear it.

**HAMLET** But he was killed?

**POLONIUS** Yes. I mean, I think— I believe— Yes, yes, he was.

**HAMLET** By whom?

**POLONIUS** I haven't a clue!

**HAMLET** I think you do. I'd bet my life on it. And yours. *(pause)* I intend to find out. By any means.

**POLONIUS** What— What are you going to do to me?

**HAMLET** Relax.

*HAMLET spins the bed around sharply. POLONIUS screams.*

It's not you I'm after. Just tell me the truth.

**POLONIUS** And you'll let me live?

**HAMLET** Not in Denmark.

**POLONIUS** In exile, then?

**HAMLET** Mmmm.

**POLONIUS** You mean, England?

**HAMLET** I mean anywhere on this bloody earth, but not here. Now who the fuck killed—

**POLONIUS** All right, all right. *(beat)* Exile. I have your word on that?

**HAMLET** Yes. But if you so much as whisper another lie, any lie, I'll hang your lungs out to dry beside the queen's bedsheets.

**POLONIUS** All right, all right. It was Claudius. Obviously. Who else? He planned it right down to the last detail. He hired two famous scoundrels, prisoners, Max and Borovitch. They botched it, left him—

**HAMLET** Who?

**POLONIUS** Theodore, they left him wounded, on the ground, choking on his own blood. Claudius had them—Max and Borovitch—executed and finished the job himself. From behind. With a pickaxe, I think. That's why the bones.... There, now you know.

**HAMLET** Yes. Now I know... *(pause)*

**POLONIUS** I'll leave at once for England. Shall I?

*HAMLET seems in a daze. He nods. POLONIUS heads for the exit.*

**HAMLET** Yes. Go to England. Drink tea.

**POLONIUS** The door is locked.

**HAMLET** Oh. Right. Sorry. *(taking out his skeleton key)* The key to the kingdom.

*HAMLET tosses him the key. Smiles. POLONIUS nervously puts it in the lock, drops it, then tries again. Succeeds, and is about to leave.*

**POLONIUS** Thank you, thank you—

**HAMLET** Wait. Question. Who is the Prince of Denmark?

**POLONIUS** Why, you, of course.

**HAMLET** Liar!

*HAMLET kicks the door shut and runs his sword through POLONIUS's body, pinning him to the door. POLONIUS gasps. Blood rises from his mouth.*

**POLONIUS** You... promised—

**HAMLET** I lied.

*POLONIUS dies.*

Skewered like a sewer rat. Bravo, Hamlet. Well done.

*Blackout.*

### Scene Eighteen

*Funeral music. CLAUDIUS, GERTRUDE, LAERTES, OPHELIA, OSRIC, and EMILIA march in. The moment they are seated HAMLET enters from the side. He and CLAUDIUS exchange glances. A short silence. OPHELIA makes a sound that alternates between laughing and crying. Eventually the laughter wins out.*

**LAERTES** Ophelia. Stop crying.

**OPHELIA** I'm not. I mean, I can't help it. I mean, I d-d-don't know what I m-m-mean… *(continues laughing)*

**GERTRUDE** Hush. Show respect, Ophelia, for goodness sake. He was your father.

**OPHELIA** S-s-s-s-sorry… *(another peal of laughter)*

**LAERTES** Shut up! *(to CLAUDIUS)* I want to know who murdered him.

**CLAUDIUS** The investigation is under way. We'll find out soon enough.

**HAMLET** Maybe you can reopen the investigation of Theodore's murder at the same time. Tit for tat?

**OPHELIA** T-t-t-t-tit… *(giggles)*

**LAERTES** Ophelia, I said shut up. *(HAMLET smiles.)* You shut up, too. I wanna talk to you when this is over. I think I'm just starting to figure out a few things.

**HAMLET** Bravo. Genius.

*HAMLET claps his hands. LAERTES is just about to bite.*

**CLAUDIUS** Not now, Laertes. Wait.

*The music ends. The PRIEST takes his place above the congregation. LAERTES and CLAUDIUS sit down.*

**PRIEST** Brethren and sisters. We are here to mourn the passing of a talkative man. Lord Polonius. He was felled by an unknown assailant, who goes as of yet unpunished, which means we may all be forgiven for looking over our shoulders. Even now.

*The PRIEST looks over his own shoulder. Others may do so as well.*

Funerals. Funerals are… there's no other word for it, is there? Strange! Funerals are very strange. Nonetheless, we will proceed according to God's instructions. Which, incidentally, I've written down in another beautifully bound pamphlet. And the word is that funerals call for reflection, flattery, and a dose of the miserable truth. Lord Polonius—

**OPHELIA** *(trying to control her giggles)* He is my father. He *is* my father.

**HAMLET** Was.

**OPHELIA** Was, is, who cares, he's d-d-d-dead. *(shrieks with laughter)*

**GERTRUDE** Ophelia, you're a disgrace.

**OPHELIA** S-sorry. I have to leave. Sorry…

*OPHELIA begins stumbling over the other mourners.*

**LAERTES** *(stopping her)* Ophelia…. For God's sake—

**HAMLET** Let her go.

**LAERTES** Fuck you.

*OPHELIA breaks into a high-pitched scream. LAERTES lets her go. She continues laughing and runs out of the room.*

**PRIEST** I hope that poor girl reads my pamphlet. It tells of the proper way to mourn. Twenty pfennings, more expensive than the rest because, well, death is the ultimate test, isn't it? Trifle with death and you capsize the fucking boat. Unless, of course, you happen to be king. Or the would-be king. Then, oh, well, then you just stab old death in the back, and what's the prize? You get to sex the queen.

**CLAUDIUS** *(rising)* You son of a bitch…

*Consternation. LAERTES and OSRIC make threatening moves towards the pulpit.*

**PRIEST** Yes, this is an accusation. The truth can be hidden no longer. Which means, of course, having said that, that my life is worth shit now, that I'm only safe within the sanctuary of this cathedral. That's right, sanctuary, sanctuary! Your immortal soul will be worth less than shit if you defy the Church's sanctuary.

*LAERTES looks at CLAUDIUS and backs off, as does OSRIC.*

*GERTRUDE and EMILIA have also risen and move towards the door. GERTRUDE breaks her stride and gives HAMLET an icy stare before leaving.*

On the other hand, ignore everything I'm saying. Forget what I just said. I am, after all, extremely drunk. Claudius, come back…

**CLAUDIUS** *(to OSRIC)* The moment he steps outside the door, kill him. *(exits)*

**PRIEST** Well good! Why should I leave? I'll stay in my sanctuary all night. All year! Here under the watchful eye of God I have everything I need. So there!

*The others have left now. HAMLET walks up to the altar and claps his hands.*

*(as the lights fade)* Was my voice okay? I didn't overdo it…?

*Blackout.*

## Scene Nineteen

*LAERTES and CLAUDIUS enter.*

**LAERTES** He killed my father, didn't he?

**CLAUDIUS** Yes.

**LAERTES** He admitted it straight out. Didn't even deny it, right?

**CLAUDIUS** He boasted about it.

**LAERTES** Fucker. I want revenge.

**CLAUDIUS** Good. Listen to me—

**LAERTES** There's only one problem…

**CLAUDIUS** What?

**LAERTES** He says you and Dad killed Theodore. So we're even.

**CLAUDIUS** Hamlet is a dangerous liar. Don't be fooled by his madness. It's like a shield of armour. You have to cut through it. Right to the heart.

**LAERTES** Yeah, that makes sense. But how?

*GERTRUDE enters, unnoticed.*

**CLAUDIUS** Make a firm, irrevocable decision to kill him. No matter how. The rest is mechanics, which you can leave up to me.

**LAERTES** All right. I'll do it.

**CLAUDIUS** Good. He wears the mask of a fool, but ultimately he's dangerous.

*CLAUDIUS turns and sees GERTRUDE staring at him.*

**GERTRUDE** Who's dangerous?

**LAERTES** Uh, no one.

**CLAUDIUS** Your son.

**GERTRUDE** Leave my son alone. I'll answer for him, no one else. Why are you involved in this, Laertes?

**LAERTES** Me? I'm— I'm not involved. I'm just—

**GERTRUDE** You're over your head. Plotting with the king of plotters. You'll end up in an early grave like your father if you're not careful.

**LAERTES** I think you're right. I mean, I-I th-think— Oh my G-G-God, I-I-I-I…. What's g-g-going o-on…

*LAERTES swoons and faints dead away.*

**GERTRUDE** Well. Another innocent fallen.

**CLAUDIUS** How long were you standing there?

**GERTRUDE** I wasn't. Who were you talking about?

**CLAUDIUS** Before you arrived? Fortinbras. The prince of Norway—

**GERTRUDE** I know who Fortinbras is. A very civilized gentleman, as I remember.

**CLAUDIUS** His manners are deceiving.

**GERTRUDE** As manners often are. Goodnight, Claudius.

*GERTRUDE stares at CLAUDIUS, holding her ground.*

**CLAUDIUS** I don't appreciate that tone, Gertrude. I happen to be king of this fucking castle. You happen to be the king's wife. Good night, yourself.

*CLAUDIUS turns to leave.*

**GERTRUDE** I know what you're up to. I won't let you get away with it.

*CLAUDIUS stops, stares at GERTRUDE for a beat, then exits. LAERTES wakes up, dazed.*

**LAERTES** What? Who? Where? Why? *(sees GERTRUDE)* Oh…

**GERTRUDE** Laertes. I think it's time we had a talk.

*Blackout.*

### Scene Twenty

*GERTRUDE is in bed, reading. CLAUDIUS enters. She glances up at him, but says nothing. CLAUDIUS takes off his jacket then sits at the foot of the bed.*

**CLAUDIUS** Why are you still up?

**GERTRUDE** I didn't ask you that question.

**CLAUDIUS** Politics. Affairs of state. Threats of war. *(pause)* What are you reading?

**GERTRUDE** *The Last Days of Nero.* A cautionary tale.

*Beat. CLAUDIUS stares at GERTRUDE. She stares back.*

**CLAUDIUS** I'm going to bed.

*CLAUDIUS takes off his boots. Gets up. Pours himself a drink or two. GERTRUDE returns to her book.*

Not tired?

**GERTRUDE** No, not really.

*GERTRUDE turns away, still reading. CLAUDIUS sits on the bed again, reaches over, touches her shoulder.*

**CLAUDIUS** When's the last time we had sex? *(GERTRUDE stares at him, incredulous.)* Sorry. I'm starting to crack. *(beat)* Gertrude, I can't function unless I know that you're—that you still—I need you for my sanity, Gertrude. *(beat)* Sometimes I feel the weight of mountains in this fucking crown. *(beat)* I'm no saint, Gertrude, but what I— Whatever wrongs I—

**GERTRUDE** Don't. Please. I understand everything now. All your darkest sins. That are no worse than my own. Ultimately. In silence, complicity. What you did I wanted you to do. I must have. Or else how could I have lived through the terrible pain of Theodore's death without a whimper. Without a murmur of protest. And married you. Betraying the king's memory. I was his queen, his lover, yet in love with you. I must have *wanted* this. How else could I have you, how else could we have each other, unless he died. And if he didn't die voluntarily, why not tip him into his grave prematurely. To liberate ourselves. To make these possibilities real. Yes, I know, I know what you did. And I forgive you. I have to. Because I'm as guilty as you are.

**CLAUDIUS** You weren't involved. I made sure of that.

**GERTRUDE** *(beat)* Did he die quickly?

**CLAUDIUS** Yes.

**GERTRUDE** Without pain?

**CLAUDIUS** Yes.

**GERTRUDE** Please. No more lies. I want the truth in every detail. So that I no longer have to speculate and doubt. Tell me, Claudi, so I can purge myself and finally, finally, move on.

**CLAUDIUS** All right. *(pause)* It was a botched-up job. I hired amateurs. Theodore was stronger than they thought, he fought back. They ran away and left him to suffer. When I found him he was bleeding everywhere. I tried to ease his pain, but he knew what I'd done. That I was responsible.

**GERTRUDE** You spoke with him? While he was dying?

**CLAUDIUS** Yes.

**GERTRUDE** Poor Theodore. What did he say?

**CLAUDIUS** He smiled. He blessed me. And he asked me to take care of his queen. I said I would. He nodded and kept on smiling. I don't know how long he stayed like that. Finally he stared at me with those cold grey eyes and told me he was in great pain.

**GERTRUDE** And you killed him?

**CLAUDIUS** There was no turning back. I embraced him and pressed my knife through his heart. He died without a sound.

**GERTRUDE** Will you be as gentle with me, Claudi?

**CLAUDIUS** What do you mean?

**GERTRUDE** When you kill me, or have me put to death. Don't pretend you haven't been thinking of it.

**CLAUDIUS** Thinking of it? What does that mean? The mind raving drunkenly in the middle of the night, is that a thought? Or a fear? An irrational, nightmare fear. Yes, the image of, of killing you, has entered my mind, but never lingered, never taken shape, I swear, because I trusted that eventually, when the time came for you to know, you'd understand. Gertrude, you can't run a nation with sanitized decrees. You have to take political initiatives or others will take them at your expense.

**GERTRUDE** What about loyalty, and love?

**CLAUDIUS** What about love? I'm obsessed with you, your body, your being. I want you forever as an extension of my life.

**GERTRUDE** What about *my* life? *(beat)* Never mind. I can't believe you said that.

*Beat. CLAUDIUS moves in and brings his arms around GERTRUDE's shoulders.*

**CLAUDIUS** Do you still want me? In spite of everything?

**GERTRUDE** *(closing her eyes)* Yes.

**CLAUDIUS** Love me?

**GERTRUDE** Of course.

**CLAUDIUS** More than Theodore?

**GERTRUDE** Oranges and pears, my dear.

**CLAUDIUS** What does that mean?

**GERTRUDE** Don't push it, Claudius. I said I still love you. That's enough.

**CLAUDIUS** I don't know if I believe you.

**GERTRUDE** Then you'll have to kill me, won't you? *(beat)* Perhaps I was lying. I don't love you at all.

**CLAUDIUS** I'm your royal sovereign, goddammit. I can command your love.

**GERTRUDE** You made your bed, Claudius. Don't expect me to lie in it now.

**CLAUDIUS** What do you intend to do? Look elsewhere?

**GERTRUDE** If I have to.

**CLAUDIUS** Whore.

**GERTRUDE** Murderer.

**CLAUDIUS** Maybe I will kill you.

**GERTRUDE** Not if I kill you first.

*They stare at each other. GERTRUDE smiles and sits on the bed. CLAUDIUS impulsively kneels beside her and puts his head on her lap.*

**CLAUDIUS** I can't believe it's come to this.

**GERTRUDE** You were always a bit of a child, Claudius. The poor, misunderstood baby brother. I used to pity you. Then, one day, I fell madly, head over heels for you. Overnight you grew stronger, older, strangely powerful, oddly addictive. And our dark, forbidden passion suddenly flourished. *(running her hand through his hair)* Yes, my Claudius, I did love you once. *(then breaking away)* But now we're in a state of crisis, and, in times of crisis, survival comes first. I am going to survive, Claudius. With or without you. And now, I'd like to be alone. Goodnight.

*GERTRUDE leaves. CLAUDIUS stares into space.*

*Blackout.*

**Scene Twenty-One**

*OPHELIA looks a mess. She sits on the floor in a semi-catatonic state, slowly pulling at her hair, making it wild and stringy, and occasionally putting it in her mouth. HAMLET sits in a chair beside her.*

*OPHELIA sings a religious chant in Latin.*

**HAMLET** Claudius is going to visit Genevieve tonight.

**OPHELIA** G-G-G-G-Gene-v-v-vieve…

**HAMLET** She's going to try to get him to confess. Or at least implicate himself. Myself and the judges will be listening.

**OPHELIA** C-C-Conf-fesss…

**HAMLET** He's on the ropes now. Even without a confession I could dethrone him in a minute. But I want the satisfaction. I want him to know what I've done. I want him begging. I want him helpless. I want him humiliated. I want him suffering, bleeding. I want him to die in pain. In his own shit. Like my father.

*OPHELIA sings a little more.*

So. Action. At last. Why then so empty? So futile? Feeling nothing but impossibilities.

**OPHELIA** H-H-H-Ham-l-lettt…

**HAMLET** Yes, sweet angel of mercy.

**OPHELIA** Angel of d-doom.

**HAMLET** You think we're heading for disaster?

*OPHELIA is silent. She begins putting bunches of her hair into her mouth and chewing on them.*

Oh well…. Let it come. *(beat)* Here, leave your hair alone…. Ophelia—

**OPHELIA** *(rising pitch)* No! I— Eat— I— Eat— Eat my life I— I— I eat—words— I eat—lies—eat people—eat persons—eat eat eat—eat politics—eat violence—eat murders—eat Ophelia, eat

G-G-G-Genevieve, eat father—eat eat eat happiness—eat my Hamlet—eat wedding bells— I eat— I eat mouth, eat eat eyes, eat hair—eat hair—eat myself—eat my cunt, eat my body— Eat my love fuck—eat— I eat, I eat, I eat, I eat— Eat— Eat. Eat— Eat— Eat— Eat—

**HAMLET** *(overlapping)* Stop, enough. Ophelia—

*HAMLET kisses OPHELIA hard on the mouth. She crumbles in his arms. Begins to cry softly.*

Be patient, love. It'll soon be over. I promise.

*Blackout.*

### Scene Twenty-Two

*GENEVIEVE is dressing. The PRIEST comes in, drunk and dishevelled.*

**PRIEST** Strike, ye avenging angels!

**GENEVIEVE** *(screams)* What the fuck are you doing here? Get out. The king's coming.

**PRIEST** But goes ne'er hence.

**GENEVIEVE** *What*?

**PRIEST** But goes ne'er hence. *(pulling out a sword)* I've come to dispatch the king.

**GENEVIEVE** Give me a break. There's a price on your head.

**PRIEST** You're right. I forgot. I must be incompetent.

**GENEVIEVE** Yes. And you're drunk.

**PRIEST** True. But I'm also the conscience of the day.

**GENEVIEVE** Please. Claudius is coming. Hamlet's arranged it. If you want your revenge take a number and wait outside.

**PRIEST** All right. I need another drink anyway.

*The PRIEST exits.*

**GENEVIEVE** Shit!

*GENEVIEVE quickly finishes arranging the bed. Then CLAUDIUS comes in.*

**CLAUDIUS** Are you busy?

**GENEVIEVE** *(startled)* No, not at all. I was expecting you later… that's all…

**CLAUDIUS** I came early. Security reasons.

**GENEVIEVE** Oh…

**CLAUDIUS** You look lovely. Ravishing. As always.

**GENEVIEVE** Thank you. *(a quick curtsy)* Your Majesty.

**CLAUDIUS** *(beat)* What do you have to drink?

**GENEVIEVE** I'm sorry, not a lot. Wine, brandy. Beer…

**CLAUDIUS** A beer'll be fine.

*GENEVIEVE pours a beer. CLAUDIUS takes off his boots. She hands him the beer. He hands it back to her. She drinks from it. Hands it to him again.*

Don't be nervous.

**GENEVIEVE** I'm not.

**CLAUDIUS** I may be your monarch, but this isn't an official visit. *(laughing and noticing that she is not)* Were you expecting someone else?

**GENEVIEVE** Of course not.

*Beat. CLAUDIUS stares at GENEVIEVE. She is visibly nervous. Aware of his critical gaze.*

Sorry. I'm not quite ready. I was going to change my dress.

**CLAUDIUS** Feel free. I'm in no hurry.

**GENEVIEVE** Good. *(beat, changing her robe behind a screen)* I guess I am nervous.

**CLAUDIUS** Why? You've bedded royalty before.

**GENEVIEVE** You mean Hamlet?

**CLAUDIUS** Seen much of him lately?

**GENEVIEVE** No. I think he's preoccupied.

**CLAUDIUS** What has he told you? Lately.

**GENEVIEVE** What do you mean?

**CLAUDIUS** He still talks to you, I believe. He used to say you were his only confidante.

**GENEVIEVE** Maybe. Once.

**CLAUDIUS** Not now?

**GENEVIEVE** No. Not since… *(pause)*

**CLAUDIUS** What?

**GENEVIEVE** His father's death.

**CLAUDIUS** Ah. Yes, very tragic, that. *(beat)* Come, sit on my lap. *(She does.)* Begin.

**GENEVIEVE** Just like that?

**CLAUDIUS** Yes.

**GENEVIEVE** Couldn't we—

**CLAUDIUS** Now.

**GENEVIEVE** All right. What would you like?

**CLAUDIUS** Just be inventive.

*GENEVIEVE begins to caress CLAUDIUS erotically and to rub her body against his. He seems hardly affected by this.*

Mmmm. So. No indications of his plans, one way or another?

**GENEVIEVE** Not really…. Is this what you like?

**CLAUDIUS** Yes, more of that… *(beat, she continues)* I'm very disappointed in you, Genevieve.

**GENEVIEVE** *(stopping)* What? Why?

**CLAUDIUS** That he's stopped seeing you. Unless you're lying. Carry on. *(She continues caressing, stroking, rubbing.)* Perhaps he's serious about marrying Ophelia. Faster. Perhaps he wants the throne after all. More. He thinks I killed his father. Faster. Harder.

*CLAUDIUS joins in GENEVIEVE's sexual rhythm. Then suddenly stops.*

He's deluded, the son of a bitch, but he wants revenge all the same. Is that true?

**GENEVIEVE** I don't know—

**CLAUDIUS** *(slapping her)* Lying whore—

**GENEVIEVE** I'm not—

*GENEVIEVE presses on with the sexual agenda. CLAUDIUS allows her to continue, then suddenly grabs her and throws her towards the bed. He follows and leans over her, closely.*

**CLAUDIUS** Not in love with Hamlet?

**GENEVIEVE** No!

**CLAUDIUS** Lying whore. You're in it with him, aren't you? Plotting, conspiring against me—

**GENEVIEVE** No! *(beat, then quietly)* No. It's over. *(beat)* I want you. Just you, for yourself. To be your mistress. If you'll have me…

**CLAUDIUS** *(beat)* Maybe I'm just paranoid.

*CLAUDIUS moves away and sits on the edge of the bed. GENEVIEVE looks around furtively for HAMLET, then catches CLAUDIUS's gaze. She looks at him, helpless, vulnerable.*

I went after the throne because I loved the smell of power. It was always this close, but never quite mine. Like the queen. I could smell her perfume in the air. I could kiss her hand at court. I could hear her breathing and imagine the passion smouldering beneath the dress. But, of course, she was Theodore's wife. I could only love her in secret or with the stupid, affected smile of a surrogate brother. Well, finally, what I lusted after is mine. But power is a dangerous mirror, it snaps at your nose right through the goddamn looking glass. And even the love of a beautiful queen can vanish, grow cold overnight. *(beat)* You say you want me? For myself? Then prove it.

*CLAUDIUS kisses GENEVIEVE hard on the lips, forcing her to respond. He tears at her dress and begins kissing her around the shoulders and breasts. He may stop to take off his jacket and shirt or loosen his pants. During this the PRIEST enters in awkward tiptoe fashion, his sword drawn, and advances towards CLAUDIUS. GENEVIEVE sees him and tries to ward him off with her eyes and with a hand gesture. He is about to strike. CLAUDIUS is now kissing GENEVIEVE's stomach. The PRIEST prepares to bring his sword down through CLAUDIUS's back.*

*CLAUDIUS, perhaps aware of GENEVIEVE's alarm, turns just in time to deflect the blow. The sword strikes directly into GENEVIEVE. She screams.*

**PRIEST** Oh my God. *(letting go of the sword)* I'm—horrified…

**GENEVIEVE** You ass… hole…

*GENEVIEVE coughs up a mouthful of blood.*

**PRIEST** You're an innocent victim, Genevieve. I'm sorry, truly sorry…. *In nomine padre—*

*The PRIEST suddenly notices CLAUDIUS, staring at him incredulously. The PRIEST thinks about retreating. CLAUDIUS grabs him by the throat.*

**CLAUDIUS** You goddamn lunatic!

*CLAUDIUS hurls the PRIEST against the wall. Then pulls out a dagger and advances on him slowly.*

**PRIEST** Please— I'm in poor health, spiritually that is.... I've more sins on my conscience than you, if truth be known— Oh, mercy—

*LAERTES enters.*

**LAERTES** What the hell is going on? *(sees GENEVIEVE curled up in bed, bleeding, groaning)* Oh my God.... My God...

**CLAUDIUS** What you see, Laertes, is another act of treason. Hamlet's conspiracies are all around us. None of us are safe. Are you man enough to deal with this problem? Finally?

**LAERTES** What... do you want me to do?

**CLAUDIUS** Learn to defend yourself. Here. *(giving his dagger to LAERTES)* Finish him off.

**PRIEST** Listen.... It was an honest mistake—

**LAERTES** And you'll pay for it, motherfucker.

**CLAUDIUS** What are you waiting for? Now.

**LAERTES** It's okay? We don't have to put him on trial—

**CLAUDIUS** Do it!

**LAERTES** All right. All right...

*LAERTES stabs the PRIEST lightly in the shoulder.*

**PRIEST** Ow...! If that's meant as a warning, believe me, I take the hint—

**LAERTES** Shut up. Worm.

**CLAUDIUS** Hold your sword out like a soldier. Now strike hard!

**LAERTES** Like this?

*LAERTES stabs harder, wounding the PRIEST more seriously. He is shocked by the reality of the blow. GENEVIEVE tries to pull out her own sword and falls to the floor.*

**CLAUDIUS** Better.

**GENEVIEVE** *(softly)* Help me... please...

**CLAUDIUS** And again… *(LAERTES strikes once more.)* Take your time. Focus. *(another strike)* Good. Good.

**LAERTES** Yes. Vengeance is good. I like it.

**PRIEST** Help…. I'm bleeding on the cross. *(another strike)* Oh…. Oh… *(crying)* I'm a goner now… let me crawl away. I'll die quietly, I promise…

**LAERTES** You'll die right here. Villain!

*LAERTES stabs the PRIEST in the heart. The PRIEST dies.*

**CLAUDIUS** *(slapping LAERTES on the shoulder)* Excellent. You show talent. Now do the same to Hamlet and I'll appoint you prince in his place.

*With only a parting glance in GENEVIEVE's direction, CLAUDIUS leads LAERTES out. GENEVIEVE tries to crawl back towards the bed but collapses on the floor. HAMLET enters from another door. Sees her.*

*Blackout.*

## Scene Twenty-Three

*Sound of bells. HAMLET and OPHELIA sit in a bath together, their bodies bare. They kiss each other tenderly on the eyes, lips, and cheeks.*

**HAMLET** With this ring…

**OPHELIA** I love you…

**HAMLET** …I thee wed.

**OPHELIA** Love, love, love, love you…

**HAMLET** Till death do us part?

**OPHELIA** Till death do make us one.

*OPHELIA raises her arms. She is bleeding heavily at the wrist. HAMLET raises his arms, revealing the same.*

**HAMLET** Angels of mercy…. Amen…

*They kiss again, covering each other in blood, then collapse, wrapped in each other's arms.*

*A knock on the door.*

**GERTRUDE** *(offstage)* Hamlet?

*GERTRUDE opens the door and sees them.*

No. Breathe. Deeply. Remain in… control…

*HAMLET looks up towards her.*

**HAMLET** *(a whisper)* Mother…

*HAMLET's bleeding arm reaches out to her. GERTRUDE backs out of the room slowly and closes the door. HAMLET's head falls.*

*Blackout.*

## Scene Twenty-Four

*OSRIC displays a tray of fencing foils to LAERTES and CLAUDIUS.*

**OSRIC** The ones with the silver brocade have been tipped with poison.

**LAERTES** That's okay, I'll take one of these.

**CLAUDIUS** Don't be crazy. Put something on the end of your sword.

**LAERTES** I don't need poison. Not to kill that rat.

**CLAUDIUS** He's an expert swordsman. Obsessed with revenge.

**LAERTES** So am I. *(beat)* No poison. No cheating. I'll finish him with a good right arm. Or die trying.

**CLAUDIUS** You're naive.

**LAERTES** You're corrupt.

**CLAUDIUS** But I'm alive. I'm in power. I'm rich. I have servants. I sleep with a beautiful queen. Think about it.

**LAERTES** I am. Believe me, I am. Beautiful queen, eh?

*LAERTES moves away, practising his fencing in a flamboyant manner. CLAUDIUS looks at him oddly. GERTRUDE enters.*

**GERTRUDE** Oh good. I was afraid you'd start without me.

**CLAUDIUS** Of course not. This is a grand occasion. It requires the presence of a queen.

**GERTRUDE** That sounds rather patronizing, Claudi. But you can kiss me anyway.

**CLAUDIUS** With pleasure.

*CLAUDIUS kisses GERTRUDE's hand and then her cheek. She smiles at him, then moves away.*

**GERTRUDE** You seem in good form, Laertes. Good luck today.

**LAERTES** Thanks.

*EMILIA enters, curtsies.*

**EMILIA** Your Majesties.

**GERTRUDE** Emilia, good. You can be a witness. Laertes is trying to prove his manhood.

**LAERTES** I'll prove more than that.

**CLAUDIUS** Of course you will. Osric, tell Hamlet we're ready. Where the hell is he, anyway?

**LAERTES** In some corner, probably, pissing his pants.

**CLAUDIUS** Or screwing Ophelia.

**LAERTES** Yeah, right.

**GERTRUDE** You're both unfair. Hamlet has a lot on his mind, poor boy. As for Ophelia, her sex life is no one's business but her own.

**LAERTES** She is my sister.

**GERTRUDE** Then treat her with respect, for heaven's sake. Come, I'm getting bored. Osric, wait. *(holding out the fencing foils)* Why don't you and Claudi warm up a little first? Put on a show for the girls.

**CLAUDIUS** Me? I haven't fenced in years. Mind you, I used be one of the best, if not the best.

**GERTRUDE** Well then. I'm sure you haven't lost your touch. Or have you? *(suddenly thrusting the sword in CLAUDIUS's direction, causing him to react)* Emilia, come here and watch with me.

**EMILIA** Oh yes. I love a good match.

**OSRIC** *(reaching for the practise foils)* I think these will be best for now, Your Majesty?

**CLAUDIUS** Fine. Watch, Laertes. You might learn something.

*CLAUDIUS sets aside his crown and does a few warm-up exercises, then fences a round with OSRIC. CLAUDIUS takes a few beats to find his form but soon shows his expertise and scores a hit.*

Yes!

**OSRIC** A point for you, I concede it.

*They continue playing. CLAUDIUS becoming more and more aggressive, though OSRIC manages to hold his own for a while.*

**LAERTES** *(to GERTRUDE)* He's very good.

**GERTRUDE** Yes, but you can strive for better. Hamlet's always been the best of them all.

**CLAUDIUS** Nonsense. Hamlet was just a spoiled prince. People let him win. Aha!

*CLAUDIUS scores a second hit on OSRIC, though perhaps OSRIC is not playing his best either. GERTRUDE and EMILIA clap.*

**OSRIC** *(bowing)* Well done, Your Majesty.

**EMILIA** Bravo! Bravo!

**GERTRUDE** Not bad, Claudi. Not bad.

*CLAUDIUS comes over and squeezes GERTRUDE's hand.*

**CLAUDIUS** Well my queen? Do I win the prize?

**GERTRUDE** *(teasing)* Not yet, Theo. *(beat)* I-I mean, Claudi, Claudi, of course. I don't know why I— Forgive me… *(publicly)* Osric, ask Hamlet to join us now. Laertes can take your place.

**OSRIC** Yes, my lady.

*OSRIC hands his foil to LAERTES and exits. CLAUDIUS gives GERTRUDE a penetrating look, then moves back into the arena.*

**CLAUDIUS** Sure, Laertes. Stick it to me if you can.

**LAERTES** *(to GERTRUDE)* Shall I—

**GERTRUDE** Of course. Wait, Laertes… *(going to him)* Here, you can wear my scarf for luck.

**CLAUDIUS** Are you betting against me, Gertrude?

**GERTRUDE** Yes. You're much too used to winning.

**CLAUDIUS** It's a habit I don't intend to break.

*LAERTES and CLAUDIUS square off.*

**EMILIA** I'm rooting for Claudius.

**CLAUDIUS** Come on, Laertes. I'm just finding my stride.

**LAERTES** *(hesitates, then looks at GERTRUDE)* All right.

*They fence. LAERTES begins tentatively, then gradually becomes rougher and more aggressive in his style. CLAUDIUS matches his energy though, and dominates the round.*

**CLAUDIUS** Good. Good. You'll need that. Someday you may have to go to war. Like your father. It's a big difference putting a sword through a body than aiming at a fencing vest.

**LAERTES** Not when you get used to it.

*LAERTES fights more aggressively and turns the tables. CLAUDIUS is becoming winded. LAERTES backs him up near the throne where GERTRUDE sits.*

**GERTRUDE** I think Claudius has met his match, Emilia.

**CLAUDIUS** Bullshit. *(breaking the clinch and pushing LAERTES back)* Moment of truth, Laertes.

*CLAUDIUS begins to fight dirty. However, LAERTES manages to hold his ground. CLAUDIUS finally trips LAERTES, but LAERTES rolls over and scores a point on CLAUDIUS's arm.*

**LAERTES** A hit, a hit.

**CLAUDIUS** Not at all.

**GERTRUDE** *(applauding)* Very good, a hit indeed.

**LAERTES** *(to CLAUDIUS)* Two out of three?

**CLAUDIUS** You goddamn worm. Where's Osric? I want a referee.

**GERTRUDE** Perhaps you'd do better with a pickaxe, Claudius.

**CLAUDIUS** *(warning)* Gertrude—

**GERTRUDE** Or we could bring back the scoundrels Max and Borevitch. Oh, I forgot. They're dead. Just like Theodore. No matter. You must have other thugs lurking in the corridors.

**CLAUDIUS** If you think I'll put up with—

*CLAUDIUS looks around, sees everyone staring at him. Suddenly throws his sword down and begins moving off. LAERTES stops him.*

**LAERTES** Don't even think about leaving, sir. This is between you and me now.

**CLAUDIUS** What? A fight to the death?

**LAERTES** Something like that.

*LAERTES tosses him the fallen sword.*

**GERTRUDE** A fight for justice, Claudius. If you win, I'll take a vow of silence, forget everything I know. Or drink a glass of poisoned wine and quietly disappear. So? Winner take all?

**CLAUDIUS** I've already won. I've nothing to gain—

**LAERTES** I do. Winner take all.

*LAERTES kisses GERTRUDE hard on the lips.*

**CLAUDIUS** You son of a bitch—

*CLAUDIUS takes the tip off his foil and attacks. LAERTES, his tip still protected, fights back defensively and manages to knock CLAUDIUS's foil out of his hand. LAERTES then takes the tip off his own foil. CLAUDIUS reaches for the rapier with the silver brocade.*

**LAERTES** Hey, that one's—

**CLAUDIUS** Poisoned? Too bad.

*They fight. LAERTES is caught off guard and receives a slight wound. He stops, stunned.*

**LAERTES** Oh my God, I'm— I'm—

**GERTRUDE** Don't worry, Laertes. I had the poisoned tips replaced. For once in your life, Claudius, you'll fight fairly.

*They fight again. LAERTES finally pins CLAUDIUS to the floor.*

**CLAUDIUS** Laertes. This is treason—

*LAERTES hesitates. CLAUDIUS edges away from him.*

**GERTRUDE** Don't think, Laertes. Just do it.

**CLAUDIUS** *(struggling to his feet)* Laertes…

**GERTRUDE** Laertes—

**LAERTES** All right!

*LAERTES stabs CLAUDIUS in the chest. CLAUDIUS grabs the sword, stares at LAERTES, then at GERTRUDE, then collapses to the ground. EMILIA screams.*

*OSRIC enters.*

**OSRIC** Your Majesty. Hamlet and Ophelia are dead— Oh! Oh, I-I see…

**LAERTES** What? What do you see?

*LAERTES holds the sword at OSRIC's throat.*

**OSRIC** Please, please, my lord—

**GERTRUDE** Leave him be, Laertes. He's always been an obedient lackey. Isn't that so, Osric?

**OSRIC** *(kneeling)* Yes, Your Majesty. Of course:

*GERTRUDE reaches for CLAUDIUS's crown, raises it above her head. The others quickly kneel.*

**GERTRUDE** Good. Let's have a glass of wine then. We'll drink to the triumph of goodness, and then begin a month of mourning. For Ophelia and Hamlet. And for Claudius, too. After all, I loved him very much, too much perhaps… *(beat)* Emilia, stop shaking like a leaf and get yourself a glass. That's better… *(raising her glass)* To the memory of our sorrows. Cheers.

*EMILIA, LAERTES, and OSRIC slowly raise a glass.*

*Blackout.*

## Scene Twenty-Five

*GERTRUDE brushing out EMILIA's hair.*

**GERTRUDE** Your hair is so long now. You haven't cut it since your husband died, am I right? *(EMILIA nods.)* Mmm. Perhaps we should braid it then, would you like that? I braided mine for my wedding, my first wedding. To Theodore. Braids weren't fashionable then, but soon all the women were doing it. Yes, I'll braid your hair, and afterwards you can braid mine, agreed? *(no response)*

Listen, not a sound. The halls and corridors are finally still. And life goes peacefully on. You see? Women should rule the world, I'm convinced of it. We may be as bloody as the men, but we don't make an art of it. Women are practical. We do what is necessary, and then we get on with living. And that is exactly what we shall do here. I've given instructions to the court to feed the poor and clothe the naked children, Claudius never even cared about such things. See the collective good our tragedies have wrought! *(bursting out with laughter)*

Now, shall you marry Laertes or shall I? I think you'd better, Emilia. No, I insist. His thighs are very firm, and he has a wonderful chin. With a short beard he'd look… dangerous, which would make my position… also dangerous. Yes, I think it'll be safer, much safer, if I remain celibate. At least for a while.

I'm not so young anymore, am I? Yet I need passion. Claudius was a lion, a passionate brute, though he could've been a poet, he had the sensitivity, but politics interfered. It always does. I'll have to marry a solid man, ordinary perhaps, even boring, one whom I can control. How to find passion and safety in the same net, well, that's a problem for another age. Isn't it?

*Blackout.*

*The end.*

# MAD BOY CHRONICLE

MICHAEL O'BRIEN

## *MAD BOY'S WILD RIDE*

Irish-Canadian Michael O'Brien is one of Canada's most prolific theatrical adaptors. He was born in 1965 on Salt Spring Island, raised between Kirkland Lake, Ontario, and London, England, educated at the University of Ottawa and the National Theatre School of Canada, and paid his dues travelling Canada's Fringe Theatre circuit in the late '80s and early '90s. He learned his playwriting craft in doing adaptations of Dickens's *A Christmas Carol* and *Oliver Twist, or the Street Boy's Progress*, and Robert Louis Stevenson's *Treasure Island* for Young People's Theatre, adaptations that have been widely produced elsewhere, including, recently, at Alberta Theatre Projects. In 2000 he was commissioned by Marti Maraden to undertake a very successful adaptation of Dickens's *Hard Times* for the National Arts Centre. Since then he has created a new version of Rossini's opera, *The Barber of Seville*, for Toronto's Theatre Columbus at CanStage, winning a Dora Award for best musical production in 2004, and he wrote an acclaimed new version of H.G. Wells's *The Invisible Man* for the Shaw Festival in 2006. He has also adapted Margaret Atwood's *The Handmaid's Tale* (2001) and *The Blind Assassin* (2003) for CBC radio, both of which became best-selling audio books.

In addition to his adaptations, his stage plays include *Aurora* (National Arts Centre Atelier, 1986), *The Last Temptation of Christopher Robin* (The Theatre Centre, 1992), *Freaks: A Circus Tale with Music* (National Arts Centre, 1994), *Restitution: An Irish-Canadian Rhapsody* (Factory Theatre, 2004), and *The Miracle Man* (with music by Alan Cole, Ryerson University, 2008). His CBC radio plays include *Shores of Wonder* (inspired by the *Norse Vinland Sagas*, 2000), *Someone Just for Me* (a thriller, 2005), and *The Hearts of the World* (about Mary Pickford and D.W. Griffith, 2005).

But O'Brien remains best known as a playwright for his Viking saga *Mad Boy Chronicle*, an adaptation of *Hamlet* and its sources for which he received a Governor General's Literary Award nomination when the play was published in 1996. *Mad Boy* is a wild ride. It's AD 999 and Christianity is about to come to the savage Viking "Denn-Mark" of one of *Hamlet's* source texts, the *Gesta Danorum* of Saxo Grammaticus. This play purports to predate or parallel Shakespeare's, returning to Shakespeare's own sources, removing *Hamlet*'s Renaissance veneer, and restoring a vulgar, hypocritical, and raw Viking world that could be a cartoon of Canada today: "Let's just sit back and complain and let our leaders destroy us," as the invented character/commentator Inga says. The play's action roughly mimics, or parodies, that of *Hamlet*, though the outcomes are very different. Its Helsingor stands in for Shakespeare's Elsinore, and its cast—the names coming in part from Saxo, in part from sheer exuberant invention—includes a Claudius character (Fengo), a Gertrude (Gerutha), the Hamlets, Jr. and ghostly Sr. (Horvendal and the ghost of his father), Polonius (Matthius), Laertes (Ragnar), and Ophelia (Lilja), along with a pair of Christian brothers, two old women (weird sisters who on occasion bear a striking resemblance to *Macbeth*'s three witches), various Vikings, monks, wolves, and spirits, and in one startling moment the "ragged little" ghost of Jesus Christ ("the god of being… Crucified"). Some of O'Brien's Shakespeare parodies are both hilarious and acute, as when Polonius's famous and fatuous advice to Laertes is reduced to "don't do nothing stupid will ye hey son? It int wise." The titular mad boy is, of course, Horvendal/Hamlet, here a drooling, vacillating, and confused fourteen-year-old early Christian boy, but the real centrepieces are the stalwart, if also mad, thirteen-year-old Lilja/Ophelia, and the crafty Fengo/Claudius, whose savagery, lust, and political instincts are all impeccable. But the play is as significant for its more major divergences from Shakespeare as its parodic parallels, most significantly its newly invented subplot concerning realpolitik, hypocrisy, and—another contemporary parallel that is also reminiscent of the work of Shakespeare's contemporary Christopher Marlowe—the political uses of religion at the turning point from medieval to modern world history.

*Mad Boy Chronicle* premiered at the Alberta Theatre Projects playRites Festival, Calgary, Alberta in February, 1995, with the following company:

| | |
|---|---|
| INGA | Donna Belleville |
| ANNA/Brother PETRI | Patricia Drake |
| RAGNAR/GHOST | Tom Rooney |
| FENGO | Hardee T. Lineham |
| MATTHIUS | Les Carlson |
| LILJA | Natascha Girgis |
| GERUTHA | Gale Garnett |
| HORVENDAL | Shaun Smyth |
| Brother PAAVO | Hugo Dann |
| SONGMAN | Kevin McGugan |
| VIKINGS, MONKS, et al. | Daryl Shuttleworth, Lenard Stanga, Cory Mack, Andrew Smith |

Directed by Bob White
Set design by John Dinning
Costume design by Carolyn Smith
Lighting design by Brian Pincott
Music by Kevin McGugan
Production dramaturgy by Kathy Eberle
Stage management by Colin McCracken, assisted by Rose Brow

## CHARACTERS

FENGO, Lord of Helsingor
GERUTHA, wife to Lord Fengo
HORVENDAL, The Mad Boy
MATTHIUS, friend to Lord Fengo
RAGNAR, son of Matthius
LILJA, daughter of Matthius

BROTHER PAAVO,
BROTHER PETRI, Christians

INGA, an old woman
ANNA, another old woman

The GHOST of the dead chieftain, Horvendal the Elder

Vikings, monks, wolves, spirits

The Ghost Of Jesus Christ

## SETTING

The Scene: Helsingor, Denmark.
AD 999, winter.

## PLAYWRIGHT'S NOTE

Spelling, punctuation, and syntax are erratic to suggest emphasis, dialect, and state of mind.

*This play was made possible by grants from the Canada Council for the Arts and the Ontario Arts Council's Playwright Recommender program.*

*— M. O'Brien*

# MAD BOY CHRONICLE

## ACT ONE

### Scene One

*Darkness. Night. The sound of a drum. The wind howls. Wolves howl. The smoke-filled hall at Helsingor, Denmark. Deep mid-winter, AD 999. Viking dragonhead posts stare northward.*

*Inside we hear a Viking winterfest. Singing, shouting, laughing, fighting, the smell of burning cedar in the air. Vikings rant and roar and drink and howl. One Viking sings lustily with a drum:*

**VIKING** Wealth must die, and Kindred die,
A Man himself must likewise die,
But Fame and Glory never die
For him who achieves it well.
Goats must die, and Kindred die,
A Man himself must likewise die,
But one thing is shall never die,
The Verdict on each Man who dies;
But one thing is shall never die,
The Verdict on each Man who dies…

*Drums go quieter. Meanwhile, outside the village, INGA, an ancient fishwife, huddles in the snow. The black impenetrable forest looms beyond.*

**INGA** Listen to them. Listen to them festivitatin.
Howlin yowlin. Winterfest indeed.
Not a scrap nor spot o' human decencie,
Makin us poor old wimmen sit outside
I' the wind 'n the ice 'n the snow…

**ANNA** Ahoy!

**INGA** Who's that?

**ANNA** Me!

**INGA** Who's me?

**ANNA** Your sister! Come from the feastin. Look what I filcht from the menfolk—look, dearheart, look!

*She has a cooked rabbit and a jug of ale.*

**INGA** You didn't!

**ANNA** Right off the fire.

**INGA** I'm starv'd. Naeone saw ye?

**ANNA** Too drunk they were.

**INGA** Greedy dogs. Swine.

**ANNA** I can't bide Lord Fengo. Can't bide his manner. Not that the last lord were much better. Or the one afore that. Or his father afore him.

**INGA** Aye, I'd like to flay the lot o' them, every last Viking.

**ANNA** And roll 'em in salt.

**INGA** That'd teach 'em.

**ANNA** Oh well, one day everythin'll change and the world'll be wonderful.

**INGA** Aye. And we'll be dead.

**ANNA** Aye will we. May the stars protect us.

**INGA** Now come on, give us some ale. Don't you be piggin it all, greedy.

*They devour the rabbit. Wind howls in the distance. A drum beats.*

*Behind them enters the GHOST of the late chieftain, Horvendal the Elder, in Viking burial dress. He brandishes a great war axe and green smoke issues from his nose. Glowing embers hang from his hair and beard. He hisses. INGA turns.*

Hoy sister—look, we gots company.

**ANNA** Here, piss off, we're trying to eat.

**INGA** Go on then, have ye nothin else to do?
Be off with ye! Off I say!

**ANNA** Ruffian! Hedge-hogg!

**INGA** Arse-manglin cur!

**ANNA** Aye, go cockwhallop someones else!

**INGA** That's tellin him!

*INGA throws a snowball. The GHOST vanishes. Pause.*

Hoy shite—wot was that?

**ANNA** Wot?

**INGA** Himm! That were himm!

**ANNA** Who, sister?

**INGA** Himm! The lord what's dead, sister, that were a blikkit ghost!

**ANNA** Ohh the Lord o' the Slain protect us—

**INGA** Horvendal the Elder. Oh 'twas a wicked mann. Chopt off me late husband's foot, he did, just for the fun of aseein him hopp!

**ANNA** I am agonna hide.

**INGA** Me too.

*Drums. The GHOST reappears.*

**ANNA** Naay he's back, he's gonna trundle us off to the spirit world! Inga, Inga throw a snowball at him!

**INGA** You throw a bloody snowball at him!

**ANNA** Here—we never hurt you! Haa! Go on wi' ye! Away you fierce and horrible tyrant! Back to yer grave!

*She grabs a snowball.*

**GHOST** *(a ghostly whisper)* Hoorvendaaalll… Hoorvendaaall…
Where—is—my—Sonn?

*Pause.*

**ANNA** He ain't here.

**GHOST** *(louder)* Hoorvendaaaaal… Hoorvendaaaaaal…
Where—is—my—Sonn?

**INGA** He ain't here, we say!

**GHOST** *(roaring)* HOORVENDAAAAAL… HOORVENDAAAAAAL…
WHERE—IS—MY—SONN??

**BOTH** Heeeelllppp!!

*Thunder. ANNA screams. The GHOST vanishes. Blackout. Lights up. Pause.*

**INGA** That spirit were a-howlin for his sonn.

**ANNA** Wot?

**INGA** That dead wretched spirit, sister, he were a-howlin for his sonn!

**ANNA** I int gettin involvd!

**INGA** No, don't you see? His soul, it's not yet at rest! It's up to us, to us, sister—to tells the Young Horvendal!

**ANNA** You tell the boy. I int a-tellin him. He don't believe in spooks noways.

**INGA** He will believe. He gots to believe. I'll go find the boy, and make the boy believe!

*INGA runs to the village. ANNA stays and drinks.*

**ANNA** Oh Denn-Mark, Denn-Mark, ohh bastion of the brave,
Folks int got the decencie to stay put i' their graves.

*ANNA exits.*

## Scenus Secundus

*Meanwhile. The smoke-filled hall at Helsingor.*

*Lord FENGO sits surrounded by a mob of Vikings. He is very huge and very drunk, covered with food, and wears an eye patch. He is having a laugh at the expense of LILJA, a thirteen-year-old girl. Further off sits GERUTHA, his wife.*

**FENGO** Bring the girl over here.

*Vikings bring LILJA across the room.*

Well, well prettygirl—how now, little thing? What say you to Fengo, Master o' the Northern Realm?

*LILJA hides her face. The Vikings laugh.*

I don't think yer daughter likes me, Matthius.

**MATTHIUS** Course she do, Fengo, course she do. She's just in awe of ye, that's all.

**FENGO** Have a drink with old Fengo, prettygirl.

**MATTHIUS** Go on, sweetheart, don't be afraid.

**FENGO** Don't break me heart, sweet thing, come sit on my knee.

**MATTHIUS** Aye!

**LILJA** You are a fukkin animal, Fengo.

*LILJA slaps him.*

**MATTHIUS** Lilja!

**FENGO** Haaaa! A child after me own heart! Come here! Smile at Lord Fengo, you rambunctious little filly!

**MATTHIUS** I dunno where she gots her mouth from.

**FENGO** Drink, bonnie lass. Drink Fengo's health! Heyup, hearties, hold the girl down. Your health, my little Nordic beauty!

*FENGO pours beer over her head. The Vikings laugh.*

**LILJA** Help!

**FENGO** What's the matter with the youth nowadays? They've all gone soft 'n spoiled. What's become of the Viking Spirit, Matthius? It wants reviving!

*(to LILJA)* Have ye ever seen Fengo's Hole? Fengo show yez Fengo's Hole. Nasty dirty eye socket, nothin inside! Look, prettygirl, look!

*FENGO pulls off his eye patch and opens his eye socket. LILJA screams.*

Looks a bit like a rabbit's bum, don't it?

**GERUTHA** Fengo, stop—

**FENGO** Why art afeard, girlie? It's a good honest Warr-Wound! Hoy Matthius—Matthius, look! *(MATTHIUS cringes.)* Haaa haaaa—

**GERUTHA** Fengo, for the love of your fathers, stop!

**FENGO** Ahhhh, I'm in a jolly mood.

*LILJA runs out. FENGO finishes his ale.*

I am Fengo: High Lord of Helsingor. Voted Lord Ruler by the Thunder-Godd hisself. It were Thor what struck me dead brother down, seven years ago tonight. Stuck him down with a mighty meteor! Right, Matthius?

**MATTHIUS** Aye, Fengo, aye!

**FENGO** "Coward," spake Thunder-Godd, unworthy to be called Viking! Death to Dead Brotherlord. Long Live Lord Fengo!

**MATTHIUS** Hail Hail!

**VIKINGS** Long Live Lord Fengo!

**FENGO** All hail Gerutha—Fengo's bride of seven years. Widowed wife of dead brotherlord; lawful holder of dead brother's lands!

**VIKINGS** Hurrah! Hail Gerutha!

**FENGO** So, woman, havin had both us bullies, which in yer mind were the better of us two? Was it Fengo? Hey? Was it merrie old Fengo? Was it dirty old Horvendal the Elder? Or was it Fengo? Hey? Hey missus? Hey, hey?

**GERUTHA** It were you, Fengo, it were you.

**FENGO** Haaa! Did ye hear that? Hearties, did ye hear the womann! Haaa! You saucy old thing! Give Fengo a kiss!

**ALL** HURRAAAH!!

*He kisses her obscenely. Pause.*

**FENGO** Somebody's missing. Somebody ain't here. Where's my adopted sonn? Where's my dear little boy?

**GERUTHA** Asleep, Fengo. Don't wake him.

**FENGO** Horvendal! Horvendal! I wants to talks to me sonn! HORVENDAL! Lord Fengo wants to speak to his ladd!

*Lights up on young HORVENDAL, praying in the woodshed. He is fourteen years old, short and scrawny, with crazed eyes.*

**HORVENDAL** Jesus, King of Heaven from the frozen edges of the earth,
I beseech you—

**FENGO** Hoy, ahoy, laddie!

**HORVENDAL** Let not my heart be consumed by barbarous Hate—

**FENGO** Show us yer face, shitthead!

**HORVENDAL** From the sinns of Hate and Envy, from the sinns of Pride and Anger, from all thoughts of Evil gainst mine own flesh and blood, deliver me Oh Christ Jesus, Redeemer of Men—

*FENGO bursts in, followed by the rest.*

**FENGO** What's goin on in here?

**HORVENDAL** God bless you, uncle.

**FENGO** Don't you "God bless me." What're you hidin away for?

**GERUTHA** He's makin silence, Fengo, amembrin of his daa.

**FENGO** Oohhhh faithful faithful boy. Amembrin of his daa. His daa what left him, his daa he never knew! I'm yer daa now, sonn. You know that. Get up and gives yer dadda a hugg.

**HORVENDAL** Yer not my Paa.

**FENGO** I is.

**HORVENDAL** Yer NOT!

**FENGO** I IS! Now what are you doin in here? Hey, laddie true? What're you doin in here then? Hey? Hey?

**HORVENDAL** Praying.

**FENGO** Praying?

**HORVENDAL** Aye, to the Lord Christ the Merciful, the Son of Heaven and the God of Peace—who's gonna save Denn-Mark, Fengo—save it from the likes of you.

**FENGO** Ho. Godd of Peace then, hey? Godd of Peace? See, Matthius? This is what I been talkin about. Yer a disgrace, ladd, to yer own people, yer brave forefathers what fought 'n died fer you. What is this new godd, what wrenches sonns away from their fathers, tearin families and kingdoms apart—what in fucks wrong wi' ye anyways, boy, are ye sick?

**HORVENDAL** I forgives you, uncle.

**FENGO** Forgives us—fer what?

**HORVENDAL** For the violence you committed against God's Children, and the mockerie you hold against his name.

**FENGO** Violence? Mockerie?

**MATTHIUS** The boy talks gibberish! E'er since that Book turn'd up in yer plundersack he been a weird one, Fengo.

**FENGO** Aye has he.

*HORVENDAL has a bowl and towel. He kneels at FENGO's feet and washes them.*

**HORVENDAL** In the name of the Father, the Sonn and the Holy Spirit, I bow down, and pay you this respect.

**FENGO** What're you doing?

**GERUTHA** Horvendal…

**FENGO** Here—what're you washin my feet for?

**HORVENDAL** This is what the Lord Christ did.
He lov'd his enemies, like I love you.
God bless you, Uncle Fengo, dear Uncle Fengo.
Peace.

*Pause.*

**FENGO** Ha haaa! Lookit this! A godd what washes people's feet! You see this, bullies? Now Fengo's finally heard all.

*They all laugh.*

Yer mother's been way too lenient. Way too soft on you, sonn. We'll have none of this love and peace prattle. Not while Fengo is Lord. Forgive me. He don't forgive me. He only forgives me 'cause he's afeard of me! Int that right, little laddie? Hey? Hey?

Go find yer Lord Jesus—tell him Fengo says he's a Womann! Tell him nobody never nail'd the Thunder-Godd to no Cross!

*All laugh. FENGO rips up HORVENDAL's Bible.*

Still forgives us now, sonn? Go on, take a swing at me!
Still forgives yer Uncle Fengo now? Hey? Hey?

*Pause.*

**HORVENDAL** Yes, sir, I do.

**FENGO** Liar!

*FENGO spits on him.*

**GERUTHA** Fengo, please—

**FENGO** Let's go, Matthius, afore I cripple the boy.

*FENGO turns to leave. HORVENDAL prays loudly.*

**HORVENDAL** You what laughs—tomorrow shall you weep!
Doomed are the Mightie—they shall be laid low!
Scatter'd their swords shall be, hammer'd into ploughshares!
And the Meek, the Weak, the Gentle and Oppress'd,
Shall rise, rise, to inherit the Earth!

*Pause. FENGO turns again.*

**FENGO** What's that?

**HORVENDAL** Thus spake the Christ.

**FENGO** What's this says you, 'bout the Meek?

**HORVENDAL** Praise the Power of the Lord.

*Pause.*

**FENGO** Show us these Meek. Let me at them. We'll soon see who inherits what. Meantime, nephew, piddleprophet, inherit this: I want you off my land by the crow o' the cock, the morrow.

**GERUTHA** Fengo, no—

**FENGO** Stand up and fight me, sonn!

**GERUTHA** Bless him, Fengo, he's a boy, he don't mean it!

**FENGO** Ohhh yes he does.

**HORVENDAL** Fengo, Christ, he's acomin to Helsingor;
He'll be seekin for you Fengo, so he shall.

**FENGO** Let him try it! I'll be ready. Let him stand, his Meek against my Axe-menn. By the crow o' the cock, let your gutless face be gone. That's all, ladds. Fengo has spoken.

**MATTHIUS** Haill, Fengo!

**VIKINGS** HAILL!!

**FENGO** Move, woman.

**MATTHIUS** Godd of Peace indeed.

*MATTHIUS spits on HORVENDAL and exits with FENGO. GERUTHA is alone with HORVENDAL, who gathers the pages of his Bible.*

**GERUTHA** Horvendal, sweet Horvendal...

**HORVENDAL** I nae wants to talk to you, muther.

**GERUTHA** Sonn, if din't marry him I'd be dead!

**HORVENDAL** Death int such a bad thing.

**GERUTHA** Horvendal, sweet sonn, Jesus Christ is make-believe; howcome yer fakin, makin like he's real?

**HORVENDAL** Jesus Christ is real, Momma! All the world knows except for here! Jesus, he's the Lord of Peace, he's awatchin o'er us now! He's awatchin o'er the world, Momma! He can see inside yer heart!

**GERUTHA** My heart—why do you wrench at it?

**HORVENDAL** What you get is what you choose.

**GERUTHA** Horvendal, don't tear my love in half!

**HORVENDAL** There's no love in you, woman—only Fear.

**GERUTHA** *Stop it!* Just stop it—undo this webb of ire!
I'm sworn to you both! Can't you not clasp hands?
Just ask his forgiveness—quit provokin his wrath.
Fer the love of your warr-torn mother, Horvendal—please!

**HORVENDAL** Hie off you Fengo-fucker. Go with your Mann.

*Pause.*

**GERUTHA** Yooou bastard—you blister—you vile, ungrateful hound! Fie upon you then—outt upon you—

I have no sonn!

*She spits at him and exits in tears,*

**HORVENDAL** The same to you!

Viking am I not, Viking I'll not be,
Too far and wide our bloody quest for Fame
Has devastated and disgraced the rolling earth!
And him—him—the worst and wickedest among us,
Still he stays our Chieftain—rooks me Maa!
Down down, you hateful rising furies,
Snarling massacre, back into my spleen!
I'm to Jerusalem, land of Peace and Freedom,
There will I meet Jesus, learn the ways of Peace!
Brave Horvendal, resists the urge to kill!
Brave Horvendal, shall seek a better path!
Brave Horvendal, whose name shall shine above all Saints!
Whose name shall shine beside the name of Christ!
Hallelujah!

*A knock on the door.*

Who's there?

**INGA** Young Horvendal?

**HORVENDAL** Who is it?

**INGA** A fishwife. Inga's my name.

**HORVENDAL** What do you want?

**INGA** Ooooh, young Horvendal, I gots a terrible secret, but I'm afeard to tell it ye.

**HORVENDAL** Say it, and quickly!

**INGA** There's a Ghost, ladd, a Spirit i' the Forest,
And he looks all the world like yer Daa.

**HORVENDAL** What?

**INGA** Green were his eyes, his face yellow,
And he look'd all the world like yer Daa!

**HORVENDAL** Get out!

**INGA** Hooorvendaaal, he cried, Hooorvendaaal...
Where—is—my—Sonn?
Hooorvendaaal... Hooorvendaaal...
Where—is—my—Sonn?

**HORVENDAL** *Stop it*, you old biddy what believes in goblins and trolls. You're so full o' fishtales there's nae room fer yer brains! Ghosts indeed. I had it wi' you people! Go tell it round the campfire you simple old crone. You blubbering old pagan, be off with ye!

**INGA** But sonn, sonn, yer Father he called fer ye! He wants to speak to ye. He do!

**HORVENDAL** Away at once! I'll not hear another word! Protect me Jesus from these fools…

*Pause.*

**INGA** Think what you want, sonn. Do as you will,
But choose the wrong path—it shall all come to ill.

*Pause. She exits. Pause.*

**HORVENDAL** What was this? Never mind. Come dawn,
Horvendal from out this hell-hole shall be gone…

## Scenus Tertius

*Before MATTHIUS's lodge. Morning. Enter RAGNAR and MATTHIUS.*

**MATTHIUS** Liljaaa! Liljaaa! Where is that girl?

**RAGNAR** She be starin out her window all sheepfaced again. Put her to work, hey Father?

**MATTHIUS** Aye I shall too. Gots to be good for somethin she. Daughter!

**RAGNAR** Me, I loves whale-huntin. I'll give the big fellow a extra harpoon fer you.

**MATTHIUS** That's me brave ladd. That's me stout and heartie fella. But don't do nothin stupid will ye hey son? It int wise.

**RAGNAR** Nae fuss, Dadd.

**MATTHIUS** Lilja! Lilja! Lilja, I say!

**LILJA** *(off)* What?

**MATTHIUS** Come say goodbye to yer brother. He's leavin.

**LILJA** *(off)* Yeah, yeah.

**MATTHIUS** Move it, girl. And fast!

**LILJA** *(off)* Yeah, yeah.

**RAGNAR** You keep an eye on her, Father. She's at that dangerous age.

**MATTHIUS** Nae worry fer that, sonn. I'm trainin her good. Liljaaa!

**LILJA** *(enters)* What?

**RAGNAR** Lagabout girl.

**MATTHIUS** Give yer brother a good-luck charm as is the custom.

**LILJA** Why?

**RAGNAR** And hurry up too.

**LILJA** I ain't got none.

**RAGNAR** Cmon, anything'll do.

**LILJA** Here brother, dear brother, ye want the scalp off me head? *(cutting her hair with a knife)*

**RAGNAR** Girl!

**MATTHIUS** What're ye doin?

**RAGNAR** I can't be totin that at sea!

**MATTHIUS** Give him yer stickpin instead, child, that's a nice gift.

**LILJA** You gave it me, Paa!

**MATTHIUS** Give it o'er or I'll smack ye.

*She gives it to him.*

**LILJA** Here.

**RAGNAR** Thank ye, sister.

**LILJA** Don't drown.

**RAGNAR** And you obey yer father 'cause he knows what's what.

**MATTHIUS** Aye it's true. I do.

**LILJA** Can I go back to me bed now?

**MATTHIUS** No, girl, he's not left!

**RAGNAR** Here, she's mouthin off to you, Daa—disrespectin her elders!

**MATTHIUS** What? What's this?

**LILJA** I'd never mouth off to you.

**RAGNAR** Again again! She says it but she don't mean it.
Watch her, she's double-tongued—a sheep and a serpent!

**MATTHIUS** I'm tryin to be a good father to you, girl. We gots to have order, that's all. Order! I wants the best, the best fer me girl—and fer me boy too.

**RAGNAR** We gots the best father in all of Denn-Mark.

**MATTHIUS** And I gots the best kinn.

**RAGNAR** We gotts the best Paa i' the World!

**MATTHIUS** And I got—ohh, sonn!

*They embrace. LILJA makes an obscene gesture at them both. RAGNAR sees her over MATTHIUS's shoulder. He seizes her by the hair and they fight.*

Here, children—what do I have to do fer you? Here, I loves you, I'd cut off both me arms! Think of yer Mother, had she aseen this scrappling—think of yer poor dead Mother! *Stop! (He pulls them apart.)* We gots to make us a solemn vow—to love and honour and protect one another. Sweet daughter, say yer sorry. Kiss yer brother. Now!

*Pause.*

**LILJA** Sorry, brother.

**RAGNAR** Nae fuss, sister.

**MATTHIUS** Go on—make the vow too.

**RAGNAR** I won't let nobody hurts ye, sister.

**LILJA** I won't let nobody hurts me neither.

**MATTHIUS** Now cutt palms. Clasp hands. Make a ring. All three.
Remember who we are. Who are we? We're DANES!
The proudest, mightiest race on earth!
And why? Why? The unbreakable Bond of Blood.
Without that—without the Bond of Blood—
The Lord o' the Gallows protect us—we're doomed!

**RAGNAR** Aye doomed! Long Live Blood!

**MATTHIUS** May the Great Odin himself bless and protect this good family. The Great—and the Small. *(He pats LILJA's head.)* Go, Brave Ragnar, out across the Sea—go kill a whalefish fer yer sister.

*RAGNAR holds up his sword.*

**RAGNAR** Aye, I shall, Father, I shall. In the name o' Skull-Byter, Sword o' me Granpapaa—I shall. Farewell, Father.

**MATTHIUS** Farewell, sonn.

**RAGNAR** Farewell, little sister.

**LILJA** Aye.

**RAGNAR** Ahoy—wait for me!

*He runs off. LILJA turns to leave but MATTHIUS stops her.*

**MATTHIUS** Sweet daughter, dear daughter, I know yer unhappy and fain would cheer ye.

**LILJA** You need not, Father, I'm as happy as a barnacle.

**MATTHIUS** I know it's hard to be the girl, my dear. I know it's hard, me lovin him more than you. But ye gots to accept yer lott in life. It's the godds' will.

**LILJA** Aye, I do accept it. At least I'm not a horse.

**MATTHIUS** That's the spirit. That's the familie spirit.
Oh Lilja, Lilja, me sweet sweet pride and joy.
A fine woman yer turnin out to be.

**LILJA** You too, Father.

**MATTHIUS** Come, let's inside.

*She exits. He follows.*

## Scene The Fourth

*Midnight. Miles away. The middle of a great frozen lake.*

*A full moon. Bitter cold. Wolves in the shadows.*

*HORVENDAL trudges miserably through the snow.*

**HORVENDAL** Jerusalem! I can see it now;
Gilden it is, risin up to the sky!
Soon I'll be there, in front of Jesu's Fireplace,
Away from Helsingor. Away from Fengo!
There it is! Just the other side of that Forest.
Comin, Lord Christ—comin. I'm acomin.

*He trudges on.*

Jesus, this icy lake goes on and on!
How far away's this place asposd to be?

Weren't there a star or sommet hangin over Jerusalem?
All these friggin stars, they look the same…
Christ? Lord Jesus? Is you a-heedin me?
If yer real, as yer Holybook sez,
Lift me up and fly me to yer Home!

*Pause. A wolf howls.*

Heyup Jesus, I done befaith'd in you!
Ye gots to do me miracles—that's the deal!
Jesus? Jesus? Holy Lord Christ?
Yuz gots to gimme a guide or somethin, Jesus!
Helloooo? Hello? Lord Jesus?

*Wolves howl louder. A raging voice in the wind.*

**GHOST** Hoorvendaaal… Hoorvendaaaal…
Where—is—my—Sonn?

**HORVENDAL** Who's that? Father?

**GHOST** HOORVENDAAAAL… HOORVENDAAAAL…
WHERE—IS—MY—SONNN??

*A deep bang from below.*

**HORVENDAL** Jesus, there's somethin under the ice—

*Bang. Bang.*

A walrus perhaps, or one o' them killer whales—

*Bang. Bang. Bang.*

Mercy! Protect me! Angels and ministers of grace—

*He runs. The ice bursts open. The GHOST of the dead lord rises up from the lake. He is twelve feet tall, roaring and chanting, brandishing his sword, surrounded by giant wolves.*

**GHOST** HOOORVENDAL, BELOV'D OF THORR,
CHILD OF MURDER, CHILD OF WARR!
HEAR YE NOT THE SPIRITS' CRY?
LOOK INTO THY FATHER'S EYE!
HORVENDAL—LOOK UPON THY DESTINY!

**HORVENDAL** Father? What happened to you?

**GHOST** I *died*! I'm dead, sonn—that's what's happen'd to me!
I come from Valhalla, Afterlife of the Brave.
Listen, listen to my Tale, my Sonn:
Hoorvendaaaal… Hoorvendaaaaal…

**HORVENDAL** You ain't real, Dadda—

**GHOST** Thine Uncle—

**HORVENDAL** I don't wanna hear this, Dadda—

**GHOST** THINE UNCLE—IS A MURDERER!
Sweet Sonn, to tell the tale, unmanly Coward,
How he did stalk thy sleeping father in his sleep,
And crush his VIKING HEAD WITH A ANVILL—

**HORVENDAL** It probably served you right, Dadda.

**GHOST** AND HOW—HOW—that same unmanly Coward
Calls hisself a LORD!
And took his BROTHER'S WIFE!
Oh MOCKERY!
Oh HUMILIATION and DISGRACE!
Sonn of mine—art thou a Mann?

**HORVENDAL** Please, Dadda—

**GHOST** Sonn of mine—art thou a DANE?

**HORVENDAL** Stop!

**GHOST** Sonn of mine—art thou—
HORVENDAL THE YOUNGER?
And Most Fittest True High Lord of Helsingor?

**HORVENDAL** NO! No, I renounce you, Father!
I don't wants to be no lord of Helsingor!

*The GHOST lets out a howl and the earth quakes.*

**GHOST** You *seen* me bloody murder, sonn. Quit yer hidin.
Quit this childish sealin of yer soul.
You weren't yet seven. Hidden in a tree.
YOU SEEN ME DIE, sonn! Quit blockin it out!

**HORVENDAL** You LIE!

**GHOST** I raised you to be a Warrior—
A brave and mightie conqueror!
And now—now—your people need you most.
You turn and runn like a castout dogg?

**HORVENDAL** Helllpp!

*More thunder.*

**GHOST** HOORVENDAAL, THOU ART THE ONE:
THOU ART THY FATHER'S ONLY SONN!

TURN YEE BACK TO WHENCE YE CAME,
AND PUNISH THOSE AS ARE TO BLAME!

Look in Fengo's eye. You'll see the truth.
Look into your heart, boy. You'll see the truth.

Avenge this Murder. Slay thy Wicked Uncle.
Rise, rise to conquer Denn-Mark!

**HORVENDAL** Please go back in the lake, Father.

**GHOST** Take my hand.

**HORVENDAL** Please, Father… no, Father—

**GHOST** TAKE THY FATHER'S HAND!!

**HORVENDAL** Mercy…

**GHOST** *(very softly)* Hooorvendaaal… Brave Horvendaall…
Revenge…. Revenge…

**HORVENDAL** Nooooo!!

*The GHOST kisses his hand. HORVENDAL is seized with a deathly shiver.*

**GHOST** Revenge, Horvendal, Revenge!
Remember me…. Remember me…
Horvendaaaal…. Remember me…

*The GHOST vanishes. HORVENDAL is alone. Long silence.*

**HORVENDAL** Jesus, if you got somethin to say, you better say it right now…

*Pause. A wolf howls.*

OH HELL!

I must return—the Truth to know. Oh SPITE!
Why will no one tell me what is right?

*He staggers home.*

### Scene The Fifth

*FENGO's house. Breakfast.*

*Vikings guard the door. FENGO and MATTHIUS sit by the fire, sharing a jug of ale.*

**FENGO** Ha haaaaaa! Have another splodge.

**MATTHIUS** Yer my best pal.

**FENGO** I know.

**MATTHIUS** Yer my best, best pal.

**FENGO** Yer my pal too, Matthius.

**MATTHIUS** Friends is a rare commodity. Yuz gots t' hang on to the few yuz gots, Fengo, and cherish them and give them gifts.

**FENGO** Don't fret, Matthius, I cherish your friendship.

**MATTHIUS** You and me we go waay back. Why, I was takin flak fer yer pranks when we was brats, plus I bloody well helped ye slay yer brother, dint I?

**FENGO** Yer a good egg, Matthius.

**MATTHIUS** You knows I am, Fengo, you better knows I am. You owes me a big reward.

**FENGO** You'll get what you deserve.

**MATTHIUS** Election's acomin. The Freeman's Assembly. Seven more years we'll make 'em buggers vote you.

**FENGO** And so they will, Matthius, so they will—if you remember to keep yer trap shutt.

**MATTHIUS** And what does that mean?

**FENGO** You know exactly what that means. They votes for Fengo, Matthius, they votes for gutts, soliditie. You don't go braggin, Matthius, 'bout brother-killing!

**MATTHIUS** Are you implyin—

**FENGO** I'm not implying it. I'm saying it. Keep yer stupid fat mouth shutt. You never know when to shutt up, Matthius. Plus yer always kissin my arse.

**MATTHIUS** But—

**FENGO** It looks peculiar. Stop it. At least when we're in public, you understand?

**MATTHIUS** I'm sorry, Fengo.

*A cry from outside.*

**GERUTHA** Fengo! Fengo!

**FENGO** What's that?

*GERUTHA rushes in.*

**GERUTHA** My boy, my boy!

**FENGO** What's this? Yer boy? Yer boy what's banish'd?
What's he done this time, is he dead?

**GERUTHA** They found him, Fengo, somethin's happened to my boy. They found him starvin, lyin naked in the snow!

**FENGO** Haa! Good!

**GERUTHA** My boy! Frozen and brainsick!
Please let him into the house, Fengo—look at him.

**FENGO** No! Fengo has spoken.

**GERUTHA** Husband, mercie! Fatherly mercie!
He int no hindrance to no one no more!
He int no Christian, he int much of anything,
My boy, he's—look, Fengo, look!

*Enter Vikings carrying the Mad Boy, mad and soiled, wrapped in a blanket. He is drooling.*

**HORVENDAL** Brrrr…

**GERUTHA** They found him, Fengo, barking and ahowling—chasing the thralls around, snarling and biting their feet.

**FENGO** Well I'll be.

**HORVENDAL** Mommie—

**FENGO** This is got to be some kind of joke. Here, why are you barkin and aslobberin like a hound, kidda? Look what yer doin to yer poor soft-hearted Maa.

**GERUTHA** My child, my only child—

**FENGO** He just don't wanna be banish'd! Let him go, woman. I said let him go! Menn, toss this Madd Boy back out in the snow. Nice try, kidda.

*The Vikings drag him out.*

**GERUTHA** WHAT? No, Fengo. STOP! I'll nott—I'll *nott* allow this!

**FENGO** What?

**GERUTHA** Can't you see what your hardness has done to him?
Do you not think that this is enough?

**FENGO** No.

**GERUTHA** Is there no end to yer ignorance, Fengo?

**FENGO** Are you sayin there should be?

**GERUTHA** Look at the boy, Fengo—

**FENGO** He's shamming! I pulled this trick once meself! No, woman, Fengo knows best. I know this kid better than you.

**GERUTHA** When will it end, Fengo? When will yer crueltie end?

When I'm dead, when he's dead, when you've driven all of us madd? When will you be happy? What're you tryin to prove? You bloody, thick, horrible—Coward!

**FENGO** What did you say?

**MATTHIUS** Don't take that from her, Fengo.

**FENGO** Matthius, shut up. What did you say to me?

**GERUTHA** Coward, Fengo, Coward. Coward! What else befits yer deeds?
What sort of Chieftain'd freeze a Madd Boy to death?
What sort of Chieftain bee you?
Earth and heaven! You think the godds be blind?
You think the people, Fengo, can't suss out
The reasons why you hate this boy?
Someday, someways, your deeds will come to light;
And when they do, Fengo, no more laughing.
They'll haul you up afore the High Assembly,
Vote you down, and take yer goods away!
Annul our marriage, cast you outt.
Disgrace and shame will rain upon your head!
Coward, Fengo! Coward still I say!
All the world will see you and agree;
So cast us out, kill the boy—who cares?
Let the Heavens judge what Mann you be.

*Long pause. He glares at her.*

**FENGO** Oh woman, your mouth.

**MATTHIUS** Sod the heavens, Fengo, kill 'im anyway.

**FENGO** Matthius, I thought I told you to shut up.

*Pause. The Vikings look at him.*

All right, womann. You can keep yer Madd Boy.
But ye gots to keep him tied up, understand?

**GERUTHA** Do ye hear that, sonn?

**FENGO** And if he turns out to be a-shammin, my dear,
I'll take you, and yer Madd Boy—
And naill yuz both—to that WALL.
Go on. Tie him up out in the yard.

**GERUTHA** Horvendal, sweetheart, you're home.

**FENGO** Don't say I never done nothin for ye.

*Vikings carry the Mad Boy out. GERUTHA follows.*

**MATTHIUS** Mark my words.

**FENGO** I'll mark yer face in a second.

**MATTHIUS** Yer losin yer power, Fengo. I see it comin. Yer waffling ways will ruin you. Yer doomed.

**FENGO** Shut up, Matthius.

**MATTHIUS** You'll rue the day, Fengo, you'll rue the day forever—

**FENGO** Shut up, Matthius. Shut up, shut up!

*They exit. Pause. Meanwhile. The Mad Boy is tied up and left alone. He smears himself with ashes. Drums sound. He speaks.*

**HORVENDAL** So here I sit, a stormtoss'd ladd
Who once was sane, and now is madd;
And all my foes what press'd me down
Are helpless gainst me, standing round!
Now I has him! Now he's mine!
Now I've got him, by the spine!
Horvendal who out was flung,
Has got you, Fengo, by the tongue!
For doggs have ears and fools have eyes,
That see men's secrets, hear through lies.
I'll catch those lies, and when I do,
I'll stain the earth with Fengo's grue!
But is this mine—this Heart of Hate?
Is this my Path? Is this my Fate?
Oh hide, my witts, till all I see;
Till then, a Madd Boy must I be!
I'll hound these Fates out—wait and see.
Till then, a Madd Boy must I be…

*Drums rise. He rolls in filth and ashes.*

### Scene The Sixth

*The north shore. Morning. Calm.*

*The old sisters sing an ancient, mournful song.*

*LILJA sits and watches them repairing a fishing net. She stares at the horizon.*

**LILJA** Oh Inga, which way is south?

**INGA** South, girl? Why, that way I believe.

**LILJA** Is it true what they say, Inga? There's a land to the south where it's summer all the time? And the Birds n' the Fish n' the Animals can talk? And nobody ever fights no one ever, 'cause everybody is best friends?

**INGA** So I heard tell, girl, so I heard tell.

**LILJA** How far a walk is it, Inga?

**INGA** Too far for a little one like you.

**LILJA** Ohhh. That's where he was goin. Fengo's foster-son, the Young Horvendal. But now he's gone madd they say. Out of his head! Just think of it, Inga, Madd!

**INGA** Child, yer a born romantic.

**LILJA** He used to talk of a godd called—Jesus. What was he the godd of, Inga?

**INGA** Jesus? From what I hear—he's the god of being crucified.

**LILJA** Crucified! Crucified! I think—I'd like to be Crucified!

**INGA** I'm tryin to do me chores, child. Stop yer yappin.

**LILJA** Is it true what they say, Inga? Jesus is a-comin to save us? That the high shall be made low and the low shall be made high and the wicked shall be driven hence and the good and virtuous shall prevail?

**INGA** Cah! What say you? What topsy-turvy drivel is that?

**LILJA** That's what the Angell said, Inga, last night. He came again to my bed.

**INGA** Angels, angels, yer always seein angels.
Child, yer a pain up the hole.

**LILJA** Oooh Inga, I wish I could go southways. Anywhere, anywhere away from Denn-Mark.

**INGA** Child, there int nothin outside o' Denn-Mark, 'cept Wolves perhaps. And Snakes. And Black-Menn.

**LILJA** Wolves and Snakes and Black-Menn! Just think!

**INGA** Girl, you got a death wish.

*The women leave. LILJA stays.*

**LILJA** Ocean, blue ocean, you wrench the yearnings from my heart;
Tell me, you spirits—tell me where to start!

**Scene The Seventh**

*Night. FENGO and GERUTHA's bed.*

*HORVENDAL lies at the foot of the bed like a dog. Viking guards loom outside the door.*

**FENGO** Roll over, woman, Fengo wants a shag.

**GERUTHA** No.

**FENGO** I beg yer pardon?

**GERUTHA** Not with him in the bed.

**FENGO** I said love me, mother—

**GERUTHA** Get yer paws off me!

**FENGO** That does it, that's it! By the Lord o' Thunder, by the Lord o' the Slain, that does it. I'm kickin him out—

**GERUTHA** Don't touch that boy, Fengo! I said, don't touch that boy! It's cold outside. He's sleepin in here.

*Pause.*

**FENGO** Ahh! Well, here's a fine how do ye do.
A Madd Boy sleepin in Fengo's bedd.

**HORVENDAL** Cuddle me, Dadda.

**FENGO** Get off me!

**GERUTHA** Oh Horvendal, sweet Horvendal, tell us your woes.

**HORVENDAL** Mother, is that you? What happened to my brain?

**GERUTHA** Oh, I don't know.

**HORVENDAL** Me father, where's me father?

**GERUTHA** You know where he is, son. He's dead, dead these seven years.

**HORVENDAL** Oh Father, dead Father, how I miss him. I am so sadd.

**FENGO** Sadd my arse. Yer daddy was a cockswipe. Laddie, when yer paa was alive he used to bind you and make you pull his sled.

**HORVENDAL** How did ye come lord, Fengo?

**FENGO** What?

**HORVENDAL** How did my dead dadda die?
Was it Trolls, Momma, done hauld him away?
Or was it Gnomes, Momma, spirited him off?
Or were it somethin else, Momma? Somethin green and meaner?
Somethin fatt and foul and furry—with one eye?

**FENGO** Woman…

**GERUTHA** You know how he died, son, everyone knows—
Struck down by a roaring thunderbolt—I mean…

**HORVENDAL** That int what the birds told us.

**GERUTHA** What?

**HORVENDAL** That int what the birds told Madd Boy…

**GERUTHA** Horvendal, sweet son, birds can't tell you nothin.
That's just yer madness, chirpin in yer head.

**HORVENDAL** Chirp chirp.

**GERUTHA** Now please, please get ye to sleep. Oh sleepy, happy family, we three.

*Pause.*

**FENGO** What did the birds tell you, Madd Boy?

**GERUTHA** Please, Fengo—

**FENGO** What's all this yer sayin about birds?

**HORVENDAL** I don't remember.

**FENGO** Don't you be shittin me, sonn. Look me i' the face.
What did these birds tell you—about Fengo?

*Pause. HORVENDAL squeezes FENGO's nose.*

**HORVENDAL** Honk honk.

**FENGO** I want him out of here.

**GERUTHA** Fengo!

**FENGO** I want him OUT OF HERE! NOW!

**GERUTHA** I' the name o' heaven, i' the name o' the godds,
He don't know what he sayin, Fengo—he's turn'd simple!

**FENGO** That little bastard, that little titt-clutcher, he's turnin mee simple too! Barking, snarling, mewling babytalk, hurling sniv'lling slanders in my house—

*FENGO looks right at him.*

He better pray to Jesus he is a simpleton. He better pray he don't know what he's sayin. 'Cause if I finds out he *do* know what he's sayin—I'll have his gutts thru his nose. You understand that, sonn? Do ye?

**GERUTHA** Fengo, stop!

**FENGO** Listen, sonn—I never touch'd yer paa!
Whoever says I didd—is a dead man!

**GERUTHA** Fengo! Stop! You're all riled up! You go take a walk till you're simmer'd down.

*Pause.*

**FENGO** Ahhh woman. Ahhh the two of you!
Gimme more frikkin grief than the goutt.
Thank yer stars, woman, I int brash like my brother!
Then you'd weep. Then yer boy would howl.

*He leaves. The Vikings still stand guard. GERUTHA rocks HORVENDAL gently. Pause.*

**HORVENDAL** How did my dadda die, Momma?

**GERUTHA** Stop askin that.

**HORVENDAL** Well how did he die?

**GERUTHA** Quit askin me!

**HORVENDAL** I love you, Mum.

**GERUTHA** Ohhh my blister'd heart…
If only you knew. My poor poor Madd Boy…

*She rocks him. Meanwhile. FENGO lurks outside, sharpening his axe.*

**FENGO** So he has me. So he thinks.
Let him stalk me, like a Lynx!
Boy, you know not what you do:
Fengo's eye is watching you!
Greater foes have cross'd my path,
All were crush'd beneath my wrath;
Men of Chaos, Men of Warr,
Prov'd no match for Fengo's sword!
Now it's your turn—if you cann—
Hemi-semi-demi-Man!
Come and get me, Fengo's here—

I'll slit yer throat from Ear to Ear!
Watch me, stalk me, Eye to Eye,
One of us must blink—and die!
Stare me down, boy, just you try!
One of us must blink—and die!

## Scene The Eighth

*A wooded mountain. Late afternoon.*

*MATTHIUS and LILJA are hauling firewood.*

**MATTHIUS** Come on, girl, are ye good fer nothin?

**LILJA** Yeah, yeah, Father, I'm tryin.

**MATTHIUS** Tryin, tryin. Tryin my patience. If ye can't haul kindling, girl, what'll become of ye? All the men in the community hate ye. They think yer odd.

*LILJA sits down in the snow.*

All right, girl—all right, we'll rest. But when I was a lad they used to throw weaklings like you into the sea.

Ohh, don't fret, I don't mean to rail at ye. Someday, someway we'll find something yer good at. Be strong for yer poor dead Mother; take faith in the stars and the heavens. I do, for your sake, girl. The godds'd never craft ye for no cause.

Now then, rested enough. Much to be done, girl, firewood to haul. Gots to get homeways, backafore sundown. Come on! Come on then, child! You can do it! Pull!

Hoy—hoy—did you feel that?

**LILJA** What, Father?

**MATTHIUS** A wind! A warm wind out of nowhere.

**LILJA** Aye.

**MATTHIUS** You felt it too? A hot and swoltery wind?
Tint right, girl—tint right. 'Tis not the time of year!

There be it again! Feel ye it blow?
What means this untimed current? I likes it not!
Look, look child, look—the snow's a-turnd to slush!
That dead and dormant elm's a-sprouted leaves!

**LILJA** Aye.

**MATTHIUS** Turn ye back, turn ye back, We'll no part of mysteries and strangeness; 'tis not normal, girl, 'tis not for us! Nooo! *(looking up)* What's that in the sky? A sign, a fiery sign from Heaven!

**LILJA** What is it, Paa?

**MATTHIUS** Hide yer head—

**LILJA** But what is it—

**MATTHIUS** Hide away from it, girl! Let yer father stand and ask its meaning. Obvious it wants to speak to mee!

*He approaches cautiously.*

What—in the name of the Valkyries—is that?

**LILJA** Looks like a Cross, Father!

**MATTHIUS** A what?

**LILJA** I seen the Madd Boy wearin it. It's a Cross!

**MATTHIUS** Not a Cross. Oh Filthy Retribution.
Not a Cross! Not the Sign of Christ!

**LILJA** Sign of Christ?

**MATTHIUS** Ill Omen, ill omen, this be it, this be it!
Surely the Dark Times is come!

**LILJA** What are you sayin, Father?

**MATTHIUS** The Christians! Ohh they're a bloodthirsty tribe;
They eats hot blood and they drinks men's flesh!
Plus they hangs folk, nails 'em high on wooden posts!
I seen sordid rendrins of it in their books!

**LILJA** Didn't you slaughter a bunch of Christians once, Father?

**MATTHIUS** SSSHHH child! Ssssh, they be a-listening!
They're comin! Comin to exact their revenge!

*He freezes in horror.*

Girl!

**LILJA** What?

**MATTHIUS** Yer hands—they're bleedin!
Yer feet—yer feet—they're bleedin too!

**LILJA** Wow.

**MATTHIUS** Ohhh Lord Thunderhelm, now everythin makes sense—
The signs are there for everyone to see!

The Madd Boy feignin madness. Fengo, he's a-floundering.
Wimmen and children mouthin off to the menfolk—
JESUS is coming!

**LILJA** What?

**MATTHIUS** FENGO! Laughed at me, did he? Fengo beware!
Come on, girl! Save yourself! We're doomed!

**LILJA** Father? Father? Father?

*He runs back to the village. LILJA stays. Looks at her bleeding hands. Licks them. Music. A gentle voice speaks.*

**VOICE** Liljaa…

**LILJA** Who's there?

**VOICE** Liljaa… Liljaa…

**LILJA** Who's there?

**VOICE** Don't be afraid. Child, come closer.
Wonderful, wonderful news…

*She follows.*

## Scene The Ninth

*Later. In front of FENGO's house.*

*MATTHIUS runs frantically into the village.*

**MATTHIUS** It's JESUS, Fengo! Jesus Lord of Christ!
He's a-comin—stormin unto Denn-Mark!

*FENGO looks at him. The Vikings gather.*

I seen his Cross, Fengo, blazin in the sky;
Jesus were snarlin, his tongue were made of fire;
And he sneakit up, behind me sweet and harmless daughter,
And slasht her wrists—with an Invisible Sword!

*The Vikings gasp.*

So there! There! I told ye from the beginning!
You kept snarking, "Don't fear no God of Peace!"
I say fear him! Fear him! Lookit where we be!
Our home, our homestead is being invaded!

**FENGO** You'd best be sure o' this Matthius.

*Enter GERUTHA with Mad Boy on a leash. Mad Boy is wrapped in a soiled blanket. GERUTHA has a wooden spoon and a bowl of gruel.*

**MATTHIUS** Here he is now: a-clingin to his mummie.
He int no Madd Boy, Fengo, you'll see—

**HORVENDAL** Woof woof.

**MATTHIUS** He's a Christian Spy—a Christlie Ferret!
Confess, Madd Boy! Quit sniffin at me crotch!

**HORVENDAL** Woof woof.

**MATTHIUS** How come yer eatin that mouldy straw?

**HORVENDAL** Helps digest the broken glass.

**MATTHIUS** And why do you eat broken glass, Madd Boy?

**HORVENDAL** Helps digest the stones.

**MATTHIUS** Oh? And why do you eat stones?

**HORVENDAL** Help digest sommet else.

**MATTHIUS** Oh Madd Boy, and pray tell us what's that?

**HORVENDAL** Come here Matthius, till I tells ye.

*MATTHIUS bends down. HORVENDAL grabs him by the ears. Bites his nose. Everyone laughs. MATTHIUS breaks free.*

**MATTHIUS** Aaaahh! Shut it, youz! This be Christian Treachorie!
Here's the Meek, Fengo, come to seize the Earth!
Look at him feigning, worming at our trustings—
Here—what've you got inside in that blanket?

**HORVENDAL** What?

*MATTHIUS fights with Mad Boy, tears open the blanket, discovers two huge iron fishgaffs.*

**MATTHIUS** Haaa! What's this? What's this, Fengo? This and this?
Fishgaffs, Fengo, swiped from off me shedd!
This boy were gonna snag ye like a squid!
Up, you weasel! You Christian Assassin,
Yer no more a blessed fool than mee!
Heyup hearties, break his bones—
Toss his bloody carcass in the Sea!

*MATTHIUS and Vikings pummel HORVENDAL.*

**VIKINGS** RAAAHHH!!

*GERUTHA dives into the midst of them. Beats the Vikings with her spoon. The Vikings scatter. Pause. GERUTHA defends HORVENDAL.*

**GERUTHA** DON'T ANY OF YOU touch my Madd Boy!
Matthius, get yee away!
The next one what touches my Madd Boy,
He gets this spoon up his hole!

What sort of Norsemenn are you?
What sort of leader lets this pass?
Beatin on cripples, on poor defenceless children,
Blamin all yer paranoyicies on Christ!
I'm this Boy's Mother. I say let him be!
You want to scrapp with someone—scrapp with me!

It is written—on Odin's Mighty Stone,
The Song of Havamal, which all of you should know—
That he who raises sword gainst fool or cripple
Is doom'd to die a Coward's Death;
And never ever enter the Hero's Afterlife—
But suffer his victim's affliction—forever!
NOW which among you dares persecute this Madd Boy?
Shame upon you! Shame upon you all.

**HORVENDAL** Woof woof.

*Pause.*

**VIKING 1** She's right, Fengo. The wailin womann's right.

**VIKING 2** Aye. Live ye, and live unharmed, Madd Boy.

**VIKING 1** So long as this boy's madd, we'll not scratch him, Fengo.
Shame on you, Matthius.

**VIKINGS** Aye Coward! Shame! Shame on you!

**MATTHIUS** What? But he's shammin! Fengo, call them back!
Lads, come back here! Look see—

*The Vikings walk away. Pause.*

**FENGO** Ain't you shamed of yourself?

**MATTHIUS** What?

**FENGO** Ain't you shamed of what you've said?
Get down, Matthius, thank this goodly womann
What spared you a fate worse than death.

**MATTHIUS** What're you sayin?

**FENGO** Matthius—

**MATTHIUS** She's conspirin with him too! My friend, my cohort, after all our schemes and preparation—to be undone by a Christian—a beardless puling boy—the very sonn of the mann we… er… that is to say we—I…

**FENGO** Matthius—

*He draws his knife and points it at him. HORVENDAL is watching them, sucking his little finger.*

Matthius. Get yerself home.
I'll talk to you later, Matthius.
Fengo is at the helm.

*MATTHIUS salutes and exits. FENGO watches GERUTHA, who comforts the Mad Boy.*

**GERUTHA** Why, why, does vileness beget vileness?
When, when, will patience beget peace?
Be it us, Fengo—be it us, the Nordic wimmenfolk?
Ist somethin in what we do, or say, or don't say,
That makes you think we love your Blood-feuds?
We don't, Fengo! Look at us! We don't!
See our tears, Fengo, follow to their source…

**FENGO** Ohhh strain'd, Gerutha, paragon of womanhood.
What a rack this plight of yours must be!
Faithful wife, loving mother, honourable, brave:
Sometimes, woman, I think yer too good for this world.

**GERUTHA** No I ain't.

**FENGO** Course you is! It's writt for all to see.
You liv'd a hard hard cruel life full o' pain and tragedie.
Why don't you let Fengo make it up to you, hey?
Why don't you let Fengo babysitt the boy?

**GERUTHA** I don't trust you.

**FENGO** Fengo's changing!
Fengo's sorry he railed at you before.
There, there.

*He hugs her. She sobs.*

**GERUTHA** Ohh if only I could start my life again.
If only I could turn around and change the past.

*FENGO catches HORVENDAL's eye.*

**FENGO** Now, now, mousie, no use recountin the mucky details.
What's done is done and can't be done again.
Bedways now. 'Tis past the Madd Boy's napp.
He'll be safe out here tonight, Mother, nae fear.

**GERUTHA** Oh my poor, poor Madd Boy…

*She kisses him and exits. FENGO ties HORVENDAL to a post.*

**FENGO** Peace my boy, my bonnie ladd;
May all yer dreams be sweet, not sadd.
Fengo loves ye, this is true,
He wouldna' dream o' harmin you!
And so goodnight, sweet boy, goodnight,
May heaven shield ye in yer plight;
And if ye die, afore ye wake—

*He kisses him on the forehead.*

Pray you do, for your own sake.

*Music. FENGO leaves him. Transition into night. Wolves howl.*

### Scene the Tenth

*That night. Colder. Outside FENGO's house.*

*Silence. HORVENDAL is tied up, listening at the door. Out of the dark forest, LILJA emerges. She kneels in front of him. Pause.*

**LILJA** You're the Madd Boy. Hello, Madd Boy.
Don't be afraid. It's me, Matthius's daughter.
I come to bring you a message:

I seen this fella. A fella in the woods;
Small he was, beak-nosed and raven-hair'd,
Dark his face was, brambles on his head,
He said, my child, be ye not afraid.
To Horvendal I bring this Holy Plea,
To Horvendal I issue this decree:
Fly he says, get out this bitter land,
Or else another Fengo you'll become!
Then he wept, wept for events unfolding,
Still he wept, questing where to turn,

Still he wept, blood come from his eyes,
Then he disappeared, into the drifting snow...

'Twas Jesus, Madd Boy. Jesus spake your name!
Jesus calls you, Pilgrim to his Shrine!
I'm a-goin—goin where he says,
To this city, place call'd—Jerusalem.
He calls ye, Madd Boy, back unto his fold;
He sent mee, Madd Boy, to save your tortur'd soul!

**HORVENDAL** What?

**LILJA** Believe it—

**HORVENDAL** Who put that in yer head?
Get yee back to girlie-land afore ye winds up dead!

*She reaches into her cloak.*

**LILJA** No. I'll nott.
He told me you would doubt.
He told me show you this. He took it from his brow.
A Crown of Brambles—a helmet of pain,
He bore for love of us upon the Cross!
He left his bloody markings on me, too;
On me hands, and on me feet. See?
He baptis'd me; anointed me; rockt me with such shivers!
Vaulted me up, and show'd to me—such things!
He listens, Madd Boy! He asks of you, believe!
Look you, his Love-Wounds!
Now—do you believe?

*Pause. He takes the crown of thorns. He looks at her with tears in his eyes.*

**HORVENDAL** Who are you?

**LILJA** Who are you?

**HORVENDAL** Are you an Angel?

**LILJA** Are you?
Why Angel why, do break you Jesus's heart?
Why Angel why, do feign you like yer madd?

**HORVENDAL** Oh GODDS! Oh girl, all I see is Fengo!
All muckt upp am I, a-drowning in the murk!
I feel no Love, I see no Angels—help me!
Where was Jesus when I call'd out his name?

**LILJA** Maybe, Madd Boy, you int listning hard enough.
Maybe Jesus is talking to you now.
Think of it, Madd Boy! Run away with me!
Together out of Denn-Mark. Forever to be free!

**HORVENDAL** Oh girl, girl, girl—

*They embrace. Pause.*

**MATTHIUS** *(off)* Liljaaaa!

**LILJA** Oh no—

**MATTHIUS** *(off)* Girl, what are you doing? Heeyup! Come inside!

**LILJA** I wait for you, Madd Boy, I pray for you.

**HORVENDAL** But—

*She kisses him. MATTHIUS comes out.*

**MATTHIUS** LILJAAAA!!!

**LILJA** Runn—runn—with mee!

*MATTHIUS grabs her, hauls her inside. HORVENDAL is stunned. He looks at the crown of thorns. Pause. Wolves watch HORVENDAL from the woods.*

**HORVENDAL** Is this Madness makes me sit here thus?
Is this Madness beckons me to runn?
Why, Horvendal, do these godds torment ye,
Sending out their dictums in bits and fits and starts?
Oh Girl! Oh Girl! You rip my heart in twainn!
Ohhhh, throw away the weaker half—
And let—the Strong remain…

**WOLVES** *(whispering)* Hooorvendaaaal… REVENNNGE…

*The Mad Boy grinds the crown of thorns on his face.*

**Scene Eleventh**

*Next morning. The woods. Behind the stables.*

*Dreadful screaming. FENGO, MATTHIUS, and Vikings drag LILJA through the snow.*

**LILJA** OWWW! Let go!!!

**FENGO** Further out—

**LILJA** Let go! OOWWW!!! HEEELPP!!

**FENGO** Matthius hold her firm.

**LILJA** OOOWWWW!!!

**MATTHIUS** What said he, girl? Fess up, we heard you!
What said you to Madd Boy lurking by last night?

**LILJA** Nothing, Paa!

**MATTHIUS** We know yer in league with him.

**LILJA** I'm not! I'm NOT!

**FENGO** Matthius, wrench it out.

**MATTHIUS** Something's between you. Something dark, un-Danely.
Say it, girl! This raiding spirit's took you both!

**LILJA** OOOWWW!! It has not!

**FENGO** She's shy. She needs prompting.
Hoist her smock, Matthius, let her taste my belt.

**MATTHIUS** NO! Fengo. NO! Please—no more floggings—
Faith, hear me, we'll chart the slyer way!
Crafticall—tackticall—like the Madd Boy himself!
A trapp then—to flush this marmott from his hole!

**FENGO** Well?

**MATTHIUS** Bind the girl, Fengo—leave her here alone,
Haul out the Madd Boy, let him glimpse her tied;
If he dare collude with her—if he move to free her—
If he dare unbind her, Fengo—then we have our Boy!

**FENGO** It's a stupid plan.

**MATTHIUS** Trust in mee!
If this plott mislay—let I horsewhippt be!
If he dare save her, Fengo, then he's no Madd Boy!
If he's no Madd Boy—then he's ours to slay.

**FENGO** Hmmm. All right, Matthius, try it. Bind her wrists.
And not kindlie, Matthius, not fatherly—
Harshly. Make it hurt!

*They tie her wrists to the rail.*

**LILJA** OOOWW!!!

**MATTHIUS** Oh wicked, wicked, wretched, weasling girl,
Look at me! Drove to bind you to a rail.

**FENGO** Enough, Matthius. Menn, fetch the Madd Boy.
Bide this plodger, let his tact be tried.
Meanwise, hide we in yonder spracky thicket—
Swords drawn, ladds! This lass we'll leave exposed.

*The Vikings exit.*

Your final chance, Matthius. Tread ye slithe.
Your worth to me is wayning. Fumble not.

**MATTHIUS** He'll take her, Fengo, upon my throat he shall.
If there's one thing Christian boys like to do, Fengo—
It's abducting and corrupting little girls.

**FENGO** Hmm.

*Pause. Vikings enter with Mad Boy.*

**VIKING** Here's the boy, Fengo.

**FENGO** Madd Boy! How slept you last night?

**HORVENDAL** Arf arf!

*FENGO holds him by the hair.*

**FENGO** Ahhh good Madd Boy, barkier than ever.
Look, Madd Boy. Quitt chewing of that logg.
See ladd, see how Fengo trusts ye?
He's found a task for yee, doggyskull'd or nott.
This girl boundup—she's spoutin mouthy insolence.
We'll just off to carve a slicing switch.
Keep the watch on her, Madd Boy, see she don't get free.
If she hollers, snapp her toes off—
Snapp her ears off! Got it?

**HORVENDAL** Arf arf arf!

**FENGO** Matthius, come away.
Be good, Madd Boy. Fearless Madd Boy.
Peerless Madd Boy. Stay.

*FENGO nods at the Vikings. They head off into the woods. HORVENDAL and LILJA are alone. Pause.*

**LILJA** Madd Boy, listen—quickly now and hear—

**HORVENDAL** Girl, what's happened??

**LILJA** Ohhh, what a plundring's here!
Boundup, battered on—all for my Angell!
Battered by our fathers—battered for my Christ!

**HORVENDAL** I'm yours, girl! Tell me the Path this boy's to take;
I heed you, love you! We runn for Jesus's sake.

**LILJA** Naay—all's changed now! Christ, he speaks a-fresh.
Nay come not near, they're watching with their swords!

**HORVENDAL** What? Where?

**LILJA** Look not behind—
It's you they're trappling, worry not for mee.
It's you, Christ, he beckons! Hark! He bidds you now.
Fly! Flee this trapp! Fly this place! Alone!

**HORVENDAL** Alone?

**LILJA** Now! Let Jesus guide your heels!
Leave me to bleed, love! Give my love to Christ.

**HORVENDAL** What? Leave you?
Christ—bids you say this?
Christ—he bids me leave you bleed alone?
Christ—he bids me strand you with your fathers?
Ye take this from yer menn, girl?
Ye take this from yer godd?
Look at you!

**LILJA** Doubt him nott!

**HORVENDAL** *Make him help us*, you says he thrives in you!
Jesus hear us—show your bloody love-strength!
Off yer cross, Christ, do yer Christly jobb!
Jesus?

**LILJA** Peace, love, peace. My time is over.
Your Star is risen, Angel. Rise! Shine on!

**HORVENDAL** Noo! Ohh no. Murder's in the Stars.
Now more than ever do I my tactick see;
Christ—he's no Saviour! Christ—he's asleep!
'Tis Thor what beckons! 'Tis Thor what thrives in mee!

**LILJA** No! No!

**HORVENDAL** Hush, lass—it's true!
In Thor do I flourish! This oath I swear to you:
When next we meet, yer plight will ended be,
And Fengo's head I'll naill on yonder tree!
Death to our Fathers!

**LILJA** Take nott the course of Wrath—
Peace! Peace! Take not the course of Doom!

**HORVENDAL** Enough!

**LILJA** Oh Jesus, guide this boy with fire;
Help! We lose him! Oh slaughterous desire—
Pray with me, Madd Boy—praying let us die!
Aye! Let us fly this Earth! Die! Die!
Drown, in a Bloodbath of Love!
WE HEED YOU CHRIST!

**HORVENDAL** Stop it!

**LILJA** CHRIST, TAKE OUR SOULLS!
Adds two more to your martyrd litany!
Fathers, come forth! Come slay your Christian Children!
We defy you, DEFY YOU IN THE NAME OF CHRIST!!
PRAISE GODD!!

**HORVENDAL** You'll kill us!

**MATTHIUS** We have him, Fengo!
Hah hurraah!! Forward axemenn!

*MATTHIUS runs out, followed by Vikings.*

**HORVENDAL** Nooo! Squalling lass! Not Christians! Not Christ!
No! Stop! I'm a mangling Madd Boy—

*He bites off her ear.*

**LILJA** OOOOOOOWW!!

*He runs home howling.*

**MATTHIUS** After him, men, after him, after him—

*The Vikings follow.*

**FENGO** Well, Matthius, there's your craftick plann.

**MATTHIUS** Did he try to free you, did he try to cutt yer bonds?
Thor's hounds, Fengo, he's chaw'd off her ear!

**FENGO** So he has.

**LILJA** Jesus, take me, take me from this land…
In the name of love, in the name of heavenmercie,
Someone, anyone, anyone, let me die…

*She sobs, bleeding.*

**MATTHIUS** Girl, what's got into you?

**FENGO** Matthius, this was your last chance.
You have wasted countless hours of my life.

From this time henceforth, let our paths turn twain.
Come not to my house, come not to my table,
I'm done with ye, Matthius, I renounce yee!

*He tears off MATTHIUS's medallions.*

**MATTHIUS** What? No! Fengo, Fengo noooo—
My bloodiest blood brother, give me one last chance.

**FENGO** Let go of me, Matthius. You int no Viking, nor no Dane.

**MATTHIUS** I am, I am! I'm trying—I'll show you—

**FENGO** Matthius—go play dolls with yer daughter.

*He spits on MATTHIUS and strides away. MATTHIUS kneels with his head in his hands, sobbing.*

**MATTHIUS** Ohh noo, ohh Fengo, ohh Odin, what'll come of me, I'm done for…

*LILJA talks to herself.*

**LILJA** My fault, my fault. This is all my fault…
No faith, no hope, no courage… I failed…

**MATTHIUS** Aye, that's it—you failed—yer hopeless!
Inside, you hopeless thing.

**LILJA** But—

**MATTHIUS** Inside! Get ye inside now!

*He unties her, shoves her homeward. Elsewhere, Mad Boy jumps on FENGO's back.*

**HORVENDAL** Piggyback, Nuncle Fengo—piggyback, piggyback!

**FENGO** Ladd, get down afore ye breaks yer neck.

*The Vikings hold him.*

**HORVENDAL** I did like ye said, Nuncle, I snappt at her ear!

**FENGO** Aye for that, we'll bedd you in the shedd.

**HORVENDAL** Ooh! What funn was today, Nuncle Fengo!

**FENGO** Aye. Bind him good.
What a frolick we'll have the morrow.

*The Vikings bind him firmly in the woodshed. FENGO speaks aside.*

Oh canny, canny Madd Boy; thou'rt indeed the one.
The game it is afoot, kidd; thou art thy Father's Sonn.

*They leave him in the shed. The Vikings stand watch. Elsewhere, LILJA lies weeping in her bed.*

### Twelfth Scene

*That sleepless night. MATTHIUS's house.*

*MATTHIUS and LILJA lie awake. LILJA nurses her wound. Pause.*

**LILJA** Dadda?

**MATTHIUS** What, girl?

**LILJA** Why was I born?

**MATTHIUS** Because, girl, because.

**LILJA** It ain't fair.

**MATTHIUS** Go to sleep.

**LILJA** Dadda?

**MATTHIUS** What, girl?

**LILJA** How come I'm me?

**MATTHIUS** Shut up.

**LILJA** I don't want to be alive. I want to be dead.

**MATTHIUS** Well yer not, girl. Yer alive. If everyone was dead—
Well… there'd be no point to life, would there?

**LILJA** It ain't fair.

**MATTHIUS** Go to sleep.

*Pause.*

**LILJA** I tried, I tried! Oh Jesus where were you?
I saw you, I dream'd you. I can't reach you no more.

*Pause.*

Dadda?

**MATTHIUS** What, girl?

**LILJA** I want to kill myself.

**MATTHIUS** Oh stop it.

**LILJA** I am gonna kill myself, Da. I want to die.

**MATTHIUS** Suicide's fer menn, child. It's a honourable death. You coudnt kill yerself anymor'n a dog could. Now get to sleep.

**LILJA** Says you.

**MATTHIUS** Says me.
I wish you would kill yerself, if the truth be told.

**LILJA** I'll do it, Da.

**MATTHIUS** Good. Join yer mother.

**LILJA** I mean it. I'll jump off a cliff.

**MATTHIUS** Good! Here, Take my dagger with you, slit yer throat on the way down. Here—take me bloody warr-axe too—chop yer own head off while yer at it. Well? Go on! What're you waitin for? Go on!

**LILJA** I don't think you're a very good father.

**MATTHIUS** Well, whose fault is that? Not mine.
Think I'm hard on ye, girl? Go and face the godds.
Think this world's cruel? Go and try the next!
Go on! Ye got yer axe, ye got yer dagger.
Go on—quit stallin—go do yerself in.

*She stands there a while, looking at the axe, patricide flashing through her mind.*

*At the same moment, in FENGO's bed, GERUTHA jumps up from her sleep.*

**GERUTHA** AAAH!

*LILJA drops the axe and throws her arms around MATTHIUS, weeping.*

**MATTHIUS** What's this? How come yer huggin mee?

**LILJA** I love you, Dad. I don't care what you are. I don't want to die—
I want to live—I want to live—I want to live…

**MATTHIUS** Then get to sleep.

*Meanwhile:*

**GERUTHA** I seen her, Fengo, I seen her in a dream;
Her smock, the hue of deepest, bluest sky;
She look'd at me, like sunlight did she seem,
And Love and Mercie nested in her eye;
"Gerutha," call'd she—call'd me by my name.
Told me my misdoings were forgott;
No one ever looked at me the same,

And lov'd me so, if I lov'd her or nott!
She's comin, Fengo, comin to this Land,
She and her Sonn, who some call Jesus Christ.
And all of Denn-Mark will take her by the hand,
And Light will shine, where only there was ice!
I seen it, Fengo—I seen it clear as day!
The Morning's come. Our sinns are wash'd away.

*FENGO gets out of bed.*

**FENGO** That does it, that's it,
I ain't sleepin with no crazywoman.
You been eatin rancid bugberries, that's your problem.
So now—Jesus Christ is got a mother…

*At the same moment. HORVENDAL dreams. A strange voice whispers. It sounds like LILJA.*

**LILJA** Horvendal? Horvendal? Where is my Love?

**HORVENDAL** Who's that?

**LILJA** Are you awake, Horvendal? Let me in.

**HORVENDAL** Lilja? Girl?

**LILJA** Aye, love, it's mee—
I come to gett you—together let's flee.

**HORVENDAL** Girl, forgive me!

**LILJA** Shhh… open the door!
Take me and heed me, as ye should've before—

**HORVENDAL** I do, girl, I loves you!

**LILJA** I loves ye too.

**HORVENDAL** If only the godds were hearted, as you!

*He goes to the door and opens it. A bolt of light. The GHOST of Horvendal the Elder is there instead.*

**GHOST** Hooorvendaaal. Hooorvendaaal. Revenge!!

**HORVENDAL** No, Dadda—

**GHOST** Revenge Revenge Revenge Revenge!!

**HORVENDAL** No, Dadda—no, Dadda—no—

*He slams the door.*

Hoy shite.

*Meanwhile. Outside. FENGO looks at the moon.*

**FENGO** Odin, Great Odin, speak ye to Fengo.
It's mee, yer old warrior, steadfast and true;
Who is this Lord Jesus? What does he want?
Why ain't I seen him—or even seen you?
Great Odin—wisen me. Show me what to do.
Faill me nott—or I'll wage Warr on you!

*Drums sound. Wolves whisper in the shadows.*

**WOLVES** Reveeeenge...

## Thirteenth Scene

*Early morning. The coast. High wind.*

*A remote hill overlooking the sea.*

*Enter FENGO, singing, the Mad Boy led by Vikings. They rest. FENGO waits. Slowly, the Viking guards leave.*

**FENGO** Look, Madd Boy. Look out at the Sea.
Don't it bestirr yer blood? It stirs mine.
Come closer, lad. Look back at the valley.
See; what a beautiful land we live in.

You know, lad: the poets, the ancient saga-writers,
They tell us Love's the mightiest thing on earth.
Dost believe that, son? Is't Love? Or is it Hate?
Can Love move a Mountain? Can Love win a Warr?
Can it, son? Hate can.

Witness us, us the Viking people:
Were't Love what made us rulers o' the world?
Were't Love what stood us up gainst Mother Nature's blast?
Ohhhh Nature: from Time's Dawn she despised us.
We, her batter'd children, hated her right back.
See! how we battle her, since time immemorial,
But we're winning, boy; we're winning.
Praise our swords, we rise!

Madd Boy, hear us.
It's tyme t' quitt yer shammin.
You int no Christian, nor no Fool.
All this Love talk, bout Jesus, bout Mary—
It's a plott to keep us Strongmen down!
And that ain't natural, sonn. It's perverse!

Skews the Fatal Majestie of Heaven!
Fengo won't have it.

Men of Greatness should brace themselves together,
Gainst the rising tide of mediocre muck.
Fear it, sonn, fear it—a world rul'd by weaklings—
We gots to stick together, and stand tall.
Love sputts and flickers, a faint and fleeting fyrefly;
Hate will one day engulf the sunn!
Let not our Hates drive our hearts asunder,
But bond us, boy, bond us,
Meld our hearts with shining gold!
Give us your hand…

**HORVENDAL** Gold?

**FENGO** Aye, sonn—Gold!
Gold and Power, sonn. My second in command!
Clever Madd Boy! Thour't prov'd a cunning foe,
Try usin those skills—for something grander.

**HORVENDAL** Yoooou—Coward Fengo!

**FENGO** Laddie, watch what you say.
Fengo won't bargain, after today.

**HORVENDAL** Coward! You Coward, Fengo! I've got you by the throat!
You skulking sott to bribe me with yer Gold!
What hope has Denn-Mark if you're the best it's got?
My Time is come! Yer bones are growing old.

**FENGO** Ohhhh you said it. You gone and said it now.
I see yer father—he's a-livin in yer gutts.
Fengo's a-gonna have to prowse him out!

*FENGO throws off his cloak.*

Wrassle me, sonn. Let's do this honourable.
Fair and square, no dirty tricks allowd;
No henchmen here—no mother do I see.
Just you and me, sonn. Do yer father proud.

**HORVENDAL** Did yee slay my father?

**FENGO** That ain't fer you to know.
Tear it fromm me, laddie. Give yer luck a go.

**HORVENDAL** No weapons?

**FENGO** No weapons.

**HORVENDAL** Teeth and claws?

**FENGO** Teeth and claws.
No, sonn, no trappings, no sneakrie, no bait.
Just you, boy, and me—and pure, unbridled Hate!

*Pause. HORVENDAL takes off his cloak.*

**HORVENDAL** Strengthen me godds!

**FENGO** Ahhhhh. Christian my arse!
Now yer deepest hue shines! Welcome back.
Ready boy? Ready? Stay inside the clearing.
In Thor's name, face me. Brace me. Grasp hands.

**HORVENDAL** May the best man winn.

**FENGO** If he didn't winn he'd not be the best mann, would he?
Now—on yer mark, get sett, GO!!

*FENGO kicks him in the groin then grips him in a hammerlock.*

**HORVENDAL** Oooomph!

**FENGO** You puny thing!

**HORVENDAL** You bloody ox!

**FENGO** Surrender?

**HORVENDAL** Never, Fengo—don't relax yer gripp,
I'll grind yer grimy gullet wi' me teeth!

**FENGO** Heh heh, oohhh the memories they flood;
Yer father was a hopeless fighter too!
No grace, the fucker used to bite and scratch!
Took all the funn out o' molestin him.

*HORVENDAL tries to break free.*

**HORVENDAL** Ooomph!!

**FENGO** C'mon, laddie, try and throw me!

**HORVENDAL** Oomph!

**FENGO** How yuz doin, Madd Boy?

**HORVENDAL** Help!

**FENGO** Over the shoulder, Madd Boy, over the shoulder.
Come on, Madd Boy, you can do it, you can do it.
I know ye can—OOOMPH!

*HORVENDAL flips FENGO over his shoulder and he lands with a colossal thud!*

Ooooooohhhh!

**HORVENDAL** Haaa! Madd Boy's got you now!
Praise Ye, Lord Thunder! Where's yer bullytalk now?

**FENGO** I can't breathe…

**HORVENDAL** What?

**FENGO** Me back—me back—it's broke…

**HORVENDAL** What's this then, Fengo? A dagger in yer breeks?
No dirty tricks you said! No dirty tricks!

**FENGO** Help!

**HORVENDAL** Now did yee slay my father?

**FENGO** Help!

**HORVENDAL** You slew my father dead!

**FENGO** I never touch'd him! Someone, someone help!
Yer facts are scrambled, Madd Boy, in yer head!

**HORVENDAL** I *seen* you Fengo! I seen you break his skull.
You never seen me hidin in that tree!
Seven years me mind it did deny it.
But it's back, Fengo! Me father lives in mee!

*HORVENDAL slices him across the scalp.*

**FENGO** AAAHHH!! Fuck me, you really are a Madd Boy!
Deluded sick and bloodicrazed to boot!
But as yer a mann, you'd best murder me quickly—
To torture me would bring you no credit!

**HORVENDAL** Oh noo, Fengo: I waited seven years!
I'll mapp out the bounds of my Revenge.

**FENGO** Heelp!!

**HORVENDAL** And when you feel my steel cut yer hamstrings,
Remember the abuse you heap'd on me!

**FENGO** NoooOOOO!!

*HORVENDAL slices FENGO's hamstrings with his knife.*

**HORVENDAL** No, Uncle, no, yer life ain't over;
You got many many nastie hours ahead!
Move mann—I'll spear ye thru the heels
And hoist ye up for skinnin on that tree!
Move!

**FENGO** JESUS, GOD OF MERCY hear my plea—
Deliver me from this Boy! JESUS! JESUS!—

**HORVENDAL** Fucker can't hear ye!
Wait… what's that, what's here?

*Pause. In the distance can be heard solemn singing.*

Voices singing? Bronze bells ringing?
Friends o' yours, I fear!
No! It's Latin! No, it cannot be!
Someone's comin up the road!

**FENGO** Let's see!

**HORVENDAL** You be still! No! I'll not believe!
No it ain't—mine eyes—they be deceiv'd!

*Enter a procession of travelling monks holding cowbells, crucifixes, and holy relics. One of the monks, Brother PAAVO, steps forward and faces them.*

**PAAVO** Ahoy, you wild and woolie Heathen;
Break off your squallid squabblings.
We are sent from Jesus and the Pope,
To seek the Lord of Helsingor!

**HORVENDAL** Lord of Helsingor?

**FENGO** I am he! I am he!
I am Fengo, Lord of Helsingor. What can I do fer yee?

**PAAVO** We carry a message from Rollo, King of Neustria.

**FENGO** Rollo the Bald? What does he want?

**PAAVO** An audience, Lord Fengo. An audience in private.
An audience bearing matters of importt.

*Pause. He looks at HORVENDAL.*

**FENGO** A haudience. They request a haudience of me.
Give us yer hand, good brother, I'm maimed.
Sorry, Madd Boy. Matters of State.
We'll have to finish our conversation later!

**HORVENDAL** No!

*The monks help FENGO up.*

**FENGO** Welcome all! Welcome to Helsingor! Land of heartie cheer!
Bigg feastin and ale for Fengo and the Christians!
This way, good strangers! This way!

*HORVENDAL is stunned.*

**HORVENDAL** Christians?

**FENGO** Aye, son. Christians! Who knows why or how?
Got you, Madd Boy, got you! Just watch what happens now.

*The monks sing. They exit with FENGO. HORVENDAL stares after them.*

**HORVENDAL** Christians…? Christians…?

Oh Christ!

*End of Act One.*

## ACT TWO

### Fourteenth Scene

*DRUMS. FENGO'S house at Helsingor.*

*FENGO, GERUTHA, and Vikings sit facing the Christians. The old women dress FENGO's wounds. He laughs.*

**FENGO** Well, well, well. Who woulda ever believ'd it.
Christian priests. In Helsingor.

**PAAVO** Lord Fengo, I am Brother Paavo.
This good Holy Man, this is Brother Petri.

**GERUTHA** Welcome, brothers—

**FENGO** Mind yer business, womann—
Youz gots some nerve prancin across my land.

**PETRI** We bear a message from Good King Rollo;
He'll stand your persecuting us no more.
Signed a treaty did he, with the French;
And in exchange for lands and yearly tribute,
Swore before God, Fengo—to make the Danes Christian.

**FENGO** Did he now?

**PETRI** That means all his Lords, all his Vikings,
Every Danish fisherman and blacksmith,
Must awake, and heed the rising tide,
And join Christ's People by New Year's Day.

**PAAVO** The One Thousandth Year of our Lord. Amen.

**PETRI** Wilt thou, Fengo, staunch and stubborn savage,
Take up the Cup of Jesus Christ?
Or wilt thou stay, and keep your brutish ways,
And face the wrath of Rollo, your superior?

**FENGO** Hmm…

**PAAVO** E'en as we speak, Fengo, Jesus Christ impends.
His Knights of the Purple Cross sweep North;
Lord Thorstalf, your neighbour, he refus'd our clerics;
Lo and behold, Fengo, his house burn'd down.

**PETRI** Praise the Power of the Lord.

**PAAVO** Speak, Fengo. Time's no longer with you.
Fend us back, another wave will rise.
We come to you, to offer you Salvation.
Your answer now, directly. Speak!

**FENGO** Hmmm…

**GERUTHA** I dreamed, I dreamed this day was coming—

**FENGO** Woman, I thought I told you to shut up.

*Pause.*

**PAAVO** Well?

**FENGO** Hmmm. Youz Christians, youz drives a hard bargain.
King Rollo, he's a devious old foxx.
Tell King Rollo—we accepts these prim conditions.
Tell him—Fengo wants a slice!

**PAAVO** Praise God.

**FENGO** Show us yer book. Yer Jesus book. Now!
I feels a strange new melting in my heart.

*They open a huge Bible.*

**PAAVO** Look you here—that's Tender Babie Jesus,
And Mary his Mother, and good Saint Joseph,
Riding on the Road to Bethlehem.

**FENGO** I see.

**PETRI** And this is Jesus, all grown up now,
All killed and Crucified, hanging on a Cross.

**FENGO** I like that picture.

**PAAVO** And here's Our Lord again, all Resurrected like.
Rising into the sky, to join his Father in Heaven.

**FENGO** Ahh… that's Beautiful. That's what that is. Poignant, Poetick and Beautiful, hey? More, more, tell me more about this! I can tells yer wise and goodlie menn.

**PAAVO** Jesus said, love thine enemy as thyself.

**FENGO** Aye, that'd throw 'em!

**PAAVO** He said, judge not, lest ye be judged.

**FENGO** Aye, no judgin Fengo!

**PETRI** Jesus said, verily, from the greatest to the smallest, We are all equal in the eyes of the Lord.

**FENGO** Ahhhh… we're all equal. You hear that, womann?
Why that's lovlie! That's poetickal too.

**GERUTHA** Amen.

**FENGO** And if yuz do something badd an' yer sorry, Jesus will forgive ye, int that right?

**PAAVO** Aye.

**FENGO** Now, what if ye ain't sorry? What if yer proud?
What if yer some bastard tryin to murder Fengo?

**PAAVO** What?

**FENGO** Punishments! Punishments! Yuz gots t'have punishments, boys. What've ye got?

**PETRI** Why?

**PAAVO** Penances, Fengo.

**PETRI** Excommunication.

**PAAVO** Depending on the Severity of the Sin.

**FENGO** Dependin on the Severity—of Fengo. Ha haaaa!

*Pause. The monks look at one another.*

Well, good holymen, I likes yer words. I likes your books and I likes your pictures. Plus, we don't want to be left behind, right ladds? Don't want to stand i' the way of progress!

**GERUTHA** But Fengo—

**FENGO** Let the statues of Odin be cut down,
Let great crucifixes be erected in their stead!
Tell yer Christian bosses Fengo wants aboard!
Womann—yer the first heathen I'm hex-communicatin!

**GERUTHA** What?

**FENGO** So long—Mother o' the Madd Boy!
Smell you in hell, woman! You boys drink ale?

**PAAVO** Er…

**FENGO** Ale! Ale for my celibate friends!
Let the horn be sounded and the sheep slaughterd!
Rowse the musicians! Let the Festival begin!
Jesus is come to Helsingor!!

**VIKINGS** Hurraaaay!!

*Music. Drums. FENGO rises on his crutches. The Vikings cheer, douse the monks with ale. The dragonhead posts outside FENGO's hall are taken down, and hauled off to the lumberyard.*

### Fifteenth Scene

*Down in the village. Later.*

*A Viking craftsman nails crossbeams on the dragonhead posts, to make them look like crosses. HORVENDAL and the old women watch.*

**HORVENDAL** Fengo a Christian? No, impossible!

**INGA** Aye, he's gonna to be baptis'd, Sunday morning!

**ANNA** Baptis'd in the sea!

**HORVENDAL** I was a Christian! I heard of Christ first!

**INGA** Aye, he's going to confess his sinns afore the townsfolk.

**ANNA** Aye and we'll confess too, and Fengo will absolve us!

**INGA** Fengo says Jesus murders all sinners with a Hammer!

**HORVENDAL** He *what*?

**ANNA** Aye, I believe it—and Fengo said to mee—
That Jesus, he specially hates… old wimmen!

**INGA** Oooh we better get baptis'd soon!

**HORVENDAL** Oh you Hound-Fates! Every turn is wrong!
Jesus, treachor-godd, spurn'd us all along!
Fengo's rook'd you! Christ, you took his side!
But I shall stitch my vengeance-capp with
Fengo's Danish hide.
Let him confess. The Baptism's the place,
Where I'll rubb Viking Justice in his Face!

### Scene Sixteenth

*The hall at Helsingor.*

*FENGO sits at his high seat. MATTHIUS enters sheepishly.*

**MATTHIUS** Fengo? Fengo?

**FENGO** Matthius, yer hex-communicated.

**MATTHIUS** I know, Fengo, I know. I… I got a surprise fer yee.

**FENGO** Do you, Matthius?

**MATTHIUS** I do indeed.

**FENGO** Well Matthius, don't just stand there, bring her in.

*MATTHIUS drags LILJA in.*

Well, well, Matthius. This is a surprise.
How'd yee like to be Fengo's bride, prettygirl?

**MATTHIUS** Oh, girl—it's yer lucky day!

**LILJA** I thought you gots yerself a bride already, Fengo.
What's wrong wi' the one ye got?

**FENGO** What's wrong wi' her, prettygirl? What's wrong wi' the wife I gots? I'll tell ye what's wrong with her. She stinks! That's what's wrong wi' her. You don't stink, do ye, prettygirl? Not my prettygirl! Fengo likes you.

**MATTHIUS** She dreams about ye, Fengo.

**FENGO** Does ye loves yer little Fengo, prettygirl?

**MATTHIUS** Course she do, Fengo, course she do.

**FENGO** Say somethin sweet to old Fengo. Say somethin all girlie an' sweet. Hey prettygirl? Hey, hey? Something all soft 'n girlie 'n sweet.

*Pause.*

**LILJA** Bugger yer dog.

**FENGO** Matthius, I'm gonna kill you.

**MATTHIUS** She do love you, Fengo! She do!

**FENGO** She'd best say somethin sweet to me, Matthius.

**MATTHIUS** She will, honest she will! She's just shy, that's her problem—

*MATTHIUS drags her aside.*

Girl, come here! I'm countin on you, child.
Give Fengo a kiss! Go! Sit on his knee! Now!

*He throws her on FENGO's lap. Pause.*

**FENGO** Well, bonnielass?

**LILJA** Well, what?

**FENGO** You gonna marrie Fengo like a good little girl?

*Pause.*

**LILJA** Sure I'll marrie you, Fengo.

**FENGO** You will?

**LILJA** Sure.

**FENGO** Well what do ye know?

**LILJA** Let's get married today.

**MATTHIUS** See, Fengo, see?

**FENGO** Whoa! Hold yer horses, prettygirl, hold yer horses! We'll get married, nae ye fear, soon as the Church okays it. Gots to flush out the pottie afore ye shitts in it again, right Matthius?

**MATTHIUS** Aye, Fengo, of course.

**FENGO** Cah, yer decrepit Matthius. A terrible father too. But this latest gift makes me blind to all yer faults.

**MATTHIUS** I'm only serving my friend and Lord.

**FENGO** Of course, Matthius. Of course.

**MATTHIUS** Is I… still hex-communicated, Fengo?

**FENGO** No, Matthius, yer nott. Goodnight my little choke-cherry.

**LILJA** Goodnight, my darling Fengo.

**MATTHIUS** Move, girl, let's go. Long live Lord Fengo!

*Exeunt MATTHIUS and LILJA.*

**FENGO** The Star of Fengo rises in the North,
Now the Fates unveil their gracious plann:

A new God, a new and juicy bride;
What didd Fengo to deserve such joy?
Nae ye mind; the Stars have spake their Will.
Fengo rises—and higher shall he still.

## Scene Seventeenth

*MATTHIUS's house.*

*LILJA has barred the door. She has a leather bag and is stuffing things into it. A pounding at the door. It is MATTHIUS.*

**LILJA** What?

**MATTHIUS** Open up!

**LILJA** In a minute.

**MATTHIUS** What are you doing?

**LILJA** None of your business—

**MATTHIUS** What are you— *(bursting in)* Here… yer packin a bag!

**LILJA** I am not.

**MATTHIUS** No? What's this about then?

**LILJA** I dunno.

**MATTHIUS** You dunno, you dunno? Maybe a crack on the snout'll jostle yer memory—

*He slaps her in the face.*

**LILJA** Dadda—Dadda—if you hitt me one more time I will punch you so hard i' the mouth.

**MATTHIUS** Oh girl, you'd rue the hour o' yer birth.

**LILJA** I already do. Now get out o' my way.

**MATTHIUS** Don't you mouth off to yer father, girl—

**LILJA** I'll mouth off to my father if I want. I wish you were fukkin DEAD!!

**MATTHIUS** WHAT??

*He slaps her. She punches him in the mouth.*

Why, you—

*They fight.*

**LILJA** You canna hit me no more—I won't let you.

**MATTHIUS** Cursed scourge o' my life, what's this bag about then?

**LILJA** Mind yer own business.

**MATTHIUS** You are my bastard business.

**LILJA** I int runnin away, I says!

**MATTHIUS** I'll ties you to the post, you little viper!

*He cruelly ties her up.*

**LILJA** Owwwww! Dadda—Dadda, stop and hear!
I was goin up the Seacoast, Dad—that's where I was going.
To get you some Seashells. Charms for Good Luck!
Stop, Dad! I was gonna give 'em ye as a surprise!

**MATTHIUS** Girl—if you brought me anything other than grief it would indeed be a surprise.

**LILJA** You gots to believe me, Dad—that's the truth.

**MATTHIUS** Hah! You wretch! You rotten little liar!
Hang you, serpent-tongue! Wrecker of my life!

*He gets ready to flog her. She wails.*

**LILJA** Aaaaaah! No one loves me no matter what I do!
No one cares what finally comes of me!
I was tryin to be loyall—do somethin good for once!
Ohhhh Daddy, Daddy—I want to die…

**MATTHIUS** Ohhh stopp it—stopp! Quit curdling at my blood!
Don't cry, don't cry, lass—it makes my heart hurt.

**LILJA** You hate my gutts.

**MATTHIUS** I do not hate you.

**LILJA** Yer always hitting me and hurting me, Paa.

**MATTHIUS** Well, sweetheart, yer always floutin my authority and that hurts me inside too…. I try, I try to be a good father to you girl—but, it's hard, it's hard, girl…. I… I don't know how…

**LILJA** Oh beloved Dad. Untie me?

**MATTHIUS** Girl, girl you've…
You've got your Mother's eyes…
I… I never meant to kill her, child—I swear.
I—I slappt her with my sword—
Oh GODDS!

**LILJA** I know, Dad.

**MATTHIUS** I'm so ashamed of what I am!
Oh godds forgive me… have mercy on old Matthius…

*He sobs.*

**LILJA** It ain't your fault. Nothing is your fault.
Yer faultless, Dad. Untie me?

*Pause. He looks at her. He dries his eyes.*

**MATTHIUS** You… you still gonna get me some seashells, child?

**LILJA** Can I finish packing my bag?

**MATTHIUS** You… promise you'll wedd with Fengo, girl?

**LILJA** Aye, as ever you say.

*He unties her.*

**MATTHIUS** Oh sweetheart. I'll go out and I'll carve you a giant sledd. I'll carve it myself, from solid oak, to last you five hundred lifetimes.

**LILJA** Thank you, Dad, staunchmost Dad.

**MATTHIUS** I love you, Lilja, very much.
Goodmorrow then, my sweet child,
Goodmorrow, goodmorrow…

*He kisses her. He goes. Pause. She is hiding a huge war-axe.*

**LILJA** Goodmorrow forever, you doomed son of a bitch.

## Scene Eighteenth

*The baptism scene. The North Sea. A winter morning.*

*The whole village is gathering on the beach. The new dragonhead crosses are erected. HORVENDAL wears a stolen monk's cowl.*

**HORVENDAL** So here's the place: the windy Sealand Shore.
Where one age ends, another does begin.
Old times cast-off like weather-beaten rugs,
And Denn-Mark answers to a Stranger's godd.
Ohh Powers, if Powers still you be,
Now's the time to manifest your Will:
I'll disguise me in a cowl'd hood,
And finish this, afore the gasping world!
Ssshh! Be silent! Here they do impend.
Watch. And listen. And Justice shall descend.

*HORVENDAL hoods himself and hides to the side. Enter FENGO, GERUTHA, and Vikings.*

**FENGO** Heh heh heh. This's been a bigger fuss 'n me weddingfest! Looka me, I'm the force o' wisdom and progress. Lookit, woman. Lookit Fengo in his baptismal cloak!

**GERUTHA** I can see.

**FENGO** Int Fengo a majestic sight?

**GERUTHA** Aye, Fengo, aye.

**FENGO** They e'en said I could keep this frock. Daft buggers. Here—as soon as I'm done this, I'm gonna hex-communicate yer sonn—fer slashing me haunches, woman! What do you think of that? Hey woman? Hey? Hey?

**GERUTHA** I want what you want.

**FENGO** You want what Fengo wants? Hah! I hope nott. Else you'd be out shaggin that prettygirl. Hey?

**GERUTHA** I—

**FENGO** Well, well, the Priests have arriv'd!
Lets go! Fengo's a-freezin! Do it fast so we can eat.

*The priests enter singing. They assemble. The great horn is sounded. Pause.*

**PETRI** Jesus Christ, oh Holy King of Heaven,
God the Father and God the Holy Ghost,
We are come to the village of Helsingor
To spread Thy Message of Love across the Earth.
Amen.

**ALL** Amen.

**PAAVO** God our Father, thank Ye for Thy Miracles,
Thank Ye for the Grace of Thy Son, Jesus Christ.
Amen.

**ALL** Amen.

**FENGO** Do I kneel now?

**PAAVO** Aye.

**FENGO** In the water?

**PAAVO** Aye.

**FENGO** Grrrr. Hold me crutches. Make it fast.

**PETRI** Christ, Redeemer, let your Light shine over the North Sea; let this Baptism of Fengo the Confessor bring the last of thy children unto Grace. Amen.

**FENGO** Couldn't we do this a' home in the friggin bath?

**PAAVO** Sshh! Lord Fengo—

**FENGO** Just hurry up!

**PETRI** Fengo, Lord of Helsingor, kneel before thy Maker,
And in His Eyes, confess thy Sinns,
That they may be forgiven.

**FENGO** Sins? Ye mean the bad things that I done?

**PAAVO** Aye, Lord Fengo.

**FENGO** Hmmmm, where do I start?

*HORVENDAL approaches, trembling. FENGO clears his throat disgustingly.*

I spake rudely in my time to—well, a lot of people—plus I took things what did not belong to me. Plus I have look'd at wimmen and thought nasty, dirty thoughts. These are Fengo's sins and he is so ashamed…

**PAAVO** Is that all?

**FENGO** Well… I did compare meself to the gods a lot.
Plus I swear. And I drink. A whole lot. And that's it.

**PAAVO** Nothing else?

**FENGO** Well...
I must admit I've slew a lot of folk.
Often for a reason, but just as often not;
Laugh'd at cripples, stole from peasants,
Fornicated like you wouln't believe;
Disembow'l'd Christians, tortur'd helpless animals;
Burn'd down yonder forest to starve the poor;
Betray'd everyone I've met; beat my wife,
Cockwhallop'd every child i' the village,
And said things that int completely true.
Heh heh…
These are my sinns. I am so ashamed.
Oh yeh—plus I smashed me brother's brains.

**PAAVO** Let us pray.

**FENGO** Aye, let's pray.

*HORVENDAL pounces on FENGO.*

**HORVENDAL** Murderer! Murderer! He said it so hisself!
This bastard int no Christian—he's a murderer!

**FENGO** Hey wot?

*HORVENDAL tries to drown him in the sea.*

**HORVENDAL** Murderer! Die you murdering dog!!

*The Vikings pounce on HORVENDAL.*

**VIKING** Hoy, stopp 'im!

**PAAVO** He's confessed, he's forgiven!

*They pull him off FENGO.*

**HORVENDAL** He ain't sorry—he ain't sorry, he's proud!

**FENGO** HE STABBED ME!

**PAAVO** Peace, boy, peace! Violence never solved anything!

**FENGO** Aye, lad, violence never solved anything!

**HORVENDAL** Why, you—

**FENGO** Haa haa haa haaaa!!

*Mayhem erupts.*

**PAAVO** Oh peace, peace, you riotous Danes!
Have some respect, and from this brawl refrain!

*They subdue him again.*

**FENGO** I'm forgiven lad, and yer not! Vengeance is not the Christian Way!!

**HORVENDAL** Dogs ripp your throat, Fengo, I was a Christian before you!

**FENGO** Well you sure don't look like one now!

**PAAVO** Peace!!

**HORVENDAL** I'll turn this village against you! I'll rouse the Danish Freemen against you!

**FENGO** Go ahead and try it—Madd Boy.

*The Vikings laugh. HORVENDAL breaks free.*

**HORVENDAL** You watch for me, Fengo—I'm not what I seem!
I'll haunt you forever—I'll slay you in your dreams!
I'm everywhere, Fengo—don't dare take a breath!
Once was I Madd-Boy—but now—am I DEATH!
I'm everywhere, Fengo—I'm EVERYWHERE!!

*He runs out howling. Pause.*

**PAAVO** I fear that lad might hurt somebody.

**FENGO** Aye, I knew he was up to somethin.

*GERUTHA has fallen to her knees weeping.*

You! This is all yer fault! I told ye from the beginning.
A sackful of gold to anyone what captures Young Horvendal!
That goes fer you too, woman. If ye wants to get baptis'd, you better move!

*She runs out, still in tears.*

Go on! Quit gawkin! Give me my crutches.
Fengo the Confessor has spoken!

*The Vikings cheer and run out waving swords. FENGO smiles at the priests.*

The Meek rise up; let all of Denn-Mark know,
No man on earth is safe—if Jesus is his Foe.

*The priests look at each other sadly.*

### Scene Nineteenth

*The great hall—empty and quiet.*

*HORVENDAL runs in with his dagger.*

**HORVENDAL** Mother! Mother! I know you're hiding!
Mother? This is yer Sonn!
Mother? Mother, where are you?
Where is that womann? Mother?

*GERUTHA ambushes him from behind.*

Oh!

**GERUTHA** Shut up, boy.

*She holds a dagger to his throat.*

Don't fight now—you hear me?

**HORVENDAL** Mother, is that you?

**GERUTHA** Don't argue wi' me, sonn. Drop yer dagger. Drop it!

*He drops his dagger and she picks it up.*

**HORVENDAL** Mother, you—

**GERUTHA** You said you was a halfwitt.
Now I'm the one what looks a halfwitt.
Bless you, sonn!

*She beats him, drags him by the hair.*

**HORVENDAL** But Momma—

**GERUTHA** I ain't seen no jott o' peace and quiet,
Not in fortie years o' life upon this earth,
And here I am, I nearly caught my breath—
And you come and stroy'd it, you blister'd seed!

**HORVENDAL** What're you doin?

**GERUTHA** What's it look like I'm doin?
I'm gonna slay you, afore they gets the chance.

**HORVENDAL** Momma, you can't!

**GERUTHA** No? Watch us and see!
I'll abort you, sonn—as you aborted mee!

*She chases him up the wall. He climbs into the rafters.*

**HORVENDAL** Momma—it's Horvendal—yer sweet and precious sonn!
How can you turn upon me in my darkest hour?
Remember the way I used to cry and cry,
You rock'd me in me cradle, sang me songs…
Momma—hear me! What times we used to have!
Listen: listen Momma: don't you remember?

**GERUTHA** No!

*He sings an ancient lullaby.*

**HORVENDAL** Sleep child, oh sweet child, oh ember of my soul…
The four winds protect thee, oh ember of my soul…

**GERUTHA** Stop. No! No! I hear you nott.
Noooo! My babie, my babie's dead!

*He sings it again. She staggers back. Suddenly she drops the dagger, falls to her knees, sobbing wretchedly. Pause.*

**HORVENDAL** Mother? Mother? Aye Maa, it's me.
Look ye my visage—yer sonn's here—look see.

*She looks up. Pause.*

**GERUTHA** Oh Sonn, Sonn. You were such a bonnie babie boy…
How come ye grew to be so horrible?

**HORVENDAL** Momma, I int so horrible—
I'll be yer tiny one again…
Cast aside the bitterness between us;
Danish Skies at long last shall be blue!
I'll build for you a house of finest cedar,
There you'll live, in blissful blissful rest!
Think of it, Momma, an end to Toil and Woe!
Believe me, Momma! The Truth, yer Heart doth know!

*He inches down to her. She sobs.*

**GERUTHA** Ohh child, I don't deserve no kindness.
Ohh what a wretched life I've lived…
I loves you, sonn, I always wept for you;
I ne'er could tell it ye… but I do…

*He holds her and they both cry.*

**HORVENDAL** There, there, Momma, you never meant no wrong;
Against the blast of fortune, a mother's love is strong.
Whatever else were perish'd, I knew me maa weren't dead.
Help us then, help us! Let's crush that Fengo's head!

**GERUTHA** WHAT? What say you? Yooouu devious Maggot!
Thought you could worm away my batter'd heart?
Pah! You wolfpupp! You sneagling scorpion!
Viperous mann-snake! Here's what I think of you!

*She comes at him with the daggers.*

**HORVENDAL** Momma, Momma, yer housin up with Evil—

**GERUTHA** Shut up, sonn, yer evil too.

**HORVENDAL** Momma, Momma—Fengo slew my paa!

**GERUTHA** SO WHAT?? Ye thinks he dint deserve it?
Fengo's a bunnyrabbit next to yer paa!

**HORVENDAL** Calm yerself, Momma—put down yer daggers! Drop them! Help me godds!

*He seizes her by the wrists.*

**GERUTHA** Someone! Someone!

**HORVENDAL** Drop them I sez—

**GERUTHA** Help us anyone! Fengo!

**HORVENDAL** Stop it!

**GERUTHA** Matthius! He were right to wanna see you strung—
Matthius! He spotted you, right from the start—
Matthius! Brethrens! Someone! Anyone!
They'll fix you. Help! Help!!

*Pause. Enter LILJA, covered in blood. Smiling, holding something behind her back.*

Child?

**HORVENDAL** Lilja?

**GERUTHA** What are you doing?

**LILJA** Madd Boy. Angel. Look what I done.

*She holds up her father's head.*

**HORVENDAL** Gods have mercy!

**LILJA** Haill, Fatherslayer!
Bless me, Saint Horvendal. I slew my father, too.

**HORVENDAL** Slew yer father, girl? What moved you to this? They'll ripp you apart, girl!

**LILJA** I love you, Madd Boy.

**HORVENDAL** Oh Momma—

**GERUTHA** Don't either of you move.
You ain't no children noways—you're BEASTS!

**HORVENDAL** Momma—

**GERUTHA** Nay, I heed you nott!
Twill joy me joy me to see ye both hung!
Die!!

*HORVENDAL grabs LILJA's dagger. There is a struggle, mother against son. Then GERUTHA falls back, the knife in her side.*

**HORVENDAL** Momma?

**GERUTHA** Ow, ow…

**HORVENDAL** Maa, I never—

**GERUTHA** Don't speak to me!

**HORVENDAL** You made me do it, 'twas yer own fault.
You know it was. Are you all right?

**GERUTHA** Piss off.

**HORVENDAL** I swear, Maa!

**GERUTHA** Runn—let me bleed.
What do I matter? Do as e'er ye need.

*Vikings shout offstage.*

**HORVENDAL** Oh you torture-godds, all its turn'd a-wrong!
Oh Warr unwinnable, hopeless all along!
Fengo he lives, Fengo's turn'd a Christian,
Me mother's stabb'd, the girl's lost her mind—
And mee, Mother, Mother what am I? A Dead Man!
Runn, girl. To Oblivion we go.

**LILJA** Is that near Jerusalem?

**HORVENDAL** Aye, somethere thereabouts.

*He throws his mother a rag.*

Here Momma, clean yerself up.
I'm real sorry, I am, I am.

**GERUTHA** Get lost!

**HORVENDAL** *(to LILJA)* Oh, girl, girl, girl.

*He runs out. LILJA follows. FENGO bursts in with the Vikings and monks.*

**FENGO** Cah, woman, can't you do anything?
Adds thatt to yer list of botch-ups!
*(seeing MATTHIUS's head)* Matthius! Hoy!
What happened to you?
See Holy-ladds? See what goes on up here?
Don't just stand there! After him, after him!
Come on, wifie, look alive!

*FENGO and VIKINGS and MONKS exit. GERUTHA is left alone.*

**GERUTHA** Farewell, you cancer of the womb,
May you swiftly meet your doom;
Poor old Mother's left to face
The consequence of her disgrace;
Menn like you are free to die,
And suffer not the lott of I;
Poor old Mother's trapped on earth;
What a joy—the gift of birth!

*A bleeding GERUTHA crawls off alone.*

## Twentieth Scene

*RAGNAR's return. Soon after. The same place.*

*He stands looking at the ransacked house. He sees his father's head. Pause.*

**RAGNAR** What in fuck's been going on here?
I buggers off fer two weeks and comes back to this!
FENGO, you cudgeon, you cankerous sledmutt,
What's been goin on here while Ragnar was a-whalin?
FENGO!

*Enter FENGO and the Vikings.*

**FENGO** Ragnar lad!

**RAGNAR** Who slew my father, Fengo?

**FENGO** How was yer whalin trip?

**RAGNAR** I'll give you a whalin trip, Fengo!

**FENGO** Easy, boy, easy! Remember I'm yer Lord!

**RAGNAR** You ain't no bloody lord if you don't do yer bloody jobb! Who chopp'd off me dadda's head? Where's me sister? Spit it out, Fengo, you crocodile, what have you done with my sister?

**FENGO** Fengo int done nothin so you put yer sword away. It's Horvendal, the so-call'd Madd-Boy. He's the one what done this.

**RAGNAR** Horvendal? Horvendal?

**FENGO** Aye, him and yer sister—who it turns out is nowt but a whoore!

**RAGNAR** I'll murder him!

**FENGO** They was dancin, Ragnar, on yer dead father's corpse,
Singin, Ragnar's a pixieboy, Ragnar's a pixie!
Then the two o' them friggerd off into the sunset,
Probly a-copulatin as we speak!

**RAGNAR** Enough! Enough! I'll hack out his liver!
I'll wind his steamin gutts round a tree!
Which way did he go, Fengo? Whence did they frigger?
Whence did they haulaway? Speak!

**FENGO** Easy, ladd, easy, this here's a Christian land.
We gots to take the Boy, legally.
Administer the punishment, slowly and deliberately.
This here's the Christian Way.

**RAGNAR** The Christian Way?

**FENGO** Aye, it's a New Age, innit? To everythin there be a season,
To every season a meaning.

**RAGNAR** What?

**FENGO** A time for warr, ladd, and a time fer hate.
A time for fightin, and a time fer dying;
A time for combatt, a time for wrangling,
A time for torture, a time for hackin out spleens—

**RAGNAR** I'm gonna murder him!

**FENGO** No you ain't! Yer gonna haul the boy home to Fengo!
Fengo will dispense Godd's Justice, Godd's way.
Do you believe in Godd, boy? Say yes.

**RAGNAR** Aye.

**FENGO** Good lad. Kneel down o' the ground.
I gots to baptize ye i' the new faith. Kneel down.

**RAGNAR** Why?

**FENGO** Just do it, boy!

**RAGNAR** Yer a pain i' the arse, Fengo.

**FENGO** Shh.

*FENGO pours holy water on his head.*

**RAGNAR** Hey!

**FENGO** The Lord is my shepherd what I don't want,
He maketh me lie down in green water.
He deploreth my soul, my cupp runneth over,
For we walk in the shadow of death forever, Amen.

**RAGNAR** What the fuck was that?

**FENGO** I just made you a Christian Soldier. Whatever ye do, from here on in, ye do on behalf of the Lord Jesus Christ, understand?

**RAGNAR** Lord who?

**FENGO** The fella I been talkin about!

**RAGNAR** Oh yeh, yeh right.

**FENGO** Round up every able-bodied man.

**RAGNAR** Aye, Fengo.

**FENGO** Build yerself a Christian Horde.

**RAGNAR** Aye, Fengo, aye.

**FENGO** Comb yee this icy wilderness. Bring this boy to Fengo.
But don't ye forget, kid, I want the boy—alive.

**RAGNAR** I'll bring him home to you, Fengo—I swear to you, right now.
In the name of Skull-Byter, Sword of me granpapaa, I swear
I'll deliver this boy to you.

**FENGO** Go, Brave Ragnar, go i' the name o' Christ,
Go forth and let Jesus guide yer Sword!

**RAGNAR** Did ye hear that, Skull-Byter? We gots a jobb to do!
Heighyupp, Skull-Byter! Long Live Lord Fengo!

*RAGNAR runs out bellowing.*

**FENGO** Ah youth, the promise o' the future.
What a joy to see events unfold.

*GERUTHA is still sitting there, bleeding.*

Stop sittin around here like a bump on a logg.
Get yer stupid cloak on. Go seek out the Madd Boy.

*He leaves. Drums sound. Vikings roar. GERUTHA crawls off the stage.*

## Scene Twenty-First

*Bitter wind. Midnight. Wolves howl. HORVENDAL and LILJA are in the icy fens. They huddle inside HORVENDAL's cloak.*

**HORVENDAL** Stop jumpin up and down, girl, yer wastin body heat.

**LILJA** I'm cold.

**HORVENDAL** Well huddle up.

**LILJA** I thought you said Jerusalem was a hot country.

**HORVENDAL** Well this ain't Jerusalem, is it? This is the Fenns. Where Grendel and his Mother lived. Gods' Death, it's a-freezin! Look ye around, girl. Make sure there int no gods comin. I don't wanna see no gods. They're makin me confus'd. *(long pause)* Lilja?

**LILJA** Aye?

**HORVENDAL** Girl, are you all right?

**LILJA** Aye, love, thank ye, love, I'm turn'd to a beautiful swann.

**HORVENDAL** But think what you done, girl, and with your Christ a-watchin!

**LILJA** Ohhh bleed me again, sweet saint, I done it acause Christ was watchin.

*She kisses him all over. He struggles free.*

**HORVENDAL** Come on, girl, ease up—let's build a fire. Gather up some kindling afore we perish.

**LILJA** I'll follow you to the ends of the earth, Saint Horvendal.

**HORVENDAL** Oh girl.

**LILJA** Me, I seen the light thru you.
You an' me we're gonna rid the world of Evill.
You an' me we're gonna purify the Earth.
You an' me we're gonna massacre the Devil!
Ain't we, Saint Horvendal, ain't we?

**HORVENDAL** No, girl, we ain't.

**LILJA** What? What say you? What mean ye we ain't?
Saint Horvendal? Love? What do you mean?

**HORVENDAL** Oh sweet soul, I should've heeded when you beckond,
And run away afore this all began;
I'd be sittin, sleepin in a Palm-tree now:
Not waitin to be eaten up by Wolves!
Sweet lost soul; ne'er ask'd you for this World!
Ne'er asked yee be cast in fray with me;
What god, what blind and mighty Power,
Could create both Crocodiles—and thee?

**LILJA** What're you telling me?

**HORVENDAL** Too much blood's been spilt. Way too much.
Somewhere, someways, the circle has to end.
More than this, girl, my arms and legs've hadd it.
I'm sick. I'm tired. I'm brokendown. I quit.

*Pause. She rises.*

**LILJA** Get yee upp.

**HORVENDAL** What?

**LILJA** On your FEET! We've a Holy War to wage!
I int quittin ever, EVER—till every Vikingman is dead!

**HORVENDAL** Girl, stopp it—

**LILJA** No, I'll stop it NOTT! Dint ye hear Lord Jesus a-howlin when ye plunged yer sword in Lord Fengo? Weren't he a-howlin and a-dancin and festivitatin with Joy?

*Pause.*

**HORVENDAL** Girl, I nee slay'd him.

**LILJA** WHAT??

**HORVENDAL** I nee slay'd him. He got away.

**LILJA** Fengo got away? You let Fengo get away?
You let Fengo, clobberer, cockswipe—GET AWAY?

**HORVENDAL** Forget it, girl—it's done.

**LILJA** You said you slay'd him—you said you putt him i' the ground—you said you whippd him, wiped him from the surface of God's Earth!

**HORVENDAL** I said no such thing! Calm yerself down.
The nightmare is over, girl. Let's eat.

*Pause.*

**LILJA** We're turnin back.

**HORVENDAL** What?

**LILJA** I said, we're turnin back! We're turnin around to do what you said you'd do but didn't, you lying floundering SLAVE!!

**HORVENDAL** No we ain't!

*She explodes, punching, kicking him.*

**LILJA** Coward! Coward! You lying Christless Coward!
You deceiv'd—you LIED to prettygirl!
Yooouu stoat! You pus-leech! You worthless wastrel!
You cyst-ridden changeling from a dogg's arse!
Oh, SLAVE!

**HORVENDAL** Girl, yer mouth—yer the one said runn away!

**LILJA** Well yer the one swore he would slay Fengo!

**HORVENDAL** Well, girl, I gone and chang'd me mind!

**LILJA** You chang'd yer mind one too many times! I'm makin decisions now, Madd Boy, and I say we turn back!

**HORVENDAL** No! No! I smell a foul conclusion!
Please, girl, don't go!

**LILJA** Unhand me, child, I'll do yer jobb for ye.
What mov'd me to put my faith in you?
Ha! Madd Boy! Sadd Boy more like.
Give up yer sword Sadd Boy—now!

*HORVENDAL grabs the blade and slices his hand.*

**HORVENDAL** Owww!

**LILJA** Ha. Serves ye right.
Here—give up yer woolly cloakings too.
A Mann's job requires mannly garb,
As well as a Mann to fit them.
You—can wear my dress!

**HORVENDAL** Hey!

*She pulls off his hooded cloak, throws him her mantle.*

**LILJA** There. Lookit ye. Pretty little Sadd Boy.
From this time henceforth—Lilja shall be you!
Go on Sadd Boy. Get ye to Jerusalem.
Go tell Jesus why yer dressed like a girl!

**HORVENDAL** Wait, girl!

**LILJA** What, girl?

**HORVENDAL** Thou Shalt Not Kill!
Berserkery is not a strategy enough!

**LILJA** Stay you here. You gave me nowt but pain;
The Destinie of Worlds is built with Gutts, not Brains.
A wretch like you, 'tis best had died at birth,
Than wasted precious Time upon this Earth!

**HORVENDAL** But, girl, girl—

**LILJA** No words, no more!

**HORVENDAL** Girl, don't leave me—

**LILJA** VENGEANCE!

*She runs into the night. Wind and wolf-cry rise.*

**HORVENDAL** Oh no…

## Scene Twenty-Second

*The forest at night. Very dark.*

*Enter RAGNAR with Vikings. They catch their breath.*

**RAGNAR** No relentin, fellas, no relentin.
Moon or Sunn, we're bound to do this task.

**VIKING** Haill!

**RAGNAR** Tells ye what, me boys, tells ye what,
Split we up and comb this icy Fenn.

**VIKINGS** Haill! Haill Ragnar! Haill!

**RAGNAR** Wait!

*RAGNAR speaks to his sword.*

What's the matter Skull-Byter, old boy?
Ye smell sommet? Ragnar smell sommet too.
Lie low everybody, lie low! Shh!!
Ohh stealth! Oh ambush! Here the Madd Boy comes!

*They all hide in the bushes. Enter LILJA as the Mad Boy, disguised in a cloak.*

**LILJA** Who's there? Who's that in there?
A skulking Viking. I aspose ye skulks fer mee.

Hello Plundermann. I can see yer helmet there!
Come on out the bunch o' yez,
Bring yer hellbound corses i' the light.

*They emerge.*

**RAGNAR** Well, well, well, if it int the Madd Boy.

**LILJA** Well, well, well, if it int the Dead Boys.

**RAGNAR** What've you done wi' the girl, Madd Boy?

**LILJA** Nothin youz ain't done already.
Come on—haul forth—rush me all at once.
Madd Boy's out to de-worm Denn-Mark!

*They surround her.*

**ALL** Ho ho! Brave notion! Oh Notion! Oh Brave!

**LILJA** Try and stop me, you lumbering slaves!

**RAGNAR** *(drawing his sword)* Behold yee Skull-Byter.

**LILJA** Skull-Byter? Arse-Byter more like!

**RAGNAR** Ohh laddie when I'm a-done wi' you,
There'll be nothin left o' you to burn.

**LILJA** Oh laddie when I'm a-done with you,
Oh you'll hang screamin on the gates of Hell.

**RAGNAR** Foolish Madd Boy!

**LILJA** Damn'd Dead Boy!

**RAGNAR** Prepare to die, Madd Boy!

**LILJA** Prepare yee to kiss the Devil's Arse!

**RAGNAR** HAA!

*RAGNAR swings and knocks the sword from her hands.*

Hey? What was you sayin?

*They both lunge for the sword. RAGNAR gets it and turns on LILJA with two swords.*

What was you sayin, Madd Boy, to mee?
Disgrace yee my Familie? Disgrace yee my Sword?
Hey Madd Boy? Hey? Who's a Madd Boy now?

**LILJA** *Liljaaa!!*

**RAGNAR** Axe-menn, axe-menn, let yer axes fall!
Shut up the Madd Boy once and for all!
Don't lettim get away boys—chop him! chop him!

*They all descend on her with swords and axes. Blackout. A horrible scream.*

## Scene Twenty-Third

*The next morning. The house of FENGO.*

**FENGO** Ahhh the morrow. The Christian Sunn's a-rised.
Another morn, a Golden Day is come;
Fengo's Day, the first of many pending,
What Good Deed shall Fengo render first?

**GERUTHA** Water, Fengo.

**FENGO** Nae chance, Mother.

**GERUTHA** I don't feel so good.

**FENGO** You don't feel so good?
Think how Fengo feels, seein yer gloomie face!
Go on! Quit bothrin me! Yer exploitin Fengo's charitie.

*A loud wailing offstage.*

What the hell is that?…

*Another wail.*

Sounds like bully Ragnar.

*Enter RAGNAR, weeping desperately, carrying a bloody bundle.*

**RAGNAR** Fengo!! Fengo!!

**FENGO** What's the matter with you?

**RAGNAR** Fengo—Fengo…

*He drops LILJA's mangled corpse.*

**FENGO** What have you got there?

**RAGNAR** Lilja, oh Liljaaa, oh sweet, ooh innocent child—

**FENGO** What you do to her. Ragnar?

**RAGNAR** I int done nothin! You can't pin nothin on me!
Madd Boy, he done this! I found her like that!

Oh girl, oh say something, sister!
Oh Skull-Byter—why didn't you tell me?

*FENGO prods her remains.*

**FENGO** She don't look very talkative.

**RAGNAR** Madd Boy, he done that.

**FENGO** Of course, me boy—you said.

**RAGNAR** It's true, Fengo, I dint do nothin! I barely murder'd her at all! Ohhh sister sister sister sister sister… that Madd Boy destroy'd everythin I ever lov'd…!

*He sobs convulsively.*

**FENGO** Boy, stop, ye needn't say aught else. Axemen, get this girl out of here.

**GERUTHA** I wish that was me.

*They drag the body out.*

**FENGO** Hie thee up, lad. Heft yer howlings inn.
Swabb that childish snooling from yer nose:
Suck yer pain back! Hold it in yer gutts!
Let it burn—and fuel ye for the chase!
Quit yer blubberin. She int our prioritie.
Where's the Madd Boy? He's still on the loose!

**RAGNAR** What sort of bastard chops up a little girl?
Promise, Fengo, you'll hang him on a tree!

**FENGO** Of course, boy.

**RAGNAR** With a sign on his neck, sayin "I chops up little girls"! She were my sister, Fengo, my little babie sister—
oooohhhHHHHH VENGEANCE!!

**FENGO** All right, ladd—look, ye can slay him.
But it has to seem a haccident, you hear?
Mulch him up and scrunch him up and down.
Make it look like the wolves done it.

**RAGNAR** Oh thank you, Fengo, thank you, thank you—

**FENGO** Aye, son.

**RAGNAR** Fengo, I swear o' me grave I nee done touch'd her!
I int no badmann Fengo, I int no lass-killer—

**FENGO** Course ye int, stoutie, yer a Christian Warrior. Now go.

**RAGNAR** Oh thank you, Fengo. Men, we're goin back ouside! C'mon Menn, we're allowed to kill the Madd Boy!

**ALL** Hurrrahh!

**RAGNAR** VENGEAAAANCE!!

*He storms out, followed by Vikings. Elsewhere, GERUTHA cradles the dead LILJA. She sings her lullaby.*

### Scene Twenty-Fourth

*A frozen swamp. Darkest night. Wolves run through the trees. The skeleton of a cannibalized wolf is left as they scatter. Enter HORVENDAL, delirious, wearing nothing but his breeches.*

**HORVENDAL** Where did I go wrong, fates? Where did I go wrong? Were it the time I stood by and forgave me uncle Fengo? Or the time I come to dream of this Revenge? Were it the time I came to faith in Jesus, or the time I cast him off? Or was it all those times wrong? Were it me birth what was wrong? Is anybody out there a-listenin to Horvendal? Hello? Or is the heavens dark, deserted; as empty as Fengo's Eye-hole? Aye, it's his Eye-hole, come to gulf me upp! Yawning, swirling, topless, bottomless! Help! Hello? What's here?

*He trips over the wolf skull, then lifts it up.*

I nae knew yee. I can guess ye well.
Where yer doggish soul went, there should Horvendal.
Howso died ye, sure it served you right,
And so I plummet howling, into that good night…

*He chops a hole in the ice with the skull.*

Go dead doggie! Show us the way!
Lead this Blind Boy into the Afterworld!

*He howls, plunges into the hole in the ice.*

### Scene Twenty-Fifth

*The hall at Helsingor.*

*GERUTHA crawls behind BROTHER PAAVO. She is in a terrible state.*

**GERUTHA** Brother Paavo. Brother Paavo.

**PAAVO** Aye, what is it?

**GERUTHA** I wants to ask you—

**PAAVO** Make it quick.

**GERUTHA** Is it true, Brother Paavo—is it true what it says—Jesus he lov'd even the wretchedest and lowest, the saddest, most brokedown souls on Earth?

**PAAVO** Aye.

**GERUTHA** Do ye think he'd a loved me too?

**PAAVO** Perhaps.

**GERUTHA** Ohhh if only he could! Baptize me, Brother Paavo, baptize me afore I dies…

**PAAVO** Nae, madam, I cannot.

**GERUTHA** What?

**PAAVO** Fengo said I int to baptize yee.

**GERUTHA** Not to baptize me? How am I to get to Heaven?

**PAAVO** Fengo said he don't want ye there.

**GERUTHA** Not to get to Heaven? Brother, I begs yer mercy! Take mercy on a repentant, dying woman!

**PAAVO** Sorry, madam. His whims I must permit.
Your Husband is God's Gateway to the Danes.
Without his might, our influence is naught.
For the greater good, madam. Forgive me.

*Enter FENGO, with Vikings and Brother PETRI.*

Morning, Lord Fengo.

**FENGO** What's goin on in here?
Didn't I tells you not to talk to the Bretherens?

**GERUTHA** But—

**FENGO** Didn't I tells you, woman—not to talk to the Bretherens?
Oh wife of mine! This Betrayall o' yers cuts deep!
I'm a-startin to doubts yer Loyaltie!

**GERUTHA** But I'm dyin, Fengo! I'm dyin—

**FENGO** Aye, woman, so you said.

**GERUTHA** Fengo—curse you. Look upon these eyes.
You've slain me! I—HATE you Fengo!!

**FENGO** Aaah! She hates me. Now the Truth comes out:
Now you see the source of Fengo's grief!
Hie thee hence, Old Mortality; float away you old stool,
Hasten yer demise—aquitt ye this realm.
This hand—will hoist youz up no more.

*Pause.*

**GERUTHA** Yooou'll suffer for this, Fengo, I know you will.
I don't know how, and I don't know when,
But I do know—it will be slooow, and bloody;
All the torture, all the grief what you've inflicted
Will come back upon you, Fengo, ohhh it shall!
An' I'll be laughin—my ghost will be laughin,
As you choke up bloody clumps of gore;
So die I, Fengo—free from out this hole.
At least in Hell—there's someone wants my soul…

*She dies. FENGO watches her. Pause.*

**FENGO** That woman broke my heart.

**PAAVO** She didn't mean it, Fengo, she were hysterical.

**FENGO** I gave my life to her.

**PAAVO** Peace good lord, leadership's a hard lot.

**FENGO** Alas, good brother, sometimes so it seems.
Perhaps true Loyaltie—comes only but in dreams…

*Dead LILJA sings.*

## Scene Twenty-Sixth

*The fens. Wolves howl.*

*HORVENDAL emerges from a frozen river, still alive.*

**HORVENDAL** Useless, useless—can't even drown meself.
Me gutts are e'en more guttless than me brains!
Where am I now? Further down the river.
It's washed me back, cross all the land I gain'd.

*A howl.*

Aye Wolvens, howl, howl!
Tear apart young Horvendal the fool!
Carry me off unto yer Wolfish Lair,
And do whate'er it is ye Were-wolves do.

Oh Death, tranquillity, haul me off to sleep.
Come on, come on, I'm tryin to freeze to death!

*A voice on the wind.*

**VOICE** Hoorvendaaal, Hoorvendaaal…

**HORVENDAL** Piss off! You bugger'd with my head!
Heyoff, Father, I heed you nott!
Go venge your bloodie self!

**VOICE** Hooorvendaaaal… Hooorvendaaaal…

**HORVENDAL** No! No! I'll drive you hence!
Come on out you Wormbound Warlord!
I'll crush your howling head!

*A rising light.*

What's this? Who's this? No! Not a Wolvish Spirit!
No…. No it can't be…
Where in hell were you?

*Out of the trees comes a bloody, ragged little man. He wears a crown of thorns and a loincloth. It is JESUS. The real JESUS. He cries tears of blood.*

**CHRIST** Madd Boy, Horvendal; to you the Christ must turn;
Behold your cast-out Saviour; Mankind will never learn.

**HORVENDAL** What??

**CHRIST** Ohh Horvendal: my shining shatterd Angell.
How you failed me! Failed my Path of Love.
Ohh my Hope-Child, how I tried to reach you!
All is soiled now. Listen to your Christ:

Turn Ye Back—Save my Strangled Gospel.
Turn Ye Back—Go Mend the Harm they've done.
Slay thine Uncle! Go take thy Viking Vengeance!
Stop him! Stop him! Oh Poisoned Love-Truth!
Turn Back—and Slay that Mann!

*He raises his arms. His wrists are pierced.*

**HORVENDAL** But your book says—

**CHRIST** All is soiled, Horvendal! Viking, go home.
Do as your savage heart bids you.

**HORVENDAL** Forgive me, Jesus.

**CHRIST** I wait for you…

**HORVENDAL** Forgive me!

*JESUS vanishes into the snow. Pause. HORVENDAL turns and faces north.*

Ohh Redemption. Redemption in the Night!
Ohh Shining Hope, you've found us!
We'll set these Fates aright!

Liljaa!

*He staggers back home.*

## Scene Twenty-Seventh

*An empty place by the sea. Early morning.*

*The two old sisters are weaving a shroud. ANNA has a pot of boiled seaweed.*

**INGA** Mornin, sister.

**ANNA** Aye, mornin.

**INGA** How be you today?

**ANNA** Got a splittin headache, don't I? Here, it may be my imaginin, but I'll swear when Fengo baptisd me, he delibrately pull'd my hair and shook me up and down.

**INGA** Well that's his way, innit? He loves his people, but it's a tough sort of love.

**ANNA** Aye but when I come up choking, he laughed a' me! That's not very nice. Thank Jesus I int in his family.

**INGA** Oh well, it ain't for us to question. Let's just sit back and complain and let our leaders destroy us.

**ANNA** Aye it's probly all for the best.

**INGA** Aye.

**ANNA** Here, what think ye of all this God and Jesus and Thunder-God stuff? Think ye it's true?

**INGA** Ohh, of course not. Lies and superstition. Everybody knows the world's rul'd by Elves.

*Behind them staggers a ranting HORVENDAL.*

Here, what's that? Comin over the hill!

**ANNA** Not another Ghost! Wait! It's the Madd Boy!

**INGA** Horvendal! It's the Young Horvendal!
Hoy ahoy! Good morrow, Madd Boy!

*HORVENDAL stops and looks at them.*

**HORVENDAL** I int no Coward!!

**ANNA** What did he say?

**INGA** He said I int no Coward.

**HORVENDAL** Fengo—

**INGA** And we int Fengo. We're two old wimmen.
He thinks we're Fengo!

**ANNA** You silly Madd Boy.

**HORVENDAL** Liljaaa… Liljaaaa…. Forgive me, Lilja…
Oh Liljaa… oh help—

*He collapses.*

**INGA** Well he's in a bad state.

**ANNA** Aye what do we do?

**INGA** Help him.

**ANNA** Help him? But he's an enemie o' the people!

**INGA** Enemy nothin. Look at the boy.

*INGA feeds him.*

Just think, sister, just think. To be cast out. To be a fugitive from the Law. To starve and suffer and perish. All for a-strivlin with his fates.

**ANNA** What a twitt.

**INGA** Still.

*The Mad Boy stirs.*

**HORVENDAL** Liljaaa—where is the girl Lilja?

**INGA** He speaks!

**HORVENDAL** You! Old wimmen! Where is the girl Lilja?

**ANNA** Who?

**INGA** The odd girl? The wee funnie one?

**ANNA** Funny you should ask. Sister and me we be weavin her shroud.

**HORVENDAL** Shroud? Shroud?

**ANNA** Aye, fer windin her up in! Cremation's tomorrow.

**INGA** She's died, you see.

**HORVENDAL** Died? But how?

**ANNA** Strook by a meteor. Int that what they said?

**HORVENDAL** AAAAHHHH!! DIED!! And Fengo lives! Oh spite!
I shine, I rise, girl—give us that Shroud!

**INGA** Hoy!

**HORVENDAL** Biddies, give us that Shroud—

*He grabs the shroud.*

Good wimmen assist me, I'll tell you what to do!

**INGA** Oh leave us out o' this, sonn. We're sick and feeble.

**ANNA** Aye, yer a big strong Madd Boy. You can murder Fengo by yerself.

**HORVENDAL** Wimmen, I beggs ye—

**INGA** Leave off of us, Madd Boy!

**ANNA** Here—don't be handlin my sister! Hoy!!

**INGA** Now go on—go on—or I'll hitt ye with this kelp!
We don't like ye no more. Nasty Madd Boy.

**ANNA** Aye.

*They drive him away.*

**HORVENDAL** When you and you and you and you are dead,
Who is it they'll remember? ME!
A Plague upon you lazie fatted stumps
What sitt and pick yer blisters and complain!
Who ist what fought for you? Who struggl'd for yer sinns?
Whose Tale will thunder, glorious, forever,
In lands unheard of, in glory-times to come?
ME! The Madd Boy. Horvendal—that's who!
You watch me world, watch me! I done this all for you!
SALVATION!!

*He staggers off. The old wimmen look at each other.*

**ANNA** Hmm.

**INGA** Anyway…

*They go back to work.*

### Scene Twenty-The-Eighth

*FENGO's hall.*

*FENGO is drinking with the monks and Vikings.*

**FENGO** Hah haaaaa!! Dint the ol' girl flare up? Didn't she flare up like a blob o' fish-oil? Burn'd fer hours she. Brighter than a torch! 'Spect its all the lard an' blubber like, hey? All them pancakes she ett in her stupid life! Hey, Brother Paavo, hey?

**PAAVO** She was your wife.

**FENGO** Ahhh, I'll get over it. I'll get me a new one. Besides, it int Fengo's way to be sadd. Drink up! Tomorrow we burn the little girl. Old whatisnames's girl. Haa, ye shoulda seen her knucklehead brother when he dragg'd her carcass home. Howl'd like a babie. What a twit. Cheers lads—to the clergy!

**ALL** To the clergy! To the clergy!

**FENGO** Here, Brother Paavo, watch us drink ale thru our nose.

*Enter RAGNAR, exhausted, tears in his eyes.*

**RAGNAR** Fengo!

**FENGO** Ragnar, what are you doing here?

**RAGNAR** I can't find the bugger.

**FENGO** Well I said don't come back till you did!

**RAGNAR** A man's gotta sleep.

**FENGO** A man's gotta sleep. Listen to the boy, Brother Paavo.

**PAAVO** You pixie!

**FENGO** See, laddie, the Church condemns ye!
You go right back outside and fetch the Madd Boy!

*FENGO and the monks laugh.*

**RAGNAR** You… DOGG, Fengo! You gutstuffin cur!

**FENGO** What did you say?

**RAGNAR** You int done nothin, Fengo, to help me in this task!

**FENGO** I have too.

**RAGNAR** You have NOTT! You been sittin on yer lazie arse stuffin yer face! I done everything! I been huntin him fer days! He int nowhere, I tells you! Nowhere!

**FENGO** Well you don't look good enough.

**RAGNAR** You just sit there all smarlyfaced sayin "Jesus Christ did this, Jesus Christ did that." You ain't no leader, yer a slobb!

**FENGO** Say that again?

**RAGNAR** Look at you, you fat pig! Ere, you got food in yer beard! Leaders is suppos'd to be inspirin. Yer fuckin disgustin, Fengo!

**FENGO** What did you say? *(rising)* Are you challengin Fengo in front of these Holy Brothers?

**RAGNAR** I'm sayin—

**FENGO** I'm sayin, do as yer told. Remember who I am, laddie, cripple or not. You want inspirin, I'll inspire you with this! *(swinging his crutch at him)* Now piss off—we're havin a theological conference. Go on, I say! Lagabout boy. Thank God he's got his father's brains! Ha!

*RAGNAR leaves.*

You—Songman. Writes us a song.

**VIKING** Aye, Lord Fengo.

**FENGO** Writes us a song—The Tale of Lord Fengo!
Speak of the Madd Boy, and his floundering misdeeds!!
Comb ye the northland, let it ring through every village!
Heyupp! Up yer bumms axe-menn! We're goin to a Funerall!

*Drums. Cheers. Scene change. The Viking sings:*

**VIKING** Wealth must die, and Kindred die,
A Man himself must likewise die,
But Fame and Glory never die,
For him who achieves it well;
Goats must die, and Kindred die,
A Mann himself must likewise die,
But one thing is shall never die,
The Verdict on each Man who dies…

## Scene Twenty-Ninth

*The conclusion: Morning. Music: "Dies Irae."*
*The dragonhead crosses are erected. The north coast.*
*A great funeral pyre.*

*Enter the monks, Vikings, and villagers with torches.*
*A shrouded corpse is carried in, bound on a bier. FENGO wears pious gear. The body is tossed on the pyre.*

**FENGO** Hold off yer torches just a little while;
Gots to allow for any tardie guests.
Let's remember this girl, the example that she set.
A good and gentle angel, inspirin to us all…
At times like this, we often do reflect,
Does life, does death, harbour any hope?
Or is we haccidents, toss'd upon this earth,
Doomed to fight and hack each other's bones?
I tell ye verily, look upon this girl,
And try to say to mee, there's no hope for this world.

**PAAVO** Amen.

**FENGO** Courageous men of Denn-Mark:

An elemental battle is risin on our shores!
The Winds of Barbarism howl to engulf us.
Thursday mornin marks a new momentous Year;
The One Thousandth Annum of Our Lord Jesus Christ…
Will Denn-Mark stand for Crueltie or Mercie?
Is we Animals or is we Christian Menn?
See ye Godd! A change upon us now is come,
And all the World will soon know who we be!

**ALL** Amen.

**FENGO** But enough of me, what more ist can be said?
My humble words can never heal this loss.
All a man can say is—Godd is Love;
Let's torch this child, and praise the Lord above.

**ALL** Amen.

**RAGNAR** Hang on a sec afore ye burns her.
Ragnar wants to speak some parting words.

**FENGO** Dammit boy, we done wrapt her up.

**RAGNAR** Shut up, Fengo—she's my sister and I'm gonna say my bit!

**FENGO** Grrrr. Hurry up.

*RAGNAR holds up his sword.*

**RAGNAR** I, Ragnar, sonn of dead Matthius,
Do here give up Skull-Byter, sword o' me
granpapaa.
Lie thou, Skull-Byter, keep this girl from harm,
Ragnar the Brave—shall ne'er again bear arms.

**FENGO** What are ye doing?

**RAGNAR** Farewell, sister. Fare thee well, Skull-Byter.
May all fighting men heed my example.

**FENGO** Oh fuck, not another one.

**RAGNAR** What's this?

*HORVENDAL is inside LILJA's shroud. He seizes the sword.*

**HORVENDAL** Haaaa!!

**RAGNAR** Madd Boy!!

**FENGO** Horvendal!!

*HORVENDAL leaps out and impales RAGNAR on Skull-Byter.*

**HORVENDAL** Die, bullyboy!

**PAAVO** Fly bretheren!

**HORVENDAL** And this is for you, and this is for you, and this is for you too!! *(stabbing RAGNAR)* Had enough?

**RAGNAR** Bless you, Madd Boy… thou hast served me well…

*He dies. HORVENDAL turns on the crowd.*

**HORVENDAL** Stand still! Don't any of ye move.
Madd Boy's come to claim his Shining Fate:
You rook'd my Godd—and you slew my Lovelass.
Come here, Fengo, you Cancer o the Earth.

*Commotion.*

Nobody move! Drop your weapons!
Forward Slaughterlord—I'll cutt you from this realm.

**PAAVO** Hold, stand back—beware the rage of heathens.

**FENGO** Never mind, I'll address the boy meself.

**HORVENDAL** You got no right to be wearin that Cross.

**FENGO** Boy, let us negotiate like civilized men.

**HORVENDAL** Never, Fengo! Kneel! Get yer just dessertt!
Brace yerself. It's gonna fuckin hurtt.

**FENGO** Boy, I begs ye, have mercy on a old sinner.

**HORVENDAL** Don't tell us. Tell it to Jesus Christ.

**FENGO** Haill Lord Horvendal—thou art most fitt for Lord!
Haill Lord Horvendal—and so let fall thy Sword.

*FENGO kneels. HORVENDAL raises the sword.*

**PETRI** Peace, fiend of Denn-Mark! Touch not that goodlie Man!
As Jesus spake of Mercie, you will not raise your hand!

**FENGO** Nay, it seems that Martyrdom's my Fate.
Love, as ever always, must be devour'd by Hate.

**HORVENDAL** Ohhhhh dear Uncle—at last is come the day.

**PETRI** No! We'll not allow this! Stand infidel—AWAY!!

*A Viking stabs HORVENDAL from behind. Other Vikings follow. HORVENDAL lashes violently at them all.*

**HORVENDAL** Ug....

**PAAVO** O savage, O monster, O beast!!

**HORVENDAL** O villanie, O vileness, O horror!!

*Brother PETRI seizes a wooden cross out of the ground. Impales the Mad Boy from behind. The crowd gasps. HORVENDAL drops to his knees, skewered on the dragonhead cross. Pause.*

**PETRI** And so die all murderers.

**VIKING** I int no murderer, Fengo, he swung at me first.

**FENGO** Of course, man, of course.

**PETRI** Shhhh! The heathen speaks.

*Pause.*

**HORVENDAL** Ohhh Death... oh Shining-Hope escaped us...
This little storm-bark's finally run aground...
Hear me, Denn-Mark! Behold my spatter'd Fate:
If Fengo stands for Mercy,
Then Madd Boy dies—for Hate.

*He spits blood at FENGO.*

Liljaa...

*He dies. Pause.*

**FENGO** Well done, my Christian Soldiers.

**PETRI** Hail Fengo!

**ALL** HAIL!!

**PAAVO** Oh wise and noble Lord,
How art we saved from barbarous destruction!

**PETRI** Art well, Lord Fengo—art thou unscraped?

**FENGO** Of course, Good Holy Brother, thou hast serv'd me well.

**PAAVO** Praise God!

**VIKINGS** HAIL FENGO!!

**VIKING** Fengo the Confessor—Saviour of the Danes!

**ALL** HOORRAYY!!

*Pause. FENGO stands forth. Drums sound.*

**FENGO** If aught of woe or wonder you've beheld,
Then look upon this tragic specktical;
Let a stone be raised upon this barren ground,
Telling this, the sadd and sorry tale of our children:
These boys lie, and soon will be cremated,
Consum'd by Hatred, festring in their Hearts:
How many others walk about us in our midst,
With secret venom, welling in their souls?
Let these deaths stand as grim example to us all,
And their tale retold, till the termination of the world…
The guilty are all dead, the grieving are consoled:
May Jesus Christ Almighty have mercy on our Souls.
Amen.

**ALL** Amen.

*Music. The company proceeds out. The stage is dark, empty, littered with the dead. The wind howls. Blackout.*

*The end.*

# HARLEM DUET

DJANET SEARS

## THE SHAKESPEARE'S MINE

Actor, director, playwright, and anthologist Djanet Sears is a major driving force behind contemporary AfriCanadian drama. Born Janet Sears in London, England, in 1959 to a Jamaican mother and Guyanese father, she came with her family to Saskatoon in 1974, and then Oakville, Ontario, in 1975. She studied theatre at York University in the late 1970s, and also studied at the Canadian Film Centre in 1999, and at New York University.

Sears is now known as a multi-award-winning playwright, author of *Afrika Solo* (premiered in 1987), *Double Trouble* (1988), *The Mother Project* (with Sangoma, the Woman's Co., 1991), *Who Killed Katie Ross?* (CBC radio, 1990; stage, as part of Ground Zero Productions's *Stolen Lands*), *Harlem Duet* (1997), and *The Adventures of a Black Girl in Search of God* (2002). She has won the silver prize at the 1991 Radio Festival of New York and an International Armstrong Award for outstanding radio drama for the radio version of *Afrika Solo*; the Dora and Chalmers Awards for outstanding new play for *Harlem Duet* in 1997, and the Governor General's Literary Award for published drama for *Harlem Duet* in 1998; the 1997 Phenomenal Woman of the Arts Award; the 1998 Harry Jerome Award for Excellence in the Cultural Industries; the Martin Luther King Jr. Achievement Award in 2003 in recognition of her contribution to the establishment of the black arts movement in Canada; a nomination for the Trillium Book Award in 2004 for *The Adventures of a Black Girl in Search of God*; the Stratford Festival's 2004 Timothy Findley Award for playwriting; and the Canadian Screenwriting Award for best radio play in 2005 for the radio adaptation of *Adventures*. *Harlem Duet* holds the distinctions of being the first play by an African-Canadian at Toronto's Canadian Stage company (in 1998), and the first play written by a person of African descent to be produced at the Stratford Festival (in 2006). *Adventures of a Black Girl in Search of God* has the distinction of a six-month commercial run with Mirvish Productions in Toronto. Sears was international artist-in-residence at the Joseph Papp Public Theatre in New York in 1996, in 2000 was appointed adjunct professor at the University of Toronto, and in 2004 was writer-in-residence at the University of Guelph.

But it wasn't always thus. Janet Sears was active in Toronto's small theatre scene throughout the 1980s, but her self-invention—and with herself, her virtual invention of an entire theatrical community—began with a trip to Africa that led to the writing of her first play, the autobiographical *Afrika Solo*. The play is about attempting to discover a coherent sense of self by going "home" to Africa, but "Janet" finds herself divided when she arrives there: "What the hell am I doing here in my ancestral *homeland*, my cultural *birthplace*," she asks, "feeling *homesick*" (78)? But she *does* "find," or maybe just reconstruct herself there, in part through embodiment, and she doesn't return without having undergone a transformation that recognizes her hybridized identity as "African Canadian. Not coloured, or negro. Maybe not even black. African Canadian" (88). Her transformation most significantly involves choice, and agency in the construction of a social identity that the show seems to perform into existence. Midway through, Janet visits the Saharan oasis town of "Djanet" and its nearby African rock paintings. The experience is transformational. As she writes in a postcard to her parents:

> the rock paintings in Djanet are ten thousand years old. That's four hundred generations ago. Three hundred and ninety eight point two grandmothers ago. Can you imagine, people lived ten thousand years ago in Djanet? Love Janet
>
> *She crosses out her signature and replaces in with:*
>
> D.J.A.N.E.T (54–55)

This change is understood as both a choice and a return, as she at once transforms and seizes control of her social identity. "Her metamorphosis [...] complete" (according to a stage direction), she ends the show singing "That's love" "*in her own Canadian/ Caribbean/British style over the intense African rhythm*" (94).

So ends the show, but I would suggest that the real performance has just begun, as Djanet returns to Canada newly christened to (re)iterate performatively her new identity on stage, in life, and in her cultural work. In a very real sense it was with this show that Djanet Sears shifted from being an actor named Janet to being, not just a writer, but, individually and culturally, a *performer*: the Djanet Sears we now know.

The performance of *Afrika Solo* has served to mark not only Sears's own transformation, but the beginnings, too, of her performative transformation of the African-Canadian theatrical community. She has done this not only as playwright, bringing African-Canadian work into the mainstream, but also as the founding director in 1997 of the AfriCanadian Playwrights Festival, which has virtually invented the now significant African-Canadian playwriting community; as a founder in 1999 of Obsidian Theatre Company in Toronto; as the editor of the two glorious, fat volumes of *Testifyin'* (2000, 2003), the first national anthologies of African-Canadian plays; as the editor of *Tellin' It like It Is* (2000), the first collection of audition monologues for African-Canadian actors; and as the co-editor of a special issue of *Canadian Theatre Review* on *African Canadian Theatre (Honouring the Word)*. Djanet Sears, then, has not only invented, or reinvented, herself as a cultural performer, she has, as such, been a prime mover in the invention of an African-Canadian theatre.

Part of Sears's individual and collective self-invention has involved the deconstruction of harmful representations that have been imposed upon people of African descent ever since the invention of "race" in the European so-called Renaissance. And chief among those representations are the works of Shakespeare. With *Harlem Duet* Djanet Sears at once *claims* Shakespeare for people of African descent and "talks back" to him. A compelling "prequel" to Shakespeare's play—set in 1860, 1928, and the present, and telling the story of Othello's black first wife, Billie—*Harlem* Duet claims a place for black writers in the canon of Western drama.

There are very few black characters in Shakespeare: Aaron, the villainous Moor in *Titus Andronicus*; the prince of Morocco in *The Merchant of Venice*, disliked by Portia for his "complexion"; perhaps Cleopatra, in *Antony and Cleopatra*, rarely cast as black (though her attendants often are); and above all the tragic hero Othello, "Moor of Venice," in the play named after him. Yet through these characters Shakespeare has had an overwhelming influence on the representation of Blackness throughout modern history. His Othello is a warrior: exotic, noble, savage, credulous, "one who loved not wisely but too well." He is the "other" of Western civilization.

Each of Shakespeare's black characters appears alone, stranded in a white world, devoid of history or community, and each lives, suffers rejection, or dies at the hands of an alien culture. Not so Sears's Othello, who lives in Harlem, the twentieth century's centre of African diasporic culture. In the world of *Harlem Duet*, Shakespeare is the outsider, surrounded on the bookshelves by *African Mythology* and *Black Psychology*, and in the play by central moments, speeches, and images from black history. Indeed, if on one level the play takes place at the intersection of Shakespeare and black North American culture, it most literally takes place at the heart of that culture, at the intersection of Harlem's Martin Luther King and Malcolm X Boulevards. The play's "duets" are played out between the assimilationist Othello ("at a deeper level we're all the same") and the separatist Billie ("I'm not the same"), representing the respective positions of King and Malcolm X. The play also directly represents the history of slavery and blackface minstrelsy in its crucial 1860 and 1928 actions.

Within this epic cultural canvas, *Harlem Duet* is centrally concerned with the intersection of race and gender. It is permeated by stories of black men in relationships with white women—the central fact of *Othello*, but viewed from a different angle. Sears's Othello leaves Billie for Mona because "with white women it's easier." His 1860 slave counterpart reneges on plans to escape to Canada with *his* black lover out of loyalty to the white woman who owns him. His 1928 minstrel counterpart betrays *his* black lover for the woman who casts him only in black roles, out of longing (echoing Shakespeare) for "skin as smooth as monumental alabaster." Even Billie's father, Canada, "the drunk of Dartmouth," has dated a white woman, Debbie, with her "stubby little beige legs." In this context, if the play is, as Sears says, a "rhapsodic blues tragedy," its tragedy is that of the black woman, with a history "trapped inside" her. It is a story Shakespeare failed to tell, one largely untold in drama to this day, but one that most fully represents through black women's lives "what hundreds of years of slavery did to the African American psyche."

If *Harlem Duet* invokes Shakespearean tragedy, then, as "*rhapsodic blues* tragedy," it does more than that. It evokes community, history, and agency in a world unlike Shakespeare's, where black people make choices and build communities, as Djanet Sears's own work has consistently done since her own self-invention in 1987. It soars with poetry, simmers with the blues, and finally celebrates a vibrant diasporic culture and community in which pain, loss, and betrayal occur, but healing has begun.

**Work Cited**

Sears, Djanet. *Afrika Solo*. Toronto: Sister Vision, 1990.

*Harlem Duet* premiered on April 24, 1997, as a Nightwood Theatre production at the Tarragon Extra Space, Toronto, with the following company:

| | |
|---|---|
| BILLIE | Alison Sealy-Smith |
| OTHELLO | Nigel Shawn Williams |
| MAGI | Barbara Barnes Hopkins |
| AMAH/MONA | Dawn Roach |
| CANADA | Jeff Jones |

| | |
|---|---|
| Double Bass | Lionel Williams |
| Cello | Doug Innes |

Directed by Djanet Sears, assisted by Maxine Bailey
Set and costume designed by Teresa Przybylski
Lighting design by Lesley Wilkinson
Music composition and arrangement by Lionel Williams
Music and sound design by Allen Booth
Stage Management by Cheryl Francis, assisted by Andrea Ottley
Dramaturgy by Diane Roberts and Kate Lushington

## CHARACTERS

OTHELLO, a man of forty, present day
HE, Othello, 1928
HIM, Othello, 1860

BILLIE, a woman of thirty-seven, present day
SHE, Billie, 1928
HER, Billie, 1860

CANADA, Billie's father, sixty-seven
AMAH, Billie's sister-in-law, thirty-three
MAGI, the landlady, forty-one
MONA, white, thirties (an offstage voice)

## SETTING

Late summer.

Harlem: 1928, a tiny dressing room.

Harlem: the present, an apartment in a renovated brownstone, at the corner of Martin Luther King and Malcolm X boulevards (125th & Lennox).

Harlem: 1860, on the steps to a blacksmith's forge.

# HARLEM DUET

*...That handkerchief*
*Did an Egyptian to my mother give.*
*She was a charmer...*
*There's magic in the web of it.*
*A sibyl... in her prophetic fury sewed the work.*
**—William Shakespeare, *Othello* (3.4.57–74)**

## ACT ONE

### Prologue

*Harlem, 1928: late summer—night. As the lights fade to black, the cello and the bass call and respond to a heaving melancholic blues. Martin Luther King's voice accompanies them. He seems to sing his dream in a slow polyrhythmic improvisation, as he reaches the climax of that now-famous speech given at the March on Washington. Lights up on a couple in a tiny dressing room. SHE is holding a large white-silk handkerchief, spotted with ripe strawberries. She looks at HE as if searching for something. He has lathered his face and is slowly erasing the day's stubble with a straight razor. She looks down at the handkerchief.*

**SHE** We keep doing this, don't we?

**HE** I love you... But—

**SHE** Remember... Remember when you gave this to me? Your mother's handkerchief. There's magic in the web of it. Little strawberries. It's so beautiful—delicate. You kissed my fingers... and with each kiss a new promise you made... swore yourself to me... for all eternity... remember?

**HE** Yes. Yes... I remember.

*Pause.*

**SHE** Harlem's the place to be now. Everyone who's anyone is coming here now. It's our time. In our place. It's what we've always dreamed of... isn't it?

**HE** Yes.

**SHE** You love her?

**HE** I… I wish—

**SHE** Have you sung to her at twilight?

**HE** Yes.

**SHE** Does your blood call out her name?

**HE** Yes.

**SHE** Do you finger feed her berries dipped in dark and luscious sweets?

**HE** Yes.

**SHE** Have you built her a crystal palace to refract her image like a thousand mirrors in your veins?

**HE** Yes.

**SHE** Do you let her sip nectar kisses from a cup of jade studded bronze from your immortal parts?

**HE** Yes.

**SHE** Does she make your thoughts and dreams and sighs, wishes and tears, ache sweet as you can bear?

**HE** Yes.

**SHE** Do you prepare her bed, deep in fragrant posies, rosemary, forget-me-nots, and roses, anoint her feet with civet oil, lotus musk, and perfumes, place them in gossamer slippers with coral clasps, amber beads and buckles of the purest gold, kiss her ankles and knees, caress her fragrant flower, gently unfolding each petal in search of the pearl in her velvet crown?

**HE** Yes.

**SHE** You love her.

**HE** Yes. Yes. Yes.

*He wipes his face with a towel. She stares at the handkerchief laying in her bare hand.*

**SHE** Is she white?

*Silence.*

Othello?

*Silence.*

She's white.

*Silence.*

Othello…

*She holds the handkerchief out to him. He does not take it. She lets it fall at his feet. After a few moments he picks it up.*

### Scene One

*Harlem, present: late summer—morning. The strings thump out an urban melody blues/jazz riff, accompanied by the voice of Malcolm X, speaking about the nightmare of race in America and the need to build strong black communities.*

*MAGI is on the fire escape, leaning on the railing, reading a magazine with a large picture of a blond woman on the cover. As the sound fades she closes the magazine, surveying the action on the street below.*

**MAGI** Sun up in Harlem. *(She spots the postman.)* Morning, Mr. P.! Don't bring me no bill now—I warned ya before, I'm having a baby. Don't need to get myself all worked up, given my condition… I'm gonna have me a Virgo baby, makes me due 'bout this time next year… I can count. I just haven't chosen the actual father/husband candidate as yet. Gotta find me a man to play his part. I wanna conceive in the middle of December, so I've booked the Convent Avenue Baptist church for this Saturday. The wedding's at three. You sure look to be the marrying kind. What you up to this weekend, yourself sweetness? Oh well then, wish your wife well for me. Package from where? California? Oohh. Yeh, yeh, yeh. I'll be right— Hey, hey, Amah girl… Up here… Let yourself in… *(She throws a set of keys down to AMAH.)* Mr. P., give that young lady the package… Yeh, she'll bring it up for me. *(beat)* Thank you, sugar. *(beat)* You have yourself a nice day now. All right, sweetness. Mmn, mmn, mmn!

*AMAH unlocks the door, enters, and makes her way to the fire escape.*

**AMAH** Magi, look at you, out on the terrace, watching the summer blossoms on the corner of Malcolm X and Martin Luther King Boulevards.

**MAGI** Nothing but weeds growing in the Soweto of America, honey. *(shouting out)* Billie!

**AMAH** Where is she?

**MAGI** I didn't want to wake her up till you got here. She didn't get to sleep till early morning. I could hear her wailing all the way downstairs.

**AMAH** I can see a week. A couple of weeks at the most. But what is this?

**MAGI** Two months—it's not like she's certifiable, though.

*Shouting gently to BILLIE in the bedroom.*

Billie! Billie, Amah's here!

**AMAH** Well, least she sleeps now.

**MAGI** She's stillness itself. Buried under that ocean of self-help books, like it's a tomb. Like a pyramid over her. Over the bed. *(calling out once more)*

Billie!

*BILLIE's body moves slightly and an arm listlessly carves its way to the surface, shifting the tomb of books, several dropping to the floor.*

*MAGI and AMAH make their way inside. On a large table is a vase filled with blossoming cotton branches. There is also a myriad of bottles and bags, and a Soxhlet extraction apparatus: flask, extractor, and thimble, condenser, siphoning hoses, all held up by two metal stands. A Bunsen burner is placed under the flask.*

I'm just making her some coffee, can I get you a cup?

*AMAH inspects the table and searches for a space to put the small package.*

**AMAH** Thanks, Magi. Where d'you want this? It looks like a science lab in here.

**MAGI** Some healing concoction I've been helping her make—but she's way ahead of me these days. She's got a real talent for herbs, you know. She's been sending away for ingredients—I can't even figure out what most of them are—put the package down anywhere.

**AMAH** If I can find a space.

**MAGI** Right there. On top of that alchemy book—right in the middle. Yeh. Thanks for doing this, Amah. For coming. It'll make her feel like a million dollars again.

**AMAH** Please. Billie and me go so far back, way before Andrew. Besides, sister-in-laws are family too, you know. Jenny's been simply begging to come and see her, you know, for their once-a-week thing. They eat sausages, mashed potatoes, and corn. Some Canadian delicacy I guess—

**MAGI** Aren't you guys vegetarians?

**AMAH** Vegan.

**MAGI** Vegan?

**AMAH** We don't eat anything that has eyes. The sausages are tofu. You know they eat exactly the same thing every time. I was glad for the break. I guess I was kinda… well… it bugged me. Jenny's always full of Auntie Billie this, Auntie Billie that. Now I miss our one night a week without her. I mean—our time alone. And I see how it's a kind of security for her.

**MAGI** Security for who?

**AMAH** Oh, I can't rent your ground floor. They won't give me any insurance 'cause I don't have a licence. And I can't get a licence until I get a cosmetician's certificate. And I can't get a cosmetician's certificate until I finish this two-year course on how to do white people's hair and make-up. I told them, ain't no white people in Harlem. I'd learn how to do work with chemical relaxers and Jheri curls. Now, I do dreadlocks. And do they teach that? Oh no. They're just cracking down on people who do hair in private homes—something about lost tax revenues. I don't know… I want my own salon so bad I can taste it. "The Lock Smiths."

**MAGI** "The Lock Smiths."

**AMAH** Billie's supposed to be helping me with the business plan. Besides, we've started trying for kid number two. I need the space.

**MAGI** You're trying?

**AMAH** I'm ten days late.

**MAGI** No!

**AMAH** It's still early. Don't tell Billie… you know. I'll tell her.

**MAGI** Good for you, girl! Did I tell you I was having a baby?

**AMAH** Oh yeh. How was he, that new candidate you were telling me about… Warren, no Waldo—

**MAGI** Wendel? Wedded Wendel as I've discovered.

**AMAH** He didn't tell—

**MAGI** Oh no. He believes that the nuclear family is the basis for a healthy society. That's why he's married. He keeps his own personal nuclear family at home in the event that he might someday want to spend time with it.

**AMAH** Why'd you stop seeing George. I liked George.

**MAGI** Well I liked him, too.

**AMAH** You two looked pretty serious there for a while.

**MAGI** We'd been seeing each other the better part of… what… two years. I'm just not getting any younger. I mean, I kept dropping hints I was ready for him to pop the question. Seems like he don't know what question I'm referring to. So I decided to give him some encouragement. See, I've been collecting things for my trousseau, and I have this negligee… all white, long, beautiful lacy thing. Looks like a see-through wedding gown. So, I'm out on my balcony—you know, 'cause it's too hot inside, and I still ain't got around to putting in air conditioning. Anyway, I see him coming up the street. So I rush in and put on the wedding dress negligee, thinking, he'll see me in it, all beautiful like—want to pop the question, you know. So I open the door, me in the negligee, and he… He stands there. Mouth wide open. And he says, he guess he should go get a bottle of wine, seeing how this was gonna be some kind of special occasion an' all. Now I don't know whether he got lost… or drunk… But I ain't seen or heard from him since.

**AMAH** Aahh nooo.

**MAGI** I should have margarined his butt when I had the chance.

**AMAH** Margarined his backside?

**MAGI** If you want to bind a man—

**AMAH** You don't mean what I think you mean?

**MAGI** If you want to keep a man, then you rub his backside with margarine.

**AMAH** And it works?

**MAGI** I don't know. When I'd remember I could never figure out how to get from the bed to the refrigerator.

**AMAH** Margarine, huh?

**MAGI** But you've got to be careful. He might be a fool. You don't want to be dragging no damn fool behind you the rest of your days.

**AMAH** You're a regular charmer, girl.

**MAGI** Don't get me wrong. I don't cut the heads off chickens or anything now.

**AMAH** You know, a Jamaican lady told me about one where you rinse your underwear and use the dirty water to cook the meal.

**MAGI** Nooo! Really?

**AMAH** Really.

**MAGI** Ooh, I like that. Boil down some greens in panty stock. Hmm!

**AMAH** Once I buried his socks under the blackberry bush by the front door. Sure enough, he always finds his way back home.

**MAGI** How is True Drew?

**AMAH** Oh, Andrew's real good. You know him. He was up here till late, night before last even, playing broad-shouldered brother.

**MAGI** Yep, he's a good man. They're rare. And he went all the way down to DC for the Million Man March. Yeh, he's one in a million. If you ever think of trading him in…

**AMAH** Don't even think about it!

**MAGI** Can't blame a girl for trying. *(calling out again)* Billie! Billie, you up yet?

*MAGI gets no response. She goes into the bedroom.*

Billie? Billie, sorry to wake you, but Amah's here. She waiting.

*BILLIE emerges. We recognize her as the woman in the prologue. She slowly makes her way to the edge of the bed.*

**BILLIE** If I could only stop dreaming, I might be able to get some rest.

**MAGI** You should jot them down. They're messages from other realms, you know.

**BILLIE** Jenny's in a large, white room—the walls start pressing in all around her…

**MAGI** You okay?

**BILLIE** Mm mm. Yeh. I'm fine. I'm good.

**MAGI** *(gently)* Come on, sweetheart, Amah's waiting.

**BILLIE** Let me just wash my face, and my mouth.

*MAGI leaves BILLIE to join AMAH, who is now on the fire escape.*

**MAGI** She's coming…

*AMAH hands MAGI a cup of coffee.*

Ooh… Thanks.

**AMAH** How is she?

**MAGI** Better. Dreaming hard, though. Like she's on some archeological dig of the unconscious mind.

**AMAH** His words hit her hard, huh.

**MAGI** Like a baseball bat hits a mango. Like he was trying for a home run or something. The bat breaks through the skin, smashing the amber flesh, propelling her core out of the park, into the clouds. And she lays there, floating.

**AMAH** Feeling sorry for herself.

**MAGI** A discarded fruit sitting in a dish, surrounded by its own ripening mould.

**AMAH** She feels so much.

**MAGI** Yeh. Each of her emotions sprout new roots, long, tangled things, intersecting each other like strangle weed.

**AMAH** She should go out though, get some fresh air once in a while.

**MAGI** She does. Her trips out into the real world are brief, though. The grocer's for tubs of things you add water to she calls food, the pharmacy for the pills, and the bookstore. All her money goes up in smokes and writings that tell her she really ain't out of her mind. They'd make her feel better, more beautiful, more well, until she'd see some nice chocolate brown-skinned man, dangling his prize in front of her. 'Cause all the rot inside her would begin to boil, threaten to shoot out. So she comes home, takes some pills and sleeps again that fitful sleep till she wakes.

**AMAH** So she knows?

**MAGI** Ooh she knows. She knows she's still up there in the clouds.

**AMAH** She never used to be like that, you know, about colour.

**MAGI** Guess it ain't never been personal before.

**AMAH** But it seems bigger than that…

**MAGI** Girl, you've been married what… six years?

**AMAH** Seven this February coming…

**MAGI** How'd you feel if Drew just upped and left you?

**AMAH** I can't even imagine…

**MAGI** They've been together nine.

**AMAH** She still moving?

**MAGI** So she say… asked me to pick up some boxes.

**AMAH** *(quietly)* Rumour has it he's getting married.

**MAGI** So soon. He hasn't told her anything. He still hasn't even moved his stuff yet.

**AMAH** And she sacrificed so much. Gave up her share of the trust from her mother's life insurance to send him through school.

**MAGI** No!

**AMAH** So when it's her turn to go… All those years.

**MAGI** And those babies.

**AMAH** Yeh, thank God they didn't have any babies.

**MAGI** No, no… Twice…

**AMAH** No!

**MAGI** First time, he told her he believed in a woman's right to choose, but he didn't think that the relationship was ready for—

**AMAH** We didn't—

**MAGI** Nobody did. Second time she miscarried.

**AMAH** When? I don't—

**MAGI** 'Bout the same time he left—no, it was before that. She was by herself… Set down in a pool of blood. She put it in a Ziploc bag… in the freezer… all purple and blue…

**AMAH** Oohh God… No… Really?

**MAGI** Yeh.

**AMAH** Nooo… For real. I'm serious…

**MAGI** Yeh!

**AMAH** Show me.

*MAGI turns toward the living area and heads for the kitchen; AMAH follows closely behind. They approach the fridge and MAGI is about to open the freezer door when BILLIE enters from the bedroom. AMAH and MAGI stop abruptly, as if caught in the act.*

Billie!

**MAGI** *(overlapping)* Hey girl!

*BILLIE waves to them as she exits into the bathroom. MAGI turns to AMAH.*

Or maybe I lied. Gotcha!

**AMAH** You… You… little heifer—

*MAGI laughs. AMAH gets infected and joins her.*

### Scene Two

*Harlem, 1860: late summer—twilight. The instruments sing a blues from deep in the Mississippi delta, while a mature northern-American voice reads from the Declaration of Independence. HIM steeps hot metal into cool water. He places the shackles on an anvil and hammers the metal into shape. HER is making repairs to a shawl with a needle.*

**HER** I pray Cleotis is in Heaven.

**HIM** Yeh… I… um… I…

**HER** You think Cleotis went to Heaven?

**HIM** Well, I… I don't…

**HER** You think he's in hell?

**HIM** No. No.

**HER** Probably somewhere in between, though. Not Hades. Not God's kingdom. He's probably right there in the hardware store. Probably right there watching every time that Mr. Howard proudly hoists the mason jar. Every time they pay their penny to see through the formaldehyde. Cleotis is probably right there watching them gawk at his shrivelled, pickled penis… You seen it?

**HIM** No.

**HER** You know who did the cutting, though?

**HIM** No… Oh no…

**HER** In France they got the vagina of a sister entombed for scientific research.

**HIM** No!

**HER** Venus, the Hottentot Venus. I read it in one of Miss Dessy's books. Saartjie—that's her real name, Saartjie Baartman. When Saartjie was alive they paraded her naked on a pay-per-view basis. Her derrière was amply endowed. People paid to see how big her butt was, and when she died, how big her pussy was.

**HIM** Wooo!

**HER** Human beings went and oohed and ahhed and paid money to see an endowment the creator bestowed on all of us.

**HIM** That's… that's… so… so…

**HER** They probably go to a special place though—Cleotis and Venus, Emmett. Purgatory. Venus and Cleotis fall in love, marry, but have no tools to consummate it. Must be a lot of us there walking around in purgatory without genitals.

*Beat.*

**HIM** I've been meaning to… I want… *(laughing to himself)* I would like to…

**HER** Yes…?

**HIM** Talk. We should talk.

**HER** Talk-talk?

**HIM** Talk-talk.

**HER** About what…? What's wrong?

**HIM** Why must something be wrong—

**HER** I… I just figured… figure…

*HIM takes HER's hand and kisses it, then places a white handkerchief into her palm.*

**HIM** My heart…

*HIM closes HER's fingers around the handkerchief. He kisses her fingers. Opening her hand, she examines the cloth.*

**HER** Little strawberries on a sheet of white. Berries in a field of snow… *(sighing)* Ah silk. It's beautiful.

**HIM** It was my mother's. Given her by my father… from his mother before that. When she died she gave it me, insisting that when I found… chose… chose a wife… that I give it to her… to you, heart.

**HER** Oh… It is so beautiful.

**HIM** There's magic in the web of it.

**HER** So delicate… so old.

**HIM** A token… an antique token of our ancient love.

**HER** My ancient love…

**HIM** My wife. My wife before I even met you. Let's do it. There's a war already brewing in the south. Canada freedom come.

**HER** Yes?

**HIM** Yes.

**HER** We're really gonna go?

**HIM** People will come to me and pay me for my work.

**HER** Yes sir, Mr. Blacksmith, sir.

**HIM** Can we have us a heap of children?

**HER** Four boys and four girls.

**HIM** And a big white house.

**HER** A big house on an emerald hill.

**HIM** Yeh… a white house, on an emerald hill, in Canada. *(pause)* I want to be with you till I'm too old to know. You know that.

**HER** Even when my breasts fall to my toes?

**HIM** I'll pick them up and carry them around for you.

**HER** And when I can't remember my own name?

**HIM** I'll call it out a thousand times a day.

**HER** Then I'll think you're me.

**HIM** I am you.

**HER** And when I get old, and wrinkled, and enormously fat, you'll—

**HIM** Fat? Naw. If you get fat I'll have to leave your ass.

*HIM kisses inside the crook of HER's arm.*

**HER** Oh-oh. You're prospecting again.

**HIM** I'm exploring the heightening Alleghenies of Pennsylvania.

*HIM kisses HER.*

The curvaceous slopes of California.

*HIM kisses HER.*

The red hills of Georgia, the mighty mountains of New York.

*HIM kisses HER again.*

I'm staking my claim.

**HER** I don't come cheap, you know.

**HIM** I know… I'm offering more than money can buy.

**HER** How much more?

**HIM** This much.

*HIM kisses HER.*

**HER** I could buy that.

**HIM** Could you buy this?

*HIM kisses HER deeply.*

**HER** Beloved…

*HER kisses HIM.*

## Scene Three

*Harlem, the present: late summer—morning. Strains of a melodious urban blues jazz keeps time with an oral address by Marcus Garvey on the need for African-Americans to return to Africa.*

**MAGI** No, I hate it.

**AMAH** Come on. No one hates it.

**MAGI** I do.

**AMAH** Bah humbug?

**MAGI** What?

**AMAH** Scrooge?

**MAGI** Oh no, no, no. You know what I hate about Christmas? Seven days to New Year's Eve. And I hate New Year's Eve. And you know what I really hate about New Year's Eve? It's not the being alone at midnight. It's not the being a wallflower at some bash, because you fired your escort, who asked for time and a half after 10:00 p.m. It's not even because you babysat your friend's kids the previous two.

I really hate New Year's Eve because it's six weeks to Valentine's Day. And what I really really hate about Valentine's Day—well, maybe that's too strong. No. I really hate it. What I really hate about Valentine's Day is… it's my birthday. Don't get me wrong, now. I'm glad I was born. But I look at my life—I'm more than halfway through it, and I wonder, what do I have to show for it? Anyway…

**AMAH** Well, you come and spend Kwanzaa with us this year.

**MAGI** I don't know about the seven days, girl? Look, I gotta go. I'm seeing a certain minister about a certain wedding.

**AMAH** Whose wedding?

**MAGI** Mine. And don't say a thing—you know, about him getting married, or anything.

*MAGI indicates the refrigerator.*

**AMAH** Sealed.

**MAGI** I'll drop by later.

**AMAH** All right.

**MAGI** *(shouting)* Billie? I'm gonna drop by later with some boxes, okay?

**BILLIE** *(offstage)* Thanks, Magi.

*MAGI exits. AMAH goes to the table and examines the small chemical factory.*

**AMAH** Saracen's Compound… Woad… Hart's tongue… Prunella vulgaris…

*She picks up a book lying among the small packages and vials.*

*Egyptian Alchemy: A Chemical Encyclopedia…*

*She puts the book back in its place and picks up another vial.*

Nux Vomica, warning: Extremely poisonous. Can be ingested on contact with skin…

*AMAH quickly replaces the vial, wiping her hand on her clothes. She turns her attention to the kitchen. She cautiously approaches the refrigerator, and is about to open the freezer section when BILLIE comes out of the bathroom.*

**BILLIE** Hey, Amah.

**AMAH** Oh—hi, girl, how you feeling?

**BILLIE** Thanks for making the house call, Amah.

**AMAH** Child, you look so thin.

**BILLIE** Well, I'm trying to lose a little baby fat before I die.

**AMAH** Coffee?

**BILLIE** Oh… Thanks. *(pours coffee)* You didn't have to come. I'm fine, you know.

**AMAH** You're very welcome. Come sit down.

*AMAH hands her the cup.*

**BILLIE** I didn't mean… Thank you.

**AMAH** You washed your hair?

**BILLIE** Yesterday.

**AMAH** Good. A package came for you this morning.

**BILLIE** Where?

**AMAH** I put it beside the chemistry set. What is all that?

**BILLIE** Don't touch anything!

**AMAH** All right—all right. I—

**BILLIE** No. No. I—I mean, some of this stuff can be deadly unless mixed… or… or diluted. Some ancient-Egyptian rejuvenation tonic. If it don't kill me, it'll make me brand new—or so it says. How's my baby?

**AMAH** Jenny's fine. Andrew's taking her to her first African dance class today. You should see her in the little leotard…

**BILLIE** I should be there.

**AMAH** She's dying to come over for sausages and mashed potatoes.

**BILLIE** Yeh, yes, soon. Real soon.

*AMAH prepares to twist BILLIE's hair. She opens a jar of hair oil and takes a generous portion of the oil, rubs it onto her hands and gently works it into BILLIE's hair.*

**AMAH** She was so cute today—you know what she did? She overheard me talking to Andrew about you, and I was saying I thought your breakdown was—

**BILLIE** You told her I had a nervous breakdown?

**AMAH** Oh— No. No. She overheard me—

**BILLIE** I am not having a nervous breakdown.

**AMAH** She didn't really understand. She thinks you've broken your legs and can't walk, you can't dance. She thinks you've broken your throat, and that's why she can't talk to you on the phone, that's why you don't sing to her on the phone anymore.

**BILLIE** Please don't tell her I'm crazy.

**AMAH** I never said you were crazy.

**BILLIE** I've just been… tired. Exhausted. I… I didn't want her to see this in me. She'd feel it in me. I never want her to feel this…

**AMAH** I know.

**BILLIE** But I'm fine now. Really, I'll be fine. I registered for school, I'm only taking one course this term, but that's cool. And first thing next week I'm redoing the business plan for the salon.

**AMAH** You need to give me some of that tonic too, girl. That's the best kind of revenge, you know—living the good life.

**BILLIE** I thought I was living that life.

**AMAH** Maybe you were just dreaming.

*AMAH takes a new lock of BILLIE's hair. Taking a large dab of oil, she applies it to the lock, rubbing the strand between her palms.*

**BILLIE** Remember when we moved in? The day Nelson and Winnie came to Harlem, remember? Winnie and Nelson—our welcoming committee. They'd blocked off the whole of 125th—it took us forty-five minutes to convince the cops to let us through. And me and you and Othe and Drew went down to hear them speak. And Drew went off in search of some grits from a street vendor. And you asked me to hold baby Jenny while you went to the restroom, when this man came up to us and took our picture. Asked to take our picture. Jenny in my arms. Othello beside me. "The perfect black family." That's what he called us. "The perfect black family."

*The phone rings.*

**AMAH** I'll get it.

**BILLIE** No. Let it ring. I know who it is. I can still feel him—feel when he's thinking of me. We've spoken… Must be three times, in the last two months. Something about $500 on my portion of his American Express card, which they'd cancel if I didn't pay the bill. Seems I did me some consumer therapy. Last time he called—mad—to announce that the card had been cancelled by Amex, and that he hoped that
I was pleased.

*Beat.*

And I was. Is that crazy?

**AMAH** Don't sound crazy. Hold the hair oil for me.

**BILLIE** I used to pray that he was calling to say he's sorry. To say how he'd discovered a deep confusion in himself. But now…

*The phone stops ringing.*

I have nothing to say to him. What could I say? Othello, how is the fairer-sexed one you love to dangle from your arm, the one you love for herself and preferred to the deeper-sexed one, is she softer does she smell of tea roses and baby powder does she sweat white musk from between her toes do her thighs touch, I am not curious just want to know, do her breasts fill the cup of your hand the lips of your tongue not too dark, you like a little milk with your nipple don't you, no I'm not curious just want to know.

**AMAH** You tell Jenny colour's only skin deep.

**BILLIE** The skin holds everything in. It's the largest organ in the human body. Slash the skin by my belly and my intestines fall out.

**AMAH** Hold the hair oil up.

*AMAH takes a dab of oil from the jar.*

**BILLIE** I thought I saw them once, you know—on the subway. I had to renew my prescription. And I spot them—him and her. My chest is pounding. My legs can't move. From the back I see the sharp barber's line, separating his tightly coiled hair from the nape of the skin at the back of his neck. His skin is soft there… and I have to kick away the memory nudging its way into my brain. My lips on his neck, gently… holding him… Here, before me—his woman—all blond hair and blond legs. Her weight against his chest. His arm around her shoulders, his thumb resting on the gold of her hair. He's proud. You can see he's proud. He isn't just any Negro. He's special. That's why she's with him. And she… she… she flaunts. Yes, she flaunts. They are before. I am behind, stuck there on the platform. My tongue is pushing hard against the roof of my mouth… trying to hold up my brain, or something. 'Cause my brain threatens to fall. Fall down through the roof of my mouth and be swallowed up. Slowly, slowly, I press forward, toward them. I'm not aiming for them though. I'm aiming with them in mind. I'm aiming for beyond the yellow line, into the tracks. The tunnel all three of us will fall into can be no worse than the one I'm trapped in now. I walk—no, well hover, really. I'm walking on air. I feel sure of myself for the first time in weeks. Only to be cut off by a tall grey man in a grey uniform, who isn't looking where he's going, or maybe I'm not—Maybe he knew my aim. He looks at me. I think he looks at me. He brushes past. Then a sound emanating from… from… from my uterus, slips out of my mouth, shatters the spell. They turn their heads—the couple. They see me. It isn't even him.

*The phone rings again.*

**AMAH** It could be your father, you know. He's been trying to get in touch with you. Says he doesn't know if you're dead or alive. He was calling Drew even up to this morning.

**BILLIE** My father… I wouldn't have anything to say. It's been so long. What would I say?

*The phone stops ringing.*

**AMAH** He's been in the hospital, you know. Something about his liver.

**BILLIE** He hauled us all the way back to Nova Scotia from the Bronx, to be near Granma, when Mama died.

**AMAH** I love that Nova Scotia was a haven for slaves way before the underground railroad. I love that…

**BILLIE** He's a sot. That's academia speak for alcoholic. My dad, the drunk of Dartmouth.

**AMAH** You're still his children.

**BILLIE** A detail I'm glad he's recalled.

**AMAH** Better late than never.

**BILLIE** Too little, too late.

**AMAH** Forgiveness is a virtue.

**BILLIE** What?

**AMAH** Forgiveness is a virtue.

**BILLIE** Girl, patience is a virtue.

**AMAH** Well… forgiveness is up there…

**BILLIE** Did Drew tell you about the time my father sang to me at my high-school graduation dinner?

**AMAH** Nooo. That's lovely. My father never sang to me at my graduation.

**BILLIE** We were eating. He was standing on top of the banquet table.

**AMAH** Nooo!

**BILLIE** It's the truth!

*Pause.*

**AMAH** Can I get a glass of water?

**BILLIE** Yeh. Yeh, help yourself.

*AMAH goes into the kitchen.*

I've got OJ in the fridge, if you want.

**AMAH** Water will do, thanks. Do you have any… ice in your freezer?

**BILLIE** I'll get it.

**AMAH** I can get it.

*BILLIE gets up quickly, and heads toward the kitchen.*

**BILLIE** It's okay. It's okay. I'll get it for you.

*BILLIE opens the freezer and gets her the ice, closing the freezer door immediately behind her.*

**AMAH** Thanks. *(beat)* What's in there?

**BILLIE** Frozen shit.

*The phone begins to ring again. Both women look toward it.*

### Scene Four

*Same day: noontime. Accompanying the sound of rushing water and the polyrhythmic chorus of strings, Martin Luther King continues to assert his dream, its relationship to the American Constitution, and the Declaration of Independence.*

**OTHELLO** *(offstage)* Billie!

*Silence. He knocks again.*

Billie?! *(to MONA)* I don't think she's there.

*OTHELLO unlocks the door. He enters. We recognize him as the man in both 1860 and 1928.*

Billie? Mona and I are here to pick up the rest of my things. Billie?

*He hears the shower. He goes over to the bathroom door. He knocks.*

Billie…?

*BILLIE screams. We hear something crash.*

It's just me… I tried to call. You should get that machine fixed.

**BILLIE** *(offstage)* I'll be out in a minute.

*OTHELLO returns to MONA at the entrance. We see nothing of her but brief glimpses of a bare arm and a waft of light-brown hair.*

**OTHELLO** It's okay, Mona, she's in there. Why don't you wait in the car.

**MONA** *(offstage)* She'll have to get used to me some time.

**OTHELLO** I'll be down in a flash. It won't take me that long.

*She doesn't answer.*

Hey, hey, hey!

**MONA** *(offstage)* Hey yourself. I do have other things to take care of, you know.

*He kisses her.*

Okay… I still haven't found anything blue. I'll scour the stores. I'll be back in a couple of hours.

**OTHELLO** All right.

**MONA** *(offstage)* All right.

*He brings in several large, empty boxes. He closes the door and looks around. He sees a burning cigarette, picks it up, looks at it, then puts it out. He takes off his jacket. Then he takes several albums from a shelf and places them on the floor. He begins to form two piles. He picks up one of the albums and begins to laugh. BILLIE enters dressed in a robe.*

**BILLIE** What are you doing here?

**OTHELLO** I came over to pack my things. The movers are coming in the morning. I tried to call…

**BILLIE** You took my pot.

**OTHELLO** What…

**BILLIE** My pot. The cast-iron Dutch pot.

**OTHELLO** Oh… Well, you never use it.

**BILLIE** I want it back.

**OTHELLO** You never use it.

**BILLIE** The one with the yellow handle.

**OTHELLO** We need it to make gumbo.

**BILLIE** She uses it?

**OTHELLO** I need it to make gumbo.

**BILLIE** She needs my pot? The one with the carrying rings.

**OTHELLO** It was a gift to both of us.

**BILLIE** From my father.

**OTHELLO** I'll bring it back tomorrow.

**BILLIE** If you don't have it here for me inside of thirty minutes I will break every jazz recording on that shelf.

**OTHELLO** You want me to go all the way back for something you don't even use.

**BILLIE** Let me see…

**OTHELLO** You never used it.

**BILLIE** Abbey Lincoln…

*She takes the album from the table. Takes the record from the jacket and breaks it in two. She reaches for another album. OTHELLO picks up the broken record.*

Aah. Max Roach.

*She takes the cover off the Max Roach album.*

**OTHELLO** The Abbey Lincoln was yours.

*She breaks the Max Roach record too.*

Okay. Okay, I'll go and get it.

*He picks up his jacket and proceeds to the door.*

**BILLIE** Fine. It's fine.

**OTHELLO** Excuse me?

**BILLIE** It's fine. Tomorrow's fine.

*Pause. He turns toward her.*

**OTHELLO** Okay.

*Pause. He puts his jacket down again. Pause.*

How are you? You look well.

**BILLIE** I'm fine. And you?

**OTHELLO** Great… Good.

*Pause.*

**BILLIE** Well you know where your stuff is.

**OTHELLO** Yep… Yes.

*Pause.*

**BILLIE** Drink?

**OTHELLO** What?

**BILLIE** Would you like something to drink?

**OTHELLO** Sure… Yes. What do you—

**BILLIE** Peppermint, fennel, camomile… No… Just peppermint and fennel. Coffee, wine, cognac, water.

**OTHELLO** What are you having?

**BILLIE** Cognac.

**OTHELLO** Oh. Well… That'll do.

*BILLIE goes to the kitchen.*

Where's my suitcase?

**BILLIE** Where you left it.

*Pause.*

**OTHELLO** So you're staying on then?

**BILLIE** No.

**OTHELLO** Where are you… You know… I mean, things are tight, money-wise, but I'll still put money in your account… When I can… I mean, I hope we can keep in touch.

*She hands him a glass of cognac.*

Thank you.

**BILLIE** You're welcome.

*Pause.*

**OTHELLO** You've lost weight. You look great. *(He takes a large gulp.)* Aaahh! Yes!

*OTHELLO looks at BILLIE for a moment. He then takes one of the boxes and places it at his feet. He approaches the bookshelf. He takes down a large book.*

*African Mythology*… Is this mine or yours?

**BILLIE** Mine… I think… I don't know.

**OTHELLO** This is going to be interesting.

**BILLIE** Take what you like. I don't care.

*OTHELLO takes another book.*

**OTHELLO** *The Great Chain of Being*?

**BILLIE** From man to mollusk. The scientific foundation for why we're not human. An African can't really be a woman, you know. My department agreed to let me take only one course this year—I'm taking a reading course.

**OTHELLO** Yours... Yours... Mine... *Black Psychology*, you keeping this?

**BILLIE** Yeh. *(She takes the books from him.)* You'd think there was more information on black people and mental health. You know... Christ, we've been here, what, four hundred years. No money in it I guess...

**OTHELLO** What's money got to do with it?

**BILLIE** You know, grants... Scholarships...

**OTHELLO** Race is not an obscure idea.

*He places several books into a box.*

**BILLIE** In genetics, or the study of what's wrong with people of African descent— The Heritage Foundation will give you tons of dough to prove the innate inferiority of... The Shakespeare's mine, but you can have it.

**OTHELLO** Sure, if you don't—

**BILLIE** No. The Heritage Foundation—that's where that guy Murray, et al., got most of their money for Bell Curve—I think... There's just no one out there willing to give you a scholarship to prove that we're all mad.

**OTHELLO** We're all mad. This is the founding principle of your thesis?

**BILLIE** Well, not mad... I mean... Well... Psychologically dysfunctional, then. All cultural groups are to some degree ethnocentric: We—they. But not all intercultural relations are of an inferiorsuperior type.

**OTHELLO** Thus we're not all mad.

*He returns to the bookshelf.*

**BILLIE** No, no. In America this race shit is classic behavioural disorder. Obsessions. Phobias. Delusions. Notions of persecution. Delusions of grandeur. Any one or combination of these can produce behaviours that categorize oneself as superior and another as inferior. You see, this kind of dysfunction is systemically supported by the larger society. Psychology only sees clients who can no longer function in society. We're all mad. We just appear to be functional.

**OTHELLO** And your solution?

**BILLIE** You'll have to buy my book.

*Pause. They continue packing.*

How's the teaching?

**OTHELLO** Fine… Great…

**BILLIE** Good.

*Pause.*

**OTHELLO** I'll be heading the department's courses in Cyprus next summer.

**BILLIE** I thought you told me Christopher… What's his name?

**OTHELLO** Chris Yago?

**BILLIE** Yeh, Yago.

**OTHELLO** Well everyone thought he would get it. I thought he'd get it. So a whole bunch of them are challenging affirmative action.

**BILLIE** Rednecks in academia.

**OTHELLO** No, no… Well….. I think it's a good thing.

**BILLIE** Pul-eese.

**OTHELLO** Using discrimination to cure discrimination is not—

**BILLIE** We're talking put asides of five percent. Five percent of everything available to whites. They've still got ninety-five.

**OTHELLO** Billie… Injustice against blacks can't be cured by injustice against whites… you know that.

**BILLIE** And younger people won't have the same opportunities you had.

**OTHELLO** Now look who's sounding white.

**BILLIE** Who said you sounded white?

**OTHELLO** It's implied… No one at school tells me I don't know how to do my job… it's implied. I'll be at a faculty meeting, I'll make a suggestion, and it'll be ignored. Not five minutes later someone else will make the exact same suggestion and everyone will agree to it. Mona noticed it too. They think I'm only there because I'm black. I've tested it.

**BILLIE** So let me get this straight, you're against affirmative action in order for white people to respect you.

**OTHELLO** For my peers… my peers to respect me. You know what it's like. Every day I have to prove to them that I can do my job. I feel that any error I make only goes to prove them right.

**BILLIE** Well you must be perfect. Mona respects you.

**OTHELLO** Well, she really sees me. She was the only other faculty to support me on the MLK Day assembly. When we played the video—

**BILLIE** The "I have a dream" speech?

**OTHELLO** They understood. For a moment I got them to understand.

*He picks up several books and places them in a box.*

**BILLIE** "America has defaulted on this promissory note insofar as her…

**OTHELLO & BILLIE** …citizens of colour are concerned.

**OTHELLO** Instead of honouring this sacred obligation, America has given its coloured people a…

**OTHELLO & BILLIE** bad cheque…

**BILLIE** …a cheque that has come back marked…

**OTHELLO & BILLIE** …'insufficient funds.'"

**BILLIE** The man was a… a…

**OTHELLO** Poet… Visionary.

**BILLIE** A prophet.

**OTHELLO** After all he'd been through in his life, he could still see that at a deeper level we're all the same.

*Pause.*

**BILLIE** I'm not the same.

**OTHELLO** In the eyes of God, Billie, we're all the same.

**BILLIE** One day little black boys and little white girls—

**OTHELLO** You're delusional.

**BILLIE** You're the one looking for white respect.

**OTHELLO** Wrong again! White respect, black respect, it's all the same to me.

**BILLIE** Right on, brother man!

**OTHELLO** When I was growing up….. in a time of black pride—it was something to say you were black. Before that I'd say… My family would say we're Cuban… It takes a long time to work through some of those things. I am a member of the human race.

**BILLIE** Oh, that's a switch. What happened to all that J.A. Rogers stuff you were pushing? Blacks created the world, blacks are the progenitors of European civilization, gloriana… Constantly trying to prove you're as good, no, better than white people. White people are always the line for you, aren't they? The rule… the margin… the variable of control. We are black. Whatever we do is black.

**OTHELLO** I'm so tired of this race shit, Billie. There are alternatives—

**BILLIE** Like what? Oh yes, white.

**OTHELLO** Oh, don't be so—

**BILLIE** Isn't that really what not acting black, or feeling black means.

**OTHELLO** Liberation has no colour.

**BILLIE** But progress is going to white schools… proving we're as good as whites… like some holy grail… all that we're taught in those white schools. All that is in us. Our success is whiteness. We religiously seek to have what they have. Access to the white-man's world. The white-man's job.

**OTHELLO** That's economics.

**BILLIE** White economics.

**OTHELLO** God! Black women always—

**BILLIE** No. Don't even go there…

**OTHELLO** I… You… Forget it!

**BILLIE** *(quietly at first)* Yes, you can forget it, can't you. I don't have that… that luxury. When I go into a store I always know when I'm being watched. I can feel it. They want to see if I'm gonna slip some of their stuff into my pockets. When someone doesn't serve me I think it's because I'm black. When a clerk won't put the change into my held-out hand, I think it's because I'm black. When I hear about a crime, any crime, I pray to God the person who they think did it isn't black. I'm even suspicious of the word black. Who called us black anyway? It's not a country, it's not a racial category, its not even the colour of my skin. And don't give me this content of one's character BS. I'm sorry… I am sorry… I had a dream. A dream that one day a black man and a black woman might find… Where jumping a broom was a solemn eternal vow that… I… Let's… Can we just get this over with?

*She goes to the window.*

*Silence.*

*He moves toward her.*

**OTHELLO** I know… I know. I'm sorry…

**BILLIE** Yeh…

**OTHELLO** I care… you know that.

**BILLIE** I know.

*Silence.*

**OTHELLO** I never thought I'd miss Harlem.

*Pause.*

**BILLIE** You still think it's a reservation?

**OTHELLO** Homeland/reservation.

**BILLIE** A sea of black faces.

**OTHELLO** Africatown, USA.

*Pause.*

**BILLIE** When we lived in the Village, sometimes, I'd be on the subway and I'd miss my stop. And I'd just sit there, past midtown, past the upper west side, and somehow I'd end up here. And I'd just walk. I love seeing all these brown faces.

**OTHELLO** Yeh…

**BILLIE** Since they knocked down the old projects I can see the Schomberg Museum from here. You still can't make out Harlem Hospital. I love that I can see the Apollo from our—from my balcony.

**OTHELLO** Fire escape.

**BILLIE** Patio.

**OTHELLO** You never did find a pair of lawn chairs and a table to fit in that space.

**BILLIE** Terrace.

**OTHELLO** I never saw the beauty in it.

**BILLIE** Deck. My deck.

**OTHELLO** I wish…

*He looks at her.*

**BILLIE** That old building across the street? I didn't know this, but that used to be the Hotel Theresa. That's where Castro stayed when he came to New York… Must have been the fifties. Ron Brown's father used to run that hotel.

**OTHELLO** I… I… I miss you so much sometimes. Nine years… it's a long time.

**BILLIE** I know.

**OTHELLO** I'm really not trying to hurt you, Billie.

**BILLIE** I know.

**OTHELLO** I never meant to hurt you.

*He strokes her face.*

**BILLIE** I know.

**OTHELLO** God you're so beautiful.

*He kisses her. She does not resist.*

**BILLIE** I…. don't…. I feel…

*He kisses her again.*

What are you doing?

**OTHELLO** I… I'm… I'm exploring the heightening Alleghenies of Pennsylvania.

*He kisses her again.*

The curvaceous slopes of California.

*He kisses her again.*

The red hills of Georgia, the mighty mountains of New York. Such sad eyes.

*He kisses her again.*

I'm an equal-opportunity employer.

*Pause.*

I am an equal-opportunity employer.

*Pause.*

I say, I'm an equal-opportunity employer, then you say, I don't come…

**BILLIE** I don't come cheap, you know.

**OTHELLO** I'm offering more than money can buy.

**BILLIE** How much more?

**OTHELLO** This much.

*He kisses her.*

**BILLIE** I could buy that.

**OTHELLO** Could you buy this?

*He kisses her deeply.*

**BILLIE** Be… be… beloved.

*She kisses him.*

### Scene Five

*Same day: early afternoon. The stringed duet croons gently as Malcolm X speaks about the need for blacks to turn their gaze away from whiteness so that they can see each other with new eyes. OTHELLO is lying in the bed. BILLIE is in the living room, smoking a cigarette.*

**OTHELLO** I've missed you.

**BILLIE** That's nice.

**OTHELLO** By the looks of things, I miss you even now.

**BILLIE** I'm coming.

**OTHELLO** I noticed.

**BILLIE** Sometimes… Sometimes when we make love. Sometimes every moment lines up into one moment. And I'm holding you. And I can't tell where I end, or you begin. I see everything. All my ancestors lined up below me…… like a Makonde statue, or something. It's like… I know. I know I'm supposed to be here. Everything is here.

**OTHELLO** Sounds crowded to me.

**BILLIE** It's actually quite empty.

**OTHELLO** Not as empty as this bed is feeling right about now.

**BILLIE** I'm coming. I'm coming.

*She hurriedly stubs the cigarette out and heads toward the bedroom. The apartment buzzer rings. BILLIE goes to the intercom.*

Hi Magi. I… er… I'm kinda busy right now.

**MONA** *(through intercom)* It's Mona. Could I have a word with Othello.

**OTHELLO** *(overlapping)* Shit!

**BILLIE** One second, please.

*He rushes to the intercom while attempting to put his clothes back on. BILLIE tries to hold back her laughter. Her laughter begins to infect OTHELLO. He puts a finger over his mouth indicating to BILLIE to be quiet.*

**OTHELLO** Hey Mone… Mone, I'm not done yet. There's more here than I imagined. Why don't I call you when I'm done.

*MONA does not respond. OTHELLO's demeanour changes.*

Mone? Mona? I'm coming, okay? I'll be right… Just wait there one second, okay? Okay?

*BILLIE is unable to hide her astonishment.*

**MONA** *(through intercom)* Okay.

**OTHELLO** Okay.

*He steps away from the intercom to finish putting on his clothes. BILLIE stares at him.*

I'll be back in… Uh… I just have to go straighten… Uh… She wants to help… help pack. You'll have to get used to her sometime. I mean… I…

*BILLIE continues to stare steadily at OTHELLO as he struggles with the buttons on his shirt.*

I'm sorry… Well…… I'll be right… I'll be back.

*He exits. BILLIE does not move.*

## Scene Six

*Harlem, 1860: late summer—night. A whining delta blues slides and blurs while the deeply resonant voice of Paul Robeson talks of his forebears, whose blood is in the American soil. HIM is hammering a newly forged horseshoe, HER rushes in holding a large carrying bag.*

**HER** Oh… let me catch—catch my breath… I thought I was seen… Oh my… I… I've packed a change of clothes for both of us, some loaves… I liberated the leftover bacon from yesterday's meal, from out the pantry, seeing how it was staring me right in the face when I was cleaning. It won't be missed. I wish I could pack old Betsy in my bag. She'd be sure an' give us some good fresh milk each mornin'. Oh—and I packed a fleece blanket. I hear the nights get good and cold farther north you go. And… did I forget… no… Nothing forgotten. Oh yes, I borrowed the big carving knife—for the bacon, a' course. You still working on those shoes for Miss Dessy's stallion… Let her send it to town, or get some other slave to do that… She's going to be mad as hell you took off in any event… May as well not finish the shoes, it won't placate her none…

*HIM picks up the horseshoe with a pair of tongs. HIM inspects it carefully. HIM puts the shoe to one side and retrieves the shackles. HIM takes a chamois and begins to polish the metal.*

*(pause)* O? O? Othello? The moon'll be rising. We've got to make any headway under cover of dark… Othello, why you trying to please her? I'm so tired of pleasing her. I'm so tired of pleasing white folks. Up in Canada we won't have to please no white folks no how. I hear they got sailing ships leaving for Africa every day. Canada freedom come… O? Othello? Are you coming?

**HIM** I can't.

**HER** If we make it to the border there's people there'll help us wade that water—help us cross over.

**HIM** I'm not going.

**HER** A big white house on an emerald hill…

**HIM** I know.

**HER** You need more time, O? I can wait for you. Finish her shoes, I'll… I can wait—

**HIM** No. No.

*Pause.*

**HER** You love her.

**HIM** Her father going to war.

**HER** You love her?

**HIM** I love you. It's just… She needs me. She respects me. Looks up to me, even. I love you. It's just… When I'm with her I feel like… a man. I want… I need to do for her…

**HER** Do you love her?

**HIM** Yes.

**HER** Fight with me… I would fight with you. Suffer with me, O… I would suffer with you…

*Silence.*

**Scene Seven**

*Harlem, present: late summer—late afternoon. Dulcet blue tones barely swing as Louis Farrakhan waxes eloquent on African-Americans being caught in the gravity of American society.*

**MAGI** And you know what he says, after turning on the baseball game, in the middle of my romantic dinner? Eyes glued to the screen, he says, I bet you've never made love to a man with twenty-six-inch biceps!

**BILLIE** *(smiles)* Oh… no…

**MAGI** I'm telling you, girl. Macho Mack, spot him at any locale selling six-packs. Easily recognizable, everything about him is permanently flexed. His favourite pastime? Weekend NFL football, MondayNight Football, USFL football—even Canadian foot… You look like you're feeling better. Amah did a great job with your hair.

**BILLIE** What's her motto? We lock heads and minds.

**MAGI** Hey, can I borrow that beautiful African boubou—I got me a date with an African prince. The brother has it going on! Oh… you already have boxes.

*BILLIE begins placing some of the wrapped objects into a box.*

**BILLIE** They're his box—

**MAGI** When… He came over?

**BILLIE** I even spoke to her.

**MAGI** You saw her?

**BILLIE** No. Want this mask?

**MAGI** You met her?

**BILLIE** No. Want this mask?

**MAGI** I'll keep it for you—

**BILLIE** I… er……. I don't know how long these things will have to stay in storage.

**MAGI** You don't have to move, you know. It's not rented yet. I mean, I can always lower the—

**BILLIE** No, no… I'm moving on.

**MAGI** Good. Good. To where? Where are you going? You haven't given me a date or anything. I've got bills to pay too, you know. When d'you plan to leave? Where are you going?

**BILLIE** I might go…… stay with Jenny. I could go home.

**MAGI** I'll keep it for you—

**BILLIE** I don't want anything that's—that was ours. If you don't want it, that's okay, I'll just trash it.

*BILLIE throws the mask onto the floor. It breaks into several pieces.*

**MAGI** Something happened. What happened?

**BILLIE** Nothing.

**MAGI** Did he tell you about… What did he say to you?

**BILLIE** I'm just tired. Tired of sleeping. Tired of night. It lays over me like a ton of white feathers. Swallows me up. The movers are coming in the morning to pick up his things. It's okay. I'm fine. You know… I've lived all my life believing in lies.

**MAGI** Well getting your masters isn't a lie.

**BILLIE** It's about proving, isn't it? Proving I'm as good as… I'm as intelligent as…

**MAGI** Nothing wrong with that.

**BILLIE** I don't want anything… Believe in anything. Really. I've gotta get out of here. I don't even believe in Harlem anymore.

**MAGI** Come on…

**BILLIE** It's all an illusion. All some imagined, idealistic… I dunno.

**MAGI** When I go out my door I see all the beauty of my blackness reflected in the world around me.

**BILLIE** Yeh, and all my wretchedness by the time I get to the end of the block.

**MAGI** Billie, he's the one who wants to whitewash his life.

**BILLIE** Corporeal malediction.

**MAGI** Corp-o-re-all mal-e… Oooh that's good.

**BILLIE** A black man afflicted with Negrophobia.

**MAGI** Girl, you on a roll now!

**BILLIE** No, no. A crumbled racial epidermal schema…

**MAGI** Who said school ain't doing you no good.

**BILLIE** …causing predilections to coitus denegrification.

**MAGI** Booker T. Uppermiddleclass III. He can be found in predominantly white neighbourhoods. He refers to other blacks as "them." His greatest accomplishment was being invited to the White House by George Bush to discuss the "Negro problem."

**BILLIE** Now that is frightening.

**MAGI** No, what's frightening is the fact that I dated him.

**BILLIE** What does it say… about us?

**MAGI** Who?

**BILLIE** You and me.

**MAGI** Girl, I don't know. I can't even want to go there.

**BILLIE** Ohh… Oh well… Least he's happy though. What does he say? Now he won't have to worry that a white woman will emotionally mistake him for the father that abandoned her.

**MAGI** Isn't he worried the white woman might mistake him for the butler?

**BILLIE** He'd be oh so happy to oblige.

**MAGI** I see them do things for white women they wouldn't dream of doing for me.

**BILLIE** It is a disease. We get infected as children, and… and the bacteria… the virus slowly spreads, disabling the entire system.

**MAGI** Are we infected too?

*There is knocking at the apartment door.*

Speaking of white minds parading around inside of black bodies—you want me to stay?

**BILLIE** Don't you have a date?

**MAGI** Hakim. But I can cancel…

*There is knocking at the door again.*

**BILLIE** I'm okay. I'm okay. I'm fine… Truly.

*BILLIE opens the door. OTHELLO enters.*

**OTHELLO** The pot!

*He hands the pot to BILLIE.*

Magi!

**MAGI** How's Harlumbia?

**OTHELLO** Columbia?

**MAGI** Harlumbia—those ten square blocks of whitedom, owned by Columbia University, set smack dab in the middle of Harlem.

**OTHELLO** Harlumbia, as you call it, is dull without you.

**MAGI** You could steal honey from a bee, couldn't you. Better watch you don't get stung. Well I'm off to doll myself up. Billie…

**BILLIE** Yeh, I'll get that boubou…

*BILLIE goes into the bedroom. After a few moments of silence.*

**MAGI** Why haven't you told her yet?

**OTHELLO** About? Oh yes… Yeh… I wanted to…

*BILLIE returns with a beautiful multicoloured boubou.*

**BILLIE** He won't be able to resist you…

**MAGI** Thank you, thank you. Later you two.

**OTHELLO** I'll be in touch…

**BILLIE** I'm keeping my fingers crossed for you.

**MAGI** Good, I'm running out of time.

*MAGI exits. OTHELLO enters. BILLIE closes the door. There is a long awkward silence. BILLIE continues placing wrapped objects into her boxes. OTHELLO steps on a piece of the broken mask. He picks it up, looks at it, then places it on the mantel. He goes over to the bookshelf and begins to pack more of his possessions into his boxes.*

**OTHELLO** They're coming at nine.

**BILLIE** Oh… Er… I'll be out of your way.

**OTHELLO** You can be here…

**BILLIE** No. No. No. I have an appointment…… an early appointment.

**OTHELLO** Either way…

*They continue packing.*

Ah… I've been meaning to tell you…… things are real….. money's real tight right now, what with buying the apartment, and moving and everything… I won't be able to cover your tuition this semester. I'll try and put money in your account when I can. Maybe—

**BILLIE** I told you, I'm only taking one course. If you cover that I won't be taking a full load till next—

**OTHELLO** I know, that's what I'm saying.... I can't... I just can't do it right now.

**BILLIE** It's one course...

**OTHELLO** It's $5000.

**BILLIE** You promised...

**OTHELLO** I'm mortgaged up the wazoo. I don't have it. I just don't have $5000 right now.

**BILLIE** Ooh..... okay.

**OTHELLO** I would if I could, you know that.

*He continues to pack.*

I think I brought the bookshelf with me when we first—

**BILLIE** Take it all.

**OTHELLO** I don't want all of it.

**BILLIE** I'm keeping the bed.

**OTHELLO** What about the rest...

**BILLIE** If you don't want it... I'm giving it away...

**OTHELLO** Okay, if you're throwing it out...

**BILLIE** I'm keeping the bed.

*They continue packing in silence.*

**OTHELLO** We're getting married.

*Pause.*

Me and Mona. We're engaged... Officially.

*Very long pause.*

**BILLIE** Congratulations.

**OTHELLO** I wanted to tell you... Hear it from the horse's mouth... Hear it from me first. You know...

*Pause.*

**BILLIE** Yeh... Yes. Yes. Congratulations.

**OTHELLO** Mona wanted me to tell you.

**BILLIE** Yes. Yes. Being a feminist and everything— A woman's right to know—since we're all in the struggle.... I thought you hated feminists.

**OTHELLO** Well… I didn't mean that. I mean… the white women's movement is different.

**BILLIE** Just black feminists.

**OTHELLO** No, no… White men have maintained a firm grasp of the pants. I mean, white men have economic and political pants that white women have been demanding to share.

**BILLIE** White wisdom from the mouth of the mythical Negro.

**OTHELLO** Don't you see! That's exactly my point! You… The black feminist position, as I experience it in this relationship, leaves me feeling unrecognized as a man. The message is black men are poor fathers, poor partners, or both. Black women wear the pants that black men were prevented from wearing… I believe in tradition. You don't support me. Black women are more concerned with their careers than their husbands. There was a time when women felt satisfied, no, honoured being a balance to their spouse, at home, supporting the family, playing her role—

**BILLIE** Which women? I mean, which women are you referring to? Your mother worked all her life. My mother worked, her mother worked… Most black women have been working like mules since we arrived on this continent. Like mules. When white women were burning their bras, we were hired to hold their tits up. We looked after their homes, their children… I don't support you? My mother's death paid your tuition, not mine…

**OTHELLO** Can't we even pretend to be civil? Can't we? I know this isn't easy. It's not easy for me either. Do you ever consider that?

**BILLIE** You like it easy, don't you?

**OTHELLO** The truth is this is too fucking difficult.

**BILLIE** You wouldn't know the truth if it stood up and knocked you sideways.

**OTHELLO** You don't want the truth. You want me to tell you what you want to hear. No, no, you want to know the truth? I'll tell you the truth. Yes, I prefer white women. They are easier—before and after sex. They wanted me and I wanted them. They weren't filled with hostility about the unequal treatment they were getting at their jobs. We'd make love and I'd fall asleep not having to beware being mistaken for someone's inattentive father. I'd explain that I wasn't interested in a committed relationship right now, and not be confused with every lousy lover or husband that had ever left them lying in a gutter of unresolved emotions. It's the truth. To a black woman I represent every black man she has ever been with and with whom there was still so much to work out. The white women I loved saw me—could see me. Look, I'm not a junkie. I don't need more than one lover to prove my manhood. I have no children. I did not leave you, your mother, or your aunt, with six babies and a whole lotta love. I am a very single, very intelligent, very employed black man. And with white women it's good. It's nice. Anyhow, we're all equal in the eyes of God, aren't we? Aren't we?

*BILLIE stares at OTHELLO. He continues to pack.*

## Scene Eight

*Harlem, 1928: late summer—night. The cello and bass moan, almost dirge-like, in harmonic tension to the sound of Jesse Jackson's oratory. SHE holds a straight-edged razor in her bloodied palms. HE lies on the floor in front of her, motionless, the handkerchief in his hand.*

**SHE** Deadly deadly straw little strawberries it's so beautiful you kissed my fingers you pressed this cloth into my palm buried it there an antique token our ancient all these tiny red dots on a sheet of white my fingernails are white three hairs on my head are white the whites of my eyes are white too the palms of my hands and my feet are white you're all I'd ever and you my my I hate sssshh. Shhhhh okay. Okay. Okay. I'm okay all right don't don't don't don't my eyes on the shadow sparrow my sense in my feet my hands my head shine the light there please scream no sing sing *(SHE tries to sing.)* and if I get a notion to jump into the ocean, ain't nobody's business if I do do do do. If I go to church on Sunday then shimmy down on Monday t'ain't nobody's business if I…

## Scene Nine

*Harlem, present: late summer—early evening. The instruments sound out a deep cerulean blues, while Malcolm X almost scats the question, "What difference does colour make?" OTHELLO continues to pack. BILLIE sits on the floor by the bed watching him from the bedroom.*

**OTHELLO** I didn't mean—what I said. You know that. I just… Sometimes you make me so mad I… People change, Billie. That's just human nature. Our experiences, our knowledge transforms us. That's why education is so powerful, so erotic. The transmission of words from mouth to ear. Her mouth to my ear. Knowledge. A desire for that distant thing I know nothing of, but yearn to hold for my very own. My mama used to say, you have to be three times as good as a white child to get by, to do well. A piece of that pie is mine. I don't want to change the recipe. I am not minor. I am not a minority. I used to be a minority when I was a kid. I mean my culture is not my mother's culture—the culture of my ancestors. My culture is Wordsworth, Shaw, *Leave it to Beaver*, *Dirty Harry*. I drink the same water, read the same books. You're the problem if you don't see beyond my skin. If you don't hear my educated English, if you don't understand that I am a middle-class, educated man. I mean, what does Africa have to do with me. We struttin' around professing some imaginary connection for a land we don't know. Never seen. Never gonna see. We lie to ourselves, saying, ah yeh, mother Africa, middle passage, suffering, the whites did it to me, it's the whites' fault. Strut around in African cloth pretending we human now. We human now. Some of us are beyond that now. Spiritually beyond this race shit bullshit now. I am an American. The slaves were freed over 130 years ago. In 1967 it was illegal for a black to marry a white in sixteen states. That was less than thirty years ago… in my lifetime. Things change, Billie. I am not my skin. My skin is not me.

## Scene Ten

*Harlem, same day: night. A rhapsody of sound keeps time with Christopher Darden as he asks O.J. Simpson to approach the jury and try on the bloody glove. The apartment is virtually full of boxes. BILLIE is by the chemical factory at the table. The book of Egyptian Alchemy sits open upon it. Something is boiling in the flask and steam is coming out of the condenser. With rubber-gloved hands she adds several drops of a violet liquid into the flask. She picks up a large white handkerchief with pretty red strawberries embroidered on it.*

**BILLIE** I have a plan, my love. My mate…. throughout eternity. Feel what I feel. Break like I break. No more—no less. You'll judge me harsher. I know. While Susan Smith… She blamed some imaginary black man for the murder of her two boys and that's why authorities didn't suspect her for nearly two weeks. Stopping every black man with a burgundy sedan from Union, South Carolina, to the Oranges of New Jersey. And you're still wondering what made her do it. What was she going through to make her feel that this was her only way out. Yet I'll be discarded as some kind of unconscionable bitter shadow, or something. Ain't I a woman? This is my face you take for night—the biggest shadow in the world. I… I have nothing more to lose. Nothing. Othello? I am preparing something special for you… Othe… Othello. A gift for you, and your new bride. Once you gave me a handkerchief. An heirloom. This handkerchief, your mother's….. given by your father. From his mother before that. So far back… And now… then… to me. It is fixed in the emotions of all your ancestors. The one who laid the foundation for the road in Herndon, Virginia, and was lashed for laziness as he stopped to wipe the sweat from his brow with this kerchief. Or your great-great-grandmother, who covered her face with it, and then covered it with her hands as she rocked and silently wailed, when told that her girl child, barely thirteen, would be sent 'cross the state for breeding purposes. Or the one who leapt for joy on hearing of the Emancipation Proclamation, fifteen years late, mind you, only to watch it fall in slow motion from his hand and onto the ground when told that the only job he could now get was the same one he'd done for free all those years, and now he's forced to take it, for not enough money to buy the food to fill even one man's belly. And more… so much more. What I add to this already fully endowed cloth will cause you such…… such… wretchedness. Othe… Othello.

*The contents of the flask have been transformed from violet to clear. BILLIE places the handkerchief on a large tray. Then with tongs she takes the hot flask and pours the contents over the handkerchief. She retrieves a vial from the table, opens it.*

My sable warrior… Fight with me. I would fight with you… Suffer with me… I would suffer—

*She starts to pour, but the vial is empty. The buzzer rings. BILLIE is surprised. The buzzer rings again. BILLIE turns off the Bunsen burner. She takes the flask into the kitchen and pours it into the sink. The buzzer rings once more. Going back to the table, she carefully takes the tray and heads toward the bathroom. There is a knock at her door.*

**BILLIE** *(from the bathroom)* You have a key, let yourself in… Make yourself right at home, why don't you—

**MAGI** *(offstage)* Billie? Billie, it's me. Magi.

**BILLIE** Magi?

**MAGI** *(offstage)* Are you okay?

**BILLIE** Yes. Yes. I'm fine. Let me call you later, okay, Magi?

*We hear the sound of liquid being poured. The toilet flushes.*

*MAGI, offstage, mumbles something about BILLIE having a visitor.*

What?

*MAGI mumbles something about a visitor again.*

What? Door's open!

*MAGI enters and stands in the doorway. She is speaking quietly, as if not wanting someone to hear.*

**MAGI** Sweetie, you have a visitor. Shall I—

**BILLIE** *(entering the living area)* Look, I'm tired. He's been here practically all day already—

**MAGI** No, no, no. He said his name is Canada. *(BILLIE turns to MAGI.)* He says he's your father. That's what he said. He said he was your father.

*A man in his late sixties brushes past MAGI. He wears a hat and has a small suitcase in his hand.*

**CANADA** Sybil? Sybil! There's my girl. Come and give your daddy a big hug.

*End of ACT ONE.*

## ACT TWO

### Scene One

*Harlem, present: late summer—night. The cello and bass pluck and bow a funky rendition of Aretha Franklin's "Spanish Harlem" against the audio sound of Michael Jackson and Lisa Marie Presley's interview on ABC's Dateline. CANADA is sitting on one of the chairs, amidst stacks of boxes.*

**CANADA** The first time I came to Harlem I was scared. Must have been '68 or '69. Yeh… We were living in the Bronx, and your mother was still alive. Everything I'd ever learned told me that I wasn't safe in this part of town. The newspapers. Television. My friends. My own family. But I'm curious, see. I says, Canada, you can't be in New York City and not see Harlem. So I make my way to 125th. "A" train. I'm gonna walk past the Apollo, I'm gonna see this place. I'm gonna walk the ten city blocks to Lexington and catch the "6" train back, if it's the last thing I do. So out of the subway I put on my "baddest mother in the city" glare. I walk—head straight. All the time trying to make my stride say, "I'm mean… I'm mean. Killed somebody mean." So I'm doing this for 'bout five, ten minutes, taking short, furtive glances at this place I really want to see, when I begin to realize… No one is taking any notice of me… Not a soul. Then it dawns on me: I'm the same as them. I look just like them. I look like I live in Harlem. Sounds silly now. But I just had to catch myself and laugh out loud. Canada, where did you get these ideas about Harlem from?

*The kettle whistles.*

**BILLIE** How do you like it?

*BILLIE heads to the kitchen to make tea.*

**CANADA** Brown sugar. No milk.

**BILLIE** I don't even know why I asked, I don't have any milk anyway.

**CANADA** You can't take milk. Never could. When your mother stopped feeding you from her milk, that cow's milk just gave you colic. And those diapers… Now that's an image I'll never forget.

**BILLIE** So what brings you to these parts?

**CANADA** Just passing through. Since I was in the neighbourhood, thought I'd stop on in.

**BILLIE** Nova Scotia's nearly a thousand miles away.

**CANADA** Well, I thought I should see my grandchild. Jenny's almost six and I've only talked to her on the phone. And Andrew and his wife, and you. Nothing wrong with seeing family, is there?

**BILLIE** Strong or weak?

**CANADA** Like a bear's bottom.

**BILLIE** Polar or Grizzly?

**CANADA** Grizzly.

*BILLIE returns with a tray.*

Andrew told me what happened.

**BILLIE** He did, did he?

**CANADA** Said you were taking it kinda hard.

**BILLIE** Oh, I'll be fine. I'm a survivor. But then again, you already know that.

**CANADA** Tea should be ready. Shall I be Mother?

**BILLIE** Go ahead.

*CANADA pours the tea.*

I hear you were in the hospital.

**CANADA** My liver ain't too good. Gave out on me. I guess you reap what you sow.

**BILLIE** Still drinking?

**CANADA** Been sober going on five years now.

**BILLIE** Good. Good for you.

**CANADA** Don't mean I don't feel like it sometimes though…

**BILLIE** Well… How long do you plan to be in town?

**CANADA** Just a few days. See Andrew and his family. See the sights. I'm staying there—at Andrew's. Went by there earlier… No one home. Must have given them the wrong time. Left a note though. Told them to find me at Sybil's.

**BILLIE** Billie. I've always despised that name. Sybil.

**CANADA** I gave you that name. It's a good name. It was your grandmother's name. It means prophetess. Sorceress. Seer of the future. I like it. I don't see anything wrong with that name.

**BILLIE** Sounds like some old woman living in a cave.

*CANADA reaches for his suitcase.*

**CANADA** I brought something for you.

*He takes out a small red box.*

Go on… Open it. The box is a bit too big, but…

*BILLIE opens the box.*

It's your mother's ring. I figured she'd want you to have it.

**BILLIE** I hardly remember her anymore. I get glimpses of this ghostly figure creeping in and out of my dreams.

**CANADA** When Beryl first passed on, I couldn't get her off my mind, like she'd gone and left us somehow. Left me… With two kids, one a young girl ripening to sprout into womanhood. I was sad, but I was good and mad, too. One minute I'd be trying to etch her face into my mind, 'cause I didn't want to forget. Next thing I'd be downing another shot of rye… I couldn't carry the weight. I just couldn't do it by myself. That's when we moved to Dartmouth. What's that them old slaves used to say? "I can't take it no more, I moving to Nova Scotia."

**BILLIE** I'm thinking of heading back there myself…

*Pause.*

**CANADA** 'Cause he left you, or 'cause she's white?

*Pause.*

**BILLIE** I remember that white woman… That hairdresser you used to go with… The one with the miniskirts… What was her name?

**CANADA** That's going way back… You remember her?

**BILLIE** She was boasting about knowing how to do our kind of hair. And she took that hot comb to my head… Sounded like she was frying chicken… Burnt my ears and half the hair on my head. I hated her stubby little beige legs and those false eyelashes. She taught me how to put on false eyelashes.

**CANADA** Deborah.

**BILLIE** Debbie… Yes… Debbie.

*Pause.*

**CANADA** I wish… I wish things between…

*The buzzer rings.*

**BILLIE** That must be Drew.

*BILLIE goes to the console by the door.*

Drew?

**AMAH** *(through intercom)* It's me. Amah. Is your—

**BILLIE** He's here. Come on up.

**CANADA** You know, an old African once told me the story of a man who was struck by an arrow. His attacker was unknown. Instead of tending to his wound, he refused to remove the arrow until the archer was found and punished. In the meantime, the wound festered, until finally the poison infected his entire body, eventually killing him… Now, who is responsible for this man's death, the archer for letting go the arrow, or the man for his foolish holding on?

*There is a knock at the door. BILLIE gets up and heads toward it.*

**BILLIE** The drunk?

**CANADA** A drunken man can get sober, but a damn fool can't ever get wise.

*BILLIE opens the door. AMAH enters with some rolls of paper in her arms.*

**AMAH** *(kissing BILLIE's cheek)* Hi, sweetie. And you must be Canada.

**CANADA** Drew's wife…

**AMAH** So very pleased to meet you at last.

**CANADA** Delighted…

**AMAH** We weren't expecting you until tomorrow. We ate out tonight. We would have come to pick you up. Jenny's so excited.

**CANADA** No, no… No need to fuss. I arrived safe and sound. And Sybil—Billie's been taking good care of me.

**AMAH** Drew would have come himself. Jenny insisted he give her a bath tonight. You know, it's a father/daughter thing.

*Silence.*

Anyway, we should get going. *(to CANADA)* You're probably starving. I can rustle something up for you in no time.

*CANADA reaches for his coat.*

*(to BILLIE)* Look, I'm gonna have to bring that child of mine over here. She's driving me crazy asking for you—

**BILLIE** No. No…. not yet.

**AMAH** Well, if I go mad, you and Drew will have to take care of her. I want you to know that. Oh, Jenny asked me to give these to you. She made them 'specially for you. She wanted to give you some inspiration. You might not be able to tell, but one's of her dancing, and the other's of her singing.

**BILLIE** Tell her I miss her.

**AMAH** I will.

**BILLIE** Tell her I'll see her real soon.

**AMAH** I will.

**BILLIE** *(to AMAH)* I still have a bone to pick with you, though. *(indicating CANADA)*

**AMAH** No, no. You have a bone to pick with Drew.

**CANADA** I'll drop in again tomorrow, if that's okay with you.

**BILLIE** Tomorrow might not be so good. He's moving his stuff in the morning. We'd probably be in the way. I won't even be here until sometime in the afternoon.

**CANADA** Well then… We'll see how things go.

*He kisses BILLIE on the forehead.*

**AMAH** Come join us over something to eat—

**BILLIE** No. Thanks. I'm fine.

**CANADA** Good to see you, Sybil—Billie.

**BILLIE** Well it certainly was a surprise. Bye, y'all.

*AMAH and CANADA exit. BILLIE closes the door, then leans against it as she studies the pictures Jenny drew.*

## Scene Two

*Harlem, the present: the next day—late morning. Lyrical strains give way to an undulating rhythm while Malcolm X recounts the tale of how George Washington sold a slave for a gallon of molasses. The apartment looks empty of furniture, save for the bed, several piles of books, and boxes strewn around the living area. OTHELLO walks into the bedroom with a large green garbage bag. After a few moments the door is unlocked and BILLIE peers through the doorway. She hears someone in the bedroom. She quietly closes the door behind her and places a small brown paper bag in her pocket. She makes her way into the kitchen area. She waits. OTHELLO exits the bedroom, green garbage bag in tow. He walks to the centre of the living room, where he stands for a few moments taking it all in.*

**BILLIE** Got everything?

**OTHELLO** *(startled)* Ahh! *(Dropping the garbage bag, he turns around.)* Christ…

**BILLIE** Got everything?

**OTHELLO** God, I didn't hear you come in.

**BILLIE** My meeting ended earlier than I expected. I was able to get what I needed… I didn't see a van. I figured you'd be done by now.

**OTHELLO** They just left. I was doing a final check. See if I'd forgotten anything.

**BILLIE** So the move went well.

**OTHELLO** Yes… yeh. It's amazing how much stuff there is.

**BILLIE** Yeh. It's hard to throw things away.

**OTHELLO** I know what you mean. We've got a huge place, though.

**BILLIE** Good. Good for you.

*Pause.*

**OTHELLO** This place looks pretty huge right now, though. Remember when we first came to look at this place?

**BILLIE** Yes.

*Pause.*

**OTHELLO** Well… I guess that's it.

**BILLIE** I guess…

*Pause.*

**OTHELLO** Anyway… So when do you plan on leaving?

**BILLIE** Oh, I don't… I don't know.

**OTHELLO** Ah.

**BILLIE** I haven't decided.

**OTHELLO** I see… Well…

**BILLIE** So when's the big day?

**OTHELLO** Oh….. well… Er… Three weeks.

**BILLIE** So soon?

**OTHELLO** Just a small affair.

**BILLIE** Good. Good for you. Good for you both.

**OTHELLO** Yeh…

**BILLIE** I… I've been meaning… Well… I've been thinking.

**OTHELLO** Hmn hmn…

**BILLIE** I… er… I… um… I want to return something you gave me… centuries ago.

**OTHELLO** Oh?

**BILLIE** The handkerchief?

**OTHELLO** Oh! Really? Wow… No. No. It's not necessary. Really—

**BILLIE** No, no, let me finish. I've……. been foolish. I understand that now. You can understand why. And…… I'm sorry. That's what I wanted to tell you. And the handkerchief… it's yours. Held by me for safekeeping, really. To be passed on to our children—if we had any. Since we don't, it should be returned to you, to your line…

**OTHELLO** Why are you doing this?

**BILLIE** I just thought you might… I thought you would… After all… it's the only thing your mother left you…

**OTHELLO** I don't know what to say.

**BILLIE** I thought you'd be glad.

**OTHELLO** Oh, I'm more than glad.

**BILLIE** But I have to find it first.

**OTHELLO** Are you sure about—

**BILLIE** I'm sure. Give me a couple of days, to find it…… clean it up a bit.

**OTHELLO** I could come by.

**BILLIE** Yes. You should have it before… You know… before your… big day.

**OTHELLO** Thank you.

**BILLIE** Just trying to play my part well.

**OTHELLO** Thanks.

**BILLIE** Forgive me…

**OTHELLO** I know it's been hard.

**BILLIE** Yeh..

**OTHELLO** Okay. Well…

*He reaches to touch her face. She retreats.*

**BILLIE** I'll see you in a couple of days then.

**OTHELLO** All right.

**BILLIE** All right.

**OTHELLO** All right. And say hello to Jenny for me. *(silence)* All right.

*OTHELLO exits. BILLIE takes the small package out of her pocket. She unwraps it, revealing a small vial of fluid. She goes into the kitchen, vial in hand, turns toward the fridge, opens the freezer door, and stares into it.*

**BILLIE** Look this way and see… your death… Othe… Othe…

*She places the vial into the freezer.*

## Scene Three

*Harlem, 1862: late summer—night. Indigo blues groan as if through a delta, while echoes of a presidential voice reads from the Emancipation Proclamation. The sound fades. HER holds HIM in her arms like Mary holds Jesus in Michelangelo's* Pietà. *There is a rope around his neck. He does not move.*

**HER** *(caressing him)* Once upon a time, there was a man who wanted to find a magic spell in order to become white. After much research and investigation, he came across an ancient ritual from the caverns of knowledge of a psychic. "The only way to become white," the psychic said, "was to enter the whiteness." And when he found his ice queen, his alabaster goddess, he fucked her. Her on his dick. He one with her, for a single, shivering moment became… her. Her and her whiteness.

## Scene Four

*Harlem, present: late summer—night. A cacophony of strings grooves and collides as sound bites from the Anita Hill and Clarence Thomas hearings, the LA riots, the O.J. Simpson trial, Malcolm X, and Martin Luther King, loop and repeat the same distorted bits of sound over and over again. BILLIE is alone in the apartment. She goes into the freezer and removes the vial. Wearing rubber gloves, she places several drops of a liquid substance onto the handkerchief. She replaces the cap of the vial. BILLIE carefully folds the handkerchief, hesitates for a moment, looks around, and spots the red box on the mantle. She puts the handkerchief back down on the tray and, with her hands in the air, like a surgeon scrubbing for surgery, she gets up and goes to the red box. With one hand she takes off one of the gloves. With the ungloved hand she opens the red box and slips her mother's ring on her finger. She then takes the red box with her to the table. She very carefully replaces the one glove, picks up the handkerchief, and neatly places it in the small red box. She works slowly and is mindful not to touch the sides of the box with the handkerchief itself.*

*She removes a single rubber glove once more, picks up the cover to the box, and places it on top of the other half. She is still for a few moments, staring at the box.*

*BILLIE gets up and crosses the room, as if looking for something, only to stop in her tracks and return to the box. She paces. Her pacing appears more methodical than hysterical. Suddenly, she stops. She turns to look at the small red box.*

*She shakes her head and takes a seat on a large, full, cardboard box at her feet. Her breathing becomes more apparent as she begins to rock, almost imperceptibly at first. Finally, she places her head in her hands.*

*After several moments BILLIE's face slowly emerges from her hands.*

*She glares at the gloved hand incredulously, as she realizes that she has inadvertently transferred some of the potion onto her own skin. She quickly removes the second glove and proceeds to wipe her face with her own clothes.*

**BILLIE** *(to herself)* Oh God! Oh my God! Shit! Shit! Shit! Shit!

*BILLIE gets up and rushes to the kitchen sink, turns on the tap, and frantically washes her hands and face in the water.*

**Scene Five**

*The following day: early evening. In counterpoint to the cello and bass, the distorted sound loop becomes a grating repetition. MAGI and CANADA are on either side of a large box, sitting on two smaller ones. The larger box is covered by a scarf to resemble a tablecloth, on top of which is a small feast. They are eating. MAGI gets up and goes to the door of the bedroom. She peeks in. After a few moments she closes the door and returns to her seat.*

**MAGI** She's in distant realms. I checked in on her when I got back from church. I thought she was speaking in tongues. I couldn't understand a thing she was saying. I don't think she slept a wink all night. Those pills work like a charm, though. *(beat)* How is it?

**CANADA** Mmn! Those greens… She looks like an angel and cooks like one, too.

**MAGI** Can I get you some more?

**CANADA** No, no, I don't want to appear too greedy now.

**MAGI** Here… *(serving him another helping)* There you go. And I won't tell a soul. Promise.

**CANADA** I haven't tasted cooking like this in a long time.

**MAGI** My mama would say, some food is good for the mind, some is good for the body, and some food is good for the soul.

**CANADA** Your mama taught you how to cook like this?

**MAGI** Once she even taught me how to cook a soufflé. She used to have a restaurant downstairs from as far back as I can recall. And I guess the boys returning home from the war in Europe kept asking for the Parisian food, and it ended up on her menu. She'd say, now this Parisian food ain't good for nothing. Soufflé ain't nothing more than baked eggs. And eggs is for breakfast. Eggs don't do no one no good past noon.

**CANADA** So you've lived here all your life?

**MAGI** And my mother before me, and her mother before her. My great-grandmother worked for the family that lived here, most of her life. She never married, but she had two children by the man she worked for—seems his wife never knew they were his. One brown baby looks just like another to most white folks. And when the wife died, my great-grandmother just stayed on. Everybody thinking she's just the maid, but she was living like the queen of the manor—him being her babies' father and everything. And his other children were all grown by then. So when he died he left everything to his white children, 'cept this house. He left it in my great-grandmother's name, and it's been in my family ever since.

**CANADA** So the white man's children ever find out? About their brown-skinned relatives.

**MAGI** I don't know. The Van Dykes—they were Dutch. We used to watch the Dick Van Dyke show, and my grandmother used to always say, "That there's your relative!" But we didn't pay her too much mind. More greens?

**CANADA** If I eat another thing I will truly burst. This was wonderful. Thank you. Thank you very much.

**MAGI** You're more than welcome.

**CANADA** When I was a boy I used to love to sop the pot liquor.

**MAGI** It's nearly the best part.

**CANADA** You sure know the way to a man's heart.

**MAGI** Haven't had any luck so far.

**CANADA** Yet.

*There is an awkward silence between them, after which they both start speaking at once.*

**MAGI** *(overlapping)* Well I better get started with these dishes…

**CANADA** *(overlapping)* I should go in and check on Sybil… Let me give you a hand.

**MAGI** No, no, it's quite all right. I can handle this.

*BILLIE enters.*

**CANADA** Billie! Marjorie was kind enough to share her dinner with me.

**MAGI** Billie, come and have something to eat.

**BILLIE** I'm not hungry. I heard voices. I need to go back and lay down… get some reading done.

**MAGI** You can't have eaten anything for the day, girl.

**BILLIE** I'm fine.

**CANADA** What you need is a good meal inside you.

**BILLIE** I said I was fine.

**MAGI** I'll just take these things downstairs.

*MAGI exits.*

**CANADA** I'll make you some tea, okay.

**BILLIE** I don't—don't need any tea. I don't want anything to eat. I'm fine. I'm sorry. I don't—don't—don't mean… to be like this… But I haven't seen you in God knows how long… And you just show up and expect things to be all hunky-dory.

*Pause.*

**CANADA** Well, I'll be off then.

*He goes for his coat.*

**BILLIE** I'm sorry.

**CANADA** Me too.

*He heads for the door.*

**BILLIE** And I am glad you came… Maybe this can be… You know…. like a beginning of something… I don't know.

**CANADA** I nearly came before… Two or three times… You know, when I heard. I wished your mother was here. I really wished for her… Her wisdom. I mean, Beryl would know what to do. A girl needs her mother. And I know you didn't have her all those times… I mean, I couldn't tell you. What could I tell you? I kept seeing your face. It's your mother's face. You've got my nose. My mouth. But those eyes… The shape of your face… The way your head tilts to one side when you're thinking, or just listening. It's all her. You've got her moods. I used to call them her moods. Once 'bout every three months, on a Friday, when she'd have the weekend off, she'd come home from that hospital, take off her clothes, and lay down in her bed and stay there till Sunday afternoon. She'd say she'd done turned the other cheek so many times in the past little while, she didn't have no more smiles for anybody. She'd say, better she just face God and the pillow than shower me and the children with the evil she had bottled up inside her. See, if you spend too much time among white people, you start believing what they think of you. So I'd take you and Drew and we'd go visiting. We'd take the whole weekend and visit all the folks we knew in a fifteen-mile radius… When we'd get home she'd have cleaned the house, washed the clothes, and even made a Sunday dinner. And after I'd pluck the guitar… And she'd start to sing… And you'd dance… You remember? You'd dance. You'd stomp on that floor like you were beating out some secret code to God or something… I know you—we don't see eye to eye. I know you haven't wanted to see very much of anything of me lately. But I've known you all your life. I carried you in my arms and on my back, kissed and spanked you when you needed, and I watched you start to talk, and learn to walk, and read, and I just wanted to come… I just wanted to come. And I know I can't make everything all right. I know. But I was there when you arrived in this world. And I didn't think there was space for a child, I loved your mother so much. But there you were, and I wondered where you'd been all my life, like something I'd been missing and didn't know I'd been missing. And I don't know if you've loved anybody that long. But behind your mother's face you're wearing, I still see the girl who shrieked with laughter, and danced to the heavens sometimes…

*CANADA slowly approaches BILLIE. She does not move. He takes her in his arms. He holds her in his arms for a long time.*

### Scene Six

*Harlem, 1928: late summer—night. The strident movement of the strings is joined by the rising tempo of the distorted sound loop. HE and SHE are both in a tiny dressing room, as in the prologue. On a counter is a shaving brush, a straight-edged razor, greasepaint, and a top hat. HE wipes his face with a towel. SHE holds the handkerchief out to him. He does not take it. She lets it fall at his feet. After a few moments he picks it up.*

**HE** *(referring to the handkerchief at first)* White, red, black, green, indigo… What difference does it make? That makes no sense… makes no difference. "If virtue no delighted beauty lack, Your son-in-law is far more fair than black." Far more fair than black. I want… I need to do this… For my soul. I am an actor. I—

**SHE** *(kindly)* A minstrel. A black minstrel…

*He places the towel on the counter beside the toiletries.*

**HE** It's paid my way.

*She caresses the towel.*

**SHE** Stay, my sable warrior…

*Her hand stumbles upon the razor.*

**HE** I'll not die in blackface to pay the rent. I am of Ira Aldridge stock. I am a classical man. I long to play the Scottish king. The prince of Denmark. "The slings and arrows of outrageous…" Or… Or… "There's a divinity that shapes our ends, Rough-hew them how we will…" Those words… I love those words. They give me life. Mona sees my gift. She's cast me as the prince of Tyre. She's breathed new life into a barren dream. She… She… She has a serene calmness about her. That smile… I bet they named her Mona because even at birth she had that constant half smile, like the *Mona Lisa*. Skin as smooth as monumental alabaster… As warm as snow velvet.

*She exposes the blade.*

**SHE** My onyx prince…

**HE** Ooohh…

*She approaches him from behind.*

**SHE** My tourmaline king…

*She leans her head on his back.*

**HE** S'all right…

**SHE** My raven knight…

*She wraps her arms around him. He turns his head toward her.*

**HE** Oh sweet…

**SHE** My umber squire…

**HE** I wish… I wish—

*Her hand rises, the razor is poised, nearly touching the skin of his neck, just below his ear, within his peripheral vision.*

**SHE** My Cimmerian lord…

*He turns around, as if to see what she's holding, and in that turn his neck appears to devour the blade. The razor's shaft, at once hidden by his flesh, swiftly withdraws, leaving a rushing river of red like a scarf billowing around his neck and her hands. He yields to gravity.*

## Scene Seven

*Harlem, the present: late-summer—night. The plucked strings and the distorted audio loop have become even more dissonant. BILLIE is clutching the small red box.*

**MAGI** …You know, Hakim has seven children, and he's never been married. Brother Hakim. Spot him at any street rally where the subject is prefaced by the words "Third World." He's the one with the "Lumumba Lives" button prominently displayed on his authentic kente cloth dashi—Billie? Billie, what's up? You don't look so good.

*Pause.*

Billie?

**BILLIE** Sybil. I'm Sybil.

**MAGI** That's what your daddy calls you.

**BILLIE** Yes.

**MAGI** Your daddy sure is one good-looking gentleman.

**BILLIE** Trapped in history. A history trapped in me.

**MAGI** I'm serious. I mean… I wanna know if you mind? Really. You were still a little girl when your mama died.

**BILLIE** I don't remember Beryl's funeral. I see my father dressed in black, sewing a white button onto his white shirt with an enormous needle. He attaches the button and knots the thread so many times it's like he's trying to hold onto more than just the button. Like he can't bear for anything else in his life to leave him.

**MAGI** He's a nice man. Would you mind?

**BILLIE** Am I nice?

**MAGI** Billie, I bet you haven't eaten today.

**BILLIE** Can you keep a secret?

**MAGI** No, but that's never stopped you before.

**BILLIE** Then sorry…

**MAGI** Okay, okay. I promise.

**BILLIE** I am about to plunge into very dangerous waters. Give me your word.

**MAGI** You're not going to do something stupid, now.

**BILLIE** Your word?

**MAGI** Yeh, okay.

**BILLIE** I've drawn a line.

**MAGI** A line? A line about what?

**BILLIE** I'm returning the handkerchief—the one his mother give him. The one he gave to me when we first agreed to be together…

**MAGI** I don't understand.

**BILLIE** I've concocted something… A potion… A plague of sorts… I've soaked the handkerchief… Soaked it in certain tinctures… Anyone who touches it—the handkerchief, will come to harm.

**MAGI** Now that is not a line, Billie, that is a trench!

**BILLIE** I'm supposed to…

**MAGI** Billie, if this kind of stuff truly worked, Africans wouldn't be in the situation we're in now. Imagine all them slaves working magic on their masters—didn't make no difference. If it truly worked I'd be married to a nice man, with three little ones by now. But if it makes you feel better—

**BILLIE** He's going to marry her... Officially...

**MAGI** I know... I know. Remember, what goes around comes around. Karma is a strong and unforgiving force.

**BILLIE** I haven't seen it affect white people too much.

**MAGI** Is everything about white people with you? Is every living moment of your life eaten up with thinking about them? Do you know where you are? Do you know who you are anymore? What about right and wrong? Racism is a disease, my friend, and your test just came back positive. You're so busy reacting you don't even know yourself.

**BILLIE** No, no, no... It's about black. I love black. I really do. And it's revolutionary... Black is beautiful... So beautiful. This Harlem sanctuary...... here. This respite... Like an ocean in the middle of a desert. And in my mirror, my womb, he has a fast-growing infestation of roaches. White roaches.

**MAGI** Billie?

**BILLIE** Did you ever consider what hundreds of years of slavery did to the African-American psyche?

**MAGI** What? What are you...?

**BILLIE** Every time someone mentions traditional values or the good old days—who exactly were those days good for?

*The phone rings. BILLIE goes over to it. She sits on the bare floor but does not answer.*

Jenny... Is that you, Jenny? My beauty. My little girl. It's Sybil... Auntie Sybil... The woman who lives in the cave.

*BILLIE laughs.*

**MAGI** I'll get it for you.

*BILLIE picks up the receiver.*

**BILLIE** Yes, yes, I'm here. Oh, Othe... Othello. I didn't recognize your voice. You sound...... different. No. No, no, you can't pick it up. I mean—I've got it, yes. It's right here. No. No, I won't be in... No, no. I haven't changed my mind. But—I mean... I have to go...

Roaches. Yeh, blue roaches. Green roaches. So I have to go now. I—I just have to go.

*BILLIE replaces the receiver.*

**MAGI** He's coming over?

**BILLIE** I don't want a *Mona Lisa* smile…

**MAGI** Oh Billie… Billie, you're all in bits and pieces.

**BILLIE** I know. I know. A tumour. Suddenly apparent, but its been there, tiny, growing slowly for a long time. What kind of therapy to take? Chop it out? Radiate it? Let it eat me alive? I see roaches all around me. In me. Blue roaches. Green roaches. Aah! Get off! Get it off. I eat roaches. I pee roaches. Help! I'm losing… I don't, don't… I'm falling…

**MAGI** Billie? Billie?

**BILLIE** I have a dream today.

**MAGI** You had a dream?

**BILLIE** I have a dream that one day every valley shall be engulfed, every hill shall be exalted, and every mountain shall be made low… oh… oh… the rough places will be made plains and the crooked places will be made…

**MAGI** *(overlapping)* It's gonna be all right, Billie.

*MAGI goes to the phone and dials.*

**BILLIE** *(overlapping)* …straight and the glory of the Lord shall be revealed and all flesh shall see it together.

**MAGI** *(overlapping)* It's Magi. You all better get over here, now. No, no, no. NOW. All right. All right.

*MAGI puts down the receiver and returns to BILLIE. She gently takes the red box from out of BILLIE's hands and places it on the mantel.*

**BILLIE** *(overlapping)* …This is our hope…

**MAGI** *(overlapping)* It's gonna be all right. I know… I know…

**BILLIE** *(overlapping)* …With this faith we will be able to hew out of the mountain of despair a stone of hope…

**MAGI** *(overlapping)* It's okay. It's okay. Let's start with a little step. Come on. Come with me. *(MAGI helps BILLIE up.)* Come on… Good. Let's get some soup into you. Warm up that frozen blood of yours.

*(MAGI leads her to the door.)* Warm up your insides. Come… Come on… Chase all the roaches out…

*BILLIE breaks loose of MAGI and rushes to the window.*

*MAGI is no longer in the room. OTHELLO appears wearing a brightly coloured dashiki. He is inspecting a broom laying against the fridge. It is now fall, seven years earlier. Save for the broom and the fridge, the apartment is empty.*

**BILLIE** Look… Come, look… You can see the Apollo from the window. I love it.

**OTHELLO** Where?

**BILLIE** Over there. See.

**OTHELLO** Oh yeh— If I crane my neck.

**BILLIE** I could find some lawn chairs and table and we'd have a city terrace.

**OTHELLO** On the fire escape?

**BILLIE** We'd have our own little balcony.

**OTHELLO** Patio.

**BILLIE** Terrace…

**OTHELLO** We could buy a house up here.

**BILLIE** We can't afford to buy a house until I finish school. If I'm going to go to school full-time, this fall, like we agreed—you'd go to school, then I'd go to school—how can we afford a down payment on a house?

**OTHELLO** I know. I know.

*Pause.*

**BILLIE** I love it. Don't you love it?

**OTHELLO** I love you.

**BILLIE** I love you and I love it.

**OTHELLO** Think Chris Yago and Mona and the other faculty will feel uncomfortable coming up here… for meetings and the like…

**BILLIE** It's on the subway line.

**OTHELLO** And boy do they need to take the journey. I'll take them on a cultural field trip—blow their minds.

**BILLIE** I've longed for this sanctuary.

**OTHELLO** I know what you mean.

**BILLIE** Black boutiques.

**OTHELLO** Black bookstores.

**BILLIE** Black groceries.

**OTHELLO** Filled with black doctors and dentists. Black banks.

**BILLIE** Black streets teeming with loud black people, listening to loud jazz and reggae and Aretha… *(She sings a line from "Spanish Harlem." As the next line starts, OTHELLO joins her.)* Maybe later we could buy a place on "Strivers' Row," that's where all the rich black folks live.

**OTHELLO** Strivers' Row.

**BILLIE** Owned by blacks hued from the faintest gold to the bluest bronze. That's my dream.

**OTHELLO** By then you'd have your Ph.D.

**BILLIE** And a small lecturer's position at a prestigious Manhattan university. We might even have enough money to get a small house in the country, too.

**OTHELLO** A big house in the country, too?

**BILLIE** A big house with a white picket fence.

**OTHELLO** On a rolling emerald hill.

**BILLIE** I want 2.5 kids.

*He kisses her lightly.*

**OTHELLO** You're mad, you know that.

**BILLIE** That makes you some kinda fool for loving me, baby.

**OTHELLO** Let's do it. There's an old broom right over there. Wanna jump it with me?

*OTHELLO retrieves the broom.*

**BILLIE** Are you asking me to m—

**OTHELLO** Yes… Yes, I am asking.

**BILLIE** Yes… *(silence)* Then yes.

*OTHELLO kisses her. He places the broom in the middle of the floor. He takes BILLIE's hand. They stand in front of it.*

What will we use for rings?

**OTHELLO** Think them old slaves had rings? Slave marriages were illegal, remember. This broom is more than rings. More than any gold. *(He whispers.)* My ancient love.

**BILLIE** *(She whispers.)* My soul.

*OTHELLO kisses her hand. The couple gaze at each other, preparing to jump over the broom. They jump. They hold each other. The landlady enters.*

**MAGI** Oh—I'm sorry.

**BILLIE** No, no. We were just… just—

*OTHELLO picks up the broom and places it to one side.*

**OTHELLO** I think we'll take it.

**MAGI** I didn't mean to rush you. I can give you another few minutes if you need to make good and sure?

**BILLIE** I think we're sure. *(to OTHELLO)* You sure? *(to MAGI)* We're sure.

*MAGI looks gravely at BILLIE. They are the only ones in the room. We are back in the present. MAGI carefully approaches BILLIE. BILLIE stares at where OTHELLO stood, only moments ago.*

**MAGI** Come on. Come with me. Come on… Good. Let's get some soup into you. Warm up that frozen blood of yours. *(MAGI leads her to the door.)* Warm up your insides. Come… come on… Chase all the roaches out… One by one… One by one…

*They exit.*

## Scene Eight

*Harlem, present: late summer—afternoon. A lyrical rhapsody swings to the sound of a commentator describing the scene at the Million Man March. The apartment is virtually empty. CANADA is cleaning the kitchen, taking tubs and bags from out of the freezer. He gives them a brief once-over and then throws them into the trash. OTHELLO enters.*

**OTHELLO** Billie? Billie?

**CANADA** Othello! Othello, good to see you, son.

*They shake hands.*

Good to see you.

**OTHELLO** I didn't know… When did you get here?

**CANADA** A few days.

**OTHELLO** Billie didn't say a word.

**CANADA** Well, Billie's in… she's… Billie's not here right now.

**OTHELLO** *(scanning the apartment)* Did she leave anything for me? An envelope… A package—

*He sees the red box on the mantel.*

Oh. Maybe…

*He goes over to it.*

**CANADA** Oh, she said no one was to touch that… I'm supposed to throw it out.

**OTHELLO** Great! *(He opens the red box and takes out the handkerchief.)* It's okay, this is it. It's mine. This is what I was looking for.

**CANADA** I was just about to throw it in with the trash from the fridge.

**OTHELLO** Just in time, huh?

**CANADA** Yeh, some of this stuff's about ready to crawl out by itself.

**OTHELLO** I can imagine.

**CANADA** I swear, one thing had actually grown little feet.

**OTHELLO** Well, Billie wasn't one for cleaning… I guess neither of us was.

*There is an awkward silence between them.*

Well… I should be off.

*He takes some keys from out of his pocket and places them where the red box was laying.*

**CANADA** She tells me you're getting married.

**OTHELLO** I do confess the vices of my blood.

**CANADA** I'm real sorry it didn't work out… Between you and Billie… I mean… I was hoping…

**OTHELLO** Yes. I know.

**CANADA** She's my child, so—

**OTHELLO** I know, I know.

**CANADA** You young'uns don't know the sweetness of molasses… Rather have granulated sugar, 'stead of a deep clover honey, or cane-sugar juice from way into the Demerara. Better watch out for that refined shit. It'll kill ya. A slow kinda killin'. 'Cause it kills your mind first. So you think you living the life, when you been dead a long time.

*Silence.*

**OTHELLO** Well, sir… I should be somewhere.

**CANADA** *(nodding)* Well, I hope we can catch up sometime…

*OTHELLO goes to the door.*

**OTHELLO** That would be great. Tell Billie I came by.

**CANADA** I'll tell her that. She'll be glad to know.

**OTHELLO** Good seeing you.

**CANADA** You too… son… You too.

*OTHELLO takes one last look at the apartment, takes out a tiny cellular phone, and exits. CANADA is still for a few moments. From the hallway we hear OTHELLO.*

**OTHELLO** *(offstage)* Chris Yago, please.

*CANADA returns to the fridge and continues to clean.*

## Scene Nine

*Harlem, 1928: late summer—night. The music softly underscores the voice of Paul Robeson speaking about not being able to get decent acting roles in the US, and how fortunate he feels to be offered a contract to play OTHELLO in England. HE is alone. He proceeds to cover his face in black greasepaint. He begins to speak, as if rehearsing, at first.*

**HE** It is most true; true, I have married her.
It is most…
It is most true; true, I have married her.
For know, but that I love the gentle Desdemona,
(She) questioned me the story of my life
From year to year—the battles, sieges, fortunes,
That I have passed. These things to hear
Would Desdemona seriously incline;
But still the house affairs would draw her thence,
Which ever as she could with haste dispatch
she'd come again, and with a greedy ear
Devour up my discourse. Which I, observing,
Took once a pliant hour…

And often did beguile her of her tears,
When I did speak of some distressful stroke
That my youth suffered…

*In the background we can hear a children's song. HE begins to add a white greasepaint to his lips, completing the mask of the minstrel.*

…My story being done,
She gave me for my pains a world of sighs.
She wished she had not heard it, yet she wished
That heaven had made her such a man. She thanked me,
She thanked me…
She thanked me…
She thanked me…

## Scene Ten

*Harlem, the present: late summer—night. A beryline blues improvisation of "Mama's Little Baby" cascades alongside a reading of the Langston Hughes poem "Harlem." AMAH sits beside BILLIE in the visitors' lounge of the psychiatric ward. AMAH is clearly saddened by BILLIE's state.*

**BILLIE** *(singing)* …Step back Sal-ly, all night long.
Strut-in' down the al-ley, al-ley, al-ley,
Strut-in' down the al-ley, all night long.

**AMAH & BILLIE** I looked over there, and what did I see?
A big fat lady from Ten-nes-see.

*BILLIE gets up and begins to dance.*

I bet you five dollars I can beat that man,
To the front, to the back, to the side, side, side.
To the front, to the back, to the side, side, side.

*The two women laugh.*

**BILLIE** I haven't done that in… in years.

**AMAH** I never knew that one—I just saw Jenny do it the other day.

**BILLIE** I even remember the dance. *(singing under her breath)* …Bet you five dollars I can beat that man…

**AMAH** It's not so bad here.

**BILLIE** You'd think the doctors at Harlem hospital would be black. Especially in psychiatrics. Most of the nurses are black.

**AMAH** But they're nice to you—the doctors?

**BILLIE** They help. I don't—don't want any more pills. And that's okay. They don't really understand, though. I had this dream. Lucinda—she's my main doctor. Lucinda was sitting at the edge of a couch and I asked her a question. But she couldn't answer because her eyes kept flashing. Like neon lights. Flash, flash, flash. That was it. That was the dream. I knew it was important, but I didn't get it. And I told her. And she didn't get it either. But it gnawed away at me… For days… The flashing eyes. And that was it! The eyes were flashing blue. Her eyes were flashing blue. She could only see my questions through her blue eyes.

**AMAH** Something in you really wants to heal.

**BILLIE** Exorcism.

**AMAH** Pardon?

**BILLIE** Repossess.

**AMAH** Self-possession?

**BILLIE** I hate. I know I hate. And he loves. How he loves.

**AMAH** Billie?

**BILLIE** Why is that, you think?

**AMAH** Some of us spend our entire lives making our own shackles.

**BILLIE** Canada freedom come.

**AMAH** And the experienced shackle-wearer knows the best polish for the gilt.

**BILLIE** I wanna be free.

**AMAH** It must be hard, though. I feel for him.

**BILLIE** I'm not that evolved.

**AMAH** Forgiveness.

**BILLIE** Forgiveness…

**AMAH** If I don't forgive my enemy, if I don't forgive him, he might just set up house, inside me.

**BILLIE** I just… I—I despise—I know… I know… Moment by moment. I forgive him now. I hate— I love him so—I forgive him now. And now.

*She moves as if to speak, but stops herself.*

And I forgive him now.

**AMAH** My time's up, sweetie.

**BILLIE** I have a dream…

**AMAH** Sorry?

**BILLIE** I had a dream…

**AMAH** Yes… I know.

**BILLIE** Tell Jenny… Tell her for me… Tell her that you saw me dancing.

**AMAH** I will tell her.

**BILLIE** And tell her… Tell her that you heard me singing.

**AMAH** I will.

**BILLIE** And tell her… I'll see her real soon.

**AMAH** I will tell her, Billie. I will tell her.

*AMAH kisses BILLIE on the cheek and begins to exit. CANADA enters.*

**BILLIE** *(in the background softly)*
Betcha five dollars I can beat that man.
To the front, to the back, to the side, side, side.
To the front, to the back, to the side, side, side.

**CANADA** How's she doing?

**AMAH** Mmm, so-so.

**CANADA** Okay. Thanks.

**AMAH** We'll really miss you when you go—back to Nova Scotia.

**CANADA** Oh, I don't think I'm going anywhere just yet—least if I can help it. Way too much leaving gone on for more than one lifetime already.

*BILLIE stops singing for a moment, then segues into a version of Aretha Franklin's "Spanish Harlem," more hummed than sung.*

*CANADA pats AMAH on the back. AMAH turns and exits. CANADA approaches BILLIE and sits down beside her. Shortly, he joins her in the song. He rests his hand on hers.*

*After several moments: The lights fade to black.*

*The end.*

# SHAKESPEARE'S WILL

VERN THIESSEN

## WHERE THERE'S A WILL

In the past five years or so, Vern Thiessen has vaulted into prominence nationally and internationally as a versatile playwright capable of handling a range of styles, treating large issues with poetic precision, and subtler matters with larger resonance. Born in 1964 in Winnipeg and raised in a Mennonite family, he graduated from the University of Winnipeg in 1985 before moving to Edmonton to earn an M.F.A. in playwriting at the University of Alberta, where he has since returned to serve as an honorary research fellow in playwriting.[1] He has been Artistic Coordinator of Drama at Lakeland College in Lloydminster, playwright-in-residence at Workshop West and the Citadel Theatre, literary liaison for the Alberta Foundation for the Arts, president of Playwrights Guild of Canada and of the Writers Guild of Alberta, and Artistic Associate at the Citadel Theatre, where he worked in dramaturgy and new play development.

Thiessen has written for stage, radio, television, and film, his screenplay for Mieko Ouchi's 1999 short film, *Samurai Swing* having won the 1998 National Screen Institute Drama Prize. His stage plays, representing a broad range of styles and subjects, include *The Courier* (1987), *The Resurrection of John Frum* (1990), *I Fell in Love with an Eel* (1991), *Blowfish* (1996), *Apple* (2002), *Einstein's Gift* (2003), *Shakespeare's Will* (2005), *Back to Berlin* (2005), *Vimy* (2007), and his newest play, *A More Perfect Union*, which will premiere off-Broadway in May 2009. Plays for young audiences include *Dawn Quixote* (1995), *Bird Brain* (2007) and *Rich* (2008, with composer Olaf Pyttlik). Thiessen is the recipient of many awards and honours: *Apple* won both the Alberta Culture Play Award and the Sterling Award for outstanding new play in 2002; *Einstein's Gift* won the 1999 Jewish Playwriting Competition, was nominated for the 2003 Sterling Award for outstanding new play, the 2003 Gwen Pharis Ringwood Award for Drama from the Alberta Book Awards, and won the 2003 Governor General's Literary Award for Drama, the country's highest literary prize; and *Shakespeare's Will* won a Sterling award for outstanding production in 2005. Thiessen has also been awarded the City of Edmonton Arts Achievement Award and the University of Alberta Alumni Award for Excellence, and was shortlisted in 2008 for the prestigious Siminovitch Prize in Theatre. His prominence in Alberta is indicated by his appearance in the province's Olympic television commercial leading up to the Torino games; his prominence in Canada is indicated by many productions, particularly by the Stratford Festival's 2007 production of *Shakespeare's Will*; and his prominence abroad is indicated by the number of high-profile productions his plays, particularly *Apple*, *Einstein's Gift*, and *Shakespeare's Will*, have received in the United States (including off-Broadway) and Europe.

*Shakespeare's Will* puns, of course, in its title, on the playwright's name, intentions, last testament, and sexual appetites—as Shakespeare himself did in his sonnets and elsewhere. It takes up a question that has dogged Shakespeare scholars

[1] I am indebted for much of the biographical information on Thiessen in this introduction to Nothof.

and biographers for centuries. One of the handful of known facts about the life of Shakespeare is that when he died he left his wife, Anne Hathaway, his second-best bed and bedclothes (or "furnishings"), nothing else.

Why?

Apologists and bardolaters have long speculated that the bequest was a sentimental gesture, the second best being the marital bed, the one not reserved for guests. Besides, they argue, a spouse would automatically receive one third of the estate, explaining why no other legacy is mentioned in the will. Thiessen, however, pulls no punches. What if the last bequest of Shakespeare, the universally revered humanist, absentee husband, and father, for almost all of his married life was a vengeful gesture, punishing his wife for her perceived negligence around the death of their one son, the one child—patriarch that Shakespeare was—that truly mattered to him? What then? If you're Anne Hathaway, you curse him and move on.

The play is beautifully written in verse—Thiessen hath a way with words, as does his Anne, whose direct, earthy, and evocative language constitutes the play's action and provides its characterizations. She paints her children, her lovers, her father, and Will's sister Joan in a few bold strokes. Her first-born, Susanna, bending like a willow branch and quiet like her father, holding secrets in her eyes; the twins, Judith, like a firecracker, her bottom yellow, dripping like yolk; and Hamnet, the shipbuilder, silent as a lamb and strong as a rock. Her lovers: Alexander the fruit seller who needs another season to ripen; Matthew hung like his horses but with less between his ears; and Caleb, rough and defiant until a slap to the rear makes him canter. Shakespeare's sister, Joan, not the one imagined by Virginia Woolf, but "a bitch. / I'm sorry but she is." The only character who remains obscure—fittingly, for this is Anne's story—is the absent Will, here, as her father complains, "A CATHOLIC, a TUTOR, a SHAKE-SPEARE, and [...] AN AC-TOR"—and, ironically, "a man of few words." The closest Shakespeare comes to putting in an appearance is a makeshift portrait made of pebbles on a beach that wash away with the waves.

But this play really *is* Anne's story, about her spirit, her strength, and *her* "Will" (in every sense). I have argued in the introduction to this collection that to adapt is often to adapt *to*, as Canadians for centuries have had to adapt to the cultural revenant that is Shakespeare. But Anne Hathaway, as presented here, was surely the first who had to adapt to Shakespeare, and most urgently. He is for her, as he is for us, an absent presence—overwhelming, thrilling, frustrating, but not there. Perhaps, then, Thiessen's version of Anne provides a model of adaptation, accepting as she does his sexuality, missing him, resenting him, loving him, cursing him, and burdened with his legacy—and in the end, as her father instructs, moving on.

**Work Cited**

Nothof, Anne. "Vern Thiessen." *Canadian Theatre Encyclopedia.* 1 November 2008. http://www.canadiantheatre.com/dict.pl?term=Thiessen%2C%20Vern.

## ACKNOWLEDGEMENTS

It takes many people and organizations to help a playwright create, develop, and produce a new play. The playwright thanks the Free Will Players/River City Shakespeare Festival for commissioning the play. Thanks also to the Alberta Foundation for the Arts, the Canada Council for the Arts, the Winspear Fund, the ATP/Banff playRites Colony 2004, Alberta Playwrights Network, the Lee Fund, Epic Theatre Ensemble, Metro Stage, Theatre 40, and the Citadel New Play Development program for assisting in the writing and development of this play.

Thanks must go to the following individuals for their inspiration, support, help, and commitment to both myself and the project: Eden Philp, Ruth Dyckfehderau, Margaret Reed, Lisa O'Connell, Brian Dooley, John Kirkpatrick, John Murrell, David Brundage, James MacDonald, Maureen Labonté, Mark Haroun, Sharon Richardson, Holly Hoover, Vanessa Sabourin, Playwrights Canada Press, Seana McKenna, Miles Potter, Susan Bay Nimoy, Leonard Nimoy, JeanMarie Simpson, and Michael Petrasek.

Thanks also to Bob Baker for the risks he takes in nurturing and producing new plays, and to the Citadel Theatre audiences who have been so supportive of my work in recent years.

A special thanks must go to Geoff Brumlik for his dedication, and for his enthusiasm and passion for the play.

*Shakespeare's Will* was commissioned by Free Will Players in 2002. It premiered in 2005 at the Citadel Theatre, Edmonton, produced by the Citadel in association with Free Will Players. It was performed on the Rice Stage with the following company:

ANNE Jan Alexandra Smith

Directed by Geoffrey Brumlik
Set and costume design by Guido Tondino, assisted by Victoria Zimski
Lighting design by Del Surjik
Sound design/composition by Dave Clarke
Stage managed by Michelle Chan with apprentice Shannon Macelli
Choreography by Anita Miotti

This version of the play was developed for the Stratford Festival of Canada, and opened in June 2007 with the following company:

ANNE Seana McKenna

Directed by Miles Potter
Designed by Peter Hartwell
Lighting design by Kevin Fraser
Composed by Marc Desormeaux
Sound design by Peter McBoyle
Stage managed by Anne Murphy
Assistant stage management by Kim Lott
Production assistance by Lucy Martin
Production stage management by Marylu Moyer

*Shakespeare's Will* had its American premiere at Theatre 40 in Los Angeles, California, in June 2007, with the following company:

ANNE JeanMarie Simpson

Directed by Susan Bay Nimoy
Produced by Leonard Nimoy
Stage Management & Set Design by Crystal M. Munson
Lighting Design by Ellen Monocroussos
Sound Design by Marc Olevin
Costume Design by Shon Leblanc and Perry Ash
Makeup and hair by Debbie San Filippo and Carol Romano
Choreography by L. Martina Young
Production Assistance by Katrien Damman

## CHARACTERS

ANNE, a woman of indeterminate age

## SETTING

Anne's room, her imagination, her memory, her dreams, and the sea.

## STYLE

Although the language is poetic in structure—and the play somewhat based on historical incidents—it should be played without sentimentality, reverence, softness, or overt attempts at historical accuracy. Rather, theatricality, humour, brashness, and non-realism in acting, lighting, set, costume, movement, and music/sound design is encouraged.

Dialects are not to be used.

The play runs approximately one hour and thirty minutes without intermission.

## MOVEMENT, MUSIC, SONGS

These sections of the play are essential to the play's rhythm and must not be omitted. They "cleanse the pallet" and provide important emotional transitions for the audience and for the character of Anne. The "gist" of the music/movement is suggested in this text, but it may be as theatrical as is desired. Music inspiration for these sections include time-honoured songs such as "Miri It Is," "Scarborough Fair," "I Saw My Lady Weep," and "She Moves Through the Fair" to the more modern: "Kindertotenlieder" of Gustav Mahler and the songs of Ralph Vaughan Williams. In the text of this edition, all lyrics are those composed for the premiere production by Geoff Brumlik, and are used here with permission. Music is by Dave Clarke, who can be contacted at stancat@shaw.ca.

## NOTE TO PRODUCERS

Please consult with the playwright, his agent, or the publisher for the most recent version of the script. Should Geoff Brumlik's lyrics be used in production, he is to be credited in the house program.

# SHAKESPEARE'S WILL

*Rain.*
*She moves slowly through it.*
*She enters her house.*
*She stares at her room.*

**ANNE** I long for the sea…

Her white-toothed smile.
Her roaring laugh.
Her salt spray on my lips…

*(wry)* The sea was a far better lover than you, Bill.
When it had me
I was wet and warm.

But you:
you
were a rough rocky shore
your head worn by tide
your beard straggly as seaweed
your eyes…

*A distant bell. She listens.*
*She puts down the will.*
*She lights a lamp.*
*She removes her mourning attire.*
*She stares out the window.*

I buried you in the church
only this morning.
Fifty-two of the town's poorest
one for every year of your life
led the way
hired to mourn your passing.
Then
two-score men
riding the finest geldings
sinking in the soft mud.
Then
a dozen more

walking
the banner of arms
hanging heavy in their wet hands.
Then you
in a wagon covered with black velvet.
And then
I
and your friends from the City
and your family
trailing behind
grief
and the rain
weighing us down
soaked through we are
soggy as the sea.

*Pause.*

After
as the men go to eat
and talk
and drink down your memory,
your sister Joan
hands me your will:

*She looks at the will.*

Come Anne, says Joan
You must go home straight away
Oh? I say
I'll be by tonight, she says.
Why, I say?

And she smiles
smiles
like…

*A distant bell. She listens.*

And now. An hour left
till Joan comes
only an hour
and I haven't even…

*She regards the will.*

*Movement/Music Sequence*[2]

*Perhaps a lively, traditional song. Perhaps "The Fair."*

*(sings)* "The boys, the boys, the boys of the town
They're pretty, and witty, and brave.
They dance like the wind, and they kiss like the sea
And soon 'twill be my heart they crave, they crave
And soon 'twill be my heart they crave.
The boys, the boys, the boys of the town
Are back now from riding the waves
They'll love you so true, till the first morning dew
But then 'twill be elsewhere they'll crave, they'll crave
But then 'twill be elsewhere they'll crave."

*The song swings her into the past.*

A country town, like any other.
A square, with market.
A High Street, with shops.
*(smiles)* I meet you
at the yearly fair
in summer.
Shading our eyes
from the afternoon's sleepy sun.
We watch the players
in from the City
don't remember the name of it
don't care, really.

We stand side by side.
We watch a fat actor
play the part
of a fat actor
and you laugh
and I laugh too
more at you
than the play.

Your eyes dancing
your slender frame
hunched at the shoulders
your arms crossed
fingering your
thin red beard
dissecting every moment

---

[2] *See production notes on Movement/Music.*

your eyebrows knit
trying to understand
how it is stitched together
why it is
what it is.

*(flirting)* I'm Anne, I say.
*(shy)* Aye, you say.

*Pause.*

Of Stratford, I say.
Aye, you say.

*Pause.*

And you?
Bill.

*Pause.*

Of…?
Same.

*Pause.*

Do you come every year?
Aye.

*Pause.*

To the fair.
Aye.

*Pause.*

To see the players.
Aye.

A man of few words, I think.
I like that.
I think.

Later
in my father's barn
you fumble with my skirts.
Your hands, shaking
never having been
had
not by a woman at least

not by an older woman
at least.

*Pause.*

Afterwards:
you, staring at the stars
through the hole
in the barn roof
reliving the play
acting all the parts
making me laugh
more than I did at the fair.

*Pause.*

How old are you, I say.
Five and twenty, you say.
Liar, I say.
...Eighteen, you say.
(Oh Lord...)

And you?
...Older.
How much?
Older!
Thirty?
NO!
What then?
Six and twenty.
And I see
you look terrified
and very pleased with yourself
all in one.

You know, I say,
I don't want to marry.
Not you, not anyone.
I'm happy, I say,
to live with my father
and brothers
well-fed
well-cared for
much to do
with Mother gone
never wanted more.

Aye, you say,
me too.
Besides, you say,
I'm Catholic.
Catholic?
Aye.
Oh dear.
Aye.
I'm not.
Aye.

Besides, you say…
What…?
Nothing, I…
…What?
NOTHING!

*Pause.*

Do you… I say
…do you…
What.
I don't know… like boys?
A long pause here.
…Don't know, you say.
Don't know?!
And I laugh
and laugh:
Don't know…?!

But then I see
you are hurt.
It's fine, I say,
doesn't matter,
doesn't matter
not to me.
Tell you a secret:
Me? I like boys too,
men that is
I like the company of lots and lots of men.
Why d'you think I go to the fair?

And your eyes smile
and you laugh
and I wipe away your tears
and we know
know

there is something…
something
between us.

SHAKE-SPEARE!
My father is furious.
A Shake-speare!?
…Father…
The son of a glove maker?! The son of a papist who can't pay his bills?!
The son of the WORST MAYOR WE EVER HAD?!
Father please!
What's he do then?
Tutor! I say, *(to impress)* in Lancashire.
LANCASHIRE! Dear poaching papists!
Father!
A tutor?! A Catholic!?And a Shake-speare!?
Jesus Christ! Jesus Christ in Heaven!

But when two months pass
and no sign of blood
I know, I know
we are joined
forever
whether we like it
or not.

I'm with child, I say.

*Pause.*

Oh?

*Pause.*

Yes.

*Pause.*

What should we do, I say?
And you smile
smile
from ear to ear.
Get married?
Aye!!!
Aye!!

And we both
laugh and laugh…

JESUS CHRIST!
Father.
WITH CHILD?!
Father.
You: six and twenty?! And him: barely eighteen?! And
both of you, with
NO MONEY?!
Father please.
You'll not be married in the queen's church,
not on my life, not on my life, or your mother's certain to
RISE FROM THE DEAD TO SMITE US ALL!!
Father!
Marry a Catholic?! And with child?!
And to a Shake-speare?!
Jesus Christ! Jesus Christ in Heaven!

And so
three days later
off to Temple Grafton
five miles from town
on my father's horse.

My father
holding me round the waist
praying for forgiveness he is
from God
or my mother
I'm not sure which.
Me: a head crowned with garlands
and
a handful of rosemary.

Father and I race to get there.
Bad luck, he says,
bad luck to marry after the clock strikes noon.

We stop along the way
twice
so I can retch
the morning sickness
already upon me.

We arrive as
the church bell
tolls eleven.

But you...
you do not arrive till two.

My father
is fit to be tied.
Visions drift past his eyes:
You: drawn and disembowelled.
You: hanged and quartered.
You: beheaded and burned.
But a sideways glance from me
stays your execution
to a later date.

With you
your best friend:
Hamnet Saddler
the baker from town
on a horse
spotted with flour.
Chubby and clean
dressed in his finest
he is today
"official wedding witness."

And you.
You.
Your beard waxed
your clothes fresh
though your eyes are red
from too much ale, I presume.
Still, they sparkle
like Venus at dusk.

The priest
(John Rith by name)
deemed unsound by some,
"unsound" meaning Catholic.
His nose red with spirits
his breath reeks
so strong of Madeira
I think he himself has been bottled in Portugal.
And when the moment comes
you give me no ring.

I'll buy you one later, you say,
when we have money
I promise.
When we have money.

*Pause.*

Father Rith blesses us
and when we exchange the vows
you kiss me.

And now
I see
the red
is not from drink at all
but from tears.

I love you,
you say,
I love you so.

Alone that night
in your parents' house
you take out a sheaf of paper

*She picks up a sheaf.*

and read to me
some words
words:

"Those lips that Love's own hand did make
Breath'd forth the sound that said I hate
To me that languish'd for her sake:
But when she saw my woeful state,
Straight in her heart did mercy come.
Chiding that tongue, that ever sweet
Was used in giving gentle doom:
And taught it thus anew to greet:
'I hate' she alter'd with an end
That follow'd it as gentle day
Doth follow night, who like a fiend
From heaven to hell is flown away.
'I hate' from hate away she threw,
And sav'd my life, saying 'not you.'"[3]

[3] *Sonnet 145*

*Pause.*

...Well...
Do you like it? you say.
It's... it's beautiful.
It's about you.
Oh?
"'I hate' from hate away she threw,
And sav'd my life, saying 'not you.'"
"Hate away," "Hatheway," you see?
*(charmed)* Oh...
One day, you say,
one day, I shall write better.

And then
you hold out your hand
and I mine
and sitting on the bed
we make a vow:

To live our own lives.
To treat each other well
but allow for our
separate desires.
To have our secrets
but protect
what we each
hold most dear.

It will be
our own kind of marriage.

*Music/Movement Sequence:*

*She dances with an imaginary Bill, her movement echoing their passion. Perhaps a haunting melody, perhaps "Rushes."*

*(sings)* "On a soft bed of rushes
With my lover I lay
When a sweet tide of passion
Did whirl us away...
Warm waters swirled round us
From north and from south
My breast on his bosom
My mouth on his mouth..."

*The bell invades. Rain.*

I buried you in the church
only this morning
with that stupid headstone
with that stupid inscription
insisted on
by your stupid sister Joan.

*She picks up the will.*

You must go home straight away, she says.
Oh? I say
I'll be by tonight.
Why, I say?
Have you not read it? she says
No, I say.
And I shant.
And she smiles
smiles
like…

*She considers it. Lets it rest.*

No.
No.
Not now…

*Her mind moves to the past. Perhaps she finds a child's dress.*

Seven months, Bill. Married seven months,
and still living with your father.

It is shortly after noon
I in the kitchen
and you out
busy with your pupils
(I think)
when
inside me
something bursts
and I fall
the water running down
and I know
know
Susanna
inside me
is saying

I am coming.
Now. I am coming.

Your mother gathers
women from the town
(except Joan, who
like you
is nowhere to be found).
She has gathered them to help
And when you do finally arrive
they bar your entrance
to the house
send the men to get you drunk.
And countless hours later
after all the pain and pushing and Please God Let It Come,
Susanna
awash in blood and phlegm and
and every inch of my insides
slides
out of me
like a seal
as if
born in the water herself.
Thus she comes to us
Bill.

*A child cries.*

I do not know how
to hold a child
rock it to sleep.
My mother taught me nothing of children.
She died before she could teach me
how to hold it
calm it
speak to it
when it wants not to lay down.

I shake my head:
no don't cry
no
a nap, you need to nap,
to sleep is good! it's good!
Suddenly knowing
why mothers of old
threw their children from windows
left them to die on mountaintops

buried them under pillows.
Quiet, I say.
Quiet.
But to no avail.

Enough, I say.
Enough!
To no avail.

BAD GIRL, I say.
BAD!
To no avail.

She wants my breast
but will not suck
and when finally she does,
my nipple
raw like a skinned knee
chokes her
drowns her in my milk,
and she cries more.

And then I hear it
the sound of…
No…. No…
But there it is:
Shite.
Yellow, brown, runny SHITE
everywhere
on my arms
on my lap
on my fingers
and I
I am
COVERED IN SHITE.

And now she is SCREAMING
and crying
and
and
And now I cry
cry like a child myself
cry…

And I, I,
I must do something
focus the mind
sink the screams

loud as any gull.
And so I rock her
I rock her
and say:
*(gently)* Shhh…
Shhh…

And like the sea sweeping the shore…

Shhh

…soft as surf on sand…

Shhh…

…she drifts off…

The sweet silence of sleep.

Saved I am.

Saved by the sea.

*Pause.*

And when
almost three years later
in our own tiny house in town
Judith and Harry come to us
they come together
and I
I am glad simply to be alive.
The women of the town
wide-eyed and whispering
amazed I have survived
the birth of twins.
A miracle! they say,
a girl AND a boy! Praise God!

And you…
You are so happy.
To have a son
a son
(as well as another girl, of course, of course)
but a son!
A son!

At night
when all the children are asleep

I watch
as you start writing
late at night
poem after poem
reading them to anyone who will listen:
me
your pupils
Gnasher, the dog.

And then
for the first time
with homemade poppets
you make up plays
act them out
to make Susanna laugh.
Susanna: Your little poppet.

*Pause.*

The summers come
and with them the fair
and with the fair
the players.

You begin missing work
your pupils wondering where you are
and I saying you are ill
while you run to the square to
see all the plays
three days straight
never coming home nights
drinking with the actors
at the Bull's Head:
devising plots
making rhymes
building characters
in your mind.

And I keep my promise
to allow you your life. .
Even when
the children wonder
where you are
even when
I am exhausted from worry
even when
at night

the children asleep
I sit
alone
by the fire
try to remember
what it was like
to be
not a mother
but a woman
wanting nothing more
than for you
to hold me
talk with me.
Even then
I keep my vow.

*Pause.*

Then
one night
(Susanna three, the twins barely a year)
you stumble home
drunk
not with ale
but with a future.

A position, you say
I've been offered a position!
With the Queen's Men
at first as a player
but later, perhaps later
as a writer,
a writer!!

The excitement in your voice
the joy in your eyes
the thrill in your hands
as they dance their ideas in the air.

I'll come back every month, you say.
I'll make ten shillings a week
ten shillings!
That's more than I make now!
I'll send home money!

Please, you say,
please…

*She sighs.*

I am doubtful.

Trust me, you say.
Trust you?
Aye, you say, trust me.
You in the City and me here
with three children?
Your father'll help, you say.
Oh my father *loves* you.
Stop it.
Going off to be a writer, oh he'll love that.
Stop it!
Trust you?
STOP IT!

*Pause.*

How can I?
How can I trust something
I don't understand?
How can I…

*Pause.*

And then.
You speak, you say:
*(gently)* Listen to me.
Anne.
Listen.
We are different than others.
Since we first met
*you've* guided our way
done what's right:
marriage
children
work
and you being older
wiser
I trusted you.
I trusted you, Anne.
And now
now
you must trust me
But how, I say
how do I do that?

From here, you say
from the heart.

*She sighs again.*

Six months, I say.
THANK YOU!
Six months!
and then we shall see!

Thank you, thank you! And you
kiss me
hug me
and I can see the tears
well up like waves
behind your eyes.

You shan't regret this, you say
you shan't.
Don't worry
don't
I will be back anon.

Does that mean soon? I say.
It means…
what it means.

Jesus Christ!
Father.
A PLAYER?!
Father.
A CATHOLIC, a TUTOR, a SHAKE-SPEARE,
and now AN AC-TOR!?
Father please.
JESUS CHRIST! JESUS CHRIST IN HEAVEN!

Two days later
you borrow a horse
from Hamnet Saddler
your bag stuffed
with half-written plays and poems
Susanna on my hip
the twins with my father.

We kiss
once.

Twice.
I leave, then
run back to
kiss you again.

You look at me
your eyes wet as the day.

Don't forget me, I say,
don't forget me.

You try to speak
but…
all you can do…
…is wave.

*Music/Movement Sequence:*

*She waves goodbye, Susanna on her hip. Perhaps a melancholy song. Perhaps "My Love Doth Fly."*

*(sings)* "My love doth fly on golden wing
With golden note my love doth sing
My love doth light on highest bower
And chimes my name out every hour.
My love doth soar through golden skies
On golden breeze my love doth glide
My love doth skim o'er golden sea
and thus, so golden, my love comes to me."

*As the sequence progresses, the wave of her hand transforms into a flood of memory…*

Six months pass
and I agree to another six months.
Then another
And another
till the years blend
like sand on a shore.
Our separate lives…

*Perhaps she spots some toys. Perhaps a doll:*

Susanna shoots up
taller and taller
but is still your little poppet
lanky and thin

like the willow in front of our house
her hair
falling past her eyes
her long arms
bending like a branch
to pick up Catter, meowing.

Joan says
she is always sad
but I say no
she is only quiet
like her father
holding secrets in her eyes.

*Next, a carving, perhaps of a hen.*

And then Judith
like the firecrackers
we see from China
twirling
popping
she explodes here and there.
She has taken
to talking to the chickens
chasing the hens round the yard
naming them
speaking to them
teaching them
how to best lay eggs
demonstrating
by SITTING ON THEIR EGGS FOR THEM,
after which
she gets into a fight with me
her bottom yellow
dripping with yolk.
And so it is I call her my chick.
Judith, my chick, chick, chick.

*Next, a child's model ship.*

And of course, Hamnet.
The flip side of his twin.
He tumbled out last
but insists
on being first in everything else.
Hamnet is a stupid name
don't you think?

Very
I don't know,
German
or something.
"Hamnet" after your best friend Saddler.
Might as well call him Cornelius or Oswald
or something.
He hates it too
asks can I change it?
I like Harry, Mother, call me that
and so I do.

Judith came into the world crying
but Harry?
Silent as a lamb.
Well-built and strong,
strong in spirit, strong in mind.
He is a rock
standing tall against any wave
shining when life's sea
splashes against him
glistening in the sun
even when…
even when…

*Pause.*

Harry likes to build things.
Not plays like you
but ships.

He dreams of the sea
of visiting far-off lands
whittling boats
from any piece of wood he can find.
Collecting rocks from the yard
to fashion a harbour
old cloth from my washing
to cut into sails
stick sailors from splinters of firewood
cork from Sunday's sherry
to float them
till he has built enough
*Victory*s, *Triumph*s, and *Golden Lion*s
to battle any armada.

He plays with Saddler's son
carefully carrying their prize creations
down to the river.
They run along the banks
to watch their ships' journey.

And should a ship run aground
or disappear
in an eddy
or whirlpool
or the reeds
Harry never curses,
Bill. Never.

No, he simply runs back home
builds another ship
to save the old one
from sinking
to a watery tomb.

*Pause.*

Your prize ship, Bill.
Your prize.

*The bell and the rain return her to the present.*

Your sister Joan
is a bitch.

I'm sorry but she is.
She is bitter and nosey
and at the funeral
talks of nothing but you
never once asking about me
never once asking about the children
never once…

*She picks up the will. Puts it down.*

Have you not read it? she says.
No, I say,
and I shan't.
It's all written down, she says,
It's all there in steadfast ink.
And she smiles
smiles like…

Pff.
What does she know, eh?
Of us.
Our lives…

*She laughs.*

And when you buy me a new house
this house, Bill
Joan is FURIOUS.

He must be doing well,
she says.
Yes, I say.
Very well, she says
her eyes green
as we watch men from town
deliver…
Built chairs?!
To replace old stools.
Stitched rugs?!
To replace loose rushes.
Oak shutters?!
To replace flimsy pine.

And our bed
now stuffed with soft feathers
instead of scratchy straw
the children
so excited to
have beds of their own.

And I hire two servants,
Brundage and Nelly.

Nelly helps
to tend
the ox and hens
the goats and swine
the peacocks and pigeons
her arms sinewy and strong
as any mare.

Brundage pulls white water lilies
from our pond
and helps tend the garden:
Snapdragons and

Columbines
Daisies and
Marigolds
Sneezewort and
Yarrow
his fingers thin and delicate as
any stem.

Brundage wants to marry Nelly
desperately
but he is too shy to ask
and she too shy to say a word.
They live together
here as husband and wife
and yet I have never heard them say the words
I love you.
Never slept in the same bed
...I don't think.

Perhaps, Bill
Perhaps
Like us
They have made their own vows.

Two servants!?
Joan cannot contain
the bile brimming on her lips:
To do WHAT? she says.
To WORK, I say.
Oh! says Joan.
Oh!
And she scuttles off
like a spider running from rain.

*Pause.*

We become a kind of family:
The children and I and Brundage and Nelly.

The children are proud of their horses
Brundage of his ale,
Nelly of her butter
and I
I
I am proud of the excellence in our honeybees.

Bees love gossip, as you know Bill.
It is considered lucky to tell the bees

every bit of news.
If you don't
they may leave
and take their good luck with them.
So I must tell them all my secrets.
And so I do:

I say to them, I say:

My friends, my friends…
*(the joy of telling a secret)* I like men.
*Many* men.

It is a funny thing, my friends
I have only now discovered
being married
it is far more respectable to have many lovers.
When you are young and active
you are called
a slut
or a whore
or a strumpet
but once you are married
you are seen merely as
"dissatisfied"
or "unfaithful" or
"adventurous."
Silly
how we want to rob a young woman of her desire
and make her unwhole.

And now
with this new house
and servants
and time
I am again able to entertain the company of men.
Many men.
Men like Richard… Frederick… Alexander…

Alexander is young.
A fruit seller at the market
he likes to touch
and taste
and tease me.
But.
He thinks he knows what he wants

more than he does
and in truth needs another season
to fully ripen.

Now Matthew…
Matthew helps with the horses
and like his steeds
has much to be thankful for
between his legs.
Alack, he has
nothing so large between his ears.

And then there is Caleb.
Caleb is a stranger
passing through town
he knocks on my door
looking for a night's lodging
in the barn.
Rough face
rough mind
chest like a shelf
stomach like a rock
and his hands
hmm.
He speaks little
but his fingers
his mouth
his tongue
say more than any words.
I am wet well before the rain beats down on the barn roof,
the sharp smell of straw caught in my throat.

Come 'ere, he says
and I obey
come 'ere, he says
and I act defiant
pretending to struggle
wanting to be had.
But then
I turn the tables
ride him like my horse
control him
the reign of my hand
grabbing his long mane
galloping
through his flesh till he is snorting

and thirsty and sweating with exhaustion
begging for rest.

And then I slap his rear
and he canters off
never to return.

It's a funny thing,
my friends,
how once you've had them
they either lose interest completely
or want to marry you.
Never in between.
Always racing to the future
never enjoying the present.

*Pause.*

And yet
my friends
for all this…
for all this…

I miss my husband.
Not a man
but a husband.

A husband who is…
present.
Not "Here."
But "Present."
A difference.

What is it about men?
Eh? What is it?

But the bees never answer.
Only hum
in their hive.

The more you succeed, Bill
the less and less you come home.

At first it was every month,
then every three
then on holy days to see the children,
then once when a bout
of the Fever

briefly closes the theatres,
once when your father died,
once for your mother,
sadly Joan lives on in perpetuity.

I become a beggar for news
asking anyone who comes from the City:
Do you have any word from my husband?
Yes, his play is doing well, they say.
Yes, I know, but my husband, do you have word from him?
You should be proud, they say.
Yes, I am, but has he sent word.
But now you write even less than you visit
saving your words only for work.
Only shillings arrive,
shillings and short messages:

*She pulls some from the table.*

"Dearest Anne:
All well here.
Will write later with details
Much Love
Bill."

Or:

"Dear Anne:

Send Hamnet and the girls my best.
Love
Bill."

Or:

"Anne:
Home next month.
Bill."

But you never come.

At night…

I dream…

I am a gull
flying over
rocks, land
sliding down creeks, rivers, and roads

soaring into the City
to land atop the theatre.

I perch myself above the crowds
to see your newest
to see the players
to hear your words.

I watch them float up
the words
your words
and I
I snatch them in my beak
warm them under my wing
take them back to my nest
and like juicy worms
feed them to the children
who gobble them down.
The words.
Your words.

And when
finally
you DO come
it's unannounced
a surprise.

For "Hamnet's birthday,"
you say.
And Judith's, I say.
Of course
and Judith's…

*Pause.*

And to see you playing with Harry.
Later
when the children are asleep
and we are alone
I say, I say:
Bill.
Bill.
It's time.

For what, you say.
It's time we came to live with you.
In the City.

Oh? you say.
Yes. We are coming to the City, Bill.
No, you say.
It's no place to raise children, Anne.

There are plenty of children in the City, Bill.

Is that what you want? you say,
Is that what you really want?
Do you really want the children to see
women whoring on the streets?
Do you want them to smell Fleet Ditch
stinking to high heaven?
Do you want them to watch men
begging in the streets?
To see sometime criminals
chained to the banks of the river?
To watch them die by the washing of three tides?
Do you really want the children to see these things, Anne?
Do you?

But that's not it.
You have secrets.
I know it.
I have heard talk
of a friend
a companion
in the City.
A man.
And that's fine
for I have secrets of my own
and best we leave them
for the bees.

I miss you, Bill.
Aye…
I've had enough of this.
I want the children to know their father.
Aye…
Then let us come!

Anne…
you say.

Yes?
Our vow
to allow each other to live our own lives.
Yes?

To protect what we each hold most dear.
Yes?
I take care of you, Anne.
Yes, you take care of me and the children and I
I give you decency, respect, lineage—
No, Anne, you say.
No.
You give me more than that:
You give me my work.
You give me my life, Anne.
But my life.
In the City.

*Pause. She sighs.*

And so you go.
And so I stay.
And try
to trust what I don't understand
to respect
what I can't control
and to let go
what I want to save.

*Movement/Music Sequence:*

*Her daily routine, methodical and efficient. Perhaps an eerie, menacing song. Perhaps: "It Scirtches and Scratches."*

*(sings)* "It scirtches and scratches
And claws at the door.
It nibbles through bedding and sheets.
It steals like a thief
Through the dead dark of night
And will gnaw on your bones while you sleep,
While you sleep
It will gnaw at your bones while you sleep..."

*She flings open the windows of the past.*

A hot spring day
shedding its winter coat.
The town comes alive
with birds

the scent of lilac
a warm breeze.

*Pause.*

I walk to the market
to buy cures:
sage and bay
for Susanna's headaches.
Saffron and basil
for Father's heart.
Wormwood and mint
for Judith's ever-sensitive stomach.

*Pause.*

Walking home through the square
I pass by the church.

*(suspicious)* Outside
women praying
for sudden salvation,
men
mad with fear
lashing themselves
atoning for the evils of the world.

*Pause.*

…this is not good…

*Pause.*

Almost home, down the lane,
a scream.
A woman crying.
I see a man stumble from the door
coughing blood.

Don't touch me! he says.
Robert! she cries.
Don't touch me!
Go back, woman! Go back!
Robert!
And people near
pull her away as
he stumbles toward the next lane
pistol in hand.
No! she cries, No!

Then a shot
and he is dead.

The next day
I open my door
and stare down the street
nearly empty
save the mayor's cart
pulling through town.
They stop by the house of the woman
and paint a cross of red on her door.

News sweeps the town like a tide.
I can smell it in the wind
the spring is hot and damp
Gnasher is barking at things not there
Catter is scratching the walls of the house.
It is just like…
It is just like…

I am eight and my mother is ill.
You were lucky, Bill.
Born in the spring that year you were.
You were spared
then
when the Fever
fetched a third of the town.
A whole third.
But my mother…
Her skin
is like stew:
burn marks
the size of lentils
boiling
on her arms
she shivering
even with the sun so hot that summer.
Then
hazelnuts on her neck,
then
goose eggs on her back,
then blood
when she sneezes
then more
when she coughs

and then
then
Father knows
it is time.

Come now my sweetlings, he says,
come now.
And he settles us in
by the fire
and tells us stories
of the sea.

Father was a ship's boy
carefully tending the hourglass
turning it
and soon as the sand had run through
he would strike a bell
for all aboard to hear.
When not at the glass
Father made "the sand" for it:
taking old eggshells
scraping them
rubbing them
till their sticky crust was gone
grinding them down
so thin
that they passed like sand
through a sieve.

And so
huddled by the fire
he tells us tales:
Of ports and pirates
of black armadas
attacking by morn
of angels
lighting the ship by night
of Grimsby and Liverpool
Scarborough and Hull
of Italy and Spain
India and Africa.
And we laugh and squeal
and cry and feel
we are safe
safe as sailing, he says,
safe as sailing when the wind is up.

No matter what happens sweetlings, he says,
when the wind is up
you move on.
You always move on.

And so to save ourselves,
he says
we must leave
leave
your mother.

*Pause.*

We travel to the sea
where Father spent his youth.
He builds a small cabin
where we are safe
away from the rats
breeding in the walls of our house.
We live there for three months
playing tag with the surf
building castles in the sand
the waves rocking us to sleep
like she was our mother.

But when cool autumn comes
we return from the sea
and watch
as Father
lights fire to our house
our mother
now dead
inside
the church bells tolling
tolling.

And so
I examine the children
incessantly:
Lips
tongue
Fever
Nothing.
No cough
no sneezing

no diarrhea
nothing.

But then
I see it:
Gnasher.
Limping.
I take a cloth
carefully lift his paw.

A sore.
Could be nothing.
But…
But…

*Pause.*

Just then
Harry comes inside
holding a rat
Catter's snagged.
He's taken your old pocketknife
cut the rat through, examining its parts
his hands covered in blood.

WHAT ARE YOU DOING?
I say.
I grab the knife
careful to pick it up with a cloth
throw it out the door
I pull him to the basin
wash his hands with lye
to let him know I am serious.

NEVER! I say.
Mother! he says.
NEVER. TOUCH. THOSE. THINGS. NEVER.
Mother!
Do you want to turn out like grandmother?
…no…
Do you want that? Do you?
No.
Do you?
NO!

*Pause.*

No.
Now is the time.

I will not live another Fever
I will not.

*Pause.*

I find Brundage.
The carriage, I say.
Wot? he says
THE CARRIAGE!
Now? he says.
Go!
They're shutting the town tomorrow, ma'am.
Then we must leave tonight.
But, but where to, ma'am?
The sea.
The sea?! But that's, that's three days journey, ma'am!
Will you come?

A pause here.

Will you?
Ma'am I…
We need you.
I…
Please.

*Pause.*

And so he fetches the carriage.
And so we pack.

*She does.*

Coats and blankets.
Food and money.
Quill and ink.
Paper and seals.
Books and toys.

Mother?
Yes my chick?
Where we going?
Away, Judith.
Where?
A trip, my chick. Holiday.
To see Father?
Maybe…

Mother?
Yes, Harry.

Is Father dead?
Now why would you say such a thing?
All the children said
last week
before we had to stay inside
they said everyone in the big City is dead.
Well he's not.
How'd you know?
I know.
But how?

I know.

*Pause.*

But I don't.
Bill.
Know.

*Pause.*

Then Nelly.
A letter
from Master Will.
I snatch it from her fingers.
Finally.

Short as always:

"Dearest Anne:
Don't worry.
I am well.
Do what you must.
Much Love
Bill."

Thank God you're alive. Thank God. At least I know that.

*Pause.*

Last minute instruction to Nelly
out of the children's earshot:

*She writes quickly on paper.*

Send this to my father.
Yes ma'am.
Have him kill Gnasher.
But ma'am.
I know it's hard

but it must be done.
Yes ma'am.
Send this to Master Will
letting him know the children are safe.

Yes ma'am.
We'll be back. I promise.
But she swallows hard
fear in her eyes.

I kiss her cheek.
If she has it
I will die.
We all will.
But how can I not.
Kiss her.

*Pause.*

After midnight.
Brundage snaps the reigns
and the carriage is off.

We ride through the night
the decaying bodies
lie by the road
shadows in the moonlight.

What are those, Mother?
Nothing, Harry.
Are they dead?
No, they are sleeping,
and so should you.
Why are they sleeping outside? he says.
It's been hot, I say,
and it's cooler
to sleep out of doors.

At the edge of town
we are met by the mayor's guard.
I pay him off with jewellery.

Travelling through the night
through the countryside.
Each town
burning their dead
the fires
lighting our way.

The second day:
the sun peeks from behind
the clouds.

Are we there yet?
they ask.
And I laugh
and say,
Soon, my sweetlings.
Soon we will be safe.
Safe as sailing when the wind is up.

*Pause.*

And then
on the third day
the carriage stops.
I awake
and yawn and stretch
the children beside me.
And step down and I look to the horizon and I…
I…

*She sees it.*

You never forget, do you:
when you first see it.

Its wide smile
its salty breath
its loud laugh
its broad brow,
broad
as the shoulders of my father.

I have not been to the sea
since my mother's death,
since I myself was a child
and now
here I am
back
with my own children.

And we stand
all of us
staring at the sea.

Brundage sets up house
in our carriage
puts up a makeshift tent.
And we?
We run to the shore.

Susanna hunts for starfish
to send to you
little Judith in frilly hat
Harry launching his ships into oncoming waves
and I…
I…

I see her white-toothed smile
hear her roaring laugh
from deep in her belly
taste the shower of her spray
on my lips
feel her hands
scrubbing my skin clean.
And I say, I say:
*(laughs)* I know you!
I know you!

Mother?
Yes, Judith my chick?
What does Father look like?
Stupid! says Susanna, like his portrait!
Now now!
He looks like me! says Harry
Yes, he looks like you
but older.
But what does he LOOK like, really.
Well my sweetlings…
well…

*She creates the portrait with found items:*

Here we are at the sea yes?
Yes!
Then we will create our own portrait.
They laugh
yes, yes, let's.

His face is as shiny as the moss there on the hill.
And they all grab moss to create an outline of your face.

His eyes are like two shiny stones on the beach.
Harry carefully chooses two
and Susanna places them down.

His hair
—what's left of it—
(they laugh again)
is like the straggly seaweed there.
Judith scoops some of the slimy stuff and
we fashion a wig for you.

His beard is soft, like the rushes in the bush back there.
They all run to yank them up
and place them carefully on your chin.

Does he smile, Mother?
Yes, my chick, always.
And what's that like?
Like the sun dancing on water.
We can't collect that! they scream.
No, I say.
No you can't.
So you will have to imagine that, my sweetlings.

And when the portrait is done
we all sit on our haunches
and admire our art...

...till the surf washes
your smile
out to the sea.

*The bell. She looks around her room, the light now fading.*

Your sister Joan
is a bitch
and chronically late
I might add.
Thank God,
thank God for that today
for I haven't even...

*She fingers the will. Pause.*

Fifteen years since... I last went to the sea.
And then
last month
a note

announcing your return.
Your friends
from the City
throwing you a party
here
"in honour of your departure from the theatre."
You are coming back.
You.
Are coming back.

*She begins to dress, for both Joan and his arrival.*

And so
I prepare a feast.
Joan insists on helping
but does nothing
only talks of you
and your successes
and your wealth
and your honours
and all your friends coming back with you
as if *I* didn't feel proud of you.

Joan fusses over every part of the feast
till Brundage and Nelly
are set to commit murder.
How the sauces are too spicy
and the table settings too gauche
and *again*
telling me how badly I have raised the children
after all
Judith is now poor and plump
Susanna is married to an idiot
and Harry, Harry…
Well!

Joan has not worked a day in her life
never had a child
nor screwed a man.
Such living is unhealthy, Bill, truly, it is.

And then
after a lifetime away
you finally come home.
Home.

Funny.
Nervous as a schoolgirl
I am.
Not sure why.

You arrive
in a horse-drawn carriage.
You climb the steps to the new house:
balding
older
your eyes squinting from decades
of writing by candlelight
your brow furrowed from
building and rebuilding
burnt theatres.

*Pause.*

Hello Bill, I say.
Hello Anne.

*Pause.*

Welcome home, I say.
Thanks.

*Pause.*

You look well, I say.
Thanks.

*Pause.*

As do you, you say.
Thanks.

*Pause.*

And we kiss.
The first time in many a year
and for a brief moment
it is as if
we are back at the fair.

*Pause.*

That night, we throw the party
the great feast for your
retirement.

Your friends arrive:
Saddler and Fletcher

and Julyus Shawe and John Robinson
and Robert Whattcott and John Hemings
and Richard Burbage and Henry Condell
and Francis bloody Bacon
(Lord but he is a tedious man!)
and you all drink and eat and talk of old times.
So many people
so much laughter
in a house
that has been quiet
for so long…

But you
you do not laugh much.
You are
sad
awkward
out of place
looking for a new audience
for your old stories.

Susanna and Judith
arrive
greet you graciously
but look at you strange
call you Bill.
More like an uncle now
than a father.
You ask them little
only
how are you faring
and
I trust all is well
fearing deeper questions
would bring answers
you would not know how to respond to.

Searching too, you are.
For him.
The one I was told of
but never met.
The one who died
last summer
in the City.

*Pause.*

The next day
we travel to the graveyard
place garlands on our parents' graves.
Then
we go to the place
by the stream
underneath the ash.
But you stop.

No…
Bill.
No, you say,
I cannot.
Please, I say.
Please.
"For those things we hold most dear."

But you do not come
simply stand away
as I lay herbs from the garden:
rosemary for remembrance
sage for strength
thyme for courage.
And parsley
to take away bitterness.

A week ago
I help you to bed.
Sweat
drips down your balding head
past your cheek
like rain on the window.

I lay down beside you.
You are hot
as an oven
burning
even as
the night grows cold.
I close my eyes and…

*Pause.*

And when I open them again
I know

I know
the night has swept you away.

I go to the window.

*She does.*

Rain.
And fresh cool air
washes into the room
and rushes out again
taking you with it.
And you are gone.

*Pause. The bell. The rain.*

And now:
the tributes
the plans for a book and
the remounting of your plays.

I must play the widow.
It is so much like work
so boring
so precious
so…
not you.

Come, Anne, she says.
You must go home straight away.
Oh?
I'll be by tonight, she says.
Why?
Have you not read it? she says.
No, I say,
and I shan't.
It's all written down, she says.
It's all there in steadfast ink.
He never forgot you know, she says,
he never forgot.
And she smiles
smiles
like…

*She picks up the will.*

But why.
Why would I read it?

No one knows, Bill.
No one knows the vow we kept
what we held most dear.
No one knows that
what mattered
between us
was not written on paper
but on our hearts.
Only I know
the words written there.

But read it now I must.

*She reads.*

"In the name of God, Amen.
I, William Shakespeare
of Stratford-upon-Avon
in the county of Warwick
gentlemen
in perfect health and memory…"

Yes yes yes…

"Item:
I give and bequeath unto my daughter Judith
one-hundred-and-fifty pounds of lawful English money…
…in discharge of her marriage portion…"

Ahh. Bribing her to marry, I see.

*She flips forward a page.*

"Item:
I give, will, bequeath, and devise
unto my eldest daughter Susanna…
to have and to hold
all during the term of her natural life,
all my goods, chattel, leases, plate, jewels, and household stuff whatsoever.
And after her decease
to the first son of her body lawfully issuing, and to the heirs…

…male…

…of her body…"

*Pause.*

I see. Lineage.

*She finds another spot.*

"Item:
To Hamnet Sadler 26 shillings and eight pence to buy him a ring…
And to my fellows in the theatre
John Hemings, Richard Burbage, and Henry Condell
26 shillings and 8 pence apiece
to buy them all rings…"

*She rubs her ring finger.*

Rings… *(wry)* even though… even though…!

*She reads more.*

"Item:
I give and bequeath
unto my said sister Joan
20 pounds
and all my wearing apparel
and I do will and devise unto her…

the house in Stratford…

wherein she may dwelleth
for her natural life…"

*She rereads this to herself, confused.*

The house…
The house…?
But….

*Pause.*

"Item: I give unto my wife…"

*She turns over the leaf, reads to self, then:*

"I give unto my wife…
…my second-best bed…"

*Pause.*

"…with the furniture…"

*She flips the pages, but there is no more. Pause.*

And so this is…
this is my, my…

"He never forgot you know.
He never…"

*(steady)* It happened so silently
me reading
Susanna making sandcastles
Judith and Harry
playing together in shallow surf.

Judith runs in
teeth clacking like a skeleton
and I pull a blanket round her.
I look up
Harry is now twenty feet out
waving
laughing.

He mouths something
but the gull's cry
drowns him out

I wave back
shoo away a wasp
and look up again
to see him gone.

And I
I think
but where, where
and I look up and down the shore
but still he is, he is, and I just saw him, where?
and I run to the water's edge, call to him, and the girls
they splash in, and I say no, there are currents and I, I
look for Brundage to help but he, high above, on the cliff,
and I call for help, but he cannot hear me, and I turn back,
and I—

*She gulps air and plunges forward.*

—rush into the sea, my gowns heavy with water, and
Susanna yells:
No!
You will sink, Mother
you will sink
and so I tear it off:
my gown, my shirt, my shoes, my…

*She tears away some of her clothing.*

trying to
to become a fish
to swim to you.
Harry!!
Harry!!

*She catches her breath.*

And he
waving goodbye
like you
at the road's end
pack slung over your shoulder
waving
waving…

*Pause.*

For hours
I hoped
the ocean would take pity
throw him up
spout him out
like Jonah
alive.

*Pause.*

And
to have Brundage
deliver him to me
pulled from a grave so wet.
And to hold him in my arms
to pull away the cold kelp
wrapped round his neck like a noose.

*Pause.*

And
not to bring him home
but instead to burn him on the beach that night
for his body, bloated had…

And
to carry his ashes
in a box cut from birch
to hold him on my lap one last time
three days back in the carriage

and to lower it in the ground
and to hear the church bell toll
like a ship
so far away, so far…

*She grabs the will, her anger mounting.*

And with this
you blame me?
with this you punish me?
with these words
you break it
our promise
with this
you rip in two
our vow
with this
you
you…

*In a rage she grabs the sheaves, but does not rip them.*

No, no, no, no, no! I will not suffer this, I will not!

*She tosses the will aside.*
*A long pause.*
*Then:*
*The bell.*
*But it seems far away. She listens.*

I will go back.

*Pause.*

Yes.

*Pause.*

I will go back.

I will go back to the sea
to live like my father.
I will go back to the sea
to live where I last saw my son.
I will go back to the sea
to let the waves
wash my wounds clean
of consequence
of memory
of words.

*Pause.*

"Those lips that Love's own hand did make
Breath'd forth the sound that said I hate…
'I hate' from hate away she threw,
And sav'd my life, saying 'not you…'"

*Pause.*

To hell.
To hell with your words.

Sink them in the sea
drown them in the depths
smash them on the shore
let the waves carry them where they will.

*(smiles faintly)* For when the wind is up, you move on.

You always move on.

*The bell is clearer now.*
*It is a ship's bell.*
*Its sound draws ever closer.*

*End of play.*

## Postscript

*Shakespeare's Will* is loosely based on the life of Anne Hathaway, the woman who married William Shakespeare. Or rather, the play is based on the very few facts we actually know about Anne. Controversy surrounds many aspects of Anne's life, but historians tend to agree on the following:

- Anne married Shakespeare when she was twenty-six years old. He was eighteen.
- She was pregnant at the time of the wedding.
- They had three children: Susanna, and twins Hamnet and Judith.
- Anne lived her life in Stratford-Upon-Avon.
- Shakespeare spent most of his adult life in London.
- Hamnet died at age eleven. It is not known how he perished, although there is a record of the plague sweeping the town at that time.
- Shakespeare returned to Stratford some time after 1610.
- Shakespeare died in Stratford in 1616 at age fifty-two.
- Anne died in Stratford in 1623 at age sixty-seven.
- Joan died in 1646 at age seventy-seven.
- Susanna died in 1649 at age sixty-six leaving no male heir.
- Judith died in 1662 at age seventy-six leaving no male heir.
- Shakespeare indeed had a will.

The sections Anne reads at the end of the play are quotes from the will. These passages of the will became my primary inspiration in writing the play.

Scholars have long debated Shakespeare's directive "I give unto my wife my second-best bed with the furniture." Samuel S. Schoenbaum, author of *William Shakespeare: A Documentary Life*, suggests that it would have been Anne's right, through English common law, to one third of his estate. He also suggests that the best bed was reserved for guests, and thus the "second-best bed" was a meaningful gift of their marriage bed. Joyce Rogers in *The Second Best Bed: Shakespeare's Will in a New Light* also concludes that the will was correct, incontestable, conventional, and designed to serve the best interests of the women and children in his family. Others maintain the will was a slight on Anne. The eighteenth century scholar, Edmund Malone, appears indignant that Shakespeare cut off Anne, "not indeed with a shilling, but with an old bed." More recently, the actor Sir Ian McKellen has argued that the playwright's decision of what to leave Anne showed he had a lack of interest in her and the marriage. And still others believe, as Willard McCarty of King's College London, that all the debate surrounding Shakespeare's private life doesn't really matter to the study of Shakespearean literature, and therefore the question of the will's meaning is moot.

What we know about the creation of the will is also scant. By most accounts, William Shakespeare began finalizing his last will and testament in early 1616. It appears Francis Collins of Warwick acted as Shakespeare's attorney. Shakespeare made corrections and additions to the will and five witnesses signed the official version in March 1616. The original copy of Shakespeare's will is three large sheets of paper bound together by a narrow strip of parchment at the top margins with each page signed by Shakespeare himself.

A version of Shakespeare's last will and testament follows. As you will discover, I have played "fast and loose" with the will and its meaning. Those readers seeking a play that sheds light on Shakespeare's writings may be disappointed in my play. So too those audience members who desire a historical representation of Anne Hathaway's life. I have done neither of those things. Instead, I have used the will as a springboard for my own imagination and my artistic goal—to explore the journey of a woman who faces adversity, rises above it, and ultimately rekindles faith in herself.

—Vern Thiessen, New York City, September, 2007

## THE LAST WILL AND TESTEMANT OF SHAKESPEARE

**NOTE:** The following text of Shakespeare's will has modernized spelling, and a translation of the Latin passages. Words that are struck out in the original will are presented here in ~~strikeout~~ and additions to the will are here represented in CAPS. Sections here in ***bold italics*** indicate parts of the will directly quoted in the play.

—V.T.

Vicesimo Quinto die ~~Januarij~~ Marti Anno Regni Domini nostri Jacobi nunc Regis Anglie &c decimo quarto & Scotie xlix Annoque domini 1616. *(Translation: On the 25th day in the year of the reign of our lord James, King of England, etc., the 14th, and of Scotland the 49th, in the year of our Lord, 1616.)*

T(estamentum) of William Shackspeare.

***In the name of God, Amen. I, William Shackspeare of Stratford--upon-Avon in the county of Warwick, gent., in perfect health and memory***, God be praised, do make and ordain this my last will and testament in manner and form following. That is to say, first, I commend my soul into the hands of God my Creator, hoping and assuredly believing, through the only merits of Jesus Christ my Saviour, to be made partaker of life everlasting, and my body to the earth whereof it is made.

***Item, I give and bequeath unto my ~~Sonne in L~~ daughter Judith one hundred and fifty pounds of lawful English money***, to be paid unto her in the manner and form following; That is to say, one hundred pounds IN DISCHARGE OF HER MARRIAGE PORTION within one year after my decease, with consideration after the rate of two shillings in the pound for so long time as the same shall be unpaid unto her after my decease, and the fifty pounds residue thereof upon her surrendering OF, or giving of such sufficient security as the overseers of this my will shall like of to surrender or grant, all her estate and right that shall descend or come unto her after my decease, OR THAT SHE now hath of, in, or to one copyhold tenement, with the appurtenances, lying and being in Stratford-upon-Avon aforesaid in the said county of Warwick, being parcel or holden of the manor of Rowington, unto my daughter Susanna Hall and her heirs for ever.

Item, I give and bequeath unto my said daughter Judith one hundred and fifty pounds more, if she or any issue of her body by living at the end of three years next ensuing the day of the date of this my will, during which time my executors are to pay her consideration from my decease according to the rate aforesaid; and if she die within the said term without issue of her body, then my will is, and I do give and bequeath one hundred pounds thereof to my niece, Elizabeth Hall, and the fifty pounds to be set forth by my executors during the life of my sister, Joan Hart, and the use and profit thereof coming shall be paid to my said sister Joan, and after her decease the said fifty pounds shall remain amongst the children of my said sister, equally to be divided amongst them. But if my said daughter Judith be living at the end of the said three years, or any issue of her body, then my will is, and so I devise and bequeath the said hundred and fifty pounds to be set out BY MY EXECUTORS AND OVERSEERS for the best benefit of her and her issue, and THE STOCK not TO BE paid unto her so long as she shall be married and covert baron ~~by my executors and overseers~~; but my will is that she shall have the consideration yearly paid unto her during her life, and, after her decease the said stock and consideration to be paid to her children, if she have any, and not to her executors or assigns, she living the said term after my decease. Provided that if such husband as she shall at the end of the said three years be married unto or attain after do sufficiently assure unto her and the issue of her body lands answerable to the portion by this my will given unto her and to be adjudged so by my executors and overseers, then my will is that the said 150 pounds shall be paid to such husband as shall make such assurance, to his own use.

***Item, I give and bequeath unto my said sister Joan 20 pounds and all my wearing apparel***, to be paid and delivered within one year after my decease; ***and I do will and devise unto her THE HOUSE*** with the appurtenances ***in Stratford, wherein she dwelleth, for her natural life***, under the yearly rent of twelvepence.

Item, I give and bequeath unto her three sonns, William Hart, —— Hart, and Michael Hart, five pounds a piece, to be paid within one year after my decease ~~to be set out for her within one year after my descease by my executors with the advise and directions of my overseers for her best profit until her marriage and then the same with the increase thereof to be paid unto her.~~

Item, I give and bequeath unto THE SAID ELIZABETH HALL, all my plate, EXCEPT MY BROAD SILVER AND GILT BOWL, that I now have at the date of this my will.

Item, I give and bequeath unto the poor of Stratford aforesaid ten pounds; to Mr. Thomas Combe my sword; to Thomas Russell, Esquire, five pounds; and to Francis Collins, of the borough of Warwick in the county of Warwick, gent., thirteen pounds, six shillings, and eightpence, to be paid within one year after my decease.

***Item,*** I give and bequeath ***to*** ~~Mr. Richard Tyler~~ the elder ***HAMLET SADLER 26 s. 8 d. to buy him a ring***; TO WILLIAM REYNOLDS, GENT., 26 S. 8 D. TO BUY HIM A RING; to my godson, William Walker, 20 s. in gold; to Anthony Nashe, gent., 26 s. 8 d. and to Mr.

John Nashe 26 s. 8 d., ***AND TO MY FELLOWS JOHN HEMINGS, RICHARD BURBAGE, AND HENRY CONDELL, 26 S. 8 D. A PIECE TO BUY THEM RINGS.***

***Item, I give, will, bequeath, and devise, unto my daughter Susanna*** Hall, FOR BETTER ENABLING OF HER TO PERFORM THIS MY WILL AND TOWARDS THE PERFORMANCE THEREOF, all that capital messuage or tenement with the appurtenances, IN STRATFORD AFORESAID, called the New Place, wherein I now dwell, and two messuages or tenements with the appurtenances situate, lying, and being in Henley Street, within the borough of Stratford aforesaid; and all my barns, stables, orchards, gardens, lands, tenements, and hereditaments, whatsoever, situate, lying, and being, or to be had, received, perceived, or taken, within the towns, hamlets, villages, fields, and grounds, of Stratford-upon-Avon, Old Stratford, Bushopton, and Welcombe, or in any of them in the said county of Warwick; and also all that messuage or tenement with the appurtenances, wherein one John Robinson dwelleth, situate, lying and being in the Black friars in London, near the Wardrobe; and all my other lands, tenements, and hereditaments whatsoever, ***to have and to hold*** all and singular the said premises, with their appurtenances, unto the said Susanna Hall, for and ***during the term of her natural life, and after her decease, to the first son of her body lawfully issuing,*** and ***to the heirs males of the body*** of the said first son lawfully issuing; and for default of such issue to the second son of her body, lawfully issuing, and ~~so~~ to the heirs males of the body of the said second son lawfully issuing; and for default of such heirs, to the third son of the body of the said Susanna lawfully issuing, and of the heirs males of the body of the said third son lawfully issuing; and for default of such issue, the same so to be and remain to the fourth, fifth, sixth, and seventh sons of her body lawfully issuing, one after another, and to the heirs males of the bodies of the bodies of the said fourth, fifth, sixth, and seventh sons lawfully issuing in such manner as it is before limited, to be and remain to the first, second, and third sons of her body, and to their heirs males. And for default of such issue, the said premises to be and remain to my said niece Hall and the heirs males of her body lawfully issuing; and for default of such issue, to my daughter Judith, and the heirs males of her body lawfully issuing; and for default of such issue, to the right heirs of me the said William Shackspeare for ever.

***ITEM, I GIVE UNTO MY WIFE MY SECOND BEST BED WITH THE FURNITURE.***

Item, I give and bequeath to my said daughter Judith my broad silver gilt bowl. All the rest of ***my goods, chattel, leases, plate, jewels, and household stuff whatsoever***, after my debts and legacies paid and my funeral expenses discharged, I give, devise, and bequeath to my son-in-law, John Hall, gent., and my daughter Susanna, his wife, whom I ordain and make executors of this my last will and testament. And I do entreat and appoint THE SAID Thomas Russell, Esquire, and Francis Collins, gent., to be overseers hereof, and do revoke all former wills, and publish this to be my last will and testament. In witness whereof I have hereunto put my ~~seal~~ hand, the day and year first above written by me, William Shakspeare.

Witnesses to the publishing hereof:

Fra: Collins<br>
Julyus Shawe<br>
John Robinson<br>
Hamnet Sadler<br>
Robert Whattcott

# DEATH OF A CHIEF

YVETTE NOLAN AND
KENNEDY C. MACKINNON

## ABUSE OF GREATNESS

As artistic director of Native Earth Performing Arts since January 2003, Yvette Nolan is a major driving force behind a rejuvenated Native Theatre community in Canada. As founder and artistic director of Shakespeare Link Canada and its anti-AIDS "Africa Project" (in collaboration with Montes Namuli in Mozambique), Kennedy C. MacKinnon has been working on several fronts since 2005 to bring Shakespeare to bear on issues of social justice. Between them, they set out in *Death of a Chief* to provide access to Shakespearean language for Native actors: "We both believe that he talks about things that reflect in almost everybody's communities," Nolan says, "and that everyone should be able to say those words if they feel like it. He coined so many words that are in the English language and so many phrases. We all go around quoting him, fighting him all the time without knowing it. That's a pretty hefty influence on language. And language is power" ("Death" 2).

Kennedy C. MacKinnon has a BFA in acting from the University of Windsor and an M.F.A. in acting, together with a diploma in voice-teacher training, from York University. She is also a graduate of the Stratford Conservatory for Classical Theatre training. She has worked as a voice coach for film, television, and radio, and for three seasons at the Stratford Festival, where she was the recipient of two Tyrone Guthrie Awards. She now teaches full-time at Humber College in Toronto, where she is Head of Voice and founder and coordinator of the Summer Shakespeare Intensive. She also teaches at Equity Showcase Theatre and George Brown College. Her training as an adapter began with the English Shakespeare Company on *God Say Amen* in 1991, based on themes from the ESC's *Wars of the Roses* production of Shakespeare's history cycles. With Shakespeare Link Canada in Mozambique she has co-directed and co-adapted Shakespeare's *A Tempestade* (*The Tempest*), and *Sonho Nocturno—Dream at Night* (*A Midsummer Night's Dream*), and in the summer of 2008 adapted and directed two one-person shows, *Hamlet, Alone*, and *Drowning Ophelia*, and directed *A Midsummer Night's Dream* at the inaugural Shakespeare Link International Festival at the Living Willow Globe Theatre in Wales.

Yvette Nolan was born in Prince Albert, Saskatchewan to an Algonquin mother (from the Kitiganzibi reserve in Quebec) and immigrant Irish–Canadian father. She grew up in Winnipeg, where she graduated from the University of Manitoba in 1997, and reputedly held a job as manager of Swenson's Ice Cream, where she presumably learned her considerable administrative and diplomatic skills. Nolan is an actor (in her professional debut she played the corpse in Joe Orton's *Loot*), a director, a dramaturg who works nationwide, a playwright, an educator and mentor, an anthologist, an administrator, and an advocate for the arts and for Aboriginal peoples in Canada. She has worked with Agassiz Theatre, Popular Theatre Alliance of Manitoba, Theatre Projects Manitoba, Manitoba Association of Playwrights, the Manitoba Theatre Centre, Nakai Theatre in Whitehorse, and the Society of Yukon Artists of Native Ancestry, and in 1996 was the first writer-in-residence at Brandon University. From 1998 to 2001 she was President of Playwrights Union of Canada, and from 2003 to 2005 President of Playwrights Canada Press, for whom she co-edited *Beyond the Pale II: Dramatic Writing from First Nations Writers and Writers of Colour* in 2004. In 2006 and 2007 she worked as Festival Dramaturg for the Saskatchewan Playwrights Centre Spring Festival and in 2008 was Playwright in Residence at the National Arts Centre. She remains President of the Indigenous Performing Arts Alliance as well as Artistic Director of Native Earth Performing Arts, and she served on the advisory committee for The Status of Women in Canadian Theatre report in 2007.

As a playwright, Nolan's credits include *Blade* (first produced 1990), *Everybody's Business* (1990), *Some of My Best Friends Are…* (1991), *Smaller* (1992), *Job's Wife* (1992), *Six Women* (1993), *Video* (1993), *A Marginal Man* (1994), *Child* (1994), *Shakedown Shakespeare* (with Philip Adams, 1997), *Annie Mae's Movement* (1998, revised 2006), *Donne In* (1999), *Finish Line* (2000), *Traps* (2003), *Faithless* (2003), *Freeman's Wake* (2005), *The Starlight Tour* (2007), and *Scattering Jake* (2008), as well as the libretto to *Hilda Blake* (2000), and the radio play *Owen* (2002). She has been nominated for the John Hirsch Award for Most Promising New Writer (1995) and the James Butler Award for Playwriting from the Centre for Indigenous Theatre in 1997. In 2007 she won the prestigious Maggie Bassett Award, which celebrates the achievements of an Ontario-based artist who has made a sustained and significant contribution to the development of theatre in the province of Ontario.

*Death of a Chief* is not your standard Shakespeare adaptation. For one thing, it is one of a very small group of plays—Robert Lepage's *Elsinore* is another—that actually uses Shakespeare's own language almost exclusively in adapting him, albeit rearranged and recontextualized. For another, it doesn't "talk back" to Shakespeare or his cultural authority as much as it *claims access* to that authority for Aboriginal peoples while using Shakespeare's story of sickness at the roots of western civilization to explore problems of leadership—"the abuse of greatness"—within the Aboriginal community in Canada. For yet another, it mounts a subtle gender critique of Aboriginal leadership simply by recasting Caesar, Cassius, Antony, and others as women (played in the original production by the formidable trio of Monique Mojica, Michelle St. John, and Jani Lauzon), leaving Brutus alone among the leads to be played by a man.

But primarily *Death of a Chief* is less "an" adaptation—a product—than part of an ongoing process of adaptation, negotiation, and reconciliation, not only with Shakespeare but across differences within the Native community in Canada. The cast and co-creators of the show came from many different First Nations; the creation process involved negotiations among them about ritual, language, culture, and tradition; the play itself includes, in its opening sequence and throughout, a negotiated mélange of cultural formations and a number of different Aboriginal languages, all filtered through the "foreign" but dominant language of Shakespearean English. *Death of a Chief* adapts to Shakespeare as part of an ongoing negotiation with a history of representations that is at once rich, contestable, powerful, and in process: adaptation that doesn't simply affirm, contest, claim, or reject the "Shakespearean," but that also and primarily enters into, and aspires to gain equal access to,

Shakespearean authority while becoming part of that rich history of representation that will no longer exclude or oppress Native peoples. As a process, *Death of a Chief* uses Shakespeare's representation of divisions and betrayals at the roots of Western civilization to help the Native community in Canada explore real pain over real betrayals within that community, as well as filtering through Shakespeare the real pain of exposing those betrayals publicly. But it also works with Shakespeare as a real negotiation across many cultures, a negotiation that constitutes part of the healing of the wounds inflicted by five hundred years of colonization: "*If we can work it out in this play*," as Nolan says of the process, "*then maybe we can work it out in our lives too.*"

## Work Cited

Nolan, Yvette. "Death of a Chief: An Interview with Yvette Nolan" Interview with Sorouja Moll. Native Earth Performing Arts Office, Distillery District, Toronto. 12 March 2006. http://www.canadianshakespeares.ca/i_ynolan2.cfm. Accessed 2 November 2008.

*Death of a Chief* premiered in the NAC Studio at the National Arts Centre in Ottawa, 21 February 2008, co-produced by NAC English Theatre and Native Earth Performing Arts, with the following company:

| | |
|---|---|
| Marcus BRUTUS | Keith Barker |
| CALPURNIUS | Lorne Cardinal |
| ORACLE | Waawaate Fobister |
| DECIUS | Falen Johnson |
| Marc ANTONY | Jani Lauzon |
| PORTIA | Cheri Maracle |
| Julius CAESAR | Monique Mojica |
| CASSIUS | Michelle St. John |
| CASCA/OCTAVIUS | Michaela Washburn |
| Musicians | Wayne Lavalee and Dale Yim |

Directed by Yvette Nolan and Kennedy C. MacKinnon
Set and costume design by Camellia Koo
Lighting design by Michelle Ramsay
Musical direction by Micah Barnes
Sound design by Richard Lee
Choreography by Michelle Olson
Fight direction by Siobhan Richardson
Stage management by Fiona Jones, assisted by Yvette Martin
Production management by André Du Toit

## CHARACTERS

Marcus BRUTUS
CALPURNIUS
ORACLE
DECIUS
Marc ANTONY
PORTIA
Julius CAESAR
CASSIUS
CASCA
OCTAVIUS
PLEBEIANS
POET
CONSPIRATORS
MESSALA
STRATO
MUSICIANS

## NOTE

The roles of CAESAR, ANTONY, PORTIA, and CASSIUS are played by women; BRUTUS is played by a man. Other roles are gender neutral (i.e. can be played by women or men).

# DEATH OF A CHIEF

*A medicine wheel, a circle of stones, laid in the middle of a road somewhere. The horizon is butter-coloured. The wheel is twenty-two stones or so; thirteen of them make the circle and another nine make spokes within the wheel. In the low light, the stones throw long shadows. A drum begins and the lights fade.*

*In the darkness, we hear a low double thrum, the heartbeat of the very earth. Five times. With the final bah-dum, the lights warm, revealing human forms in the places where there were only rocks before. Here a woman, here a man, here another woman. Nine human forms curled around their rocks, nine human forms that wake now, moving from fetal position to child's pose, still covering their rocks.*

*Pulling themselves onto their knees, the people begin to sweep the ground around their rocks. One by one, they execute a series of gestures, raising their rocks to the sky, rocking them like children. One by one they struggle to all fours, and then they stand. Standing, they draw a half-circle in the earth. One by one, they come to stillness, arms extended, in circle. They see each other. Someone begins to dance, suddenly all are dancing, each in his or her own way. There is no sound, no fiddle, no drum, yet here are the stately traditional dances of the women, the Métis jig, the grass dance.*

*And then there is sound. One voice begins to sing, and is joined by another.*

Whey ya no hey
Whey ya ha no way‿yo‿way na ha you hey
Way na ya way na yaa
Way ya no way ya
Way no way ya naaa [1]

[1] "Deathless Voice," reclaimed by the company from one of the Indianist composers of the nineteenth century.

*The people clear the rocks, setting them in small piles on either side of the road.*

Whey ya no hey
Whey ya ha no way‿yo‿way na ha you hey
Way na ya way na yaa
Way ya no way ya
Way no way ya naaa

*The people come together, joining the song, touching each other. Then look to the sky. Four silk banners drop: red at centre stage, white stage right, yellow and black further upstage and left.*

Whey ya no hey
Whey ya ha no way‿yo‿way na ha you hey
Way na ya way na yaa
Way ya no way ya
Way no way ya naaa

*The people lift a young man skyward. His fingers touch the bottom of the red banner. He grasps and pulls; yards of red silk pour from the sky. The people pair themselves along the length of the silk, facing each other. "Deathless Voice" ends and immediately someone begins a rabbit dance song.* [2]

hi yo hi yo hey ya nay no hi yo ho ho
hi yo hey ya nay no hiyo ho o
hi yo hey ya nay no hiyo way ya hey yo
ya ho way na hey ya way ya hey

*Everyone joins the song, and then they begin to move, two steps with the left foot, one step back with the right.*

hi yo hi yo hey ya nay no hi yo ho ho
hi yo hey ya nay no hiyo ho o
hi yo hey ya nay no hiyo way ya hey yo
ya ho way na hey ya way ya hey

*After a complete circle of the space, the silk is raised as a canopy and everyone travels under it. Now the end of the procession is at the beginning and the people proceed down the middle of the road, all facing the same direction. The rabbit dance song ends and the people lay the silk down the middle of the road. At the upstage left end of the silk, one prepares to step onto the red road.*

---

[2] A Mohawk community dance song

*She is stately and imposing. As she goes to step on the road, a young man blocks her way, catching her foot before she can set it on the road. He is the young man who pulled down the red silk; he is the ORACLE.*

**ORACLE** Aaniin minik dasing awiya ge-ichigewaad
owe ge-ini-izhiwebag,
bebakaan miziwe gaye, bebakaan ezhi-giigidong?[3]

*But it is too late, for always, she is CAESAR. She pushes the ORACLE, who falls away from her, and she sets her foot down on the road.*

*At the other end a woman begins to drum and the people begin a new song. The drummer is Marc ANTONY, and the song is a dirge. As CAESAR proceeds along the road, the people assume their roles. Here is CALPURNIUS, trying to warn CAESAR, just as PORTIA tries to warn BRUTUS. Here are CASCA and DECIUS, genuflecting and plotting. CASSIUS and BRUTUS pull up the red road behind CAESAR, and as PORTIA sings her warning, shroud CAESAR.*

*The people cheer, wave the red silk above them, and exit, still shouting and clamouring, leaving BRUTUS and CASSIUS alone on stage.*

**BRUTUS** What meanes this Showting?
I do feare, the People choose Caesar
For their Chief.

**CASSIUS** I, do you feare it?
Then must I thinke you would not have it so.

**BRUTUS** I would not Cassius, yet I love her well:
But wherefore do you hold me heere so long?
What is it, that you would impart to me?
If it be ought toward the generall good,
Set Honour in one eye, and Death i'th other,
And I will looke on both indifferently:
For let the Gods so speed mee, as I love
The name of Honour, more then I feare death.

*Through this next, we see in silhouette the procession of CAESAR. Backed by CALPURNIUS, urged on by the*

---

3 Ojibway colloquial translation of *How many Ages hence*
*Shall this our lofty Scene be acted over,*
*In State unborne, and Accents yet unknowne?*

*PLEBEIANS, CAESAR moves towards Marc ANTONY, who carries a staff. When they meet, ANTONY offers the staff to CAESAR, who puts it by. The PLEBEIANS react with shock and amazement. Again ANTONY offers the staff; again CAESAR puts it by, passing ANTONY as if to continue her progress. The PLEBEIANS crowd behind ANTONY, urging yet another offer. CALPURNIUS follows her, catching her by the arm. CAESAR stops, turns, considers the crowd, the staff, and Marc ANTONY. CAESAR walks to ANTONY, touches the staff, and suddenly the two women are dancing, the staff between them.*

**CASSIUS** I know that vertue to be in you Brutus,
As well as I do know your outward favour.
Well, Honour is the subject of my Story:
I cannot tell, what you and other men
Thinke of this life: But for my single selfe,
I had as liefe not be, as live to be
In awe of such a Thing, as I my selfe.
I was borne free as Caesar, so were you,
We both have fed as well, and we can both
Endure the Winters cold, as well as shee.
For once, upon a Rawe and Gustie day,
The troubled Tyber, chafing with her Shores,
Caesar saide to me, Dar'st thou Cassius now
Leape in with me into this angry Flood,
And swim to yonder Point? Upon the word,
Accoutred as I was, I plunged in,
And bade her follow: so indeed she did.
The Torrent roar'd, and we did buffet it
With lusty Sinewes, throwing it aside,
And stemming it with hearts of Controversie.
But ere we could arrive the Point propos'd,
Caesar cride, Helpe me Cassius, or I sinke.
I (as Aeneas, our great Ancestor,
Did from the Flames of Troy, upon his shoulder
The old Anchyses beare) so, from the waves of Tyber
Did I the tyred Caesar: And this One,
Is now become a God, and Cassius is
A wretched Creature, and must bend her body,
If Caesar carelessly but nod on her.
She had a Feaver when she was in Spaine,
And when the Fit was on her, I did marke
How she did shake: 'Tis true, this God did shake,

Her Coward lippes did from their colour flye,
And that same Eye, whose bend doth awe the World,
Did loose her Lustre: I did heare her grone:
I, and that Tongue of hers, that bade the Romans
Marke her, and write her Speeches in their Bookes,
Alas, it cried, Give me some drinke Titinius,
As a sicke Girle: Ye Gods, it doth amaze me,
That one of such a feeble temper should
So get the start of the Majesticke world,
And beare the Palme alone.

*With shouts and a flourish, the procession of CAESAR arrives on stage at the opposite end of the road from BRUTUS and CASSIUS. The PLEBEIANS spill out on the stage around CAESAR, lining the roadside.*

**BRUTUS** Another generall shout?
I do believe, that these applauses are
For some new Honours, that are heap'd on Caesar.

**CASSIUS** Why man, she doth bestride the narrow world
Like a Colossus, and we petty men
Walke under her huge legges, and peepe about
To finde ourselves dishonourable Graves.
Men at sometime, are Masters of their Fates.

**ORACLE** Caesar!

**PLEBEIAN 1** How do you un-ring the bell?

**CAESAR** Ha! Who calls?

**PLEBEIAN 2** If we could have back what's been lost and stolen,

**PLEBEIAN 3** Could we rebuild what's been lost and stolen?

**ORACLE** Caesar!

**PLEBEIAN 4** What will we look like in a different light
or will the light simply illuminate
the emptiness that can never be filled?

**PLEBEIAN 5** How then does one stand alone?

**CAESAR** Who is it in the press, that calls on me?
I hear a tongue shriller than all music
cry, Caesar: Speak, Caesar is turned to hear.

**ORACLE** Beware the Ides of March.

**CAESAR** What man is that?

**CALPURNIUS** A soothsayer bids you beware the Ides of March.

**PLEBEIAN 6** If we are all we have in the end then how can we defer to a decided greatness that not all can agree to?

**CAESAR** Set him before me, let me see his face.

**CALPURNIUS** Fellow, come from the throng, look upon Caesar.

**CAESAR** What say'st thou to me now? Speak once again.

**ORACLE** Beware the Ides of March.

**CAESAR** He is a dreamer. Let us leave him. Pass.

**CASSIUS** The fault (deere Brutus) is not in our Starres,
But in our Selves, that we are underlings.

**CAESAR** Antonia.

**ANTONY** Caesar.

**CASSIUS** Brutus and Caesar: What should be in that Caesar?
Why should that name be sounded more than yours
Write them together: Yours, is as faire a Name:
Sound them, it doth become the mouth as well:
Weigh them, it is as heavy: Conjure with 'em,
Brutus will start a Spirit as soone as Caesar.
Now in the names of all the Gods at once,
Upon what meate doth this our Caesar feede,
That she is growne so great? Age, thou art sham'd.

**CAESAR** Let me have men about me, that are fat,
Sleeke-headed men, and such as sleepe a-nights:
Yond Cassius has a leane and hungry looke,
She thinkes too much: such ones are dangerous.

**ANTONY** Feare her not Caesar, she's not dangerous,
She is a Noble Roman, and well given.

**CASSIUS** Rome, thou hast lost the breed of Noble Bloods.
When went there by an Age, since the great Flood,
But it was fam'd with more then with one chief?
When could they say (till now) that talk'd of Rome,
That her wide Walkes incompast but one chief?
Now is it Rome indeed, and Roome enough
When there is in it but one only chief.
O! you and I, have heard our Fathers say,
There was a Brutus once, that would have brook'd
Th' eternall Divell to keepe his State in Rome,
As easily as a King.

**CAESAR** Would she were fatter; But I feare her not:
Yet if my name were lyable to feare,
I do not know the one I should avoyd
So soone as that spare Cassius. She reades much,
She is a great Observer, and she lookes
Quite through the Deeds of men. She loves no Playes,
As thou dost Antony: she heares no Musicke;
Seldome she smiles, and smiles in such a sort
As if she mock'd herselfe, and scorn'd her spirit
That could be mov'd to smile at any thing.
Women as she, be never at hearts ease,
Whiles they behold a greater than themselves,
And therefore are they very dangerous.

**BRUTUS** That you do love me, I am nothing jealous:
What you would worke me too, I have some ayme:
How I have thought of this, and of these times
I shall recount heereafter. For this present,
I would not so (with love I might entreat you)
Be any further moov'd: What you have said,
I will consider: what you have to say
I will with patience heare, and finde a time
Both meete to heare, and answer such high things.

Till then, my Noble Friend, chew upon this:
Brutus had rather be a Villager,
Then to repute himselfe a Sonne of Rome
Under these hard Conditions, as this time
Is like to lay upon us.

**CASSIUS** I am glad that my weake words
Have strucke but thus much shew of fire from Brutus.

**BRUTUS** For this time I will leave you:
Tomorrow, if you please to speak with me,
I will come home to you: or if you will,
Come home to me, and I will wait for you.

*CASSIUS exits.*

**CAESAR** I rather tell thee what is to be fear'd,
Then what I feare: for alwayes I am Caesar.
Come on my right hand, for this eare is deafe,
And tell me truely, what thou think'st of her.

*CAESAR and ANTONY exit, followed by the PLEBEIANS.*

**BRUTUS**

It must be by her death: and for my part,
I know no personall cause, to spurne at her,
But for the generall. She would be crown'd:
How that might change her nature, there's the question?
It is the bright day, that brings forth the Adder,
And that craves warie walking: Crowne her that,
And then I graunt we put a Sting in her,
That at her will she may doe danger with.
Th' abuse of Greatnesse, is, when it disjoynes
Remorse from Power: And to speake truth of Caesar,
I have not knowne, when her Affections sway'd
More then her Reason. But 'tis a common proofe,
That Lowlynesse is young Ambitions Ladder,
Whereto the Climber upward turnes his Face:
But when he once attaines the upmost Round,
He then unto the Ladder turnes his Backe,
Lookes in the Clouds, scorning the base degrees
By which he did ascend: so Caesar may;
Then least she may, prevent. And since the Quarrell
Will beare no colour, for the thing she is,
Fashion it thus; that what she is, augmented,
Would runne to these, and these extremities:
And therefore thinke her as a Serpents egge,
Which hatch'd, would as her kinde grow mischievous;
And kill her in the shell.

**PORTIA**

Brutus, my Lord.

**BRUTUS**

Portia: What meane you? wherfore rise you now?
It is not for your health, thus to commit
Your weake condition, to the raw cold morning.

**PORTIA**

Nor for yours neither. Y'have ungently Brutus
Stole from my bed: and yesternight at Supper
You sodainly arose, and walk'd about,
Musing, and sighing, with your armes a-crosse
And when I ask'd you what the matter was,
You star'd upon me, with ungentle lookes.
I urg'd you further, then you scratch'd your head,
And too impatiently stampt with your foote:
Yet I insisted, yet you answer'd not,
But with an angry wafter of your hand
Gave signe for me to leave you: So I did,
Fearing to strengthen that impatience
Which seem'd too much inkindled; and withall,
Hoping it was but an effect of Humour,

Which sometime hath his houre with every man.
It will not let you eate, nor talke, nor sleepe;
And could it worke so much upon your shape,
As it hath much prevayl'd on your Condition,
I should not know you Brutus. Deere my Lord,
Make me acquainted with your cause of greefe.

**BRUTUS** I am not well in health, and that is all.

**CONSPIRATORS** It must be by her death.

**PORTIA** Brutus is wise, and were he not in health,
He would embrace the meanes to come by it.

**BRUTUS** Why so I do: good Portia go to bed.

*Lights upstage begin to reveal figures behind the scrim, listening, watching, plotting. Upstage left a couple sleeps under a red silk.*

**PORTIA** Is Brutus sicke? And is it Physicall
To walke unbraced, and sucke up the humours
Of the danke Morning? What, is Brutus sicke?
And will he steale out of his wholsome bed
To dare the vile contagion of the Night?
And tempt the Rhewmy, and unpurged Ayre,
To adde unto his sicknesse? No my Brutus,
You have some sicke Offence within your minde,
Which by the Right and Vertue of my place
I ought to know of: And upon my knees,
I charme you, by my once commended Beauty,
By all your vowes of Love, and that great Vow
Which did incorporate and make us one,
That you unfold to me, your selfe; your halfe
Why you are heavy: and what men to night
Have had resort to you: for heere have beene
Some sixe or seven, who did hide their faces
Even from darknesse.

**CONSPIRATORS** It must be by her death; it must be by
Her death; it must be by her death; it must.

*The couple wakes. CAESAR leaves the bed upstage and enters the playing space, followed by CALPURNIUS. Upstage of the scrim, the shadowy figures create images of the most horrid sights.*

**CALPURNIUS** What mean you Caesar? Think you to walk forth?
You shall not stirre out of your house to day.

**CAESAR** Caesar shall forth; the things that threaten'd me,
Ne're look'd but on my backe: When they shall see
The face of Caesar, they are vanished.

**CALPURNIUS** Caesar, I never stood on Ceremonies,
Yet now they fright me: There is one within,
Besides the things that we have heard and seene,
Recounts most horrid sights seene by the Watch.
A Lionnesse hath whelped in the streets,
And Graves have yawn'd, and yeelded up their dead;
Fierce fiery Warriours fight upon the Clouds
In Rankes and Squadrons, and right forme of Warre
Which drizel'd blood upon the Capitall:
The noise of Battell hurtled in the Ayre:
Horses do neigh, and dying men did grone,
And Ghosts did shrieke and squeale about the streets.
O Caesar, these things are beyond all use,
And I do feare them.

**CAESAR** What can be avoyded
Whose end is purpos'd by the mighty Gods?
Yet Caesar shall go forth: for these Predictions
Are to the world in generall, as to Caesar.

**CALPURNIUS** When Beggers dye, there are no Comets seen,
The Heavens themselves blaze forth the death of Princes

**CAESAR** Cowards dye many times before their deaths,
The valiant never taste of death but once:
Of all the Wonders that I yet have heard,
It seemes to me most strange that men should feare,
Seeing that death, a necessary end
Will come, when it will come.

**BRUTUS** Kneele not gentle Portia.

**PORTIA** I should not neede, if you were gentle Brutus.
Within the Bond of Marriage, tell me Brutus,
Is it excepted, I should know no Secrets
That appertaine to you? Am I your Selfe,
But as it were in sort, or limitation?
To keepe with you at Meales, comfort your Bed,
And talke to you sometimes? Dwell I but in the Suburbs
Of your good pleasure? If it be no more,
Portia is Brutus Harlot, not his Wife.

**BRUTUS** You are my true and honourable Wife,
As deere to me, as are the ruddy droppes
That visit my sad heart.

**PORTIA** If this were true, then should I know this secret.
I graunt I am a Woman; but withall,
A woman that Lord Brutus tooke to Wife:
I graunt I am a Woman; but withall,
A Woman well reputed: Cato's Daughter.
Thinke you, I am no stronger then my Sex
Being so Father'd, and so Husbanded?
Tell me your Counsels, I will not disclose 'em:
I have made strong proofe of my Constancie,
Giving my selfe a voluntary wound
Heere, in the Thigh: Can I beare that with patience,
And not my Husbands Secrets?

**BRUTUS** O ye Gods!
Render me worthy of this Noble Wife.

**CONSPIRATORS** Speake, strike, redress.
Speake, strike, redress.
Speake, strike, redress.

*The CONSPIRATORS begin to make their way on stage to BRUTUS, slithering under the scrim, rolling through CAESAR's space, backing in to the scene. Their hoods are up, masking their identities.*

**BRUTUS** Harke, harke, one knockes: Portia go in a while,
And by and by thy bosome shall partake
The secrets of my Heart.
All my engagements, I will construe to thee,
All the Charractery of my sad browes:
Leave me with hast.

*PORTIA exits, turning as she does, trying to identify the hooded visitor who passes her in her doorway.*

**CASSIUS** I thinke we are too bold upon your Rest:
Good morrow Brutus, doe we trouble you?

**BRUTUS** I have beene up this howre, awake all Night:
Know I these men, that come along with you?

**CASSIUS** Yes, every one of them; and no one here
But honours you: and every one doth wish,
You had but that opinion of your selfe,

Which every Noble Roman beares of you.
This is Trebonius.

**BRUTUS** He is welcome hither.

**CASSIUS** This, Decius, Brutus.

**BRUTUS** She is welcome too.

**CASSIUS** This, Casca;

**BRUTUS** You are all welcome.
What watchfull Cares doe interpose themselve
Betwixt your Eyes, and Night?

**CASSIUS** Shall I entreat a word?

**DECIUS** Think you he may be one with us tonight?

**TREBONIUS** If he would not then I would not myself.

**CASCA** If there's a point I think needs to be made
I will not hesitate to make that call.

**TREBONIUS** Who speaks the loudest now, who shall I hear?

**DECIUS** His honour makes our Peece of work more just.

**TREBONIUS** Who do I listen to, who do I trust?

**BRUTUS** Give me your hands all over, one by one.

**CASSIUS** And let us sweare our Resolution.

**BRUTUS** No, not an Oath: if not the Face of men,
The sufferance of our Soules, the times Abuse;
If these be Motives weake, breake off betimes,
And every man hence, to his idle bed:
So let high-sighted Tyranny range on,
Till each man drop by Lottery. But if these
(As I am sure they do) beare fire enough
To kindle Cowards, and to steele with valour
The melting Spirits of women. Then Countrymen,
What neede we any spurre, but our owne cause
To pricke us to redresse? What other Bond,
Than secret Romans, that have spoke the word,
And will not palter? And what other Oath,
Then Honesty to Honesty ingag'd,
That this shall be, or we will fall for it.
Sweare Priests and Cowards, and men Cautelous
Old feeble Carrions, and such suffering Soules
That welcome wrongs: Unto bad causes, sweare

Such Creatures as men doubt; but do not staine
The even vertue of our Enterprize,
Nor th' insuppressive Mettle of our Spirits,
To thinke, that or our Cause, or our Performance
Did neede an Oath. When every drop of blood
That every Roman beares, and Nobly beares
Is guilty of a severall Bastardie,
If he do breake the smallest Particle
Of any promise that hath past from him.

**CASSIUS** But what of Cicero? Shall we sound him?
I thinke he will stand very strong with us.

**CASCA** Let us not leave him out.

**DECIUS** No, by no meanes.

**CASCA** O let us have him, for his Silver haires
Will purchase us a good opinion:
And buy mens voyces, to commend our deeds:
It shall be sayd, his judgment rul'd our hands,
Our youths, and wildenesse, shall no whit appeare,
But all be buried in his Gravity.

**BRUTUS** O name him not; let us not breake with him,
For he will never follow any thing
That other men begin.

**CASSIUS** Then leave him out.

**CASCA** Indeed, he is not fit.

**DECIUS** Shall no one else be toucht, but onely Caesar?

**CASSIUS** Decius well urg'd: I thinke it is not meet,
Marc Antony, so well belov'd of Caesar,
Should out-live Caesar, we shall finde of her
A shrew'd Contriver. And you know, her meanes
If she improve them, may well stretch so farre
As to annoy us all: which to prevent,
Let Antony and Caesar fall together.

**BRUTUS** Our course will seeme too bloody, Caius Cassius,
To cut the Head off, and then hacke the Limbes:
Like Wrath in death, and Envy afterwards:
For Antony, is but a Limbe of Caesar.
Let's be Sacrificers, but not Butchers Caius:
We all stand up against the spirit of Caesar,
And in the Spirit of men, there is no blood:
O that we then could come by Caesars Spirit,

And not dismember Caesar! But (alas)
Caesar must bleed for it. And gentle Friends,
Let's kill her Boldly, but not Wrathfully:
Let's carve her, as a Dish fit for the Gods,
Not hew her as a Carkasse fit for Hounds:
And let our Hearts, as subtle Masters do,
Stirre up their Servants to an acte of Rage,
And after seeme to chide 'em. This shall make
Our purpose Necessary, and not Envious.
Which so appearing to the common eyes,
We shall be call'd Purgers, not Murderers.
And for Marc Antony, thinke not of her:
For she can do no more than Caesars Arme,
When Caesars head is off.

**CASSIUS** Yet I feare her,
For in the ingrafted love she beares to Caesar.

**BRUTUS** Alas, good Cassius, do not thinke of her:
If she love Caesar, all that she can do
Is to herselfe; take thought, and dye for Caesar,
And that were much she should: for she is given
To sports, to wildenesse, and much company.

**TREBONIUS** There is no feare in her; let her not dye,
For she will live, and laugh at this heereafter.

*Clocke strikes.*

**BRUTUS** Peace, count the Clocke.

**CASSIUS** The Clocke hath stricken three.

**TREBONIUS**
'Tis time to part.

**CASSIUS** But it is doubtfull yet,
Whether Caesar will come forth to day, or no:
For she is Superstitious growne of late,
Quite from the maine Opinion she held once,
Of Fantasie, of Dreames, and Ceremonies:
It may be, these apparant Prodigies,
The unaccustom'd Terror of this night,
And the perswasion of her Augurers,
May hold her from the Capitoll to day.

*The ORACLE enters downstage right, passing the oblivious conspirators, dancing his way up the road to CAESAR's house.*

**DECIUS** Never feare that: If she be so resolv'd,
I can ore-sway her: For she loves to heare,
That Unicornes may be betray'd with Trees,
And Beares with Glasses, Elephants with Holes,
Lyons with Toyles, and men with Flatterers.
But, when I tell her, she hates Flatterers,
She sayes, she does; being then most flattered.
Let me worke:
For I can give her humour the true bent;
And I will bring her to the Capitoll.

*The conspirators melt away, as the ORACLE passes upstage of CAESAR.*

**CAESAR** What say the Augurers?

**ORACLE** Upon a heape a hundred ghastly women,
Men all in fire walk up and down the streets.

**CALPURNIUS** They would not have you to stirre forth to day.
Plucking the intrailes of an Offering forth,
They could not finde a heart within the beast.

**CAESAR** The Gods do this in shame of Cowardice:
Caesar should be a Beast without a heart
If she should stay at home to day for feare:
No Caesar shall not;

**ALL** Danger knowes full well
That Caesar is more dangerous then he.

**CAESAR** We heare two Lyons litter'd in one day,
And I the elder and more terrible,
And Caesar shall go foorth.

**CALPURNIUS** Alas my Love,
Your wisedome is consum'd in confidence:
Do not go forth to day: Call it my feare,
That keepes you in the house, and not your owne.
Wee'l send Marc Antony to the Senate house,
And she shall say, you are not well to day:
Let me upon my knee, prevaile in this.

**CAESAR** Marc Antony shall say I am not well,
And for thy humour, I will stay at home.

**CONSPIRATORS** Speake, strike, redress.

*DECIUS enters.*

**DECIUS** Caesar, all haile: Good morrow worthy Caesar,
I come to fetch you to the Senate house.

**CAESAR** And you are come in very happy time,
To beare my greeting to the Senators,
And tell them that I will not come to day:
Cannot, is false: and that I dare not, falser:
I will not come to day, tell them so Decius.

**CALPURNIUS** Say she is sicke.

**CAESAR** Shall Caesar send a Lye?
Have I in Conquest stretcht mine Arme so farre,
To be afear'd to tell Grey-beards the truth:
Decius, go tell them, Caesar will not come.

**DECIUS** Most mighty Caesar, let me know some cause
Lest I be laught at when I tell them so.

**CAESAR** The cause is in my Will, I will not come,
That is enough to satisfie the Senate.
But for your private satisfaction,
Because I love you, I will let you know.
Calpurnius heere my love, stayes me at home:
He dreamt to night, he saw my Statue,
Which like a Fountaine, with an hundred spouts
Did run pure blood: and many lusty Romans
Came smiling, and did bathe their hands in it:
And these does he apply, for warnings and portents,
And evils imminent; and on his knee
Hath begg'd, that I will stay at home to day.

**DECIUS** This Dreame is all amisse interpreted,
It was a vision, faire and fortunate:
Your Statue spouting blood in many pipes,
In which so many smiling Romans bath'd,
Signifies, that from you great Rome shall sucke
Reviving blood, and that great men shall presse
For Tinctures, Staines, Reliques, and Cognisance.
This by Calpurnius's Dreame is signified.

**CAESAR** And this way have you well expounded it.

**DECIUS** I have, when you have heard what I can say:
And know it now, the Senate have concluded
To give this day, a Crowne to mighty Caesar.

**BRUTUS** *(off)* And then I grant we put a sting in her
That at her will she may do danger with.

**DECIUS** If you shall send them word you will not come,
Their mindes may change. Besides, it were a mocke
Apt to be render'd, for some one to say,
Breake up the Senate, till another time:
When Caesars wife shall meete with better Dreames.
If Caesar hide herselfe, shall they not whisper
Loe Caesar is affraid?

**CONSPIRATORS** Caesar's afraid.

**DECIUS** Pardon me Caesar, for my deere deere love
To your proceeding, bids me tell you this
And reason to my love is liable.

*The CONSPIRATORS begin to slip onstage, under and through the scrim, creeping, rolling.*

**TREBONIUS** My ancestors did from the streets of Rome
The tarquin drive when he was called the king.

**CAESAR** How foolish do your fears seeme now Calpurnius?
I am ashamed I did yeeld to them.

**CASSIUS** And this one is now become a God.

**CAESAR** Give me my Robe, for I will go.

*Upstage of the scrim the ORACLE has been preparing CAESAR's robe. He now steps into the entrance and offers the robe to CALPURNIUS, who refuses it and exits. Downstage, BRUTUS enters, the last of the CONSPIRATORS. Now all the CONSPIRATORS are onstage, circling CAESAR, fawning when they are in her sight, threatening when they are not. One picks up a rock from the downstage pile, hides it behind his back.*

**BRUTUS** Th' abuse of greatnesse, is,
When it disjoynes remorse from power.

**CAESAR** What Brutus?

**BRUTUS** I kisse thy hand, but not in flattery Caesar:

**CASSIUS** Pardon Caesar: Caesar pardon:
As lowe as to thy foote doth Cassius fall,
To begge infranchisement for Publius Cymber.

**CAESAR** I could be well mov'd, if I were as you,
If I could pray to moove, Prayers would moove me:
But I am constant as the Northerne Starre,
Of whose true fixt, and resting quality,

There is no fellow in the Firmament.
The Skies are painted with unnumbred sparkes,
They are all Fire, and every one doth shine:
But, there's but one in all doth hold her place.
So, in the World; 'Tis furnish'd well with Men,
And Men are Flesh and Blood, and apprehensive;
Yet in the number, I do know but One
That unassayleable holds on her Ranke,
Unshak'd of Motion: and that I am she,
Let me a little shew it, even in this:
That I was constant Cymber should be banish'd,
And constant do remaine to keepe him so.

**CASSIUS** O Caesar.

**CAESAR** Hence: Wilt thou lift up Olympus?

**DECIUS** Great Caesar.

**CAESAR** Doth not Brutus bootlesse kneele?

**CASCA** Speake hands for me.

*The drumbeat, now evident, increases in speed and intensity as the CONSPIRATORS attack CAESAR with their rocks. CASCA strikes her in the neck, the others in the chest, the side. They pull off the robe, which CASSIUS holds. One pulls her up by the hair, only to stab her in the gut. Their blows become more frenzied, a pattern emerges. It becomes a dance of fury, predators attacking a wounded beast. Only BRUTUS does not participate. CAESAR crawls towards him, crawls up his body. For a moment, time stops, the CONSPIRATORS looking at BRUTUS, BRUTUS looking into CAESAR's eyes.*

**CAESAR** Et Tu, Brute?

*BRUTUS stabs CAESAR in the back of the neck.*

Then fall Caesar.

*Drum ceases, except for a slowing, deep bah-dum, the heartbeat. BRUTUS lays CAESAR down, arranging her braid on her chest.*

**BRUTUS** Stoope Romans, stoope,
And let us bathe our hands in Caesars blood
Up to the Elbowes, and besmeare our Swords:
Then walke we forth, even to the Market place,

And waving our red Weapons o're our heads,
Let's all cry Peace, Freedome, and Liberty.

*The drum is gone.*

**CASSIUS** Stoop then, and wash. How many Ages hence
Shall this our lofty Scene be acted over,
In State unborne, and Accents yet unknowne?

**ORACLE** Aaniin minik dasing awiya ge-ichigewaad owe ge-ini-izhiwe-bag, bebakaan miziwe gaye, bebakaan ezhi-giigidong?

**CASCA** Liberty, Freedome; Tyranny is dead,
Run hence, proclaime, cry it about the Streets.

**CASSIUS** Some to the common Pulpits, and cry out
Liberty, Freedome, and Infranchisement.

**BRUTUS** People and Senators, be not affrighted:
Fly not, stand still: Ambitions debt is paid.

*From offstage, we hear keening.*

**CASCA** Go to the Pulpit Brutus.

**BRUTUS** Where is Antony?

**CASCA** Go to the Pulpit Brutus.

*ANTONY enters.*

**BRUTUS** But heere comes Antony:
Welcome Marc Antony.

**ANTONY** O mighty Caesar! Dost thou lye so lowe?
Are all thy Conquests, Glories, Triumphes, Spoiles,
Shrunke to this little Measure? Fare thee well.
I know not Gentlemen what you intend,
Who else must be let blood, who else is ranke:
If I my selfe, there is no houre so fit
As Caesars deaths houre; nor no Instrument
Of halfe that worth, as those your Swords; made rich
With the most Noble blood of all this World.
I do beseech yee, if you beare me hard,
Now, whil'st your purpled hands do reeke and smoake,
Fulfill your pleasure. Live a thousand yeeres,
I shall not finde my selfe so apt to dye.
No place will please me so, no meane of death,
As heere by Caesar, and by you cut off,
The Choice and Master Spirits of this Age.

**BRUTUS** O Antony! Begge not your death of us:
Though now we must appeare bloody and cruell,
As by our hands, and this our present Acte
You see we do: Yet see you but our hands,
And this, the bleeding businesse they have done:
Our hearts you see not, they are pittifull:
And pitty to the generall wrong of Rome,
As fire drives out fire, so pitty, pitty
Hath done this deed on Caesar. For your part,
To you, our Swords have leaden points Marc Antony:
Our Armes in strength of malice, and our Hearts
Of Brothers temper, do receive you in,
With all kinde love, good thoughts, and reverence.

**PLEBEIANS** We will be satisfied; let us be satisfied.

Anmar nabir ittogoe; anmar nabir ittomala.[4]

**CASSIUS** Your voyce shall be as strong as any mans,
In the disposing of new Dignities.

**PLEBEIANS** Ya day yuong gwa erdeezay; day yuong gwa erdeezay.[5]

**BRUTUS** Onely be patient, till we have appeas'd
The Multitude, beside themselves with feare,
And then, we will deliver you the cause,
Why I, that did love Caesar when I strooke her,
Have thus proceeded.

**PLEBEIANS** Ninga-na' endaamin; bizaanigo ninga-na' endaamin.[6]

**BRUTUS** Then follow me, and give me Audience friends.

**PLEBEIAN 1** I will heare Brutus speake.

**PLEBEIAN 2** The Noble Brutus is ascended: Silence.

*During BRUTUS's speech, ANTONY pulls down the white silk banner that hangs above her. Yards and yards of silk pour down onto the stage. She arranges CAESAR's body, covers her with the silk, performs a ritual over her.*

**BRUTUS** Be patient till the last.
Romans, Countrey-men, and Lovers, heare mee for my cause, and be silent, that you may heare. Believe me for mine Honour, and have respect to mine Honour, that you may believe. Censure me in your Wisedom, and awake

[4] Kuna colloquial translation of *We will be satisfied; let us be satisfied.*
[5] Mohawk colloquial translation of *We will be satisfied; let us be satisfied.*
[6] Ojibway colloquial translation of *We will be satisfied; let us be satisfied.*

your Senses, that you may the better Judge. If there bee any in this Assembly, any deere Friend of Caesars, to him I say, that Brutus love to Caesar, was no lesse then his. If then, that Friend demand, why Brutus rose against Cae-sar, this is my answer: Not that I lov'd Caesar lesse, but that I lov'd Rome more. Had you rather Caesar were living, and dye all Slaves; then that Caesar were dead, to live all Free-men? As Caesar lov'd mee, I weepe for her; as she was Fortunate, I rejoyce at it; as she was Valiant, I honour her: But, as she was Ambitious, I slew her. There is Teares, for her Love: Joy, for her Fortune: Honour, for her Valour: and Death, for her Ambition. Who is heere so base, that would be a Bondman? If any, speak, for him have I offended. Who is heere so rude, that would not be a Roman? If any, speak, for him have I offended. Who is heere so vile, that will not love his Countrey? If any, speake, for him have I offended. I pause for a Reply.

**ALL** None Brutus, none. Gongego Brutus, gongego.[7]

**BRUTUS** Then none have I offended. I have done no more to Caesar, then you shall do to Brutus. The Question of her death, is inroll'd in the Capitoll: her Glory not extenuated, wherein she was worthy; nor her offences enforc'd, for which she suffered death.
Heere comes her Body, mourn'd by Marc Antony, who though she had no hand in her death, shall receive the benefit of her dying, a place in the Commonwealth, as which of you shall not. With this I depart, that as I slewe my best Lover for the good of Rome, I have the same Dagger for my selfe, when it shall please my Country to need my death.

**ALL** Live Brutus, live, live.

**PLEBEIAN 1** Bring him with Triumph home unto his house.

**PLEBEIAN 2** Give him a Statue with his Ancestors.

**PLEBEIAN 3** Let him be Caesar.

**PLEBEIAN 4** Caesars better parts,
Shall be Crown'd in Brutus.

**PLEBEIAN 1** Wee'l bring him to his House,
With Showts and Clamours.

---

[7] Ojibway colloquial translation of *None, Brutus, none.*

**BRUTUS** My Country-men.

**PLEBEIAN 2** Peace, silence, Brutus speakes.

**PLEBEIAN 1** Peace ho.

**BRUTUS** Good Countrymen, let me depart alone,
And (for my sake) stay heere with Antony:
Do grace to Caesars Corpes, and grace her Speech
Tending to Caesars Glories, which Marc Antony
(By our permission) is allow'd to make.
I do intreat you, not a man depart,
Save I alone, till Antony have spoke.

*BRUTUS exits, followed by CASSIUS.*

**PLEBEIAN 1** Stay ho, and let us heare Marc Antony.

**PLEBEIAN 3** Let her go up into the publike Chaire,
Wee'l heare her: Noble Antony go up.

**ANTONY** For Brutus sake, I am beholding to you.

**PLEBEIAN 4** What does she say of Brutus?

**PLEBEIAN 3** She sayes, for Brutus sake,
She findes herselfe beholding to us all.

**PLEBEIAN 4** 'Twere best she speake no harme of Brutus heere?

**PLEBEIAN 1** This Caesar was a Tyrant.

**PLEBEIAN 3** Nay that's certaine:
We are blest that Rome is rid of her.

**PLEBEIAN 2** Peace, let us heare what Antony can say.

**ANTONY** You gentle Romans.

**ALL** Peace hoe, let us heare her.

**ANTONY** Friends, Romans, Countrymen, lend me your ears:
I come to bury Caesar, not to praise her:
The evil that men do, lives after them,
The good is oft enterred with their bones,
So let it be with Caesar. The Noble Brutus,
Hath told you Caesar was Ambitious:
If it were so, it was a greevous Fault,
And greevously hath Caesar answer'd it.
Heere, under leave of Brutus, and the rest
(For Brutus is an Honourable man,
So are they all; all Honourable men)
Come I to speake in Caesars Funerall.

She was my Friend, faithfull, and just to me;
But Brutus sayes, she was Ambitious,
And Brutus is an Honourable man.
She hath brought many Captives home to Rome,
Whose Ransomes, did the generall Coffers fill:
Did this in Caesar seeme Ambitious?
When that the poore have cride, Caesar hath wept:
Ambition should be made of sterner stuffe,
Yet Brutus sayes, she was Ambitious:
And Brutus is an Honourable man.
You all did see, that on the Lupercall,
I thrice presented her a Kingly Crowne,
Which she did thrice refuse. Was this Ambition?
Yet Brutus sayes, she was Ambitious:
And sure he is an Honourable man.
I speake not to disproove what Brutus spoke,
But heere I am, to speake what I do know;
You all did love her once, not without cause,
What cause with-holds you then, to mourne for her?
O Judgment! thou are fled to brutish Beasts,
And Men have lost their Reason. Beare with me,
My heart is in the Coffin there with Caesar,
And I must pawse, till it come backe to me.

**PLEBEIAN 1** Me thinkes there is much reason in her sayings.

**PLEBEIAN 2** If thou consider rightly of the matter,
Caesar ha's had great wrong.

**PLEBEIAN 3** Ha's shee Masters? I feare there will a worse come in her place.

*The PLEBEIANS have arranged themselves onstage, looking out at the audience. During ANTONY's speech, they begin to dance his prophecy. They pull the rocks from their pockets, stab the air, lunge. The dance disintegrates into a civil war, brother against sister, citizen against citizen. By the end of ANTONY's speech, all are singing a war song. It is an adapted haka[8], with echoes of a yoik[9].*

**ANTONY** O pardon me, thou bleeding peece of Earth:
That I am meeke and gentle with these Butchers.
Thou art the Ruines of the Noblest Chief

---

[8] Maori war song.

[9] Sami song.

That ever lived in the Tide of Times.
Woe to the hand that shed this costly Blood.
Over thy wounds, now do I Prophesie,
(Which like dumbe mouthes do ope their Ruby lips,
To begge the voyce and utterance of my Tongue)
A Curse shall light upon the limbes of men;
Domesticke Fury, and fierce Civill strife,
Shall cumber all the parts of Canada:
Blood and destruction shall be so in use,
And dreadfull Objects so familiar,
That Mothers shall but smile, when they behold
Their Infants quartered with the hands of Warre:
All pitty choak'd with custome of fell deeds,
And Caesars Spirit ranging for Revenge,
With Ate by her side, come hot from Hell,
Shall in these Confines, with a Monarkes voyce,
Cry havocke, and let slip the Dogges of Warre,
That this foule deede, shall smell above the earth
With Carrion men, groaning for Buriall.

*ANTONY finishes her speech and begins to haka. CAESAR rises and assumes the stance of a warrior, joins the haka. She moves through the escalating war, unseen by the combatants, but agitating them nonetheless. The PLEBEIANS leap and tear down the other two banners, and suddenly all four banners are undulating onstage. The PLEBEIANS catch a civilian in the banners. He becomes the centre of a web of waving silks.*

**PLEBEIAN 1** What is your name?

**PLEBEIAN 2** Whether are you going?

**PLEBEIAN 1** Where do you dwell?

**PLEBEIAN 2** Your name sir, truly.

**POET** Truly, my name is Cinna.

**PLEBEIAN 1** Teare him to peeces, hee's a Conspirator.

**POET** I am Cinna the Poet, I am Cinna the Poet.

**PLEBEIAN 3** Teare him for his bad verses, teare him for his bad Verses.

**POET** I am not Cinna the Conspirator.

**PLEBEIAN 3** It is no matter, his name's Cinna, plucke but his name out of his heart, and turne him going.

**PLEBEIAN 1** Teare him, teare him; Come Brands Hoe, Firebrands:
to Brutus, to Cassius, burne all. Awas[10], go. Húnh nyo![11]

*All release their silks, some exit, some fall where they are as BRUTUS enters downstage of the silks.*

**BRUTUS** You must note beside,
That we have tride the utmost of our Friends:
Our Legions are brim full, our cause is ripe,
The Enemy encreaseth every day,
We at the height, are readie to decline.
There is a Tide in the affayres of men,
Which taken at the Flood, leades on to Fortune:
Omitted, all the voyage of their life,
Is bound in Shallowes, and in Miseries.
On such a full Sea are we now a-float,
And we must take the current when it serves,
Or loose our Ventures.

*CASSIUS enters.*

**CASSIUS** Most Noble Brother, you have done me wrong.

**BRUTUS** Judge me you Gods; wrong I mine Enemies?
And if not so, how should I wrong a Brother.

**CASSIUS** Brutus, this sober forme of yours, hides wrongs,
And when you do them—

**BRUTUS** Cassius, be content,
Speake your greefes softly, I do know you well.
Before the eyes of both our Armies heere
(Which should perceive nothing but Love from us)
Let us not wrangle. Bid them moue away:
Then in my Tent Cassius enlarge your Greefes,
And I will give you Audience.

**CASSIUS** Strato,
Bid our Commanders leade their Charges off
A little from this ground.
That you have wrong'd me, doth appear in this:
You have condemn'd, and noted Lucius Pella
For taking Bribes heere of the Sardians;
Wherein my Letters, praying on his side,
Because I knew the man was slighted off.

**BRUTUS** You wrong'd your selfe to write in such a case.

---

[10] Ojibway, *Go!*
[11] Mohawk, *Let's go!*

**CASSIUS** In such a time as this, it is not meet
That every nice offence should beare his Comment.

**BRUTUS** Let me tell you Cassius, you your selfe
Are much condemn'd to have an itching Palme,
To sell, and Mart your Offices for Gold
To Undeservers.

**CASSIUS** I, an itching Palme?
You know that you are Brutus that speakes this,
Or by the Gods, this speech were else your last.

**BRUTUS** The name of Cassius Honours this corruption,
And Chasticement doth therefore hide his head.

**CASSIUS** Chasticement?

**BRUTUS** Remember March, the Ides of March reme[m]ber:
Did not great Julius bleede for Justice sake?
What Villaine touch'd her body, that did stab,
And not for Justice? What? Shall one of Us,
That strucke the Formost one of all this World,
But for supporting Robbers: shall we now,
Contaminate our fingers, with base Bribes?
And sell the mighty space of our large Honours
For so much trash, as may be grasped thus?
I had rather be a Dogge, and bay the Moone,
Then such a Roman.

**CASSIUS** Brutus, baite not me,
Ile not indure it: you forget your selfe
To hedge me in. I am a Souldier, I,
Older in practice, Abler then your selfe
To make Conditions.

*Upstage of the silk divide, ANTONY, LEPIDUS, and OCTAVIUS enter.*

**ANTONY** These many then shall die, their names are prickt.

**OCTAVIUS** Your Brother too must dye: consent you Lepidus?

**LEPIDUS** I do consent.

**OCTAVIUS** Pricke him downe Antony.

**LEPIDUS** Upon condition Publius shall not liue,
Who is your Sisters sonne, Marc Antony.

**ANTONY** He shall not liue; looke, with a spot I dam him.
But Lepidus, go you to Caesars house:

Fetch the Will hither, and we shall determine
How to cut off some charge in Legacies.

**LEPIDUS** What? shall I finde you heere?

**OCTAVIUS** Or heere, or at the Capitoll.

*Exit LEPIDUS.*

**ANTONY** This is a slight unmeritable man,
Meet to be sent on Errands: is it fit
The three-fold World divided, he should stand
One of the three to share it?

**OCTAVIUS** So you thought him,
And tooke his voyce who should be prickt to dye
In our blacke Sentence and Proscription.

**ANTONY** Octavius, I have seene more dayes than you,
And though we lay these Honours on this man,
To ease our selves of divers sland'rous loads,
He shall but beare them, as the Asse beares Gold,
To groane and swet under the Businesse,
Either led or driven, as we point the way:
And having brought our Treasure, where we will,
Then take we downe his Load, and turne him off
(Like to the empty Asse) to shake his eares,
And graze in Commons.

**OCTAVIUS** You may do your will:
But hee's a tried, and valiant Souldier.

**ANTONY** So is my Horse Octavius, and for that
I do appoint him store of Provender.
It is a Creature that I teach to fight,
To winde, to stop, to run directly on:
His corporall Motion, govern'd by my Spirit,
And in some taste, is Lepidus but so:
He must be taught, and train'd, and bid go forth:
A barren spirited Fellow; one that feeds
On Objects, Arts, and Imitations.
Which out of use, and stal'de by other men
Begin his fashion. Do not talke of him,
But as a property: and now Octavius,
Listen great things. Brutus and Cassius
Are levying Powers; We must straight make head:
Therefore let our Alliance be combin'd,
Our best Friends made, our meanes stretcht,
And let us presently go sit in Councell,

How covert matters may be best disclos'd,
And open Perils surest answered.

**OCTAVIUS** Let us do so: for we are at the stake,
And bayed about with many Enemies,
And some that smile have in their hearts I feare
Millions of Mischeefes.

*They exit.*

**BRUTUS** Go too: you are not Cassius.

**CASSIUS** I am.

**BRUTUS** I say, you are not.

**CASSIUS** Urge me no more, I shall forget my selfe:
Have minde upon your health: Tempt me no farther.

**BRUTUS** Away slight man.

**CASSIUS** Is't possible?

**BRUTUS** Heare me, for I will speake.
Must I give way, and roome to your rash Choller?
Shall I be frighted, when a Madman stares?

**CASSIUS** O ye Gods, ye Gods, Must I endure all this?

**BRUTUS** All this? I more: Fret till your proud hart break.
Go shew your Slaves how Chollericke you are,
And make your Bondmen tremble. Must I budge?
Must I observe you? Must I stand and crouch
Under your Testie Humour? By the Gods,
You shall digest the Venom of your Spleene
Though it do Split you. For, from this day forth,
Ile use you for my Mirth, yea for my Laughter
When you are Waspish.

**CASSIUS** Is it come to this?

**BRUTUS** You say, you are a better Souldier:
Let it appeare so; make your vaunting true,
And it shall please me well. For mine owne part,
I shall be glad to learne of Noble men.

**CASSIUS** You wrong me every way:
You wrong me Brutus:
I saide, an Elder Souldier, not a Better.
Did I say Better?

**BRUTUS** If you did, I care not.

**CASSIUS** When Caesar liv'd, she durst not thus have mov'd me.

**BRUTUS** Peace, peace, you durst not so have tempted her.

**CASSIUS** I durst not.

**BRUTUS** No.

**CASSIUS** What? durst not tempt her?

**BRUTUS** For your life you durst not.

**CASSIUS** Do not presume too much upon my Love,
I may do that I shall be sorry for.

**BRUTUS** You have done that you should be sorry for.
There is no terror Cassius in your threats:
For I am Arm'd so strong in Honesty,
That they passe by me, as the idle winde,
Which I respect not. I did send to you
For certaine summes of Gold, which you deny'd me,
For I can raise no money by vile meanes:
By Heaven, I had rather Coine my Heart,
And drop my blood for Drachmaes, then to wring
From the hard hands of Peazants, their vile trash
By any indirection. I did send
To you for Gold to pay my Legions,
Which you deny'd me: was that done like Cassius?
Should I have answer'd Caius Cassius so?
When Marcus Brutus growes so Covetous,
To locke such Rascall Counters from his Friends,
Be ready Gods with all your Thunder-bolts,
Dash him to peeces.

**CASSIUS** I deny'd you not.

**BRUTUS** You did.

**CASSIUS** I did not. He was but a Foole
That brought my answer back. Brutus hath riv'd my hart:
A Friend should beare his Friends infirmities;
But Brutus makes mine greater then they are.

**BRUTUS** I do not, till you practice them on me.

**CASSIUS** You love me not.

**BRUTUS** I do not like your faults.

**CASSIUS** A friendly eye could never see such faults.

**BRUTUS** A Flatterers would not, though they do appeare
As huge as high Olympus.

**CASSIUS** Come Antony, and young Octavius come,
Revenge your selves alone on Cassius,
For Cassius is a-weary of the World:
Hated by one she loves, brav'd by her Brother,
Check'd like a bondman, all her faults observ'd,
Set in a Note-booke, learn'd, and con'd by roate
To cast into my Teeth. O I could weepe
My Spirit from mine eyes. There is my Dagger,
And heere my naked Breast: Within, a Heart
Deerer then Pluto's Mine, Richer then Gold:
If that thou bee'st a Roman, take it foorth.
I that deny'd thee Gold, will give my Heart:
Strike as thou did'st at Caesar: For I know,
When thou did'st hate her worst, y loved'st her better
Then ever thou loved'st Cassius.

*Suddenly the POET rises from the centre of the silks, still tangled. The others hold him in place by the silks.*

**POET** Let me go in to see the Generals,
There is some grudge betweene 'em, 'tis not meete
They be alone. Nothing but death shall stay me.

**BRUTUS** How now? What's the matter?

**POET** For shame you Generals; what do you meane?
Love, and be Friends, as two such souls should bee,
For I have seene more yeeres I'me sure then yee.

**CASSIUS** Ha, ha, how wildely doth this Cynicke rime?

**BRUTUS** Get you hence sirra: Sawcy Fellow, hence.

**CASSIUS** Beare with him Brutus, 'tis his fashion.

**BRUTUS** Ile know his humour, when he knowes his time:
What should the Warres do with these Jigging Fooles?
Companion, hence.

**CASSIUS** Away, away be gone.

*The POET exits, dragging the white and yellow silks behind him.*

**BRUTUS** Sheath your Dagger:
Be angry when you will, it shall have scope:
Do what you will, Dishonour, shall be Humour.
O Cassius, you are yoaked with a Lambe

That carries Anger, as the Flint beares fire,
Who much inforced, shewes a hastie Sparke,
And straite is cold agen.

**CASSIUS** Hath Cassius liv'd
To be but Mirth and Laughter to her Brutus,
When greefe and blood ill-temper'd, vexeth her?

**BRUTUS** When I spoke that, I was ill-temper'd too.

**CASSIUS** Do you confesse so much? Give me your hand.

**BRUTUS** And my heart too.

**CASSIUS** O Brutus!

**BRUTUS** What's the matter?

**CASSIUS** Have not you love enough to beare with me,
When that rash humour which my Mother gave me
Makes me forgetfull.

**BRUTUS** Yes Cassius, and from henceforth
When you are over-earnest with your Brutus,
Hee'l thinke your Mother chides, and leave you so.
Speak no more of this: Give me a bowl of wine,
In this I bury all unkindnesse Cassius.

**CASSIUS** My heart is thirsty for that Noble pledge.
Fill Brutus, till the Wine ore-swell the Cup:
I cannot drinke too much of Brutus love.

**BRUTUS** Well, to our worke alive. What do you thinke
Of marching to Philippi presently.

**CASSIUS** I do not thinke it good.

**BRUTUS** Your reason?

**CASSIUS** This it is:
'Tis better that the Enemie seeke us,
So shall she waste her meanes, weary her Souldiers,
Doing herselfe offence, whil'st we lying still,
Are full of rest, defence, and nimblenesse.

*BRUTUS moves to the rocks downstage, using them to illustrate his plan.*

**BRUTUS** Good reasons must of force give place to better:
The people 'twixt Philippi, and this ground
Do stand but in a forc'd affection:
For they have grug'd us Contribution.

The Enemy, marching along by them,
By them shall make a fuller number up,
Come on refresht, new added, and encourag'd:
From which advantage shall we cut them off.
If at Philippi we do face them there,
These people at our backe.

**CASSIUS** Then with your will go on: wee'l along
Our selves, and meet them at Philippi.

**BRUTUS** The deepe of night is crept upon our talke,
And Nature must obey Necessitie,
Which we will put off with a little rest:
There is no more to say.

**CASSIUS** No more, good night,
Early to morrow will we rise, and hence.

**BRUTUS** Noble, Noble Cassius,
Good night, and good repose.

**CASSIUS** O my deere Brother:
This was an ill beginning of the night:
Never come such division 'tweene our soules:
Let it not Brutus.

*CASSIUS exits. Enter the ghost of CAESAR. Outside, one of the PLEBEIANS begins to sing "Deathless Voice." Throughout the scene, CAESAR continues to travel from the bottom of the road downstage right to the top upstage left. She turns occasionally as she travels, but she does not stop.*

**BRUTUS** How ill this Taper burnes. Ha! Who comes heere?
I thinke it is the weakenesse of mine eyes
That shapes this monstrous Apparition.
It comes upon me: Art thou any thing?
Art thou some God, some Angell, or some Divell,
That mak'st my blood cold, and my haire to stare?
Speake to me, what thou art.

**CAESAR** Thy evill Spirit Brutus?

**BRUTUS** I slewe my best Lover for the good of Rome.

**CAESAR** Octavius, Antony, and Lepidus,
Have put to death, an hundred Senators.
By their proscriptions, Cicero being one.

**BRUTUS** Cicero one?

**CAESAR** Cicero is dead, and by that order of proscription.
No man beares sorrow better.
Portia is dead.

*A gasp from the PLEBEIANS, and the singer pauses.*

**BRUTUS** Ha? Portia?

**CAESAR** She is dead.

**BRUTUS** O insupportable, and touching losse!
Upon what sicknesse?

**CAESAR** Impatient of your absence,
And greefe, that young Octavius with Marc Antony
Have made themselves so strong: For with her death
That tydings came. With this she fell distract,
And (her Attendants absent) swallow'd fire.

**BRUTUS** And dy'd so?

**CAESAR** Even so.

**BRUTUS** O ye immortall Gods!
Eyther there is a Civill strife in Heaven,
Or else the World, too sawcie with the Gods,
Incenses them to send destruction.

**CAESAR** O Brutus, we have left you all the Walkes,

**PLEBEIANS** East into the lakes, wetlands to the west

**CAESAR** The private Arbours, and new-planted Orchards,

**PLEBEIANS** Be stewards of our traditional lands

**CAESAR** On this side Tyber, we have left them you,

**PLEBEIANS** streams and rivers, fresh and tidal waters,

**CAESAR** And to your heyres for ever: common pleasures

**PLEBEIANS** the singing firs, the dusk, and—you, and—you.

**CAESAR** To walke abroad, and recreate your selves.

*CAESAR exiting, followed by a PLEBEIAN.*

**BRUTUS** O Spirit, I would hold more talke with thee.

**CAESAR** I tell thee thou shalt see me at Philippi.

**BRUTUS** Well: then I shall see thee againe?

**CAESAR** I, at Philippi.

**BRUTUS** Why I will see thee at Philippi then:
Now I have taken heart, thou vanishest.

*Enter OCTAVIUS, ANTONY, and their army.*

**OCTAVIUS** Now Antony, our hopes are answered,
You said the Enemy would not come downe,
But keepe the Hilles and upper Regions:
It proves not so: their battailes are at hand,
They meane to warne us at Philippi heere:
Answering before we do demand of them.

*ANTONY uses the same rocks downstage to illustrate the strategy of their enemies.*

**ANTONY** Tut I am in their bosomes, and I know
Wherefore they do it: They could be content
To visit other places, and come downe
With fearefull bravery: thinking by this face
To fasten in our thoughts that they have Courage;
But 'tis not so.

*Enter a MESSENGER.*

**MESSENGER** Prepare you Generals,
The Enemy comes on in gallant shew:
Their bloody signe of Battell is hung out,
And something to be done immediately.

**ANTONY** Octavius, leade your Battaile softly on
Upon the left hand of the even Field.

**OCTAVIUS** Upon the right hand I, keepe thou the left.

**ANTONY** Why do you crosse me in this exigent.

**OCTAVIUS** I do not crosse you: but I will do so.

*Drum. Enter BRUTUS, CASSIUS, and their army. The two sides stand on either side of the silks.*

**BRUTUS** They stand, and would have parley.

**CASSIUS** Stand fast Messala, we must out and talke.

**OCTAVIUS** Marc Antony, shall we give signe of Battaile?

**ANTONY** No Caesar, we will answer on their Charge.
Make forth, the Generals would have some words.

**OCTAVIUS** Stirre not until the Signall.

**BRUTUS** Words before blowes: is it so Countrymen?

**OCTAVIUS** Not that we love words better, as you do.

**BRUTUS** Good words are better then bad strokes Octavius.

**ANTONY** In your bad strokes Brutus, you give good words.
Witnesse the hole you made in Caesars heart,
Crying long live, Haile Caesar.

**CASSIUS** Antony,
The posture of your blowes are yet unknowne;
But for your words, they rob the Hibla Bees,
And leave them Hony-lesse.

**ANTONY** Not stinglesse too.

**BRUTUS** O yes, and soundlesse too:
For you have stolne their buzzing Antony,
And very wisely threat before you sting.

**ANTONY** Villains: you did not so, when your vile daggers
Hackt one another in the sides of Caesar:
You shew'd your teethes like Apes,
And fawn'd like Hounds,
And bow'd like Bondmen, kissing Caesars feete;
Whil'st damned Casca, like a Curre, behinde
Strooke Caesar on the necke. O you Flatterers.

**CASSIUS** Flatterers? Now Brutus thanke your selfe,
This tongue had not offended so to day.
If Cassius might have rul'd.

**OCTAVIUS** Come, come, the cause. If arguing make us swet,
The proofe of it will turne to redder drops:
Looke, I draw a Sword against Conspirators,
When thinke you that the Sword goes up againe?
Never till Caesars three and thirtie wounds
Be well aveng'd; or till another Caesar
Have added slaughter to the Sword of Traitors.

**BRUTUS** Caesar, thou canst not dye by Traitors hands.
Unlesse thou bring'st them with thee.

**OCTAVIUS** So I hope:
I was not borne to dye on Brutus Sword.

**BRUTUS** O if thou wer't the Noblest of thy Straine,
Woman, thou could'st not dye more honourable.

**CASSIUS** A peevish School-girl, worthles of such Honour
Joyn'd with a Masker, and a Reveller.

**ANTONY** Old Cassius still.

**OCTAVIUS** Come Antony: away:
Defiance Traitors, hurle we in your teeth.
If you dare fight to day, come to the Field;
If not, when you have stomackes.

*OCTAVIUS, ANTONY, and army move upstage right and begin to prepare for battle.*

**CASSIUS** Why not blow winde, swell Billow,
And swimme Barke:
The Storme is up, and all is on the hazard.

Messala, this is my Birth-day: at this very day
Was Cassius borne. Give me thy hand Messala:
Be thou my witnesse, that against my will
(As Pompey was) am I compell'd to set
Upon one Battell all our Liberties.
You know, that I held Epicurus strong,
And his Opinion: Now I change my minde,
And partly credit things that do presage.
Comming from Sardis, on our former Ensigne
Two mighty Eagles fell, and there they pearch'd,
Gorging and feeding from our Soldiers hands,
Who to Philippi heere consorted us:
This Morning are they fled away, and gone,
And in their steeds, do Ravens, Crowes, and Kites
Fly ore our heads, and downward looke on us
As we were sickely prey; their shadowes seeme
A Canopy most fatall, under which
Our Army lies, ready to give up the Ghost.

**MESSALA** Beleeve not so.

**CASSIUS** I but beleeve it partly,
For I am fresh of spirit, and resolv'd
To meete all perils, very constantly.

Now most Noble Brutus,
The Gods to day stand friendly, that we may
Lovers in peace, leade on our dayes to age.
But since the affayres of men rests still incertaine,
Let's reason with the worst that may befall.
If we do lose this Battaile, then is this
The very last time we shall speake together:
What are you then determined to do?

**BRUTUS** Even by the rule of that Philosophy,
By which I did blame Cato, for the death
Which he did give himselfe, I know not how:
But I do finde it Cowardly, and vile,
For feare of what might fall, so to prevent
The time of life, arming my selfe with patience,
To stay the providence of some high Powers,
That governe us below.

**CASSIUS** Then, if we loose this Battaile,
You are contented to be led in Triumph
Thorow the streets of Rome.

**BRUTUS** No Cassius, no:
Thinke not thou Noble Romane,
That ever Brutus will go bound to Rome,
He beares too great a minde. But this same day
Must end that worke, the Ides of March begun.
And whether we shall meete againe, I know not:
Therefore our everlasting farewell take:
For ever, and for ever, farewell Cassius,
If we do meete againe, why we shall smile;
If not, why then this parting was well made.

**CASSIUS** For ever, and for ever, farewell Brutus:
If we do meete againe, wee'l smile indeede;
If not, 'tis true, this parting was well made.

*They kiss.*

**BRUTUS** Why then leade on. O that a man might know
The end of this dayes businesse, ere it come:
But it sufficeth, that the day will end,
And then the end is knowne. Come now, away.

*The drum takes over as the two sides engage. The fight becomes the dance of the civil war. In the midst of the battle, CAESAR appears upstage, the ORACLE sees her. The people pick up the red and black silks, creating a shimmering, shuddering pathway through which the ORACLE leads CAESAR. They sing BRUTUS 49*[12] *as BRUTUS sees CAESAR's progress. Elsewhere on the field, CASSIUS is seeing the same vision.*

Wenh ah hih yanh‿ya
Yanh heh yanh heh hih yenh‿ah

[12] A 49 is a social song often sung at powwow gatherings outside of the arbour. 49's often tell stories of everyday life.

Yanh heh yanh honh hih yanh
Wenh hih yanh heh yonh‿oh
Yanh henh yanh yanh honh‿oh hih yanh
Wenh ah hih yanh
Wenh ah hih yonh

Oh my darling
Caesar's ghost is calling me
As I hug my sword so closely
I am thinking of you hih yanh
I slew my best lover for the good of Rome, hih yanh
Wenh yanh hanh, wenh yanh hanh yonh

Oh my darling,
I will see thee at Philippi
Now I have taken heart, thou vanishest, hih yanh
I kill'd not thee with half so good a will, hih yanh
Wenh yanh hanh, wenh yanh hanh yonh

Wenh ah hih yanh‿ya
Yanh heh yanh heh hih yenh‿ah
Yanh heh yanh honh hih yanh
Wenh hih yanh heh yonh‿oh
Yanh henh yanh yanh honh‿oh hih yanh
Wenh ah hih yanh
Wenh ah hih yonh

*As CAESAR, the ORACLE, and ANTONY fade into the scrim, BRUTUS turns to see PORTIA eating fire.*

**BRUTUS** Come hither, good Volumnius, list a word.

*PORTIA steps out of BRUTUS's vision, becoming VOLUMNIUS.*

**VOLUMNIUS** What sayes my Lord?

**BRUTUS** Why this, Volumnius:
The Ghost of Caesar hath appear'd to me
Two severall times by Night: at Sardis, once;
And this last Night, here in Philippi fields:
I know my houre is come.

**VOLUMNIUS** Not so, my Lord.

*Elsewhere on the field.*

**CASSIUS** O Coward that I am, to live so long.
Come hither Strato: In Parthia did I take thee Prisoner,
And then I swore thee, saving of thy life,
That whatsoever I did bid thee do,

Thou should'st attempt it. Come now, keepe thine oath,
Now be a Free-soul, and with this good Sword
That ran through Caesars bowels, search this bosome.
Stand not to answer: Heere, take thou the Hilts,
And when my face is cover'd, as 'tis now,
Guide thou the Sword. Caesar, thou art reveng'd,
Even with the Sword that kill'd thee.

*CASSIUS covers her head with the red silk, and opens her arms. She embraces STRATO, her sword, and her death. STRATO lies her body down gently and covers her with the silk.*

*As if he sees CASSIUS's death:*

**BRUTUS** It is more worthy, to leape in our selves,
Then tarry till they push us. Good Volumnius,
Thou know'st, that we two went to Schoole together:
Even for that our love of old, I prethee
Hold thou my Sword Hilts, whilest I runne on it.

**VOLUMNIUS** That's not an Office for a friend, my Lord.

*Alarum still.*

**CLYTUS** Flye, flye my Lord, there is no tarrying heere.

**BRUTUS** Farewell to you, and you, and Volumnius.
Strato, thou hast bin all this while asleepe:
Farewell to thee, to Strato, Countrymen:
My heart doth joy, that yet in all my life,
I found no man, but he was true to me.
I shall have glory by this loosing day
More then Octavius, and Marc Antony,
By this vile Conquest shall attaine unto.
So fare you well at once, for Brutus tongue
Hath almost ended his lives History:
Night hangs upon mine eyes, my Bones would rest,
That have but labour'd, to attaine this houre.

*Alarum. Cries from every side of the stage.*

**CLYTUS** Flye my Lord, flye.

**BRUTUS** Hence: I will follow:
I prythee Strato, stay thou by thy Lord,
Thou art a Woman of a good respect:
Thy life hath had some smatch of Honour in it,
Hold then my Sword, and turne away thy face,
While I do run upon it. Wilt thou Strato?

**STRATO** Give me your hand first.

*Behind STRATO, CAESAR appears to BRUTUS.*

**STRATO & CAESAR** Fare you wel my Lord.

**BRUTUS** Farewell good Strato. Caesar, now be still,
I kill'd not thee with halfe so good a will.

*He reaches for CAESAR, pulling himself onto his sword. STRATO slips out, leaving BRUTUS in CAESAR's embrace for a moment. Then falls BRUTUS. As he dies, CAESAR's spirit takes flight.*

*STRATO covers BRUTUS's face with the other end of the red silk. She begins to sing the dirge.*

*Enter ANTONY, OCTAVIUS, MESSALA, and the army. One of the people picks up the dirge from STRATO.*

**OCTAVIUS** What woman is that?

**MESSALA** My Masters woman. Strato, where is thy Master?

**STRATO** Free from the Bondage you are in my friends,
The Conquerors can but make a fire of him:
For Brutus onely ouercame himselfe,
And no man else hath Honour by his death.

**MESSALA** How dyed my Master Strato?

**STRATO** I held the Sword, and he did run on it.

**MESSALA** Octavius, then take her to follow thee,
That did the latest service to my Master.

**ANTONY** This was the Noblest Roman of them all:
All the Conspirators save onely hee,
Did that they did, in envy of great Caesar:
He, onely in a generall honest thought,
And common good to all, made one of them.
His life was gentle, and the Elements
So mixt in him, that Nature might stand up,
And say to all the world; This was a man.

**OCTAVIUS** According to his Vertue, let us use him
Withall Respect, and Rites of Buriall.
Within my Tent his bones to night shall lye,
Most like a Souldier ordered Honourably:
So call the Field to rest, and let's away,
To part the glories of this happy day.

*The people lay their rocks down, leaving a semicircle around the bodies of BRUTUS and CASSIUS. As the lights begin to fade, we hear the low double thrum, the heartbeat, five times. STRATO is the last to lay her rock down, in the middle of the road, in the centre of the partially reconstructed medicine wheel.*

*The end.*

**Ric Knowles** is Professor of Theatre Studies at the University of Guelph, editor of *Canadian Theatre Review*, and past editor of *Modern Drama* (1999–2005). He is author of *The Theatre of Form and the Production of Meaning*, *Shakespeare and Canada*, and *Reading the Material Theatre*, co-author (with the Cultural Memory Group) of *Remembering Women Murdered by Men*, editor of *Theatre in Atlantic Canada*, *Judith Thompson*, and *The Masks of Judith Thompson*, and co-editor (with Joanne Tompkins and W.B. Worthen) of *Modern Drama: Defining the Field*. Ric co-edited, with Monique Mojica, *Staging Coyote's Dream*, volume I (2003) and volume II (2008). He is general editor of the book series, *Critical Perspectives on Canadian Theatre*, from Playwrights Canada Press.